Signal processing is a ubiquitous part of modern technology. Its mathematical basis and many areas of application are the subject of this book, based on a series of graduate-level lectures held at the Mathematical Sciences Research Institute. Emphasis is on current challenges, new techniques adapted to new technologies, and certain recent advances in algorithms and theory.

The book covers two main areas: computational harmonic analysis, envisioned as a technology for efficiently analyzing real data using inherent symmetries; and the challenges inherent in the acquisition, processing, and analysis of images and sensing data in general — ranging from sonar on a submarine to a neuroscientist's fMRI study.

Mathematical Sciences Research Institute
Publications

46

Modern Signal Processing

Mathematical Sciences Research Institute Publications

Volumes 1–4 and 6–27 are published by Springer-Verlag

Modern Signal Processing

Edited by

Daniel N. Rockmore
Dartmouth College

Dennis M. Healy, Jr.
University of Maryland

Daniel N. Rockmore
Department of Mathematics
Dartmouth College
Hanover, NH 03755
United States
  rockmore@cs.dartmouth.edu

Dennis M. Healy, Jr.
Department of Mathematics
University of Maryland
College Park, MD 20742-4015
United States
  dhealy@math.umd.edu

Series Editor
Silvio Levy
Mathematical Sciences
  Research Institute
17 Gauss Way
Berkeley, CA 94720
United States

MSRI Editorial Committee
Hugo Rossi (chair)
Alexandre Chorin
Silvio Levy
Jill Mesirov
Robert Osserman
Peter Sarnak

The Mathematical Sciences Research Institute wishes to acknowledge support by
the National Science Foundation. This material is based upon work supported by
NSF Cooperative Agreement DMS-9810361.

PUBLISHED BY THE PRESS SYNDICATE OF THE UNIVERSITY OF CAMBRIDGE
The Pitt Building, Trumpington Street, Cambridge, United Kingdom

CAMBRIDGE UNIVERSITY PRESS
The Edinburgh Building, Cambridge CB2 2RU, UK
40 West 20th Street, New York, NY 10011-4211, USA
477 Williamstown Road, Port Melbourne, VIC 3207, Australia
Ruiz de Alarcón 13, 28014 Madrid, Spain
Dock House, The Waterfront, Cape Town 8001, South Africa

http://www.cambridge.org

Printed in the United States of America

A catalogue record for this book is available from the British Library.

Library of Congress Cataloging in Publication data available

ISBN 0 521 82706 X hardback

Contents

Modern Signal Processing
MSRI Publications
Volume **46**, 2003

Introduction
A New Generation of Signal Processing

In many ways, the late 1950s marked the beginning of the digital age, and with
it, the beginning of a new age for the mathematics of signal processing. High-
speed analog-to-digital converters had just been invented. These devices were
capable of taking analog signals like time series (think of continuous functions
of time like seismograms which measure the seismic activity — the amount of
bouncing — at a fixed location, or an EEG, or an EKG) and converting them to
lists of numbers. These numbers were obtained by *sampling* the time series, that
is, recording the value of the function at regular intervals, which at that time
could be as fast as 300,000 times every second. (Current technology permits
sampling at much higher rates where necessary.) Suddenly, reams and reams of
data were being generated and new mathematics was needed for their analysis,
manipulation and management.

So was born the discipline of Digital Signal Processing (DSP), and it is no
exaggeration to say that the world has not been the same. In the mathematical
sciences the DSP revolution has, among other things, helped drive the development of disciplines like algorithmic analysis (which was the impetus behind
the creation of computer science departments), communication and information theory, linear algebra, computational statistics, combinatorics, and discrete
mathematics. DSP tools have changed the face of the arts (electroacoustic music and image processing), health care (medical imaging and computed imaging),
and, of course, both social and economic commerce (i.e., the internet). Suffice
to say that the mathematics of DSP is one of the pillars supporting the amazing
technological revolution that we are experiencing today.

Some fifty years later, as we turn the corner on the twenty-first century, we find
ourselves facing an analogous paradigm shift in the world of signal processing.
Ubiquitous networked computing has once again changed the order of magnitude
of the size of datasets that are routinely interrogated and manipulated by an
increasingly large and diverse set of customers. New sensing modalities are
changing the form of the data that researchers need to consider, as well as making
necessary techniques for integrating data from different sources in order to best
understand the information they contain. This information is presented in a
variety of formats, ranging from simple one-dimensional time domain signals,

through the 2-D, 3-D and 4-D realms of basic imagery and video, and on to increasingly higher-dimensional data of various sorts. The growing mathematical sophistication of the signal processor's toolbox is driven by the need to collect, manage, analyze, and exploit data that are growing in complexity, size, and diversity.

This volume contains a collection of papers which gives some idea of the spectrum of mathematical tools that researchers are now bringing to bear on the new challenges of what might be called *modern signal processing*. It is the outgrowth of the Summer Graduate Program in Modern Signal Processing which we ran at the Mathematical Sciences Research Institute in June 2001.

The program was divided into two main parts: fundamentals and current research. Each morning was devoted to introductory lectures on some of the standard mathematical tools which currently comprise DSP. These included a brief tour of Fourier-based DSP (sampling theory, algorithms) group theoretic generalizations, several lectures on adaptive wavelet-based approaches, basic statistical signal processing ideas including detection and estimation theory, and information theoretic tools including source and channel coding (data compression and error correction).

Afternoons were given over to a series of invited outside lectures sampling directions of current research. Some of the papers included here are derived from those lectures, while others were solicited, and all were refereed. Applications areas touched upon here range among robotics, phylogeny, radar antennae design, imaging, sensing, and optical communication. The mathematical tools used include noncommutative harmonic analysis, differential geometry, time-frequency analysis, and mathematical statistics. This body of work gives some indication of the wide range of disciplines and methodologies that currently comprise the frontier of signal processing, as well as the wide range of working environments and application areas where signal processing is studied (academia, industry, defense laboratories, etc.).

We like to think that the breadth of mathematical research represented by this volume is at least reminiscent of the wide range of topics presented at the famous 1968 Arden Conference devoted to the FFT. That meeting brought together mathematicians and statisticians, physicists interested in astronomical and atomic calculations, M.D.s interested in spectral analysis for medical sensing, radar and sonar engineers, hardware and software developers, and it exemplifies the excitement that surrounded the birth of the digital revolution. In a June 1967 special issue of the the the *IEEE Transactions on Audio and Electroacoustics* (which has turned into the *IEEE Transactions on Signal Processing*), B. Bogert closes his guest editorial with the words "What lies over the horizon in digital processing is anyone's guess, but I think it will surprise us all." We hope that the papers collected here are an indication of the beginnings of a similarly intellectually exciting and fertile era.

In closing, we'd like to thank everyone who made the summer program possible: our friends and colleagues who contributed time and lectures, as well as MSRI's friendly and professional staff who kept everything running so smoothly. Special thanks to all of those who contributed papers to this volume, and to Silvio Levy, without whose patience and technical savvy this volume would have never seen the light of day. Rockmore gratefully acknowledges the support of NSF, AFOSR, and the Santa Fe Institute over the course of the production of this volume.

Daniel N. Rockmore
Dennis M. Healy, Jr.
Hanover, NH, and College Park, MD

Modern Signal Processing
MSRI Publications
Volume **46**, 2003

Hyperbolic Geometry, Nehari's Theorem, Electric Circuits, and Analog Signal Processing

JEFFERY C. ALLEN AND DENNIS M. HEALY, JR.

ABSTRACT. Underlying many of the current mathematical opportunities in digital signal processing are unsolved analog signal processing problems. For instance, digital signals for communication or sensing must map into an analog format for transmission through a physical layer. In this layer we meet a canonical example of analog signal processing: the electrical engineer's *impedance matching problem*. Impedance matching is the design of analog signal processing circuits to minimize loss and distortion as the signal moves from its source into the propagation medium. This paper works the matching problem from theory to sampled data, exploiting links between H^∞ theory, hyperbolic geometry, and matching circuits. We apply J. W. Helton's significant extensions of operator theory, convex analysis, and optimization theory to demonstrate new approaches and research opportunities in this fundamental problem.

CONTENTS

Allen gratefully acknowledges support from ONR and the IAR Program at SCC San Diego. Healy was supported in part by ONR.

1. The Impedance Matching Problem

Figure 1 shows a twin-whip HF (high-frequency) antenna mounted on a superstructure representative of a shipboard environment. If a signal generator is connected directly to this antenna, not all the power delivered to the antenna can be radiated by the antenna. If an *impedance mismatch* exists between the signal generator and the antenna, some of the signal power is reflected from the antenna back to the generator. To effectively use this antenna, a *matching circuit* must be inserted between the signal generator and antenna to minimize this wasted power.

Figure 2 shows the matching circuit connecting the generator to the antenna. Port 1 is the input from the generator. Port 2 is the output that feeds the antenna.

The matching circuit is called a 2-*port*. Because the 2-port must not waste power, the circuit designer only considers *lossless* 2-ports. The mathematician knows the lossless 2-ports as the 2×2 inner functions. The matching problem is to find a lossless 2-port that transfers as much power as possible from the generator to the antenna.

The mathematical reader can see antennas everywhere: on cars, on rooftops, sticking out of cell phones. A realistic model of an antenna is extremely complex because the antenna is embedded in its environment. Fortunately, we only need to know how the antenna behaves as a 1-port device. As indicated in Figure 2, the

Courtesy of Antenna Products

Figure 1

antenna's *scattering function* or *reflectance* s_L characterizes its 1-port behavior. The mathematician knows s_L as an element in the unit ball of H^∞.

Figure 3 displays $s_L : j\mathbb{R} \to \mathbb{C}$ of an HF antenna measured over the frequency range of 9 to 30 MHz. (Here $j = +\sqrt{-1}$ because i is used for current.) At each radian frequency $\omega = 2\pi f$, where f is the frequency in Hertz, $s_L(j\omega)$ is a

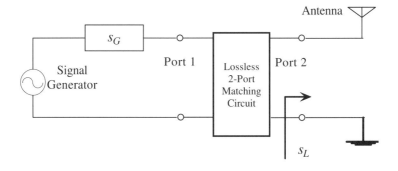

Figure 2. An antenna connected to a lossless matching 2-port.

complex number in the unit disk that specifies the relative strength and phase of the reflection from the antenna when it is driven by a pure tone of frequency ω. $s_L(j\omega)$ measures how efficiently we could broadcast a pure sinusoid of frequency ω by directly connecting the sinusoidal signal generator to the antenna. If $|s_L(j\omega)|$ is near 0, almost no signal is reflected back by the antenna towards

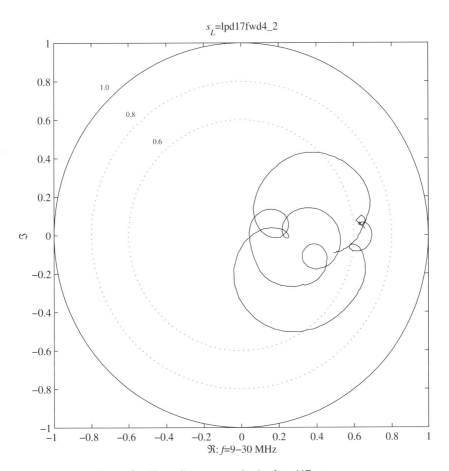

Figure 3. The reflectance $s_L(j\omega)$ of an HF antenna.

the generator or, equivalently, almost all of the signal power passes through the antenna to be radiated into space. If $|s_L(j\omega)|$ is near 1, most of this signal is reflected back from the antenna and so very little signal power is radiated.

Most signals are not pure tones, but may be represented in the usual way as a Fourier superposition of pure tones taken over a band of frequencies. In this case, the reflectance function evaluated at each frequency in the band multiplies the corresponding frequency component of the incident signal. The net reflection is the superposition of the resulting component reflections. To ensure that an undistorted version of the generated signal is radiated from the antenna, the circuit designer looks for a lossless 2-port that "pulls $s_L(j\omega)$ to 0 over all frequencies in the band." As a general rule, the circuit designer must pull s_L inside the disk of radius 0.6 at the very least.

To take a concrete example, the circuit designer may match the HF antenna using a transformer as shown in Figure 4. If we put a signal into in Port 1

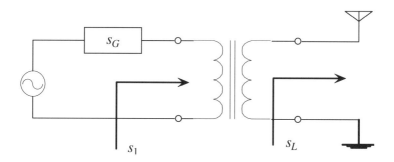

Figure 4. An antenna connected to a matching transformer.

of the transformer and measure the reflected signal, their ratio is the scattering function s_1. That is, s_1 is how the antenna looks when viewed through the transformer. The circuit designer attempts to find a transformer so that the "matched antenna" has a small reflectance. Figure 5 shows the optimal transformer does provide a minimally acceptable match for the HF antenna. The grey disk shows all reflectances $|s| \leq 0.6$ and contains $s_1(j\omega)$ over the frequency band.

However, this example raises the following question: *Could we do better with a different matching circuit?* Typically, a circuit designer selects a circuit topology, selects the reactive elements (inductors and capacitors), and then undertakes a constrained optimization over the acceptable element values. The difficulty of this approach lies in the fact that there are many circuit topologies and each presents a highly nonlinear optimization problem. This forces the circuit designer to undertake a massive search to determine an optimal network topology with no stopping criteria. In practice, often the circuit designer throws circuit after circuit at the problem and hopes for a lucky hit. And there is always the nagging question: *What is the best matching possible?* Remarkably, "pure" mathematics has much to say about this analog signal processing problem.

2. A Synopsis of the H^∞ Solution

Our presentation of the impedance matching problem weaves together many diverse mathematical and technological threads. This motivates beginning with the big picture of the story, leaving the details of the structure to the subsequent sections. In this spirit, the reader is asked to accept for now that to every N-port (generalizing the 1- and 2-ports we have just encountered), there

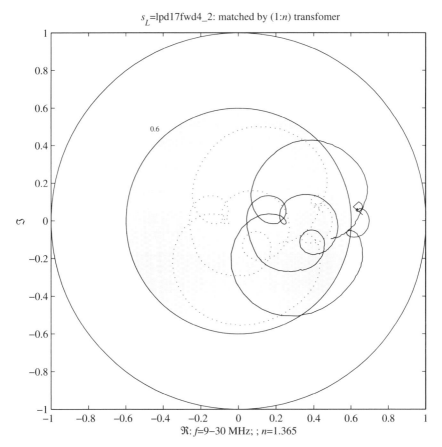

Figure 5. The reflectance s_L (solid line) of an HF antenna and the reflectance s_1 (dotted line) obtained by a matching transformer.

corresponds an $N \times N$ *scattering matrix* $S \in H^\infty(\mathbb{C}_+, \mathbb{C}^{N \times N})$, whose entries are analytic functions of frequency generalizing the reflectances of the previous section. Mathematically, $S : \mathbb{C}_+ \to \mathbb{C}^{N \times N}$ is a mapping from open right half plane $\mathbb{C}_+$ (parameterizing complex frequency) to the space of complex $N \times N$ matrices that is analytic and bounded with sup-norm

$$\|S\|_\infty := \text{ess.sup}\{\|S(j\omega)\| : \omega \in \mathbb{R}\} < \infty.$$

For a 1-port, S is scalar-valued and, as we saw previously, is called a scattering function or *reflectance*. Scattering matrix entries for physical circuits are not arbitrary functions of frequency. The circuits in this paper are linear, causal, time-invariant, and solvable. These constraints force their scattering matrices into H^∞; see [3; 4; 31].

Figure 6 presents the schematic of the matching 2-port. The matching 2-port is characterized by its 2×2 scattering matrix

$$S(j\omega) = \begin{bmatrix} S_{11}(j\omega) & S_{12}(j\omega) \\ S_{21}(j\omega) & S_{22}(j\omega) \end{bmatrix}.$$

The matrix entries measure the output response of the 2-port. For example, s_{22}

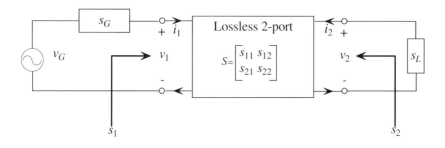

Figure 6. Matching circuit and reflectances.

measures the response reflected from Port 2 when a unit signal is driving Port 2; s_{12} is the signal from Port 1 in response to a unit signal input to Port 2. If the 2-port is consumes power, it is called *passive* and its corresponding scattering matrix is a contraction on $j\mathbb{R}$:

$$S(j\omega)^H S(j\omega) \leq \begin{bmatrix} 1 & 0 \\ 0 & 1 \end{bmatrix}$$

almost everywhere in frequency (a.e. in ω), or equivalently that S belongs to the closed unit ball: $S \in \bar{B}H^\infty(\mathbb{C}_+, \mathbb{C}^{2\times2})$. The reflectances of the generator and load are assumed to be passive also: $s_G, s_L \in \bar{B}H^\infty(\mathbb{C}_+)$. Because the goal is to avoid wasting power, the circuit designer matches the generator to the load using a *lossless* 2-port:

$$S(j\omega)^H S(j\omega) = \begin{bmatrix} 1 & 0 \\ 0 & 1 \end{bmatrix} \quad \text{a.e.}$$

Scattering matrices satisfying this constraint provide the most general model for lossless 2-ports. These are the 2×2 *real inner functions*, denoted by $U^+(2) \subset H^\infty(\mathbb{C}_+, \mathbb{C}^{2\times2})$. The circuit designer does not actually have access to all of $U^+(2)$ through practical electrical networks. Instead, the circuit designer optimizes over a practical subclass $\mathcal{U} \subset U^+(2)$. For example, some antenna applications restrict the total number d of inductors and capacitors. In this case, $\mathcal{U} = U^+(2, d)$ consists of the real, rational, inner functions of Smith–McMillan degree not exceeding degree d (d defined in Theorem 6.2).

The figure-of-merit for the matching problem of Figure 6 is the transducer power gain G_T defined as the ratio of the power delivered to the load to the maximum power available from the generator [44, pages 606-608]:

$$G_T(s_G, S, s_L) := |s_{21}|^2 \frac{1 - |s_G|^2}{|1 - s_1 s_G|^2} \frac{1 - |s_L|^2}{|1 - s_{22} s_L|^2}, \tag{2–1}$$

where s_1 is the reflectance seen looking into Port 1 of the matching circuit at the load s_L terminating Port 2. This is computed by acting on s_L by a linear-fractional transform parameterized by the matrix S:

$$s_1 = \mathcal{F}_1(S, s_L) := s_{11} + s_{12} s_L (1 - s_{22} s_L)^{-1} s_{21}. \tag{2–2}$$

Likewise, looking into Port 2 with Port 1 terminated in s_G gives the reflectance

$$s_2 = \mathcal{F}_2(S, s_G) := s_{22} + s_{21} s_G (1 - s_{11} s_G)^{-1} s_{12}. \tag{2–3}$$

The worst case performance of the matching circuit S is represented by the minimum of the gain over frequency:

$$\|G_T(s_G, S, s_L)\|_{-\infty} := \text{ess.inf}\{|G_T(s_G, S, s_L; j\omega)| : \omega \in \mathbb{R}\}.$$

In terms of this gain we can formulate the *Matching Problem:*

MATCHING PROBLEM. *Maximize the worst case of the transducer power gain* G_T *over a collection* $\mathcal{U} \subseteq U^+(2)$ *of matching 2-ports:*

$$\sup\{\|G_T(s_G, S, s_L)\|_{-\infty} : S \in \mathcal{U}\}.$$

The current approach is to convert the 2-port matching problem to an equivalent 1-port problem and optimize over an orbit in the hyperbolic disk. Specifically, the transducer power gain can be written

$$G_T(s_G, S, s_L) = 1 - \Delta P(\mathcal{F}_2(S, s_G), s_L)^2 = 1 - \Delta P(s_G, \mathcal{F}_1(S, s_L))^2,$$

where the *power mismatch*

$$\Delta P(s_1, s_2) := \left| \frac{\overline{s_1} - s_2}{1 - s_1 s_2} \right|$$

is the *pseudohyperbolic distance* between $\bar{s}_1$ and s_2. The *orbit* of the generator's reflectance s_G under the action of $\mathcal{U}$ is the set of reflectances

$$\mathcal{F}_2(\mathcal{U}, s_G) := \{\mathcal{F}_2(S, s_G) : S \in \mathcal{U}\} \subseteq \bar{B} H^\infty(\mathbb{C}_+).$$

Thus, the matching problem is equivalent to maximizing the transducer power gain over this orbit. The transducer power gain is bounded as follows:

$$\sup\{\|G_T(s_G, S, s_L)\|_{-\infty} : S \in \mathcal{U}\} = 1 - \inf\{\|\Delta P(\mathcal{F}_2(S, s_G), s_L)\|_\infty^2 : S \in \mathcal{U}\}$$

$$= 1 - \inf\{\|\Delta P(s_2, s_L)\|_\infty^2 : s_2 \in \mathcal{F}_2(\mathcal{U}, s_G)\}$$

$$\leq 1 - \inf\{\|\Delta P(s_2, s_L)\|_\infty^2 : s_2 \in \bar{B} H^\infty(\mathbb{C}_+)\}.$$

Expressing matching in terms of power mismatch in this way manifests the underlying hyperbolic geometry approximation problem. The reflectance of the generator is transformed to various new reflectances in the hyperbolic disk under the action of the possible matching circuits. We look for the closest approach of this orbit to the load s_L with respect to the (pseudo) hyperbolic metric. The last bound is reducible to a matrix calculation by a hyperbolic version of Nehari's Theorem [42], a classic result relating analytic approximation to an operator norm calculation. The resulting Nehari bound gives the circuit designer an upper limit on the possible performance for any class $\mathcal{U} \subseteq U^+(2)$ of matching circuits. For some classes, this bound is tight, telling the circuit designer that the benchmark is essentially obtainable with matching circuits from the specified class. For example, when $\mathcal{U}$ is the class of all lumped lossless 2-ports (networks of discrete inductors and capacitors)

$$U^+(2,\infty) := \bigcup_{d \geq 0} U^+(2,d)$$

and $s_G = 0$, Darlington's Theorem establishes that

$$\sup\{\|G_T(s_G = 0, S, s_L)\|_{-\infty} : S \in U^+(2,\infty)\}$$
$$= 1 - \inf\{\|\Delta P(s_2, s_L)\|_\infty^2 : s_2 \in \bar{B}H^\infty(\mathbb{C}_+),$$

provided s_L is sufficiently smooth. In this case, the circuit designer knows that there are lumped, lossless 2-ports that get arbitrarily close to the Nehari bound. The limitation of this approach is the requirement that the generator reflectance $s_G = 0$, which is not always true. Thus, a good research topic is to relax this constraint, or to generalize Darlington's Theorem. Another limitation of the techniques described in this paper is that the Nehari methods produce only a bound — they do not supply the matching circuit. However, the techniques do compute the optimal s_2, leading to another excellent research topic — the "unitary dilation" of s_2 to a scattering matrix with $s_2 = s_{22}$. That such substantial research topics naturally arise shows how an applied problem brings depth to mathematical investigations.

3. Technical Preliminaries

The real numbers are denoted by $\mathbb{R}$. The complex numbers are denoted by $\mathbb{C}$. The set of complex $M \times N$ matrices is denoted by $\mathbb{C}^{M \times N}$. I_N and 0_N denote the $N \times N$ identity and zero matrices. Complex frequency is written $p = \sigma + j\omega$. The open right-half plane is denoted by $\mathbb{C}_+ := \{p \in \mathbb{C} : \text{Re}[p] > 0\}$. The open unit disk is denoted by $\mathbf{D}$ and the unit circle by $\mathbf{T}$.

3.1. Function spaces.

- $L^\infty(j\mathbb{R})$ denotes the class of Lebesgue-measurable functions defined on $j\mathbb{R}$ with norm $\|\phi\|_\infty := \text{ess.sup}\{|\phi(j\omega)| : \omega \in \mathbb{R}\}$.
- $C_0(j\mathbb{R})$ denotes the subspace of those continuous functions on $j\mathbb{R}$ that vanish at $\pm\infty$ with sup norm.

- $H^\infty(\mathbb{C}_+)$ denotes the Hardy space of functions bounded and analytic on $\mathbb{C}_+$ with norm $\|h\|_\infty := \sup\{|h(p)| : p \in \mathbb{C}_+\}$.

$H^\infty(\mathbb{C}_+)$ is identified with a subspace of $L^\infty(j\mathbb{R})$ whose elements are obtained by the pointwise limit $h(j\omega) = \lim_{\sigma \to 0} h(\sigma + j\omega)$ that converges almost everywhere [39, page 153]. Convergence in norm occurs if and only if the H^∞ function has continuous boundary values. Those H^∞ functions with continuous boundary values constitute the *disk algebra*:

- $A_1(\mathbb{C}_+) := 1 \dotplus H^\infty(\mathbb{C}_+) \cap C_0(j\mathbb{R})$ denotes those continuous $H^\infty(\mathbb{C}_+)$ functions that are constant at infinity.

These spaces nest as

$$A_1(\mathbb{C}_+) \subset H^\infty(\mathbb{C}_+) \subset L^\infty(j\mathbb{R}).$$

Tensoring with $\mathbb{C}^{M \times N}$ gives the corresponding matrix-valued functions:

$$L^\infty(j\mathbb{R}, \mathbb{C}^{M \times N}) := L^\infty(j\mathbb{R}) \otimes \mathbb{C}^{M \times N}$$

with norm $\|\phi\|_\infty := \mathrm{ess.sup}\{\|\phi(j\omega)\| : \omega \in \mathbb{R}\}$ induced by the matrix norm.

3.2. The unit balls. The *open unit ball* of $L^\infty(j\mathbb{R}, \mathbb{C}^{M \times N})$ is denoted as

$$BL^\infty(j\mathbb{R}, \mathbb{C}^{M \times N}) := \left\{ \phi \in L^\infty(j\mathbb{R}, \mathbb{C}^{M \times N}) : \|\phi\|_\infty < 1 \right\}.$$

The *closed unit ball* of $L^\infty(j\mathbb{R}, \mathbb{C}^{M \times N})$ is denoted as

$$\bar{B}L^\infty(j\mathbb{R}, \mathbb{C}^{M \times N}) := \left\{ \phi \in L^\infty(j\mathbb{R}, \mathbb{C}^{M \times N}) : \|\phi\|_\infty \leq 1 \right\}.$$

Likewise, the open unit ball of $H^\infty(\mathbb{C}_+, \mathbb{C}^{M \times N})$ is

$$BH^\infty(\mathbb{C}_+, \mathbb{C}^{M \times N}) := BL^\infty(j\mathbb{R}, \mathbb{C}^{M \times N}) \cap H^\infty(\mathbb{C}_+, \mathbb{C}^{M \times N}).$$

3.3. The real inner functions. The class of *real* $H^\infty(\mathbb{C}_+, \mathbb{C}^{M \times N})$ functions is denoted

$$\mathrm{Re}\, H^\infty(\mathbb{C}_+, \mathbb{C}^{M \times N}) = \{S \in H^\infty(\mathbb{C}_+, \mathbb{C}^{M \times N}) : \overline{S(\bar{p})} = S(p)\}.$$

A function $S \in H^\infty(\mathbb{C}_+, \mathbb{C}^{M \times N})$ is called *inner* provided

$$S(j\omega)^H S(j\omega) = I_N \quad \text{a.e.}$$

The class of *real inner* functions is denoted

$$U^+(N) := \{S \in \mathrm{Re}\, \bar{B}H^\infty(\mathbb{C}_+, \mathbb{C}^{N \times N}) : S(j\omega)^H S(j\omega) = I_N \quad \text{a.e.}\}.$$

LEMMA 3.1. $U^+(N)$ *is closed subset of the boundary of* $\mathrm{Re}\, \bar{B}H^\infty(\mathbb{C}_+, \mathbb{C}^{N \times N})$.

PROOF. It suffices to show closure. If $\{S_m\} \subset U^+(N)$ converges to $S \in H^\infty(\mathbb{C}_+, \mathbb{C}^{N \times N})$, then $S_m(j\omega) \to S(j\omega)$ almost everywhere so that

$$I_N = \lim_{m \to \infty} S_m(j\omega)^H S_m(j\omega) = S(j\omega)^H S(j\omega) \quad \text{a.e.}$$

That is, $S(j\omega)$ is unitary almost everywhere or $S \in U^+(N)$.   □

3.4.   The weak-∗ topology. We use the weak-∗ topology on $L^\infty(j\mathbb{R}) = L^1(j\mathbb{R})^*$. A weak-∗ subbasis at $0 \in L^\infty(j\mathbb{R})$ is the collection of weak-∗ open sets

$$O[w, \varepsilon] := \{\phi \in L^\infty(j\mathbb{R}) : |\langle w, \phi \rangle| < \varepsilon\},$$

where $\varepsilon > 0$, $w \in L^1(j\mathbb{R})$, and

$$\langle w, \phi \rangle := \int_{-\infty}^{\infty} w(j\omega)\phi(j\omega)d\omega.$$

Every weak-∗ open set that contains $0 \in L^\infty(j\mathbb{R})$ is a union of finite intersections of these subbasic sets. The Banach–Alaoglu Theorem [47, Theorem 3.15] gives that the unit ball $\bar{B}L^\infty(j\mathbb{R})$ is weak-∗ compact. The next lemma shows that the same holds for a distorted version of the unit ball, a fact that will have significant import for the optimization problems we consider later.

LEMMA 3.2. *Let $c, r \in L^\infty(j\mathbb{R})$ with $r \geq 0$ define the disk*

$$\bar{D}(c, r) := \{\phi \in L^\infty(j\mathbb{R}) : |\phi - c| \leq r \quad \text{a.e.}\}.$$

Then $\bar{D}(c, r)$ a closed, convex subset of $L^\infty(j\mathbb{R})$ that is also weak-∗ compact.

PROOF. Closure and convexity follow from pointwise closure and convexity. To prove weak-∗ compactness, let $M_r : L^\infty(j\mathbb{R}) \to L^\infty(j\mathbb{R})$ be multiplication: $M_r\phi := r\phi$. Observe $\bar{D}(k, r) = k + M_r\bar{B}L^\infty(j\mathbb{R})$. Assume for now that M_r is weak-∗ continuous. Then $M_r\bar{B}L^\infty(j\mathbb{R})$ is weak-∗ compact, because $\bar{B}L^\infty(j\mathbb{R})$ is weak-∗ compact, and the image of a compact set under a continuous function is compact. This forces $\bar{D}(k, r)$ to be weak-∗ compact, provided M_r is weak-∗ continuous. To see that M_r is weak-∗ continuous, it suffices to shows that M_r pulls subbasic sets back to subbasic sets. Let $\varepsilon > 0$, $w \in L^1(j\mathbb{R})$. Then

$$\psi \in M_r^{-1}(O[w, \varepsilon]) M_r\psi \in O[w, \varepsilon] \iff |\langle w, r\psi \rangle| < \varepsilon$$
$$\iff |\langle rw, \psi \rangle| < \varepsilon \iff \psi \in O[rw, \varepsilon],$$

noting that $rw \in L^1(j\mathbb{R})$.   □

If K is a convex subset $L^\infty(j\mathbb{R})$, then K is closed $\iff$ K is weak-∗ closed [17, page 422]. Because $H^\infty(\mathbb{C}_+)$ is a closed subspace of $L^\infty(\mathbb{C}_+)$, is it also weak-∗ closed. Intersecting weak-∗ closed $H^\infty(\mathbb{C}_+)$ with the weak-∗ compact unit ball of $L^\infty(j\mathbb{R})$ forces $\bar{B}H^\infty(\mathbb{C}_+)$ to be weak-∗ compact.

3.5. The Cayley transform. Many computations are more conveniently placed in function spaces defined on the open unit disk $\mathbf{D}$ rather than on the open right half-plane $\mathbb{C}_+$. The notation for the spaces on the disk follows the preceeding nomenclature with the unit disk $\mathbf{D}$ replacing $\mathbb{C}_+$ and the unit circle $\mathbf{T}$ replacing $j\mathbb{R}$. $H^\infty(\mathbf{D})$ denotes the collection of analytic functions on the open unit disk with essentially bounded boundary values. $C(\mathbf{T})$ denotes the continuous functions on the unit circle, $\mathcal{A}(\mathbf{D}) := H^\infty(\mathbf{D}) \cap C(\mathbf{T})$ denotes the disk algebra, and $L^\infty(\mathbf{T})$ denotes the Lebesgue-measurable functions on the unit circle $\mathbf{T}$ with norm determined by the essential bound. A Cayley transform connects the function spaces on the right half plane to their counterparts on the disk.

LEMMA 3.3 ([27, page 99]). *Let the Cayley transform* $\mathbf{c} : \mathbb{C}_+ \to \mathbf{D}$

$$\mathbf{c}(p) := \frac{p-1}{p+1}$$

extend to the composition operator $\mathbf{c} : L^\infty(\mathbf{T}) \to L^\infty(j\mathbb{R})$ *as*

$$h(p) := H \circ \mathbf{c}(p) \quad (p = j\omega).$$

Then $\mathbf{c}$ *is an isometry mapping* $\left\{ \begin{array}{c} \mathcal{A}(\mathbf{D}) \\ H^\infty(\mathbf{D}) \\ C(\mathbf{T}) \\ L^\infty(\mathbf{T}) \end{array} \right\}$ onto $\left\{ \begin{array}{c} \mathcal{A}_1(\mathbb{C}_+) \\ H^\infty(\mathbb{C}_+) \\ 1 \dot{+} C_0(j\mathbb{R}) \\ L^\infty(j\mathbb{R}) \end{array} \right\}$.

3.6. Factoring H^∞ functions. The boundary values and *inner-outer* factorization of H^∞ functions are notions most conveniently developed on the unit disk and then transplanted to the right half-plane by the Cayley transform [35]. Let $\phi \in L^1(\mathbf{T})$ have the Fourier expansion in $z = \exp(j\theta)$

$$\phi(z) = \sum_{n=-\infty}^{\infty} \widehat{\phi}(n) z^n; \quad \widehat{\phi}(n) := \int_{-\pi}^{\pi} e^{-jn\theta} \phi(e^{j\theta}) \frac{d\theta}{2\pi}.$$

For $1 \le p \le \infty$, define $H^p(\mathbf{D})$ as the subspace of $L^p(\mathbf{T})$ with vanishing negative Fourier coefficients [27, page 77]:

$$H^p(\mathbf{D}) := \{ h \in L^p(\mathbf{T}) : \widehat{h}(n) = 0 \text{ for } n = -1, -2, \dots \}.$$

Then $H^p(\mathbf{D})$ is a closed subspace of $L^p(\mathbf{T})$ and as [27, page 3]:

$$H^\infty(\mathbf{T}) \subset H^{p_2}(\mathbf{T}) \subset H^{p_1}(\mathbf{T}) \subset H^1(\mathbf{T}) \quad (1 \le p_1 \le p_2 \le \infty)$$

Each $h \in H^p(\mathbf{D})$ admits an analytic extension on the open unit disk [27, p. 77]:

$$h(z) = \sum_{n=0}^{\infty} \widehat{h}(n) z^n \quad (z = re^{j\theta}).$$

From the analytic extension, define $h_r(e^{j\theta}) := h(re^{j\theta})$ for $0 \le r \le 1$. For $r < 1$, h_r is continuous and analytic. As r increases to 1, h_r converges to h in the L^p norm, provided $1 \le p < \infty$. For $p = \infty$, h_r converges to h in the weak-∗ topology (discussed on page 10). If h_r does converge to h in the L^∞ norm, convergence is uniform and forces $h \in \mathcal{A}(\mathbf{D})$. Although disk algebra $\mathcal{A}(\mathbf{D})$ is a strict subset of $H^\infty(\mathbf{D})$ in the norm topology, it is a weak-$*$ dense subset.

If ϕ is a positive, measurable function with $\log(\phi) \in L^1(\mathbf{T})$ then the analytic function [48, page 370]:

$$q(z) = \exp\left(\int_{-\pi}^{\pi} \frac{e^{jt} + z}{e^{jt} - z} \log|\phi(e^{jt})| \frac{dt}{2\pi}\right) \quad (z \in \mathbf{D}),$$

is called an *outer function*. The magnitude of $q(z)$ matches ϕ [48, page 371]:

$$\lim_{r \to 1} |q_r(re^{j\theta})| = \phi(re^{j\theta}) \quad \text{(a.e.)}$$

and leads to the equivalence: $\phi \in L^p(\mathbf{T}) \iff q \in H^p(\mathbf{D})$. We call $q(z)$ a *spectral factor* of ϕ. Every $h \in H^\infty(\mathbf{D})$ admits an inner-outer factorization [48, pages 370-375]:

$$h(z) = e^{j\theta_0} b(z)s(z)q(z),$$

where the outer function $q(z)$ is a spectral factor of $|h|$ and the inner function consists of the *Blaschke product* [48, page 333]

$$b(z) := z^k \prod_{n=1}^{\infty} \frac{z_n - z}{1 - \bar{z}_n z} \frac{\bar{z}_n}{z_n},$$

$z_n \neq 0$, $\sum(1 - |z_n|) < \infty$, and the *singular inner function*

$$s(z) = \exp\left(-\int_{-\pi}^{\pi} \frac{e^{jt} + z}{e^{jt} - z} d\mu(t)\right),$$

for μ a finite, positive, Borel measure on $\mathbf{T}$ that is singular with respect to the Lebesgue measure. In the electrical engineering setup, we will see that the Blaschke products correspond to lumped, lossless circuits while a transmission line corresponds to a singular inner function.

4. Electric Circuits

The impedance matching problem may be formulated as an optimization of certain natural figures of merit over structured sets of candidate electrical matching networks. We begin the formulation in this section, starting with an examination of the sorts of electrical networks available for impedance matching. Consideration of various choices of coordinate systems parameterizing the set of candidate matching circuits leads to the scattering formalism as the most suitable choice. Next we consider appropriate objective functions for measuring the utility of a candidate impedance matching circuit. This leads to description and characterization of power gain and mismatch functions as natural indicators of the suitability of our circuits. With the objective function and the parameterization of the admissible candidate set, we are in position to formulate impedance matching as a constrained optimization problem. We will see that hyperbolic geometry plays a natural and enabling role in this formulation.

4.1. Basic components. Figure 7 represents an N-port—a box with N pairs of wire sticking out of it. The use of the word "port" means that each pair of wires obeys a *conservation of current*—the current flowing into one wire of the pair equals the current flowing out of the other wire. We can imagine

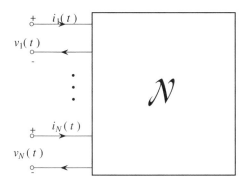

Figure 7. The N-port.

characterizing such a box by supplying current and voltage input signals of given frequency at the various ports and observing the current and voltages induced at the other ports. Mathematically, the N-port is defined as the collection $\mathcal{N}$ of voltage $\mathbf{v}(p)$ and current $\mathbf{i}(p)$ vectors that can appear on its ports for all choices of the frequency $p = \sigma + j\omega$ [31]:

$$\mathcal{N} \subseteq L^2(j\mathbb{R}, \mathbb{C}^N) \times L^2(j\mathbb{R}, \mathbb{C}^N).$$

If $\mathcal{N}$ is a linear subspace, then the N-port is called a *linear* N-port. Figures 8 and 9 present the fundamental linear 1-ports and 2-ports. These examples show

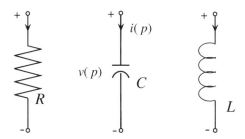

Figure 8. The lumped elements: resistor $v(p) = Ri(p)$; capacitor $i(p) = pCv(p)$; inductor $v(p) = pLi(p)$.

that $\mathcal{N}$ can have the finer structure as the graph of a matrix-valued function: for instance, with the inductor $\mathcal{N}$ is the graph of the function $i(p) \mapsto pLi(p)$.

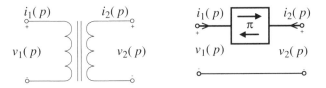

Figure 9. The transformer and gyrator.

More generally, if the voltage and current are related as $\mathbf{v}(p) = Z(p)\mathbf{i}(p)$ then $Z(p)$ is called the *impedance matrix* with real and imaginary parts $Z(p) = R(p) + jX(p)$ called the resistance and reactance, respectively. If the voltage and current are related as $\mathbf{i}(p) = Y(p)\mathbf{v}(p)$ then $Y(p)$ is called the *admittance matrix* with real and imaginary parts $Y(p) = B(p) + jG(p)$ called the conductance and susceptance, respectively. The *chain matrix* $T(p)$ relates 2-port voltages and currents as

$$\left[\begin{array}{c} v_1 \\ i_1 \end{array} \right] = \left[\begin{array}{cc} t_{11}(p) & t_{12}(p) \\ t_{21}(p) & t_{22}(p) \end{array} \right] \left[\begin{array}{c} v_2 \\ -i_2 \end{array} \right].$$

The ideal transformer has chain matrix [3, Eq. 2.4]:

$$\left[\begin{array}{c} v_1 \\ i_1 \end{array} \right] = \left[\begin{array}{cc} n^{-1} & 0 \\ 0 & n \end{array} \right] \left[\begin{array}{c} v_2 \\ -i_2 \end{array} \right], \tag{4-1}$$

where n is the *turns ratio* of the windings on the transformer. The gyrator has chain matrix [3, Eq. 2.14]:

$$\left[\begin{array}{c} v_1 \\ i_1 \end{array} \right] = \left[\begin{array}{cc} 0 & \alpha \\ \alpha^{-1} & 0 \end{array} \right] \left[\begin{array}{c} v_2 \\ -i_2 \end{array} \right].$$

Figure 10 shows how the 1-ports can build the series and shunt 2-ports with chain matrices

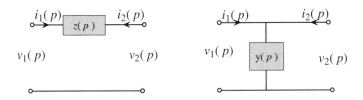

Figure 10. Series and shunt 2-ports.

$$T_{\text{series}}(p) = \left[\begin{array}{cc} 1 & z(p) \\ 0 & 1 \end{array} \right] \quad T_{\text{shunt}}(p) = \left[\begin{array}{cc} 1 & 0 \\ y(p) & 1 \end{array} \right]$$

using the using the impedance $z(p)$ and admittance $y(p)$. Connecting the series and shunts in a "chain" produces a 2-port called a ladder. The ladder's chain matrix is the product of the individual chain matrices of the series and shunt 2-ports. For example, the low-pass ladders are a classic family of lossless matching

2-ports. Figure 11 shows a low-pass ladder with Port 2 terminated in a load z_L. The low-pass ladder has chain matrix

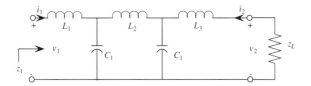

Figure 11. A low-pass ladder terminated in a load.

$$T(p) = \begin{bmatrix} 1 & pL_1 \\ 0 & 1 \end{bmatrix} \begin{bmatrix} 1 & 0 \\ pC_1 & 1 \end{bmatrix} \begin{bmatrix} 1 & pL_2 \\ 0 & 1 \end{bmatrix} \begin{bmatrix} 1 & 0 \\ pC_2 & 1 \end{bmatrix} \begin{bmatrix} 1 & pL_3 \\ 0 & 1 \end{bmatrix}.$$

The impedance looking into Port 1 is computed

$$z_1 = \frac{v_1}{i_1} = \frac{t_{11}z_L + t_{12}}{t_{21}z_L + t_{22}} =: \mathcal{G}(T, z_L).$$

Thus, the chain matrices provide a natural parameterization for the *orbit of the load* z_L *under the action of the low-pass ladders*. Section 1 showed that these orbits are fundamental for the matching problem. Even at this elementary level, the mathematician can raise some pretty substantial questions regarding how these ladders sit in $U^+(2)$ or how the orbit of the load sits in the unit ball of H^∞.

Unfortunately, the impedance, the admittance, and the chain formalisms do not provide ideal representations for all circuits of interest. For example, there are N-ports that do not have an impedance matrix (i.e., the transformer does not have an impedance matrix). There are difficulties inherent in attempting the matching problem in a formalism where the some of the basic objects under discussion fail to exist.

In fact, much of the debate in electrical engineering in the 1960's focused on finding the right formalism that guaranteed that every N-port had a representation as the graph of a linear operator. For example, the existence of the impedance matrix $Z(p)$ is equivalent to

$$\mathcal{N} = \left\{ \begin{bmatrix} Z\mathbf{i} \\ \mathbf{i} \end{bmatrix} : \mathbf{i} \in L^2(j\mathbb{R}, \mathbb{C}^N) \right\}.$$

but this formalism is not so useful when we need to describe circuits with transformers in them. The claim is that any linear, passive, time-invariant, solvable N-port always admits a *scattering matrix* $S \in \bar{B}H^\infty(\mathbb{C}_+, \mathbb{C}^{N \times N})$; see [3; 4; 31]. Consequently, we work the matching problem in the scattering formalism, which we now describe.

4.2. The scattering matrices. Specializing to the 2-port in Figure 12, define

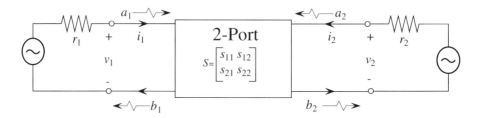

Figure 12. The 2-port scattering formalism.

the *incident signal* (see [3, Eq. 4.25a] and [4, page 234]):

$$\mathbf{a} = \tfrac{1}{2}\{R_0^{-1/2}\mathbf{v} + R_0^{1/2}\mathbf{i}\} \tag{4-2}$$

and the *reflected signal* (see [3, Eq. 4.25b] and [4, page 234]):

$$\mathbf{b} = \tfrac{1}{2}\{R_0^{-1/2}\mathbf{v} - R_0^{1/2}\mathbf{i}\}, \tag{4-3}$$

with respect to the normalizing[1] matrix

$$R_0 = \begin{bmatrix} r_1 & 0 \\ 0 & r_2 \end{bmatrix}.$$

The scattering matrix maps the incident wave to the reflected wave:

$$\mathbf{b} = \begin{bmatrix} b_1 \\ b_2 \end{bmatrix} = \begin{bmatrix} s_{11} & s_{12} \\ s_{21} & s_{22} \end{bmatrix} \begin{bmatrix} a_1 \\ a_2 \end{bmatrix} = S\mathbf{a}.$$

The scattering description can be readily related to other representations when the latter exist. For instance, the scattering matrix determines the impedance matrix as

$$\tilde{Z} := R_0^{-1/2} Z R_0^{-1/2} = (I + S)(I - S)^{-1}.$$

To see this, invert Equations 4–2 and 4–3 and substitute into $\mathbf{v} = Z\mathbf{i}$. Conversely, if the N-port admits an impedance matrix, normalize and Cayley transform to get

$$S = (\tilde{Z} - I)(\tilde{Z} + I)^{-1}.$$

Usually, $R_0 = r_0 I$ with $r_0 = 50$ ohms so the normalizing matrix disappear. The math guys always take $r_0 = 1$. The EE's have endless arguments about normalizations. Unless stated otherwise, we'll always normalize with respect to r_0.

---

[1]Two accessible books on the scattering parameters are [3] and [4]. The first of these omits the factor $\tfrac{1}{2}$ but carries this rescaling onto the power definitions. Most other books use the *power-wave normalization* [16]: $\mathbf{a} = R_0^{-1/2}\{\mathbf{v} + Z_0\mathbf{i}\}/2$, where the normalizing matrix $Z_0 = R_0 + jX_0$ is diagonal with diagonal resistance $R_0 > 0$ and reactance X_0.

4.3. The chain scattering matrix. Closely related to the scattering matrix is the *chain scattering matrix* Θ [25, page 148]:

$$\begin{bmatrix} b_1 \\ a_1 \end{bmatrix} = \Theta \begin{bmatrix} a_2 \\ b_2 \end{bmatrix} = \begin{bmatrix} \theta_{11} & \theta_{12} \\ \theta_{21} & \theta_{22} \end{bmatrix} \begin{bmatrix} a_2 \\ b_2 \end{bmatrix}.$$

When multiple 2-ports are connected in a chain the chain scattering matrix of the chain is the product of the individual chain scattering matrices. The mappings between the scattering and chain scattering matrices are [25]:

$$S \mapsto s_{21}^{-1} \begin{bmatrix} -\det[S] & s_{11} \\ -s_{22} & 1 \end{bmatrix} = \Theta \mapsto \theta_{22}^{-1} \begin{bmatrix} \theta_{12} & \det[\Theta] \\ 1 & -\theta_{21} \end{bmatrix} = S. \qquad (4\text{--}4)$$

Although every 2-port has a scattering matrix, it admits chain scattering matrix only if s_{21} is invertible.

4.4. Passive terminations. In Figure 6, Port 2 is terminated with the load reflectance s_L so that

$$a_2 = s_L b_2. \qquad (4\text{--}5)$$

Then the reflectance looking into Port 1 is obtained by the chain-scattering matrix:

$$s_1 := \frac{b_1}{a_1} = \frac{\theta_{11} a_2 + \theta_{12} b_2}{\theta_{21} a_2 + \theta_{22} b_2} = \frac{\theta_{11} s_L + \theta_{12}}{\theta_{21} s_L + \theta_{22}} =: \mathcal{G}_1(\Theta, s_L).$$

Equation 4–4 also allows us to express s_1 in terms of the linear-fractional form of the scattering matrix introduced in Equation 2–2: $s_1 = \mathcal{F}_1(S, s_L)$. Similarly, if Port 1 of the 2-port is terminated with the load reflectance s_G, then the reflectance looking into Port 2 is

$$s_2 = \mathcal{G}_2(\Theta, s_G) := \frac{\theta_{22} s_G + \theta_{21}}{\theta_{12} s_G + \theta_{11}} = \mathcal{F}_2(S, s_G),$$

with $\mathcal{F}_2(S, s_G)$ as introduced in Equation 2–3.

4.5. Active terminations. Equation 4–5 admits a generalization to include the generators. Figure 13 shows the labeling convention of the scattering variables. The generalization includes the scattering of the generator in terms of the

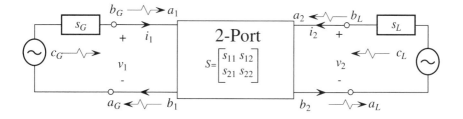

Figure 13. Scattering conventions.

voltage source [16, Eq. 3.2]:

$$b_G = s_G a_G + c_G; \quad c_G := \frac{r_0^{-1/2}}{z_G + r_0} v_G. \tag{4-6}$$

To get this result, use Equations 4–2 and 4–3 to write $v_1 = r_0^{1/2}(a_1 + b_1)$ and $i_1 = r_0^{-1/2}(a_1 - b_1)$. Substitute this into the voltage drops $v_G = z_G i_1 + v_1$ of Figure 13 to get

$$c_G = \frac{r_0^{-1/2} v_G}{z_G + r_0} = a_1 - \frac{z_G - r_0}{z_G + r_0} b_1 = b_G - s_G a_G.$$

We can now analyze the setup in Figure 13. Equations 4–5 and 4–6 give

$$\mathbf{a} = \begin{bmatrix} a_1 \\ a_2 \end{bmatrix} = \begin{bmatrix} s_G & 0 \\ 0 & s_L \end{bmatrix} \begin{bmatrix} b_1 \\ b_2 \end{bmatrix} + \begin{bmatrix} c_G \\ c_L \end{bmatrix} =: S_X \mathbf{b} + \mathbf{c}_X.$$

Substitution into $\mathbf{b} = S\mathbf{a}$ solves the 2-port scattering as

$$\mathbf{a} = (I_2 - S_X S)^{-1} \mathbf{c}_X.$$

4.6. Power flows in the 2-port. With respect to an N-port, the complex power[2] is [4, page 241]:

$$W(p) := \mathbf{v}(p)^H \mathbf{i}(p).$$

Because $\mathbf{v}(p)$ has units volts second and $\mathbf{i}(p)$ has units ampères second, $W(p)$ units of watts/Hz^2. The average power delivered to the N-port is [21, page 19]

$$P_{\text{avg}} := \tfrac{1}{2} \text{Re}[W] = \tfrac{1}{2}\{\mathbf{a}^H \mathbf{a} - \mathbf{b}^H \mathbf{b}\} = \tfrac{1}{2}\mathbf{a}^H \{I - S^H S\}\mathbf{a}. \tag{4-7}$$

We're dragging the $1/2$ along so our power definitions coincide with [21]. If the N-port consumes power ($P_{\text{avg}} \geq 0$) for all its voltage and current pairs, then the N-port is said to be passive. If the N-port consumes no power ($P_{\text{avg}} = 0$) for all its voltage and current pairs, then the N-port is said to be lossless. In terms of the scattering matrices [28]:

- Passive: $S^H(j\omega)S(j\omega) \leq I_N$
- Lossless: $S^H(j\omega)S(j\omega) = I_N$

for all $\omega \in \mathbb{R}$. Specializing these concepts to the 2-port of Figure 14, leads to the following power flows:

- The average power delivered to Port 1 is

$$P_1 := \tfrac{1}{2}(|a_1|^2 - |b_1|^2) = \frac{|a_1|^2}{2}(1 - |s_1|^2).$$

- The average power delivered to Port 2 is

$$P_2 := \tfrac{1}{2}(|a_2|^2 - |b_2|^2) = -P_L.$$

---

[2]Baher uses [3, Eq. 2.17]: $W(p) = \mathbf{i}(p)^H \mathbf{v}(p)$.

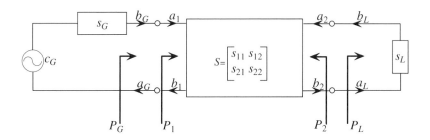

Figure 14. Matching circuit and reflectances.

- The average power delivered to the load is [21, Eq. 2.6.6]

$$P_L := \tfrac{1}{2}(|a_L|^2 - |b_L|^2) = \frac{|b_2|^2}{2}(1 - |s_L|^2).$$

- The average power delivered by the generator:

$$P_G = \tfrac{1}{2}(|b_G|^2 - |a_G|^2).$$

To compute P_G, observe that Figure 14 gives $a_G = b_1$ and $b_G = a_1$. Substitute these and $b_1 = s_1 a_1$ into Equation 4–6 to get $c_G = (1 - s_G s_1)a_1$. Then

$$P_G = \tfrac{1}{2}(|a_1|^2 - |b_1|^2) = \frac{|a_1|^2}{2}(1 - |s_1|^2) = \frac{|c_G|^2}{2}\frac{1 - |s_1|^2}{|1 - s_G s_1|^2}. \qquad (4\text{--}8)$$

LEMMA 4.1. *Assume the setup of Figure 14. There always holds $P_2 = -P_L$ and $P_G = P_1$. If the 2-port is lossless, $P_1 + P_2 = 0$.*

4.7. The power gains in the 2-port. The matching network maps the generator's power into a form that we hope will be more useful at the load than if the generator drove the load directly. The modification of power is generically described as "gain." The matching problem puts us in the business of gain computations, and we need the maximum power and mismatch definitions. The maximum power available from a generator is defined as the average power delivered by the generator to a conjugately matched load. Use Equation 4–8 to get [21, Eq. 2.6.7]:

$$P_{G,\max} := P_G|_{s_1 = \overline{s_G}} = \frac{|c_G|^2}{2}(1 - |s_G|^2)^{-1}.$$

The *source mismatch factor* is [21, Eq. 2.7.17]:

$$\frac{P_G}{P_{G,\max}} = \frac{(1 - |s_G|^2)(1 - |s_1|^2)}{|1 - s_G s_1|^2}.$$

The maximum power available from the matching network is defined as the average power delivered from the network to a conjugately matched load [21, Eq. 2.6.19]:

$$P_{L,\max} := P_L|_{s_L = \overline{s_2}} := \frac{|b_2|_{s_L = \overline{s_2}}|^2}{2}(1 - |s_2|^2).$$

Less straightforward to derive is the *load mismatch factor* [21, Eq. 2.7.25]:

$$\frac{P_L}{P_{L,\max}} = \frac{(1-|s_L|^2)(1-|s_2|^2)}{|1-s_L s_2|^2}.$$

These powers lead to several types of power gains [21, page 213]:

- Transducer power gain

$$G_T := \frac{P_L}{P_{G,\max}} = \frac{\text{power delivered to the load}}{\text{maximum power available from the generator}}.$$

- Power gain or operating power gain

$$G_P := \frac{P_L}{P_1} = \frac{\text{power delivered to the load}}{\text{power delivered to the network}}.$$

- Available power gain

$$G_A := \frac{P_{L,\max}}{P_{G,\max}} = \frac{\text{maximum power available from the network}}{\text{maximum power available from the generator}}.$$

LEMMA 4.2. *Assume the setup of Figure 14. If the 2-port is lossless,*

$$G_T = \frac{(1-|s_G|^2)(1-|s_1|^2)}{|1-s_G s_1|^2}.$$

PROOF.

$$G_T = \frac{P_L}{P_{G,\max}} \overset{\text{Lemma 4.1}}{=} \frac{-P_2}{P_{G,\max}} \overset{\text{lossless}}{=} \frac{P_1}{P_{G,\max}} \overset{\text{Lemma 4.1}}{=} \frac{P_G}{P_{G,\max}}.$$

$\square$

What's nice about the proof is that it makes clear that the equality holds because the power flowing into the lossless 2-port is the power flowing out of the 2-port. The key to analyzing the transducer power gain is the power mismatch.

4.8. Power mismatch. Previously we established that the power mismatch is the key to the matching problem. In fact, this is a concept that brings together ideas from pure mathematics and applied electrical engineering, as seen in the engineer's Smith Chart—a disk-shaped analysis tool marked with coordinate curves which look compellingly familiar to the mathematician. A standard engineering reference observes the connection [51]:

> The transformation through a lossless junction [2-port] ... leaves invariant the *hyperbolic distance* ... The hyperbolic distance to the origin of the [Smith] chart is the *mismatch*, that is, the standing-wave ratio expressed in decibels: It may be evaluated by means of the proper graduation on the radial arm of the Smith chart. For two arbitrary points W_1, W_2, the hyperbolic distance between them may be interpreted as the mismatch that results from the load W_2 seen through a lossless network that matches W_1 to the input waveguide.

Hyperbolic metrics have been under mathematical development for the last 200 years, while Phil Smith introduced his chart in the late 1930's with a somewhat different motivation. It is fascinating to see how hyperbolic analysis transcribes to electrical engineering. Mathematically, we start with the *pseudohyperbolic metric*[3] on $\mathbf{D}$ defined as follows (see [58, page 58]):

$$\rho(s_1, s_2) := \left| \frac{s_1 - s_2}{1 - \overline{s_1} s_2} \right| \quad (s_1, s_2 \in \mathbf{D}).$$

The Möbius group of symmetries of $\mathbf{D}$ consists of all maps $\mathbf{g} : \mathbf{D} \to \mathbf{D}$ [20, Theorem 1.3]:

$$\mathbf{g}(s) = e^{j\theta} \frac{s - a}{1 - \bar{a}s},$$

where $a \in \mathbf{D}$ and $\theta \in \mathbb{R}$. That ρ is invariant under the Möbius maps $\mathbf{g}$ is fundamental (see [20] and [58, page 58]):

$$\rho(\mathbf{g}(s_1), \mathbf{g}(s_2)) = \rho(s_1, s_2). \tag{4-9}$$

The *hyperbolic metric*[4] on $\mathbf{D}$ is [58, page 59]:

$$\beta(s_1, s_2) = \tfrac{1}{2} \log \left(\frac{1 + \rho(s_1, s_2)}{1 - \rho(s_1, s_2)} \right).$$

Because ρ is Möbius-invariant, it follows that β is also Möbius-invariant:

$$\beta(\mathbf{g}(s_1), \mathbf{g}(s_2)) = \beta(s_1, s_2).$$

One can visualize the matching problem in terms of the action of this group of symmetries. At fixed frequency, a given load reflectance s_L corresponds to a point in $\mathbf{D}$. Attaching a matching network to the load modifies this reflectance by applying to it the Möbius transformation associated with the chain scattering matrix of the matching network. By varying the choice of the matching network, we vary the Möbius map applied to s_L and sweep the modified reflectance around the disk to a desirable position.

The series inductor of Figure 10 provides an excellent example of this action of a circuit as Möbius map acting on the reflectances parameterized as points of the unit disk. The series inductor has the chain scattering matrix [25, Table 6.2]:

$$\Theta(p) = \left[\begin{array}{cc} 1 - Lp/2 & Lp/2 \\ -Lp/2 & 1 + Lp/2 \end{array} \right].$$

that acts on $s \in \mathbf{D}$ as

$$\mathcal{G}(\Theta; s) = \frac{\Theta_{11} s + \Theta_{12}}{\Theta_{21} s + \Theta_{22}} = -\frac{\bar{a}}{a} \frac{s - a}{1 - \bar{a}s} \bigg|_{a = (1 + j2/(\omega L))^{-1}}.$$

---

[3] Also known as the Poincaré hyperbolic distance function; see [50].

[4] Also known as the Bergman metric or the Poincaré metric.

Figure 15 shows the Möbius action of this lossless 2-port on the disk. Frequency is fixed at $p = j$. The upper left panel shows the unit disk partitioned into radial segments. Each of the other panels show the action of an inductor on the points of this disk. Increasing the inductance warps the radial pattern to the boundary. The radial segments are geodesics of ρ and β. Because the Möbius maps preserve both metrics, the resulting circles are also geodesics. More generally, the geodesics of ρ and β are either the radial lines or the circles that meet the boundary of the unit disk at right angles.

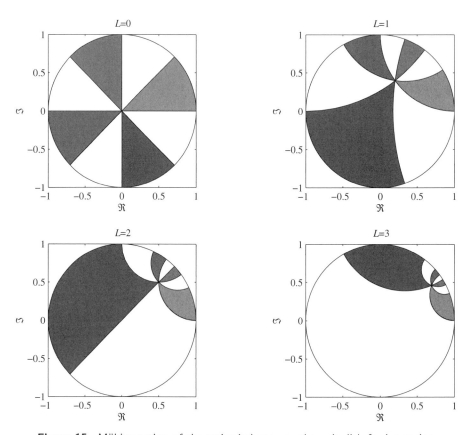

Figure 15. Möbius action of the series inductor on the unit disk for increasing inductance values (frequency fixed at $p = j$).

Several electrical engineering figures of merit for the matching problem are naturally understood in terms of the geometry of the hyperbolic disk. We are concerned primarily with three: (1) the power mismatch, (2) the VSWR, (3) the transducer power gain. The power mismatch between two passive reflectances s_1, s_2 is [29]:

$$\Delta P(s_1, s_2) := \left| \frac{\overline{s_1} - s_2}{1 - s_1 s_2} \right| = \rho(\bar{s}_1, s_2), \qquad (4\text{--}10)$$

or the pseudohyperbolic distance between $\bar{s}_1$ and s_2 measured along their geodesic. Thus, the geodesics of ρ attach a geometric meaning to the power mismatch and illustrate the quote at the beginning of this section.

The voltage standing wave ratio (VSWR) is a sensitive measure of impedance mismatch. Intuitively, when power is pushed into a mismatched load, part of the power is reflected back measured by the reflectance $s \in \mathbf{D}$. Superposition of the incident and reflected wave sets up a voltage standing wave pattern. The VSWR is the ratio of the maximum to minimum voltage in this pattern: [6, Equation 3.51]:

$$\text{VSWR}(s) = 20 \log_{10} \left(\frac{1 + |s|}{1 - |s|} \right) \quad \text{[dB]}.$$

Referring to Figure 15, the VSWR is a scaled hyperbolic distance from the origin to s measured along its radial line. Thus, the geodesics of β attach a geometric meaning to the VSWR.

The transducer power gain G_T links to the power mismatch ΔP by the classical identity of the hyperbolic metric [58, page 58]:

$$1 - \rho(s_1, s_2)^2 = \frac{(1 - |s_1|^2)(1 - |s_2|^2)}{|1 - \overline{s_1} s_2|^2} \quad (s_1, s_2 \in \mathbf{D}), \quad (4\text{--}11)$$

and Lemma 4.2 provided the matching 2-port is lossless.

LEMMA 4.3. *If the 2-port is lossless in Figure 14, $G_T = 1 - \Delta P(s_G, s_1)^2$.*

That is, *maximizing G_T is equivalent to minimizing the power mismatch.* As the next result shows, we can use either Port 1 or Port 2 (Proof in Appendix B).

LEMMA 4.4. *Assume the 2-port is lossless in Figure 6: $S \in U^+(2)$. Assume s_G and s_L are strictly passive: $s_G, s_L \in BH^\infty(\mathbb{C}_+)$. Then $s_1 = \mathcal{F}_1(S, s_L)$ and $s_2 = \mathcal{F}_2(S, s_G)$ (defined in Equations 2–2 and 2–3 respectively) are well-defined and strictly passive with the LFT (Linear Fractional Transform) law*

$$\Delta P(s_G, \mathcal{F}_1(S, s_L)) = \Delta P(\mathcal{F}_2(S, s_G), s_L)$$

and the TPG (Transducer Power Gain) law

$$G_T(s_G, S, s_L) = 1 - \Delta P(s_G, \mathcal{F}_1(S, s_L))^2 = 1 - \Delta P(\mathcal{F}_2(S, s_G), s_L)^2$$

holding on $j\mathbb{R}$.

The LFT law is not true if S is strictly passive. For $S^H S < I_2$, define the gains at Port 1 and 2 as follows:

$$G_1(s_G, S, s_L) := 1 - \Delta P(s_G, \mathcal{F}_1(S, s_L))^2$$

$$G_2(s_G, S, s_L) := 1 - \Delta P(\mathcal{F}_2(S, s_G), s_L)^2.$$

Lemma 4.4 gives that $G_T = G_1 = G_2$, provided S is lossless. If S is only passive, we can only say $G_T \leq G_1, G_2$. To see this, Equation 4–11 identifies G_1 and G_2 as mismatch factors:

$$G_1(s_G, S, s_L) = 1 - \Delta P(s_G, s_1)^2 = \frac{P_G}{P_{G,\max}},$$

$$G_2(s_G, S, s_L) := 1 - \Delta P(s_2, s_L)^2 = \frac{P_L}{P_{L,\max}}.$$

If we believe that a passive 2-port forces the available gain $G_A \leq 1$ and power gain $G_P \leq 1$ of Section 4.7, the inequalities $G_T \leq G_1$, G_2 are explained as

$$G_T = \frac{P_L}{P_{G,\max}} = \frac{P_{L,\max}}{P_{G,\max}} \frac{P_L}{P_{L,\max}} = G_A G_2$$

$$G_T = \frac{P_L}{P_{G,\max}} = \frac{P_1}{P_{G,\max}} \frac{P_L}{P_1} = G_P G_1.$$

4.9. Sublevel sets of the power mismatch. We have just seen that impedance matching reduces to minimization of the power mismatch. We can obtain some geometrical intuition for the behavior of this by examining Figure 16, which shows the isocontours of the function $s_2 \mapsto \Delta P(s_2, s_L)$ for a fixed reflectance s_L in the unit disk (at a fixed frequency). The key observation is that for each fixed frequency, the sublevel sets $\{s_2 \in \mathbf{D} : \Delta P(s_2, s_L) \leq \rho\}$ comprise a family of concentric disks with hyperbolic center $\overline{s_L}$. Of course, we must actually consider power mismatch over a range of frequencies. To this end, the next lemma characterizes the corresponding sublevel sets in $L^\infty(j\mathbb{R})$.

LEMMA 4.5 (ΔP DISKS). *Let* $s_L \in BL^\infty(j\mathbb{R})$. *Let* $0 \leq \rho \leq 1$. *Define the center function*

$$k := \bar{s}_L \frac{1 - \rho^2}{1 - \rho^2 |s_L|^2} \in BL^\infty(j\mathbb{R}), \tag{4-12}$$

the radius function

$$r := \rho \frac{1 - |s_L|^2}{1 - \rho^2 |s_L|^2} \in \bar{B}L^\infty(j\mathbb{R}), \tag{4-13}$$

and the disk

$$\bar{D}(k, r) := \{\phi \in L^\infty(j\mathbb{R}) : |\phi(j\omega) - k(j\omega)| \leq r(j\omega)\}.$$

Then,

D-1: $\bar{D}(k,r)$ *is a closed, convex subset of* $L^\infty(j\mathbb{R})$.
D-2: $\bar{D}(k,r) = \{\phi \in \bar{B}L^\infty(jR) : \rho \geq \|\Delta P(\phi, s_L)\|_\infty\}$.
D-3: $\bar{D}(k,r)$ *is a weak-∗ compact, convex subset of* $L^\infty(j\mathbb{R})$.

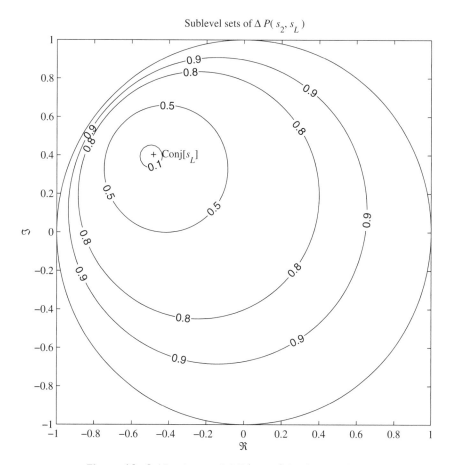

Figure 16. Sublevel sets of $\Delta P(s_2, s_L)$ in the unit disk.

PROOF. Under the assumption that $\|s_L\|_\infty < 1$, it is straightforward to verify that the center and radius functions are in the open and closed unit balls of $L^\infty(j\mathbb{R})$, respectively.

D-1: Convexity and closure follow from pointwise convexity and closure.

D-2: Basic algebra computes $\bar{D}(k,r) = \{\phi \in L^\infty(jR) : \rho \geq \|\Delta P(\phi, s_L)\|_\infty\}$. The "free" result is that $\|\bar{D}(k,r)\|_\infty \leq 1$. To see this, let $s := \|s_L\|_\infty$. The norm of any element in $\bar{D}(k,r)$ is bounded by

$$\|k\|_\infty + \|r\|_\infty \leq s\frac{1-\rho^2}{1-\rho^2 s^2} + \rho\frac{1-s^2}{1-\rho^2 s^2} =: u(s,\rho).$$

For $s \in [0,1)$ fixed, we obtain

$$\frac{\partial u}{\partial \rho} = -\frac{-1+s^2}{(\rho s + 1)^2}.$$

Thus, $u(s, \circ)$ attains its maximum on the boundary of $[0, 1]$: $u(s, 1) = 1$. Thus, $\|\bar{D}(k, r)\|_\infty \leq 1$.

D-3: D-1 and Lemma 3.2. $\square$

4.10. Continuity of the power mismatch. Consider the mapping $\Delta\rho :$ $\bar{B}L^\infty(j\mathbb{R}) \to \mathbb{R}_+$

$$\Delta\rho(s_2) := \|\Delta P(s_2, s_L)\|_\infty,$$

for fixed $s_L \in BL^\infty(j\mathbb{R})$. The main problem of this paper concerns the minimization of this functional over feasible classes (ultimately, the orbits of the reflectance under classes of matching circuits). This problem is determined by the structure of the sublevel sets of $\Delta\rho$. What we have just seen is that the sublevel sets are disks in function space, a very nice structure indeed. As the "level" of $\Delta\rho$ is decreased, these sets neck down; the question of existence of a minimizer in a feasible class comes down to the intersection of the feasible class with these sublevel sets.

DEFINITION 4.1. [48, pages 38–39], [57, page 150] Let γ be a real or extended-real function on a topological space X.

- γ is lower semicontinuous provided $\{x \in X : \gamma(x) \leq \alpha\}$ is closed for every real α.
- γ is lower semicompact provided $\{x \in X : \gamma(x) \leq \alpha\}$ is compact for every real α.

These properties produce minimizers by the Weierstrass Theorem.

THEOREM 4.1 (WEIERSTRASS). [57, page 152] *Let K be a nonempty subset of a a topological space X. Let γ be a real or extended-real function defined on K. If either condition holds:*

- *γ is lower semicontinuous on the compact set K, or*
- *γ is lower semicompact,*

then $\inf\{\gamma(x) : x \in K\}$ admits minimizers.

Lemma 4.5 demonstrates that $\Delta\rho$ is both weak-$*$ lower semicontinuous and weak-$*$ lower compact. The minimum of $\Delta\rho$ in $\bar{B}L^\infty(j\mathbb{R})$ is $0 = \Delta\rho(\overline{s_L})$ that corresponds to a perfect match over all frequencies. However, the matching functions at our disposal are not arbitrary, and this trivial solution is typically not obtainable with real matching circuits. The constraints on allowable matching functions lead us to consider minimizing $\Delta\rho$ restricted to $\bar{B}H^\infty(\mathbb{C}_+)$, $\bar{B}A_1(\mathbb{C}_+)$, and associated orbits. Finally, straight-forward sequence arguments show that $\Delta\rho$ is also continuous as a function on $\bar{B}L^\infty(j\mathbb{R})$ in the norm topology.

LEMMA 4.6. *If $s_L \in BL^\infty(j\mathbb{R})$, then $\Delta\rho : \bar{B}L^\infty(j\mathbb{R}) \to \mathbb{R}_+$ is continuous.*

PROOF. Define $\Delta P_1 : \bar{B}L^\infty(j\mathbb{R}) \to L^\infty(j\mathbb{R})$ as $\Delta P_1(s) := (\bar{s} - s_L)(1 - ss_L)^{-1}$. If we show that ΔP_1 is continuous then composition with $\|\circ\|_\infty$ shows continuity of $\Delta\rho$. The first task is to show ΔP_1 is well-defined. For each $s \in \bar{B}L^\infty(j\mathbb{R})$, $\Delta P_1(s)$ is measurable and

$$\left|\frac{\bar{s} - s_L}{1 - ss_L}\right| \leq \frac{2}{1 - \|s\|_\infty\|s_L\|_\infty} \leq \frac{2}{1 - \|s_L\|_\infty}.$$

Thus, $\Delta P_1(s) \in L^\infty(j\mathbb{R})$ so is well-defined. For continuity, let $\{s_n\} \subset \bar{B}L^\infty(j\mathbb{R})$ and $s_n \to s$. Then

$$\Delta P_1(s_n) - \Delta P_1(s) = \frac{\overline{s_n} - s_L}{1 - s_n s_L} - \frac{\bar{s} - s_L}{1 - ss_L}$$

$$= \frac{1}{(1 - s_n s_L)(1 - ss_L)}\{(\overline{s_n} - s_L)(1 - ss_L) - (\bar{s} - s_L)(1 - s_n s_L)\}$$

$$= \frac{1}{(1 - s_n s_L)(1 - ss_L)}\{\overline{s_n} - \bar{s} + s_L(\bar{s}s_n - \overline{s_n}s) + (s - s_n)s_L^2\}.$$

In terms of the norm,

$$\|\Delta P_1(s_n) - \Delta P_1(s)\|$$
$$\leq (1 - \|s_L\|_\infty)^{-2}\{\|\overline{s_n} - \bar{s}\|_\infty + \|s_L\|_\infty\|\bar{s}s_n - \overline{s_n}s\|_\infty + \|s - s_n\|_\infty\|s_L\|_\infty^2\},$$

so that the difference converges to zero. With ΔP_1 a continuous mapping, the continuity of the norm $\| \circ \|_\infty : L^\infty(j\mathbb{R}) \to \mathbb{R}_+$ makes the mapping $\Delta\rho(s) := \|\Delta P_1(s)\|_\infty$ also continuous. $\qquad\square$

5. H^∞ Matching Techniques

Recalling the matching problem synopsis of Section 2, our goal is to maximize the transducer power gain G_T over a specified class $\mathcal{U}$ of scattering matrices. By Lemma 4.3, we can equivalently minimize the power mismatch:

$$\sup\{\|G_T(s_G, S, s_L)\|_{-\infty} : S \in \mathcal{U}\} = 1 - \inf\{\|\Delta P(\mathcal{F}_2(S, s_G), s_L)\|_\infty^2 : S \in \mathcal{U}\}$$
$$= 1 - \inf\{\|\Delta P(s_2, s_L)\|_\infty^2 : s_2 \in \mathcal{F}_2(\mathcal{U}, s_G)\}$$
$$\leq 1 - \inf\{\|\Delta P(s_2, s_L)\|_\infty^2 : s_2 \in \bar{B}H^\infty(\mathbb{C}_+)\}.$$

The next step in our program is to develop tools for computing the upper bound at the end of this chain of expressions, based on what we know of s_L. Ultimately, we will try to make this a tight bound given the right properties of the admissible matching circuits parameterized by $\mathcal{U}$. The key computation is a hyperbolic version of Nehari's Theorem that computes the minimum power mismatch from the Hankel matrix determined by s_L.

We start towards this in Section 5.1 by reviewing the concept of Hankel operators and their relation to best approximation from H^∞ as expressed by the linear Nehari theory. Section 5.2 extends this to a nonlinear framework that includes the desired hyperbolic Nehari bound on the power mismatch as a special case.

Having computed a bound on our ability to match a given load, we consider how closely one can approach this in a practical implementation with real circuits. The key matching circuits we consider in practice are the lumped, lossless 2-ports with scattering matrices in $U^+(2, \infty)$. Later on, Section 7 demonstrates that the orbit of $s_G = 0$ under $U^+(2, \infty)$ is dense in the real disk algebra, $\operatorname{Re} \bar{B} A_1(\mathbb{C}_+)$ (Darlington's Theorem), so that smallest mismatch approachable with lumped circuits is

$$\inf\{\|\Delta P(s_2, s_L)\|_\infty : s_2 \in \mathcal{F}_2(U^+(2, \infty), 0)\}$$
$$= \inf\{\|\Delta P(s_2, s_L)\|_\infty : s_2 \in \operatorname{Re} \bar{B} A_1(\mathbb{C}_+)\}.$$

If we can relate the latter infimum to the minimization over the larger space $H^\infty(\mathbb{C}_+)$, then minimizing the power mismatch over the lumped circuits can be related to the computable hyperbolic Nehari bound. This seems plausible from experience with the classical linear Nehari Theory, where ϕ real and continuous implies that the distance from the real subset of disk algebra is the same as the distance to H^∞:

$$\|\phi - H^\infty(\mathbb{C}_+)\|_\infty = \|\phi - \operatorname{Re} A_1(\mathbb{C}_+)\|_\infty.$$

Section 5.3 obtains similar results for the nonlinear hyperbolic Nehari bound using metric properties of the power mismatch ΔP.

Thus, the results of this section will provide the desired result: the Nehari bound for the matching problem is both computable and tight in the sense that a sequence of lumped, lossless 2-ports can be found that approach the Nehari bound.

5.1. Nehari's theorem. The Toeplitz and Hankel operators are most conveniently defined on $L^2(\mathbf{T})$ using the Fourier basis. Let $\phi \in L^2(\mathbf{T})$ have the Fourier expansion

$$\phi(z) = \sum_{n=-\infty}^\infty \widehat{\phi}(n) z^n \quad (z = e^{j\theta}).$$

Let P denote the orthogonal projection of $L^2(\mathbf{T})$ onto $H^2(\mathbf{D})$:

$$P\phi(z) = \sum_{n=0}^\infty \widehat{\phi}(n) z^n.$$

The *Toeplitz operator* with symbol $\phi \in L^\infty(\mathbf{T})$ is the mapping $\mathcal{T}_\phi : H^2(\mathbf{D}) \to H^2(\mathbf{D})$

$$\mathcal{T}_\phi h := P(\phi h).$$

The *Hankel operator* with symbol $\phi \in L^\infty(\mathbf{T})$ is the mapping $\mathcal{H}_\phi : H^2(\mathbf{D}) \to H^2(\mathbf{D})$

$$\mathcal{H}_\phi h := U(I - P)(\phi h),$$

where $U : H^2(\mathbf{D})^{\perp} \to H^2(\mathbf{D})$ is the unitary "flipping" operator:

$$Uh\,(z) := z^{-1}h(z^{-1}).$$

These operators admit matrix representations with respect to the Fourier basis [56, page 173]:

$$\mathfrak{T}_{\phi} = \begin{bmatrix} \widehat{\phi}(0) & \widehat{\phi}(1) & \widehat{\phi}(2) & \ddots \\ \widehat{\phi}(-1) & \widehat{\phi}(0) & \widehat{\phi}(1) & \ddots \\ \widehat{\phi}(-2) & \widehat{\phi}(-1) & \widehat{\phi}(0) & \ddots \\ \ddots & \ddots & \ddots & \ddots \end{bmatrix}$$

and [56, page 191]

$$\mathfrak{H}_{\phi} = \begin{bmatrix} \widehat{\phi}(-1) & \widehat{\phi}(-2) & \widehat{\phi}(-3) & \cdots \\ \widehat{\phi}(-2) & \widehat{\phi}(-3) & \widehat{\phi}(-4) & \cdots \\ \widehat{\phi}(-3) & \widehat{\phi}(-4) & \widehat{\phi}(-5) & \cdots \\ \vdots & \vdots & \vdots & \end{bmatrix}.$$

The operator norm is

$$\|\mathfrak{H}_{\phi}\| := \sup\{\|\mathfrak{H}_{\phi}h\|_{\infty} : h \in \bar{B}H^{\infty}(\mathbf{D})\}.$$

The essential norm is

$$\|\mathfrak{H}_{\phi}\|_e := \inf\{\|\mathfrak{H}_{\phi} - K\| : K \text{ is a compact operator}\}.$$

The following version of Nehari's Theorem emphasizes existence and uniqueness of best approximations.

THEOREM 5.1 (NEHARI [56; 45]). *If $\phi \in L^{\infty}(\mathbf{T})$, then ϕ admits best approximations from $H^{\infty}(\mathbf{D})$ as follows:*

N-1: $\|\phi - H^{\infty}(\mathbf{D})\|_{\infty} = \|\mathfrak{H}_{\phi}\|$.
N-2: $\|\phi - \{H^{\infty}(\mathbf{D}) + C(\mathbf{T})\}\|_{\infty} = \|\mathfrak{H}_{\phi}\|_e$.
N-3: *If $\|\mathfrak{H}_{\phi}\|_e < \|\mathfrak{H}_{\phi}\|$ then best approximations are unique.*

Thus, Nehari's Theorem computes the distance from ϕ to $H^{\infty}(\mathbf{D})$ using the Hankel matrix. However, solving the matching problem with lumped circuits forces us to minimize from the disk algebra $\mathcal{A}(\mathbf{D})$. Because the disk algebra is a proper subset of $H^{\infty}(\mathbf{D})$, there always holds the inequality:

$$\|\phi - \mathcal{A}(\mathbf{D})\|_{\infty} \geq \|\phi - H^{\infty}(\mathbf{D})\|_{\infty} = \|\mathfrak{H}_{\phi}\|.$$

Fortunately for our application, equality holds when ϕ is continuous.

THEOREM 5.2 (Adapted from [39, pages 193–195], [33; 34]). *If $\phi \in 1\dot{+}C_0(j\mathbb{R})$,*

$$\|\phi - \mathcal{A}_1(\mathbb{C}_+)\|_\infty = \|\phi - H^\infty(\mathbb{C}_+)\|_\infty$$

and there is exactly one $h \in H^\infty(\mathbb{C}_+)$ such that

$$\|\phi - \mathcal{A}_1(\mathbb{C}_+)\|_\infty = |\phi(j\omega) - h(j\omega)| \quad \text{a.e.}$$

Thus, continuity forces unicity and characterizes the minimum by the *circularity of the error $\phi - h$*. To get existence in the disk algebra requires more than continuity. Let $\phi : \mathbb{R} \to \mathbb{C}$ be periodic with period 2π. The *modulus of continuity* of ϕ is the function [18, page 71]:

$$\omega(\phi; t) := \sup\{|\phi(t_1) - \phi(t_2)| : t_1, t_2 \in \mathbb{R}, |t_1 - t_2| \le t\}.$$

Let Λ_α denote those functions that satisfy a *Lipschitz condition of order $\alpha \in (0,1]$*:

$$|\phi(t_1) - \phi(t_2)| \le A|t_1 - t_2|^\alpha.$$

Let $C^{n+\alpha}$ denote those functions with $\phi^{(n)} \in \Lambda_\alpha$ [5]. Let C_ω denote those functions that are *Dini-continuous*:

$$\int_0^\varepsilon \omega(\phi; t) t^{-1} dt < \infty,$$

for some $\varepsilon > 0$. A sufficient condition for a function $\phi(t)$ to be Dini-continuous is that $|\phi'(t)|$ be bounded [19, section IV.2]. Carleson & Jacobs have an amazing paper that addresses best approximation from the disk algebra [5]:

THEOREM 5.3 (CARLESON & JACOBS [5]). *If $\phi \in L^\infty(\mathbf{T})$, then there always exists a best approximation $h \in H^\infty(\mathbf{D})$:*

$$\|\phi - h\|_\infty = \|\phi - H^\infty(\mathbf{D})\|_\infty.$$

If $\phi \in C(\mathbf{T})$, then the best approximation is unique. Moreover,

(A): *If $\phi \in C_\omega$ then $h \in C_\omega$.*
(B): *If $\phi^{(n)} \in C_\omega$ then $h^{(n)} \in C_\omega$.*
(C): *If $0 < \alpha < 1$ and $\phi \in \Lambda_\alpha$ then $h \in \Lambda_\alpha$.*
(D): *If $0 < \alpha < 1$, $n \in N$, and $\phi \in C^{n+\alpha}$ then $h \in C^{n+\alpha}$.*

As noted by Carleson & Jacobs [5]: "the function-theoretic proofs ... are all of a local character, and so all the results can easily be carried over to any region which has in each case a sufficiently regular boundary." Provided we can guarantee smoothness across $\pm j\infty$, Theorem 5.3 carries over to the right half-plane.

COROLLARY 5.1. *If $\phi \in 1\dot{+}C_0(j\mathbb{R})$, then the best approximation*

$$\|\phi - h\|_\infty = \|\phi - H^\infty(\mathbb{C}_+)\|_\infty$$

exists and is unique. Moreover, if $\phi \circ \mathbf{c}^{-1} \in C_\omega$, then $h \circ \mathbf{c}^{-1} \in C_\omega$ so that

$$\|\phi - h\|_\infty = \|\phi - H^\infty(\mathbb{C}_+)\|_\infty = \|\phi - \mathcal{A}_1(\mathbb{C}_+)\|_\infty.$$

Thus, the smoothness of the target function ϕ is invariant under the *best approximation operator* of H^∞.

5.2. Nonlinear Nehari and simple matching bounds.

Helton [28; 31; 29; 32] is extending Nehari's Theorem into a general Theory of Analytic Optimization. Let $\Gamma : j\mathbb{R} \times \mathbb{C} \to \mathbb{R}_+$ be continuous. Define $\gamma : L^\infty(j\mathbb{R}) \to \mathbb{R}_+ \cup \infty$ by

$$\gamma(h) := \text{ess.sup}\{\Gamma(j\omega, h(j\omega)) : \omega \in \mathbb{R}\}.$$

and consider the minimization of γ on $K \subseteq L^\infty(j\mathbb{R})$:

$$\min\{\gamma(\phi) : \phi \in K\}.$$

Helton observed that many interesting problems in electrical engineering and control theory have the form of this minimization problem and furthermore in many cases the objective functions have sublevel sets that are disks [32]:

$$[\gamma \leq \alpha] := \{\phi \in \bar{B}L^\infty(j\mathbb{R}) : \gamma(\phi) \leq \alpha\} = \bar{D}(c_\alpha, r_\alpha).$$

This is certainly the case for the matching problem. For a given load $s_L \in BL^\infty(j\mathbb{R})$, we want to minimize the worst case mismatch

$$\gamma(s_2) = \Delta\rho(s_2) := \text{ess.sup}\{\Delta P(s_2(j\omega), s_L(j\omega)) : \omega \in \mathbb{R}\}$$

over all $s_2 \in \bar{B}H^\infty(\mathbb{C}_+)$. In this special case, Lemma 4.5 shows explicitly that the sublevel sets of $\Delta\rho$ are disks. These sublevel sets govern the optimization problem. For a start, the sublevel sets determine the existence of minimizers.

LEMMA 5.1. *Let $\gamma : \bar{B}L^\infty(j\mathbb{R}) \to \mathbb{R}$. Assume γ has sublevel sets that are disks contained in $\bar{B}L^\infty(j\mathbb{R})$:*

$$[\gamma \leq \alpha] = \bar{D}(c_\alpha, r_\alpha) \subseteq \bar{B}L^\infty(j\mathbb{R}).$$

Then γ has a minimizer $h_{\min} \in \bar{B}H^\infty(\mathbb{C}_+)$.

PROOF. Lemma 3.2 gives that γ is lower semicontinuous in the weak-$*$ topology. Because $\bar{B}H^\infty(\mathbb{C}_+)$ is weak-$*$ compact, the Weierstrass Theorem of Section 4.10 forces the existence of H^∞ minimizers. $\qquad\square$

In particular, an H^∞ minimizer of power mismatch does exist. This is only the beginning; we'll see that the disk structure of the sublevel sets also couples with Nehari's Theorem to to characterize such minimizers using Helton's fundamental link between disks and operators. Ultimately, this line of inquiry permits us to *calculate* the matching performance for real problems.

THEOREM 5.4 (HELTON [29, Theorem 4.2]). *Let C, P, $R \in L^\infty(\mathbf{T}, \mathbb{C}^{N \times N})$. Assume P and R are uniformly strictly positive. Define the disk*

$$\bar{D}(C, R, P) := \{\Phi \in L^\infty(\mathbf{T}, \mathbb{C}^{N \times N}) : (\Phi - C)P^2(\Phi - C)^H \leq R^2\}$$

and $\check{R}(j\omega) := R(-j\omega)$. Then

$$\varnothing \neq \bar{D}(C, R, P) \cap H^\infty(\mathbf{D}, \mathbb{C}^{N \times N}) \quad \Longleftrightarrow \quad \mathcal{H}_C \mathcal{T}_{P^{-2}}^{-1} \mathcal{H}_C^* \leq \mathcal{T}_{\check{R}^2},$$

For the impedance matching problem, γ is the power mismatch ΔP whose sublevel sets are contained in $\bar{B}L^\infty(j\mathbb{R})$:

$$\bar{D}(c_\alpha, r_\alpha) \cap \bar{B}H^\infty(\mathbb{C}_+) = \bar{D}(c_\alpha, r_\alpha) \cap H^\infty(\mathbb{C}_+).$$

Consequently, in our problem the unit ball constraint may be ignored and we may apply Theorem 5.4 specialized to the disk theory under this stronger assumption.

COROLLARY 5.2. *Let $\gamma : \bar{B}L^\infty(j\mathbb{R}) \to \mathbb{R}$. Assume γ has sublevel sets that are disks:*

$$[\gamma \leq \alpha] = \bar{D}(c_\alpha, r_\alpha) \subseteq \bar{B}L^\infty(j\mathbb{R}).$$

Let $C_\alpha := c_\alpha \circ \mathbf{c}^{-1}$ and $R_\alpha = r_\alpha \circ \mathbf{c}^{-1}$ where $\mathbf{c}$ is the Cayley transform of Lemma 3.3. Assume R_α is strictly uniformly positive with spectral factor $Q_\alpha \in H^\infty(\mathbf{D})$: $R_\alpha = |Q_\alpha|$. Then the following are equivalent:

(A): $\bar{D}(c_\alpha, r_\alpha) \cap \bar{B}H^\infty(\mathbb{C}_+) \neq \varnothing$
(B): $\mathcal{H}_{C_\alpha} \mathcal{H}_{C_\alpha}^* \leq \mathcal{T}_{\check{R}_\alpha^2}$
(C): $\|Q_\alpha^{-1} C_\alpha - H^\infty(\mathbf{D})\|_\infty \leq 1$.

PROOF. By Theorem 5.4, all that is needed is to prove (a) $\Longleftrightarrow$ (c). If (a) is true, there exists an $H \in \bar{B}H^\infty(\mathbf{D})$ such that $|H - C_\alpha| \leq R_\alpha = |Q_\alpha|$ a.e. Because R_α is strictly uniformly positive on $\mathbf{T}$, we may divide by $|Q_\alpha|$ to get $|Q_\alpha^{-1}H - Q_\alpha^{-1}C_\alpha| \leq 1$ a.e. Because Q_α is outer, $Q_\alpha^{-1}H \in H^\infty(\mathbf{D})$ so that(c) must be true. Conversely, suppose (c) is true. Because Q_α is outer, $Q_\alpha^{-1}C_\alpha \in L^\infty(j\mathbb{R})$. The Cayley transform of Nehari's Theorem forces the existence of a $G \in H^\infty(\mathbf{D})$ such that $\|G - Q_\alpha^{-1}C_\alpha\|_\infty \leq 1$. Because Q_α is outer, $H = Q_\alpha G \in H^\infty(\mathbf{D})$ and $|H - C_\alpha| \leq R_\alpha$ a.e. Then $H \in \bar{D}(C_\alpha, R_\alpha) \cap H^\infty(\mathbb{C})$. Because $\bar{D}(C_\alpha, R_\alpha)$ is assumed to be contained in the unit ball of $L^\infty(\mathbf{T})$, the Cayley transform forces(a) to hold.   □

Part (b) amounts to an eigenvalue test that admits a nice graphical display of the minimizing α. Let $\lambda_{\inf}(\alpha)$ denote the smallest "eigenvalue" of $\mathcal{T}_{\check{R}^2} - \mathcal{H}_{C_\alpha} \mathcal{H}_{C_\alpha}^*$. A plot of α versus $\lambda_{\inf}(\alpha)$ reveals that $\lambda_{\inf}(\alpha)$ is a decreasing function of α that crosses zero at a minimum. The next result verifies this assertion regarding the minimum.

COROLLARY 5.3. *Let $\gamma : \bar{B}L^\infty(j\mathbb{R}) \to \mathbb{R}$. Assume γ has sublevel sets that are disks contained in $\bar{B}L^\infty(j\mathbb{R})$:*

$$[\gamma \leq \alpha] = \bar{D}(c_\alpha, r_\alpha) \subseteq \bar{B}L^\infty(j\mathbb{R}).$$

Then γ has a minimizer $h_{\min} \in \bar{B}H^\infty(\mathbb{C}_+)$:

$$\gamma_{\bar{B}H^\infty} := \min\{\gamma(h) : h \in \bar{B}H^\infty(\mathbb{C}_+)\}.$$

Let $c_{\min}$ and $r_{\min}$ denote the $L^\infty(j\mathbb{R})$ center and radius functions of the sublevel disk at the minimum level: $[\gamma \le \gamma_{\bar{B}H^\infty}]$. Let $C_\alpha := c_\alpha \circ \mathbf{c}^{-1}$ and $R_\alpha = r_\alpha \circ \mathbf{c}^{-1}$ where $\mathbf{c}$ is the Cayley transform of Lemma 3.3. Assume $R_{\min}$ is strictly uniformly positive with spectral factor $Q_{\min}$. Then the following are equivalent:

MIN-1: $\bar{D}(c_{\min}, r_{\min}) \cap \bar{B}H^\infty \ne \varnothing$
MIN-2: $0 = \lambda_{\inf}(\gamma_{\bar{B}H^\infty})$
MIN-3: $\|Q_{\min}^{-1}C_{\min} - H^\infty(\mathbf{D})\|_\infty = 1$.

Moreover, if $Q_{\min}^{-1}C_{\min} \in C(\mathbf{T})$ the minimizer $h_{\min}$ is unique.

PROOF. Min-1 $\Longrightarrow$ Min-3: If the inequality were strict, $|C_{\min} - H| < R_{\min}$ a.e. for some $H \in H^\infty(\mathbf{D})$. Then $h = H \circ \mathbf{c}$ belongs to $H^\infty(\mathbb{C}_+)$ and drops γ below its minimum: $\gamma(h) < \alpha_{\min}$. This contradiction forces equality at the minimum. Min-3 $\Longrightarrow$ Min-1: Corollary 5.2.

Min-1 $\Longrightarrow$ Min-2: Theorem 5.4 forces $\mathcal{H}_{C_{\min}}\mathcal{H}_{C_{\min}}^* \le \mathcal{T}_{\bar{R}_{\min}^2}$ or $0 \le \lambda_{\inf}(\gamma_{\bar{B}H^\infty})$. This operator inequality is equivalent to $1 \ge \|\mathcal{H}_{Q_{\min}^{-1}C_{\min}}\|$ [29, page 42]. By Nehari's Theorem, $1 \ge \|\mathcal{H}_{Q_{\min}^{-1}C_{\min}}\| = \|Q_{\min}^{-1}C_{\min} - H^\infty(\mathbf{D})\|_\infty = 1$, where the equivalence of Min-1 and Min-3 gives the last equality. Thus, the inequality must be an equality. Min-2 $\Longrightarrow$ Min-1: $0 = \lambda_{\inf}(\gamma_{\bar{B}H^\infty})$ forces $1 = \|\mathcal{H}_{Q_{\min}^{-1}C_{\min}}\|$. By Nehari's Theorem, $1 = \|Q_{\min}^{-1}C_{\min} - H^\infty(\mathbf{D})\|_\infty$. The Cayley transform of Nehari's Theorem gives an $H \in H^\infty(\mathbf{D})$ such that $1 = \|Q_{\min}^{-1}C_{\min} - H\|_\infty$. Multiply by the spectral factor to get $R_{\min} = |C_{\min} - Q_{\min}H\|$ or that $\bar{D}(c_{\min}, r_{\min}) \cap H^\infty(\mathbf{D}) \ne \varnothing$. Use the assumption that the sublevel sets are contained in the close unit ball to get Min-1. For unicity, Min-3 forces $H_{\min} = h_{\min} \circ \mathbf{c}^{-1}$ to be a minimizer of $1 = \|Q_{\min}^{-1}C_{\min} - H^\infty(\mathbf{D})\|_\infty = \|Q_{\min}^{-1}C_{\min} - H_{\min}\|_\infty$. Because $Q_{\min}^{-1}C_{\min}$ is continuous, the Cayley transform of Corollary 5.1 forces unicity. $\square$

Lumped matching circuits have continuous scattering matrices. This requires us to constrain our minimization of power mismatch yet further to the disk algebra. For minimization of a general γ over the disk algebra, we always have

$$\gamma_{\bar{B}H^\infty} \le \gamma_{\bar{B}\mathcal{A}_1} := \inf\{\gamma(h) : h \in \bar{B}\mathcal{A}_1(\mathbb{C}_+)\}.$$

Under smoothness and continuity conditions, equality between the disk algebra and H^∞ can be established.

COROLLARY 5.4. *In addition to the assumptions of Corollary 5.3, assume $Q_{\min}^{-1}C_{\min}$ is Dini-continuous. Then*

$$\gamma_{\bar{B}H^\infty} = \gamma_{\bar{B}\mathcal{A}_1} = \min\{\gamma(h) : h \in \bar{B}\mathcal{A}_1(\mathbb{C}_+)\}.$$

PROOF. By Corollary 5.3, there is a unique minimizer $H_{\min} \in H^\infty(\mathbf{D})$

$$1 = \|Q_{\min}^{-1} C_{\min} - H^\infty(\mathbf{D})\|_\infty = \|Q_{\min}^{-1} C_{\min} - H_{\min}\|_\infty.$$

By Corollary 5.1, Dini-continuity forces $H_{\min}$ to be Dini-continuous or $h_{\min} = H \circ \mathbf{c} \in \mathcal{A}_1(\mathbb{C}_+)$, Thus, the inclusion of the H^∞ minimizer in the disk algebra forces $\gamma_{\bar{B}H^\infty} = \gamma_{\bar{B}\mathcal{A}_1}$. $\square$

This is a useful general result, but for our matching problem the requirement of Dini-continuity can in fact be relaxed. An easier approach, specialized to the case of γ is the power mismatch, gives equality between the minimum over the disk algebra and that over H^∞ using only continuity (proof in Appendix D).

THEOREM 5.5. *Assume $s_L \in B\mathcal{A}_1(\mathbb{C}_+)$. Then*

$$\min\{\|\Delta P(s_2, s_L)\|_\infty : s_2 \in \bar{B}H^\infty(\mathbb{C}_+)\} = \inf\{\|\Delta P(s_2, s_L)\|_\infty : s_2 \in \bar{B}\mathcal{A}_1(\mathbb{C}_+)\}.$$

5.3. The real constraint. Examination of the circuits in Section 4 shows the scattering matrices are real: $S(p) = \overline{S(\bar{p})}$ In fact, the scattering matrices that are used in the matching problem must satisfy this *real constraint*. Those H^∞ functions satisfying this real constraint form a proper subset $\operatorname{Re} H^\infty(\mathbb{C}_+)$, which generally forces the inequality:

$$\inf\{\|\phi - h\|_\infty : h \in \operatorname{Re} H^\infty(\mathbb{C}_+)\} \geq \|\phi - H^\infty(\mathbb{C}_+)\|_\infty$$

However, equality is obtained provided ϕ is also real. That the best approximation operator preserves the real constraint is an excellent illustration of the general principle: That the best approximation operator preserves symmetries.

LEMMA 5.2. *Let $(\mathcal{X}, d)$ be a metric space. Assume $A : \mathcal{X} \to \mathcal{X}$ is a contractive map: $d(A(x), A(y)) \leq d(x, y)$. Let $\mathcal{V} \subseteq \mathcal{X}$ be nonempty. Define $\operatorname{dist}(x, \mathcal{V}) := \inf\{d(x, v) : v \in \mathcal{V}\}$. Assume*

A-1: *$\mathcal{V}$ is A-invariant: $A(\mathcal{V}) \subseteq \mathcal{V}$.*
A-2: *$x \in \mathcal{X}$ is also A-invariant $A(x) = x$.*

Then equality holds: $\operatorname{dist}(x, A(\mathcal{V})) = \operatorname{dist}(x, \mathcal{V})$.

PROOF. Let $\{v_n\}$ be a minimizing sequence: $d(x, v_n) \to \operatorname{dist}(x, \mathcal{V})$. Because x is A-invariant, $d(x, A(v_n)) = d(A(x), A(v_n)) \leq d(x, v_n) \to \operatorname{dist}(x, \mathcal{V})$. Thus, $\operatorname{dist}(x, A(\mathcal{V})) \leq \operatorname{dist}(x, \mathcal{V})$ forces equality. $\square$

Lemma 5.2 makes explicit the structure to handle the real constraint in the matching problem.

COROLLARY 5.5. *If $s_L \in B \operatorname{Re} L^\infty(j\mathbb{R})$, there holds*

$$\inf\{\|\Delta P(s_2, s_L)\|_\infty : s_2 \in \bar{B}\mathcal{A}_1(\mathbb{C}_+)\} = \inf\{\|\Delta P(s_2, s_L)\|_\infty : s_2 \in \operatorname{Re} \bar{B}\mathcal{A}_1(\mathbb{C}_+)\}.$$

Proof. Apply Lemma 5.2 identifying $BL^\infty(j\mathbb{R})$ as the metric space, $\widetilde{\phi}(j\omega) = \overline{\phi(\overline{j\omega})}$ as the contraction, $\mathrm{Re}\, B\mathcal{A}_1(\mathbb{C}_+)$ as the $\sim$-invariant subset, and s_L as the $\sim$-invariant target function. Recall that the power mismatch $\Delta P(s_2, s_L)$ is the pseudohyperbolic metric $\rho(\overline{s_2}, s_L)$ (Section 4.8). Because ρ is a metric, it follows that $\|\rho\|_\infty$ is also metric that is $\sim$-invariant: $\|\rho(\widetilde{s_2}, \widetilde{s_L})\|_\infty = \|\rho(s_2, s_L)\|_\infty$. The technical complication is that $\Delta P(s_2, s_L)$ is well-defined only when one of its arguments is restricted to the open unit ball $BL^\infty(j\mathbb{R})$. With $s_L \in B\,\mathrm{Re}\,L^\infty(j\mathbb{R})$, Lemma 4.6 asserts that $s_2 \mapsto \|\Delta P(s_2, s_L)\|_\infty$ is a continuous mapping on $\bar{B}L^\infty(j\mathbb{R})$. Thus, we use continuity to drop the $\bar{B}$ constraint, apply Lemma 5.2 to the open ball with the real contraction "$\sim$", and apply continuity again to close the open ball:

$$\inf\{\|\Delta P(s_2, s_L)\|_\infty : s_2 \in \mathrm{Re}\,\bar{B}\mathcal{A}_1(\mathbb{C}_+)\}$$

$$\overset{\text{Lemma 4.6}}{=} \inf\{\|\Delta P(s_2, s_L)\|_\infty : s_2 \in \mathrm{Re}\,B\mathcal{A}_1(\mathbb{C}_+)\}$$

$$\overset{\text{Eq. 4-10}}{=} \inf\{\|\rho(\overline{s_2}, s_L)\|_\infty : s_2 \in \mathrm{Re}\,B\mathcal{A}_1(\mathbb{C}_+)\}$$

$$\overset{\text{Corollary 5.5}}{=} \inf\{\|\rho(\overline{s_2}, s_L)\|_\infty : s_2 \in B\mathcal{A}_1(\mathbb{C}_+)\}$$

$$\overset{\text{Eq. 4-10}}{=} \inf\{\|\Delta P(s_2, s_L)\|_\infty : s_2 \in B\mathcal{A}_1(\mathbb{C}_+)\}$$

$$\overset{\text{Lemma 4.6}}{=} \inf\{\|\Delta P(s_2, s_L)\|_\infty : s_2 \in \bar{B}\mathcal{A}_1(\mathbb{C}_+)\}. \quad \square$$

Not surprisingly, Helton has also uncovered another notion of "real-invariance" for general nonlinear minimization [32].

6. Classes of Lossless 2-Ports

The matching problems are optimization problems over classes of $U^+(2)$:

$$U^+(2, d) \subset U^+(2, \infty) \subset U^+(2) \subset \mathrm{Re}\,\bar{B}H^\infty(\mathbb{C}_+, \mathbb{C}^{2 \times 2}).$$

On the left, $U^+(2, d)$ corresponds to the lumped, lossless 2-ports. Optimization over this set represents an electrical engineering solution. On the right, the H^∞ solution provided in the last section is computable from the measured data but may not correspond to any lossless scattering matrix. The gap between the H^∞ solution and the various electrical engineering solutions may be closed by continuity conditions.

The first result on gives the correspondence between the lumped N-ports and their scattering matrices.

The Circuit-Scattering Correspondence [52, Theorems 3.1, 3.2]. *Any N-port composed of a finite number of lumped elements (positive resistors, capacitors, inductors, transformers, gyrators) admits a real, rational, lossless scattering matrix $S \in U^+(N)$. Conversely, to any real, rational, scattering matrix $S \in U^+(N)$ there corresponds an N-port composed of a finite number of lumped elements*

This equivalence permits us to delineate the following class of lossless 2-ports by their scattering matrices:

$$U^+(2, d) := \{S \in U^+(2) : \deg_{\mathrm{SM}}[S(p)] \le d\},$$

where $\deg_{\mathrm{SM}}[S(p)]$ denotes the Smith–McMillan degree (defined in Theorem 6.2). The second result establishes compactness (Appendix C contains the proof).

THEOREM 6.1. *Let* $d \ge 0$. $U^+(N, d)$ *is a compact subset of* $\mathcal{A}_1(\mathbb{C}_+, \mathbb{C}^{N \times N})$.

It is straight-forward but tedious to demonstrate that the gain function $S \mapsto \|G_T(s_G, S, s_L)\|_{-\infty}$ is a continuous function on $U^+(2, d)$. Thus, the matching problem on $U^+(2, d)$ has a solution. The third result on $U^+(2, d)$ is the Belevitch parameterization.

BELEVITCH'S THEOREM [53] $S \in U^+(2, d)$ *if and only if*

$$S(p) = \left[\begin{array}{cc} s_{11}(p) & s_{12}(p) \\ s_{21}(p) & s_{22}(p) \end{array} \right] = \frac{1}{g(p)} \left[\begin{array}{cc} h(p) & f(p) \\ \pm f_*(p) & \mp h_*(p) \end{array} \right],$$

where $f_*(p) := f(-p)$ *and*

B-1: $f(p)$, $g(p)$, *and* $h(p)$ *are real polynomials,*

B-2: $g(p)$ *is strict Hurwitz[5] of degree not exceeding* d,

B-3: $g_*(p)g(p) = f_*(p)f(p) + h_*(p)h(p)$ *for all* $p \in \mathbb{C}$.

Belevitch's Theorem lets us characterize several classes of 2-ports, such as the low-pass and high-pass ladders. The low-pass ladders (Figure 11) admit the scattering matrix characterization [3, page 121]:

$$s_{21}(p) = \frac{1}{g(p)}.$$

These scattering matrices ($f(p) = 1$) form a closed and therefore compact subset of $U^+(2, d)$. Consequently, the matching problem admits a solution over the class of low-pass ladders. Figure 17 shows a high-pass ladder. A high-pass ladder admits the scattering matrix characterization [3, page 122]:

$$s_{21}(p) = \frac{p^{\partial g}}{g(p)},$$

where ∂g denotes the degree of the polynomial $g(p)$. The high-pass ladders form

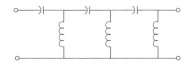

Figure 17. A high-pass ladder.

---

[5]The zeros of $g(p)$ lie in the open left half-plane.

a closed and therefore compact subset of $U^+(2,d)$. Consequently, the matching problem admits a solution over the class of high-pass ladders.

The fourth result on $U^+(2,d)$ is the state-space parameterization illustrated in Figure 18. The N-port has a scattering matrix $S \in U^+(N,d)$, where $d = \deg_{\mathrm{SM}}[S(p)]$ counts the number of inductors and capacitors, The figure shows that by pulling all the d reactive elements into the *augmented load* $S_L(p)$. What's left is an $(N+d)$-port with has a *constant* scattering matrix S_a called the *augmented scattering* matrix. Then S_a models the $(N+d)$-port as a collection of wires, transformers, and gyrators. Consequently, S_a is a real, unitary, and *constant* matrix. Thus, $S(p)$ is the image of the augmented load viewed through the augmented scattering matrix. Theorem 6.2 gives the precise statement of this *state-space representation*.

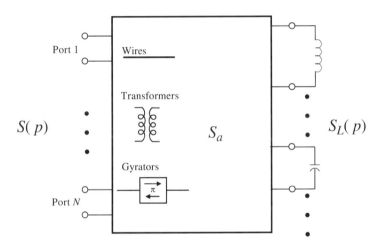

Figure 18. State-space representation of a lumped, lossless N-port containing d reactive elements.

THEOREM 6.2 (STATE-SPACE [52, pages 90–93]). *Every lumped, lossless, casual, time-invariant N-port admits a scattering matrix $S(p)$ and conversely. If $S(p)$ has degree d, $S(p)$ admits the following state-space representation:*

$$S(p) = \mathcal{F}(S_a, S_L; p) := S_{a,11} + S_{a,12}S_L(p)(I_d - S_{a,22}S_L)^{-1}S_{a,21},$$

where the augmented load is

$$S_L(p) = \frac{p-1}{p+1} \begin{bmatrix} I_{N_L} & 0 \\ 0 & -I_{N_C} \end{bmatrix}$$

and $N_L+N_C = d$ counts the number of inductors and capacitors. The augmented scattering matrix is

$$S_a = \begin{bmatrix} S_{a,11} & S_{a,12} \\ S_{a,21} & S_{a,22} \end{bmatrix} \begin{matrix} N \\ d \end{matrix}$$
$$\quad\quad\quad N \quad d$$

is a constant, real, orthogonal matrix.

This representation reveals the structure of the lumped, lossless N-ports, offers a numerically efficient parameterization of $U^+(N,d)$ in terms of the orthogonal group, proves the Circuit-Scattering Correspondence, generalizes to lumped, passive N-ports, and provides an approach to non-lumped or distributed N-ports.

A natural generalization drops the constraint on the number of reactive elements in the 2-port and asks: *What is the matching set that is obtained as* $\deg_{SM}[S(p)] \to \infty$? Define

$$U^+(2,\infty) = \overline{\bigcup_{d\geq 0} U^+(2,d)}.$$

The physical meaning of $U^+(2,\infty)$ is that it contains the scattering matrices of all lumped, lossless 2-ports. It is worthwhile to ask: *Has the closure has picked up additional circuits?* Mathematically, a lossless matching N-port has a scattering matrix $S(p)$ that is a real inner function. Inner functions exhibit a fascinating behavior at the boundary. For example, inner functions can interpolate a sequence of closed, connected subsets $K_m \subseteq \overline{\mathbf{D}}$ [12]: $\lim_{r\to 1} S(re^{j\theta_m}) = K_m$. In contrast to this boundary behavior, if the lossless N-port is lumped, then S is rational and so must continuous. The converse is true and demonstrated in Appendix A.

COROLLARY 6.1. *Let* $S \in H^\infty(\mathbb{C}_+, \mathbb{C}^{N\times N})$ *be an inner function. The following are equivalent:*

(A): $S \in \mathcal{A}_1(\mathbb{C}_+, \mathbb{C}^{N\times N})$.
(B): S *is rational*

Corollary 6.1 answers our question above with the negative:

$$U^+(2,\infty) = \bigcup_{d\geq 0} U^+(2,d).$$

Thus, continuity forces $S \in U^+(2,\infty)$ to be rational and the corresponding lossless 2-port to be lumped. It is natural to ask: *What lossless 2-ports are not in* $U^+(2,\infty)$?

EXAMPLE 6.1 (TRANSMISSION LINE). A uniform, lossless transmission line of characteristic impedance Z_c and *commensurate* length l is called a unit element (UE) with chain matrix [3, Equation 8.1]

$$\begin{bmatrix} v_1 \\ i_1 \end{bmatrix} = \begin{bmatrix} \cosh(\tau p) & Z_c\sinh(\tau p) \\ Y_c\sinh(\tau p) & \cosh(\tau p) \end{bmatrix} \begin{bmatrix} v_2 \\ -i_2 \end{bmatrix},$$

where τ is the commensurate one-way delay $\tau = l/c$ determined by the speed of propagation c.

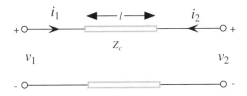

Figure 19. The unit element (UE) transmission line.

The scattering matrix of the transmission line **normalized to Z_c** is

$$S_{\mathrm{UE}}(p) = \begin{bmatrix} 0 & e^{-\tau p} \\ e^{-\tau p} & 0 \end{bmatrix}$$

and gives rise to two observations: First, $S_{\mathrm{UE}}(j\omega)$ oscillates out to $\pm\infty$, so $S_{\mathrm{UE}}(j\omega)$ cannot be continuous across $\pm\infty$. Thus, $U^+(2,\infty)$ cannot contain such a transmission line. Second, a physical transmission line cannot behave like this near $\pm\infty$. Many electrical engineering books mention only in passing that their models are applicable only for a given frequency band. One rarely sees much discussion that the models for the inductor and capacitor are essentially low-frequency models. This holds true even for the standard model of wire. One cannot shine a light in one end of a 100-foot length of copper wire and expect much out of the other end. These model limitations notwithstanding, the circuit-scattering correspondence will be developed using these standard models. The transmission line on the disk is

$$S_{\mathrm{UE}} \circ \mathbf{c}^{-1}(z) = \begin{bmatrix} 0 & \exp\!\left(-\tau\dfrac{1+z}{1-z}\right) \\ \exp\!\left(-\tau\dfrac{1+z}{1-z}\right) & 0 \end{bmatrix}$$

and is recognizable as the simplest singular inner function [35, pages 66–67] analytic on $\mathbb{C} \setminus \{1\}$ [35, pages 68–69]. Figure 20 shows the essential singularity of the real part of the $(1,2)$ element of $S_{\mathrm{UE}} \circ \mathbf{c}^{-1}(z)$ as z tends toward the boundary of the unit circle.

7. Orbits and Tight Bounds for Matching

The following equalities convert a 2-port problem into a 1-port problem. Let $\mathcal{U}$ be a subset of $U^+(2)$. Let

$$\mathcal{F}_1(\mathcal{U}, s_L) := \{\mathcal{F}_1(S, s_L) : S \in \mathcal{U}\}, \quad \mathcal{F}_2(\mathcal{U}, s_G) := \{\mathcal{F}_2(S, s_G) : S \in \mathcal{U}\}$$

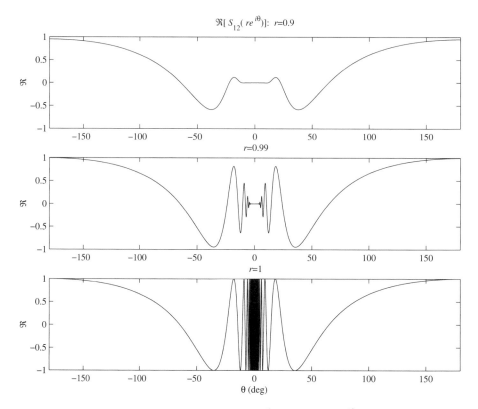

Figure 20. Behavior of $\mathrm{Re}[S_{\mathrm{UE},12} \circ \mathbf{c}^{-1}(z)]$ for $z = re^{j\theta}$ as $r \to 1$.

denote the orbit of the load and the orbit of the generator, respectively. By Lemma 4.4,

$$\sup\{\|G_T(s_G, S, s_L)\|_{-\infty} : S \in \mathcal{U}\} = 1 - \inf\{\|\Delta P(s_G, S, s_L)\|_\infty^2 : S \in \mathcal{U}\}$$
$$= 1 - \inf\{\|\Delta P(s_G, s_1)\|_\infty^2 : s_1 \in \mathcal{F}_1(\mathcal{U}; s_L)\},$$
$$= 1 - \inf\{\|\Delta P(s_2, s_L)\|_\infty^2 : s_2 \in \mathcal{F}_2(\mathcal{U}; s_G)\},$$

or maximizing the gain on $\mathcal{U}$ is equivalent to minimizing the power mismatch on either orbit. Darlington's Theorem makes explicit a class of orbits.

THEOREM 7.1 (DARLINGTON [3]). *The orbits of zero under the lumped, lossless 2-ports are equal*

$$\mathcal{F}_2(U^+(2,\infty), 0) = \mathcal{F}_1(U^+(2,\infty), 0)$$

and strictly dense in $\mathrm{Re}\,\bar{B}\mathcal{A}_1(\mathbb{C}_+)$.

PROOF. Let $S \in U^+(2,\infty)$. Corollary 6.1 and Belevitch's Theorem give that

$$S(p) = \frac{1}{g} \begin{bmatrix} h & f \\ \pm f_* & \mp h_* \end{bmatrix} \in \mathrm{Re}\,\mathcal{A}_1(\mathbb{C}_+, \mathbb{C}^{2\times 2}),$$

where (f, g, h) is a Belevitch triple. With $s_L = 0$ and $s_G = 0$, both $s_1 = \mathcal{F}_1(S, 0) = h/g$ and belong to $\text{Re } \bar{B}\mathcal{A}_1(\mathbb{C}_+)$. However, Corollary 6.1 restricts S to be rational so the orbits cannot be all of $\text{Re } \bar{B}\mathcal{A}_1(\mathbb{C}_+)$. By relabeling S with $1 \leftrightarrow 2$, we get equality between the orbits. To show density, suppose $s \in \text{Re } \bar{B}\mathcal{A}_1(\mathbb{C}_+)$. Because the rational functions in $\text{Re } \bar{B}\mathcal{A}_1(\mathbb{C}_+)$ are a dense[6] subset, we may approximate $s(p)$ by a real rational function: $s \approx h/g \in \text{Re } \bar{B}\mathcal{A}_1(\mathbb{C}_+)$, where $h(p)$ and $g(p)$ may be taken as real polynomials with $g(p)$ strict Hurwitz and for all $\omega \in \mathbb{R}$: $g(j\omega)g_*(j\omega) - h(j\omega)h_*(j\omega) \geq 0$. By factoring $g(p)g_*(p) - h(p)h_*(p)$ or appealing to the Fejér–Riesz Theorem [46, page 109], we can find a real polynomial $f(p)$ such that

$$f(p)f_*(p) = g(p)g_*(p) - h(p)h_*(p).$$

The conditions of Belevitch's Theorem are met and

$$S(p) = \frac{1}{g(p)} \begin{bmatrix} h(p) & f(p) \\ f_*(p) & -h_*(p) \end{bmatrix}$$

is a lossless scattering matrix that represents a lumped, lossless 2-port. That is, $h(p)/g(p)$ dilates to a lossless scattering matrix $S(p)$ for which $s \approx s_{11}$. Consequentially, both orbits are dense in $\text{Re } \bar{B}\mathcal{A}_1(\mathbb{C}_+)$. □

At this point we are in position to obtain a tight bound on matching performance in the special case of vanishing generator reflectance, $s_G = 0$. For any given load $s_L \in BH^\infty(\mathbb{C}_+)$. Lemma 4.6 shows that $s_2 \mapsto \|\Delta P(s_2, s_L)\|_\infty$ is continuous. This continuity, coupled with the density claims of Darlington's Theorem, gives:

$$\max\{G_T(0, S, s_L) : S \in U^+(2, d)\}$$

$$= 1 - \min\{\|\Delta P(s_2, s_L)\|_\infty^2 : s_2 \in \mathcal{F}_2(U^+(2, d); 0)\}$$

$$\leq 1 - \inf\{\|\Delta P(s_2, s_L)\|_\infty^2 : s_2 \in \mathcal{F}_2(U^+(2, \infty); 0)\}$$

$$\overset{\text{Darlington}}{=} 1 - \inf\{\|\Delta P(s_2, s_L)\|_\infty^2 : s_2 \in \text{Re } \bar{B}\mathcal{A}_1(\mathbb{C}_+)\}$$

$$\leq 1 - \inf\{\|\Delta P(s_2, s_L)\|_\infty^2 : s_2 \in \bar{B}H^\infty(\mathbb{C}_+)\}.$$

The "max" and the "min" are used because $U^+(2, d)$ is compact (Theorem 6.1) and G_T is continuous. The last infimum is attained by a minimizer by the Weierstrass Theorem using the weak-$*$ compactness of $\bar{B}H^\infty(\mathbb{C}_+)$ (page 10) and the weak-$*$ lower semicontinuity of the power mismatch (Section 4.10). The minimum can be computed using the Nonlinear Nehari Theorem (See the comments following Corollary 5.2 and Corollary 5.3). Thus, the impedance matching problem has a *computable* bound:

---

[6]Density claims on unbounded regions can be tricky. However, Lemma 3.3 isometrically maps $\mathcal{A}_1(\mathbb{C}_+) = \mathcal{A}_1(\mathbf{D}) \circ \mathbf{c}$ and preserves the rational functions. Therefore, the dense rational functions in $\mathcal{A}(\mathbf{D})$ map to a set of rational functions in $\mathcal{A}_1(\mathbb{C}_+)$ that must be dense.

$$\max\{G_T(0, S, s_L) : S \in U^+(2, d)\}$$

$$= \quad 1 - \min\{\|\Delta P(s_2, s_L)\|_\infty^2 : s_2 \in \mathcal{F}_2(U^+(2, d); 0)\}$$

$$\leq \quad 1 - \inf\{\|\Delta P(s_2, s_L)\|_\infty^2 : s_2 \in \mathcal{F}_2(U^+(2, \infty); 0)\}$$

$$\overset{\text{Darlington}}{=} \quad 1 - \inf\{\|\Delta P(s_2, s_L)\|_\infty^2 : s_2 \in \operatorname{Re}\bar{B}\mathcal{A}_1(\mathbb{C}_+)\}$$

$$\leq \quad 1 - \overset{\text{Corollary 5.3}}{\min} \{\|\Delta P(s_2, s_L)\|_\infty^2 : s_2 \in \bar{B}H^\infty(\mathbb{C}_+)\} \text{ (computable)}.$$

The real constraint can be relaxed for real loads s_L by Corollary 5.5:

$$\max\{G_T(0, S, s_L) : S \in U^+(2, d)\}$$

$$= \quad 1 - \min\{\|\Delta P(s_2, s_L)\|_\infty^2 : s_2 \in \mathcal{F}_2(U^+(2, d); 0)\}$$

$$\leq \quad 1 - \inf\{\|\Delta P(s_2, s_L)\|_\infty^2 : s_2 \in \mathcal{F}_2(U^+(2, \infty); 0)\}$$

$$\overset{\text{Darlington}}{=} \quad 1 - \inf\{\|\Delta P(s_2, s_L)\|_\infty^2 : s_2 \in \operatorname{Re}\bar{B}\mathcal{A}_1(\mathbb{C}_+)\}$$

$$\overset{\text{Corollary 5.5}}{=} \quad 1 - \inf\{\|\Delta P(s_2, s_L)\|_\infty^2 : s_2 \in \bar{B}\mathcal{A}_1(\mathbb{C}_+)\}$$

$$\leq \quad 1 - \overset{\text{Corollary 5.3}}{\min} \{\|\Delta P(s_2, s_L)\|_\infty^2 : s_2 \in \bar{B}H^\infty(\mathbb{C}_+)\} \text{ (computable)}.$$

Finally, the last inequality is actually equality if s_L is sufficiently smooth, using Theorem 5.5. Rolling it all up, we see that $s_L \in \operatorname{Re}B\mathcal{A}_1(\mathbb{C}_+)$ forces a lot of equalities:

$$\max\{G_T(0, S, s_L) : S \in U^+(2, d)\}$$

$$= \quad 1 - \min\{\|\Delta P(s_2, s_L)\|_\infty^2 : s_2 \in \mathcal{F}_2(U^+(2, d); 0)\}$$

$$\leq \quad 1 - \inf\{\|\Delta P(s_2, s_L)\|_\infty^2 : s_2 \in \mathcal{F}_2(U^+(2, \infty); 0)\}$$

$$\overset{\text{Darlington}}{=} \quad 1 - \inf\{\|\Delta P(s_2, s_L)\|_\infty^2 : s_2 \in \operatorname{Re}\bar{B}\mathcal{A}_1(\mathbb{C}_+)\}$$

$$\overset{\text{Corollary 5.5}}{=} \quad 1 - \inf\{\|\Delta P(s_2, s_L)\|_\infty^2 : s_2 \in \bar{B}\mathcal{A}_1(\mathbb{C}_+)\}$$

$$\overset{\text{Theorem 5.5}}{=} \quad 1 - \overset{\text{Corollary 5.3}}{\min} \{\|\Delta P(s_2, s_L)\|_\infty^2 : s_2 \in \bar{B}H^\infty(\mathbb{C}_+)\} \text{ (computable)}.$$

Physically, this tight Nehari bound means that a lossless 2-port can be found with smallest possible power mismatch and that there is a sequence of lumped, lossless 2-ports that can get arbitrarily close to this bound. Furthermore, this bound can be computed from measured data on the load.

8. Matching an HF Antenna

Recent measurements were acquired on the forward-mast integrated HF antenna on the LPD 17, an amphibious transport dock. The problem is match this antenna over 9-30 MHz to a 50-ohm line impedance using the simplest matching circuit possible. The goal is to find a simple matching circuit that gets the smallest power mismatch or the smallest VSWR (Section 4.8) Thus, a practical matching problem is complicated by not only minimizing the VSWR but making a tradeoff between VSWR and circuit complexity.

We start with a transformer, consider low- and high-pass ladders, and then show how the Nehari bound benchmarks these matching efforts. The transformer has chain and chain scattering matrices parameterized by its turns ratio n (see [3, Eq. 2.4] and [25, Table 6.2]; see also Figure 4 and Equation 4–1):

$$T_{\text{transformer}} = \begin{bmatrix} n^{-1} & 0 \\ 0 & n \end{bmatrix} \quad \Theta_{\text{transformer}} = \frac{1}{2n} \begin{bmatrix} 1+n^2 & 1-n^2 \\ 1-n^2 & 1+n^2 \end{bmatrix}.$$

Figure 21 displays the power mismatch as a function of the turns ratio n. This optimal n produced Figure 5 in the introduction. The antenna's load s_L is plotted as the solid curve in the unit disk. The solid disk corresponds to those reflectances with VSWR less than 4. The dotted line plots the reflectance looking to Port 1 of the optimal transformer with Port 2 terminated in the antenna: $s_1 = \mathcal{G}_1(\Theta_{\text{transformer}}, s_L)$. Lemma 4.4 demonstrates that matching at either port is equivalent when the 2-port is lossless.

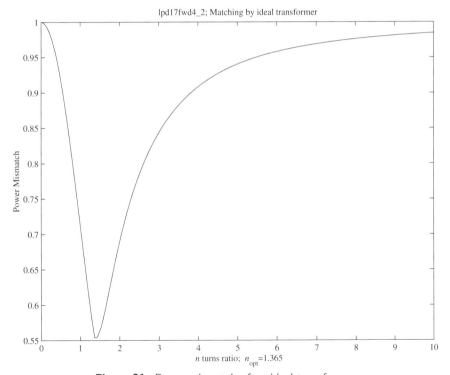

Figure 21. Power mismatch of an ideal transformer.

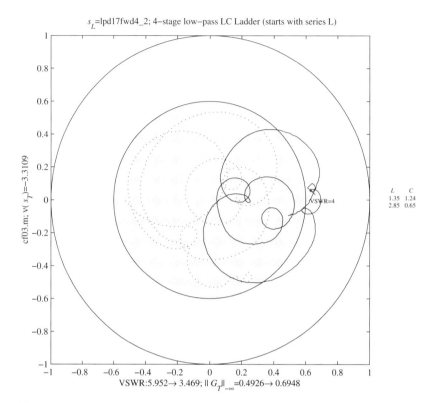

s_L=lpd17fwd4_2; 4–stage low–pass LC Ladder (starts with series L)

VSWR:5.952→ 3.469; ‖ G_T‖$_{-\infty}$=0.4926→ 0.6948

L	C
1.35	1.24
2.85	0.65

Figure 22. The antenna's reflectance s_L (solid) and the reflectance s_1 after matching with a low-pass ladder of order 4.

Figure 22 matches the antenna with a low-pass ladder of order 4 (See Figure 11). Comparison with the transformer shows little is to be gained with the extra complexity. So it is very tempting to try longer ladders, or switch to high-pass ladders, or just start throwing circuits at the antenna. The first step to gain control over the matching processes is conduct a search over all lumped, lossless 2-port of degree not exceeding d:

$$d \mapsto \min\{\|\Delta P(\mathcal{F}_2(S, s_G), s_L)\|_\infty : S \in U^+(2, d)\}.$$

The state-space representation of Theorem 6.2 provides a numerically efficient parameterization of these lossless 2-ports. Figure 23 reports on matching from $U^+(2, 4)$. What is interesting is that s_2 is starting to take a circular shape. This circular shape is no accident. Mathematically, Nehari's Theorem implies that the error is constant at optimum s_2:

$$\Delta P(s_2(j\omega), s_L(j\omega)) = \rho_{\min}.$$

The electrical engineers know the practical manifestation of Nehari's Theorem. For example, a broadband matching technique is described as follows [55]: The

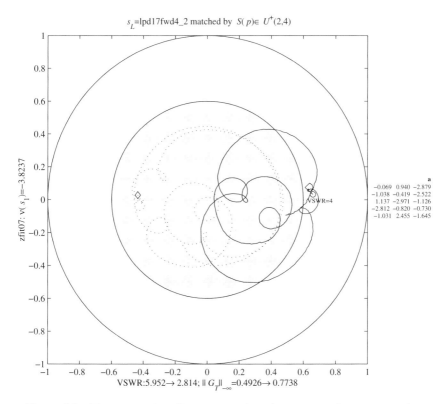

Figure 23. The antenna's reflectance s_L (solid) and the reflectance s_1 after matching over $U^+(2,4)$.

load impedance z_L is plotted in the Smith chart. The engineer is to terminate this load with a cascade of lossless two-ports. By repeatedly applying "shunt-stub/series-line cascades, a skilled designer using simulation software can see [the terminated impedance z_T] form into a fairly tight circle around $z = 1$." The appearance of a circle is a real-world demonstration that Nehari's Theorem is heuristically understood by microwave engineers.

The final step for bounding the matching process is to estimate the Nehari bound. Combine the eigenvalue test of Corollary 5.2 with the characterization of the power mismatch disks in Lemma 4.5: There is an $s_2 \in \bar{B}H^\infty(\mathbb{C}_+)$ with

$$\|\Delta(s_2, s_L)\|_\infty \leq \rho \iff \mathcal{T}_{\tilde{R}_\rho}{}^2 \geq \mathcal{H}_{C_\rho}\mathcal{H}_{C_\rho}^*,$$

where the center and radius functions are

$$C_\rho = k_\rho \circ \mathbf{c}^{-1}, \quad k_\rho = \bar{s}_L \frac{1 - \rho^2}{1 - \rho^2 |s_L|^2},$$

$$R_\rho = r_\rho \circ \mathbf{c}^{-1}, \quad r_\rho = \rho \frac{1 - |s_L|^2}{1 - \rho^2 |s_L|^2}.$$

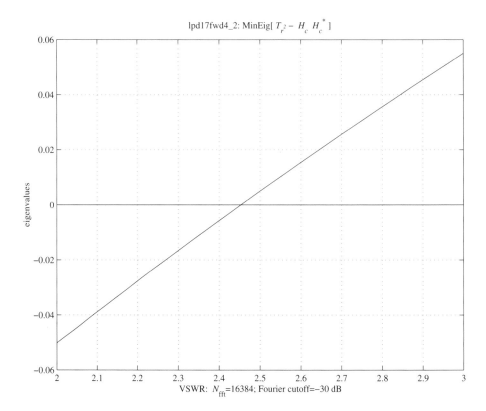

Figure 24. Estimate of $\lambda_{\inf}(\rho)$ versus ρ in terms of the VSWR

Let $\lambda_{\inf}(\rho)$ denote the smallest real number in the spectrum of $\mathcal{T}_{\check{R}_{\rho}{}^2} - \mathcal{H}_{C_{\rho}}\mathcal{H}_{C_{\rho}}^{*}$. Figure 24 plots an estimate of $\lambda_{\inf}(\rho)$. The optimal VSWR occurs near the zero-crossing point.

Figure 25 uses these VSWR bounds to benchmark several classes of matching circuits. Each circuit's VSWR is plotted as a function of the degree d (the total number of inductors and capacitors). The dashed lines are the VSWR from the low- and high-pass ladders containing inductors and capacitors constrained to practical design values. The solid line is the matching estimated from $U^{+}(2,d)$. A transformer performs as well as any matching circuit of degree 0 and as well as the low-pass ladders out to degree 6. The high-pass ladders get closer to the VSWR bound at degree 4. A perfectly coupled transformer (coefficient of coupling $k = 1$) offers only a slight improvement over the transformer. In terms of making the tradeoff between VSWR and circuit complexity, Figure 25 directs the circuit designer's attention to the $d = 2$ region. There exist matching circuits of order 2 with performance comparable to high-pass ladders of order 4. Thus, the circuit designer can graphically assess trade-offs between various circuits in the context of knowing the best match possible for any lossless 2-port.

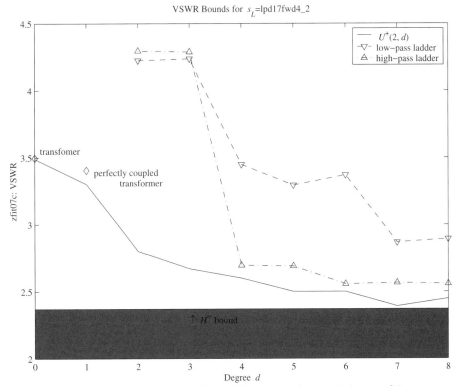

Figure 25. Comparing the matching performance of several classes of 2-ports with the Nehari and $U^+(2, d)$ bounds.

9. Research Topics

This paper shows how to apply the Nehari bound to measured, real-world impedances. The price of admission is learning the scattering formalism and a few common electric circuits. The payoff is that many substantial research topics can be tastefully guided by this concrete problem. For immediate applications, several active and passive devices explicitly use wideband matching to improve performance:

- antenna [49; 2; 8; 1];
- circulator [36];
- fiber-optic links [7; 26; 23];
- satellite links [40];
- amplifiers [11; 22; 37].

The H^∞ applications to the transducers, antenna, and communication links are immediate. The amplifier is an active 2-port that requires a more general approach. The matching problem for the amplifier is to find input and output matching 2-ports that simultaneously maximize transducer power gain, minimize the noise figure, and maintain stability. Although a more general problem, this amplifier-matching problem fits squarely in the H^∞ framework [28; 29; 30] and is a current topic in ONR's H^∞ Research Initiative [41].

9.1. Darlington's Theorem and orbits. Parameterizing the orbits currently limit the H^∞ approach and leads to a series of generalization on Darlington's Theorem. An immediate application of Nehari's Theorem asks for a "unit-ball" characterization of an orbit:

QUESTION 9.1. For what $s_G \in BH^\infty(\mathbb{C}_+)$ is it true that $\mathcal{F}_1(U^+(2,\infty), s_G)$ is dense in Re $\bar{B}\mathcal{A}_1(\mathbb{C}_+)$?

This question of characterization is subsumed by the problem of computing orbits:

QUESTION 9.2. What is the orbit of a general reflectance $\mathcal{F}_1(\mathcal{U}, s_L)$?

We can also generalize $U^+(2,\infty)$ and ask about the orbit of s_L over all lumped 2-ports.

QUESTION 9.3. Characterize all reflectances that belong to

$$\overline{\bigcup_{d \geq 0} \mathcal{F}_1(U^+(2,d), s_L)}$$

Closely related is the question of *compatible impedances* or when a reflectance s_L belongs to the orbit of another reflectance s'_L.

QUESTION 9.4. Let $s_L, s'_L \in \bar{B}H^\infty(\mathbb{C}_+)$. Determine if there exists an $S' \in U^+(2)$ such that $s_L = \mathcal{F}_1(S', s'_L)$.

The theory of compatible impedances is an active research topic in electrical engineering [54] and has links to the Buerling–Lax Theorem [29].

9.2. $U^+(2)$ and circuits. The Circuit-Scattering Correspondence of Section 6 identified lumped, lossless N-ports and the scattering matrices of $U^+(N,d)$ [52]. By identifying an N-port as a subset of a Hilbert space, Section 1 claimed that any linear, lossless, time-invariant, causal, maximal solvable N-port corresponded to a scattering matrix in $U^+(N)$ [31]. The problem is reconcile the lumped approach, which has a concrete representation of a circuit, with Hilbert space claim, which gets a scattering matrix — not a circuit — by operator theory.

QUESTION 9.5. Does every element in $U^+(2)$ correspond to a lossless 2-port?

In terms of Kirkoff's current and voltage laws, if you were handed a collection of integro-differential partial differential equations, is it obvious that the system admits a scattering matrix?

9.3. Circuit synthesis and matrix dilations.

If matching problem with $s_G = 0$

$$\inf\{\|\Delta P(s_2, s_L)\|_\infty^2 : s_2 \in \mathcal{F}_2(U^+(2); 0)\},$$

admits a minimizer, then

$$s_2 = \mathcal{F}_2(S, s_G = 0) = s_{22} + s_{21}s_G(1 - s_{11}s_G)^{-1}s_{12}|_{s_G=0} = s_{22}.$$

How can we use s_2 to get a matching scattering matrix $S \in U^+(2)$? Thus, a circuit synthesis problem is really a question in matrix dilations.

QUESTION 9.6. Given $s_2 \in \bar{B}H^\infty(\mathbb{C}_+)$, find all $S \in U^+(2)$ such that

$$S = \begin{bmatrix} s_{11} & s_{12} \\ s_{21} & s_{22} \end{bmatrix} = \begin{bmatrix} s_{11} & s_{12} \\ s_{21} & s_2 \end{bmatrix}.$$

Not all s_2's can dilate to a lossless 2-port. Wohlers [52, page 100-101] shows that the 1-port with impedance $z(p) = \arctan(p)$ cannot dilate to an $S \in U^+(2)$. The Douglas–Helton result characterizes those elements in the unit ball of H^∞ that came from a lossless N-port.

THEOREM 9.1 ([14; 15]). *Let* $S(p) \in \bar{B}H^\infty(\mathbb{C}_+, \mathbb{C}^{N\times N})$ *be a real matrix function. The following are equivalent:*

(A): $S(p)$ *admits an real inner dilation* $\mathbf{S}(p) = \begin{bmatrix} S(p) & S_{12}(p) \\ S_{21}(p) & S_{22}(p) \end{bmatrix}.$

(B): $S(p)$ *has a meromorphic pseudocontinuation of bounded type to the open left half-plane* $\mathbb{C}_-$; *that is, there exist* $\phi \in H^\infty(\mathbb{C}_-)$ *and* $H \in H^\infty(\mathbb{C}_-, \mathbb{C}^{N\times N})$ *such that*

$$\lim_{\substack{\sigma>0 \\ \sigma\to0}} S(\sigma + j\omega) = \lim_{\substack{\sigma>0 \\ \sigma\to0}} \frac{H}{\phi}(-\sigma + j\omega) \quad \text{a.e.}$$

(C): *There is an inner function* $\phi \in H^\infty(\mathbb{C}_+)$ *such that* $\phi S^H \in H^\infty(\mathbb{C}_+, \mathbb{C}^{N\times N})$.

Let $\mathfrak{M}$ denote the subset of $\bar{B}H^\infty(\mathbb{C}_+)$ of functions that have meromorphic pseudocontinuations of bounded type. General hyperbolic Carleson–Jacob (Theorem 5.3) line of inquiry opens up to explore when the inequality

$$\inf\{\|\Delta P(s_2, s_L)\|_\infty : s_2 \in \mathfrak{M}\} \geq \min\{\|\Delta P(s_2, s_L)\|_\infty^2 : s_2 \in \bar{B}H^\infty(\mathbb{C}_+)\}$$

holds with equality.

9.4. Structure of $U^+(2)$.

Turning to the inclusion $U^+(2, \infty) \subset U^+(2)$, the preceding sections have established that $U^+(2, \infty)$ is a closed subset of $U^+(2)$ that consists of all rational inner functions parameterized by Belevitch's Theorem. Physically, $U^+(2, \infty)$ models all the lumped 2-ports, but does not model the transmission line. It is natural to wonder what subclass of $U^+(2)$ contains the lumped 2-ports and the transmission line. More precisely,

QUESTION 9.7. What constitutes a lumped-distributed network? How do we recognize its scattering matrix?

Wohlers [52] answers the first question by parameterizing the class of lumped-distributed N-ports, consisting of N_L inductors, N_C capacitors, and N_U uniform transmission lines using the model in Figure 26. Wohlers [52, pages 168–172]

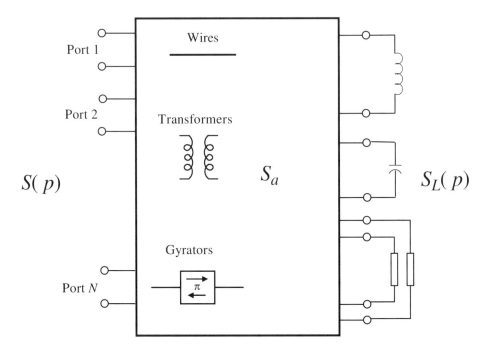

Figure 26. State-space representation of a lumped-distributed lossless 2-port.

establishes that such scattering matrices exist and have the form,

$$S(p) = \mathcal{F}(S_a, S_L; p) = S_{a,11} + S_{a,12}S_L(p)(I_d - S_{a,22}S_L(p))^{-1}S_{a,21},$$

where the augmented scattering matrix

$$S_a = \begin{bmatrix} S_{a,11} & S_{a,12} \\ S_{a,21} & S_{a,22} \end{bmatrix}$$

models a network of wires, transformers, and gyrators. Consequently, S_a is a constant, real, orthogonal matrix of size $d = N_L + N_C + 2N_U$. $S_L(p)$ is called the augmented load and models the reactive elements as

$$S_L(p) = qI_{N_L} \oplus -qI_{N_C} \oplus \left\{ I_{N_U} \otimes \begin{bmatrix} 0 & e^{-\tau p} \\ e^{-\tau p} & 0 \end{bmatrix} \right\}.$$

This decomposition assumes: (1) the first $N_L + N_C$ ports are normalized to $z_0 = 1$, and (2) the remaining N_U pairs of ports are normalized to the characteristic impedance Z_{0,n_u} of each transmission line. Although some work has be done charactering these scattering matrices, the reports in Wohlers [52, page 173] are false, as determined by Choi [10].

9.5. Error bounds. The problem is to determine if $\mathcal{T}_{r^2} \geq \mathcal{H}_c^* \mathcal{H}_c$, when all we know are noisy samples of the center and radius functions measured at a finite number of frequencies. Of the several approaches to this problem [29], we use the simple Spline-FFT Method.

THE SPLINE-FFT NEHARI ALGORITHM *Given samples* $\{(jw_k, C(j\omega_k))\}$ *and* $\{(jw_k, R(j\omega_k))\}$, *where* $0 \leq \omega_1 < \omega_2 < \cdots < \omega_K < \infty$.

SF-1: *Cayley transform the samples from* $j\mathbb{R}$ *to the unit circle* **T***:*

$$c(e^{j\theta_k}) := C \circ \mathbf{c}^{-1}(e^{j\theta_k}), \qquad r(e^{j\theta_k}) := R \circ \mathbf{c}^{-1}(e^{j\theta_k}).$$

SF-2: *Use a spline to extend* $\{e^{j\theta_k}, c(e^{j\theta_k})\}$ *and* $\{e^{j\theta_k}, r(e^{j\theta_k})\}$ *to functions on the unit circle* **T***.*

SF-3: *Approximate the Fourier coefficients using the FFT:*

$$\widehat{c}(N; n) := \frac{1}{N} \sum_{n'=0}^{N-1} e^{-j2\pi nn'/N} c(e^{+j2\pi n'/N}),$$

$$\widehat{r}(N; n) := \frac{1}{N} \sum_{n'=0}^{N-1} e^{-j2\pi nn'/N} r(e^{+j2\pi n'/N}).$$

SF-4: *Make the truncated Toeplitz and Hankel matrices:*

$$\mathcal{T}_{r^2, M, N} = \left[\widehat{r^2}(N; m_1 - m_2) \right]_{m_1, m_2 = 0}^{M-1},$$

$$\mathcal{H}_{c, M, N} = [\widehat{c}(N; -(m_1 + m_2))]_{m_1, m_2 = 0}^{M-1}.$$

SF-5: *Find the smallest eigenvalue of*

$$A_{M,N} := \mathcal{T}_{r^2, M, N} - \mathcal{H}_{c, M, N}^H \mathcal{H}_{c, M, N}.$$

We are aware of the following sources of error:

- The samples are corrupted by measurement errors.
- The spline extensions from sampled data to functions defined on the unit circle **T**.
- The Fourier coefficients are computed from an FFT of size N.
- The operator A is computed from $M \times M$ truncations.

QUESTION 9.8. Are these all the sources of error (neglecting roundoff)? How can the Spline-FFT Nehari algorithm adapt to account for these errors? Can we put error bars on Figure 24?

10. Epilogue

One of the great joys in applied mathematics is to link an abstract computation to a physical system. Nehari's Theorem computes the norm of a Hankel operator $\mathcal{H}_\phi$ as the distance between its symbol $\phi \in L^\infty$ and the Hardy subspace H^∞:

$$\|\mathcal{H}_\phi\| = \inf\{\|\phi - h\|_\infty : h \in H^\infty\}.$$

One of J. W. Helton's inspired observations linked this computation to a host of problems in electrical engineering and control theory. These problems, in turn, led Helton to deep and original extensions of operator theory, geometry, convex analysis, and optimization theory.

By linking H^∞ theory to the matching circuits, a physical meaning is attached to the Nehari computation and produces a plot that the electrical engineers can actually use. Along the way we encountered Darlington's Theorem, Belevitch's Theorem, Weierstrass' Theorem, the Carleson–Jacobs theorems, Nehari's Theorem, inner-function models, and hyperbolic geometry. Impedance-matching provides a case study of rather surprising mathematical richness in what may appear at first to be a rather prosaic analog signal processing issue.

A measure of the vitality of a subject is the quality of the unexplored questions. A small effort invested in circuit theory opens up a host of wonderful research topics for mathematicians. These topics discussed in this paper indicate only a few of the significant research opportunities that lie between mathematics and electrical engineering. For the mathematician, there are few engineering subjects where an advanced topic like H^∞ has such an immediate connection actual physical devices. We hope our readers do realize a rich harvest from these research opportunities.

Appendix A. Matrix-Valued Factorizations

This appendix proves Corollary 6.1 using Blaschke–Potapov factorizations. We start with the scalar-valued case.

LEMMA A.1. *Let $h \in H^\infty(\mathbf{D})$ be an inner function. The following are equivalent*:

(A): $h \in \mathcal{A}(\mathbf{D})$.
(B): h *is rational*.

PROOF. (a$\Longrightarrow$b) Factor h as $h = cbs$, where $c \in \mathbf{T}$, b is a Blaschke and s is a singular inner function. If $z_a \in \mathbf{T}$ is an accumulation point of the zeros $\{z_n\}$ of b, that is, there is a subsequence $z_{n_k} \to z_a$, then continuity of h on $\overline{\mathbf{D}}$ implies that $0 = h(z_{n_k}) \to h(z_a)$. Continuity of h on $\overline{\mathbf{D}}$ gives a neighborhood $U \subset \mathbf{T}$ of z_a for which $|h(U)| < 1$. Thus, h cannot be inner with b an infinite Blaschke product. Thus, b can only be a finite product and has no accumulation points to cancel the discontinuities of s. More formally, b never vanishes on $\mathbf{T}$ and neither

s nor $|s|$ is continously extendable to from the interior of the disk to any point in the support of the singular measure that represents s [35, pages 68–69]. Thus, h cannot have a singular part and we have $h = cb$.

(b$\implies$a) A rational h also in $H^\infty(\mathbf{D})$ cannot have a pole in $\overline{\mathbf{D}}$. Then h is continuous on $\overline{\mathbf{D}}$ so belongs to the disk algebra.   □

The result generalizes to matrix-valued inner functions. For $a \in \mathbf{D}$, define the elementary Blaschke factor [38, Equation 4.2]:

$$b_a(z) := \begin{cases} \dfrac{|a|}{a} \dfrac{a - z}{1 - \bar{a}z} & \text{if } a \neq 0, \\ z & \text{if } a = 0. \end{cases}$$

To get a matrix-valued version, let $P \in \mathbb{C}^{N \times N}$ be an orthogonal projection: $P^2 = P$ and $P^H = P$. The *Blaschke–Potapov elementary factor* associated with a and P is [38, Equation 4.4]:

$$B_{a,P}(z) := I_M + (b_a(z) - 1)P.$$

There are a couple of ways to see that $B_{a,P}$ is inner. Let U be a unitary matrix that diagonalizes P:

$$U^H P U = \begin{bmatrix} I_K & 0 \\ 0 & 0 \end{bmatrix}.$$

Then,

$$U^H B_{a,P}(z) U = \begin{bmatrix} b_a(z) I_K & 0 \\ 0 & I_{M-K} \end{bmatrix}.$$

From this, we get [38, Equation 4.5]:

$$\det[B_{a,P}(z)] = b_a(z)^{\operatorname{rank}[P]}.$$

DEFINITION A.1 ([38, pages 320–321]). The function $B : \mathbf{D} \to \mathbb{C}^{N \times N}$ is called a *left Blaschke–Potapov product* if either B is a constant unitary matrix or there exists a unitary matrix U, a sequence of orthogonal projection matrices $\{P_k : k \in \mathcal{K}\}$, and a sequence $\{z_k : k \in \mathcal{K}\} \subset \mathbf{D}$ such that

$$\sum_{k \in \mathcal{K}} (1 - |z_k|)\operatorname{trace}[P_k] < \infty$$

and the representation

$$B(z) = \left\{ \overrightarrow{\prod_{k \in \mathcal{K}}} B_{z_k, P_k}(z) \right\} U$$

holds.

DEFINITION A.2 ([38, pages 319]). Let $S \in H^\infty(\mathbf{D}, \mathbb{C}^{N \times N})$ be an inner function. S is called *singular* if and only if $\det[S(z)] \neq 0$ for all $z \in \mathbf{D}$.

THEOREM A.1 ([38, Theorem 4.1]). *Let $S \in H^\infty(\mathbf{D}, \mathbb{C}^{N \times N})$ be an inner function. There exists a left Blaschke–Potapov product and a $\mathbb{C}^{N \times N}$-valued singular inner function Ξ such that*

$$S = B\Xi.$$

Moreover, the representation is unique up to a unitary matrix U. If

$$S = B_1\Xi_1 = B_2\Xi_2,$$

then $B_2 = B_1 U$ and $\Xi_2 = U^H \Xi_1$.

Critical for our use is that the determinant maps these matrix-valued generalizations of the Blaschke and singular functions to their scalar-valued counterparts.

THEOREM A.2 ([38, Theorem 4.2]). *Let $S \in \bar{B}H^\infty(\mathbf{D}, \mathbb{C}^{N \times N})$.*

(A): $\det[S] \in \bar{B}H^\infty(\mathbf{D})$.
(B): *S is inner if and only if $\det[S]$ is inner.*
(C): *S is singular if and only if $\det[S]$ is singular.*

With these results in place, Lemma A.1 generalizes to the matrix-valued case.

PROOF OF COROLLARY A.1. (a $\Longrightarrow$ b) Lemma 3.3 and Assumption (a) give that $W = S \circ \mathbf{c}^{-1}$ is a continuous inner function in $\mathcal{A}(\mathbf{D}, \mathbb{C}^{2 \times 2})$. Theorem A.1 gives that $W = B\Xi$ for a left Blaschke–Potapov product B and singular Ξ. Observe that $\det[W] = \det[B]\det[\Xi]$. If W is inner, then $\det[W]$ is inner by Theorem A.2(a). Because W is continuous, $\det[W]$ is continuous and Lemma A.1 forces $\det[W]$ to be rational. Therefore, $\det[W]$ cannot admit the singular factor $\det[\Xi]$. Consequently, W cannot have a singular factor by Theorem A.2(c). Because $\det[W]$ is rational and

$$\det[W] = \det[B] = \prod b_{z_k}^{\mathrm{rank}[P_k]},$$

we see that B must be a *finite* left Blaschke–Potapov product. Consequently, $S = W \circ \mathbf{c}$ is rational. Finally, this gives that S is rational.

(b $\Longrightarrow$ a) Let

$$S(p) = \frac{1}{g(p)} H(p),$$

where $g(p)$ is a real polynomial

$$g(p) = g_0 + g_1 p + \cdots + g_L p^L,$$

of degree K that is strict Hurwitz (zero only in $\mathbb{C}_-$) and $H(p)$ is a real $N \times N$ polynomial

$$H(p) = H_0 + H_1 p + \cdots + H_M p^M$$

of degree L. Boundedness forces $L \geq M$. Then,

$$\frac{H(p)}{g(p)} = \frac{H_0 + \cdots + H_M p^M}{g_0 + \cdots + g_L p^L} \overset{p \to \infty}{\longrightarrow} \begin{cases} 0 & \text{if } L > M, \\ H_N/g_N & \text{if } L = M. \end{cases}$$

Thus, $H(p)/g(p)$ is continuous across $p = \pm j\infty$. Thus, $S(p)$ is continuous at $\pm j\infty$.   □

Appendix B. Proof of Lemma 4.4

The chain scattering representations are [25]:

$$\mathcal{G}(\Theta_1; s) := \mathcal{F}_1(S, s), \quad \Theta_1 \sim \frac{1}{s_{21}} \begin{bmatrix} -\det[S] & s_{11} \\ -s_{22} & 1 \end{bmatrix},$$

$$\mathcal{G}(\Theta_2; s) := \mathcal{F}_2(S, s), \quad \Theta_2 \sim \frac{1}{s_{12}} \begin{bmatrix} -\det[S] & s_{22} \\ -s_{11} & 1 \end{bmatrix},$$

where "$\sim$" denotes equality in homogeneous coordinates: $\Theta \sim \Phi$ if and only if $\mathcal{G}(\Theta) = \mathcal{G}(\Phi)$. Because $S(p)$ is unitary on $j\mathbb{R}$, $\Theta_1(p)$ and $\Theta_2(p)$ are J-unitary on $j\mathbb{R}$ [29]:

$$\Theta^H J \Theta = J = \begin{bmatrix} 1 & 0 \\ 0 & -1 \end{bmatrix}.$$

Fix $\omega \in \mathbb{R}$. Define the maps $\mathbf{g}_1$ and $\mathbf{g}_2$ on the unit disk $\mathbf{D}$ as

$$\mathbf{g}_1(s) := \mathcal{G}(\Theta_1(j\omega), s), \qquad \mathbf{g}_2(s) := \mathcal{G}(\Theta_2(j\omega), s).$$

Because $\Theta_1(p)$ and $\Theta_2(p)$ are J-unitary on $j\mathbb{R}$, it follows that $\mathbf{g}_1$ and $\mathbf{g}_2$ are invertible automorphisms of the unit disk onto itself with inverses:

$$\mathbf{g}_1^{-1}(s) = \mathcal{G}(\Theta_1(j\omega)^{-1}, s), \quad \Theta_1(j\omega)^{-1} \sim \begin{bmatrix} -1 & s_{11}(j\omega) \\ -s_{22}(j\omega) & \det[S(j\omega)] \end{bmatrix}$$

$$\mathbf{g}_2^{-1}(s) = \mathcal{G}(\Theta_2(j\omega)^{-1}, s), \quad \Theta_2(j\omega)^{-1} \sim \begin{bmatrix} -1 & s_{22}(j\omega) \\ -s_{11}(j\omega) & \det[S(j\omega)] \end{bmatrix}.$$

Because the $\mathbf{g}_k$'s and their inverses are invertible automorphisms, Equation 4–9 gives that

$$\left| \frac{\mathbf{g}(s_1) - \mathbf{g}(s_2)}{1 - \mathbf{g}(s_1)\overline{\mathbf{g}(s_2)}} \right| = \left| \frac{s_1 - s_2}{1 - s_1 \bar{s}_2} \right|,$$

for s_1, $s_2 \in \mathbf{D}$ and $\mathbf{g}$ denoting either $\mathbf{g}_1$, $\mathbf{g}_2$, $\mathbf{g}_1^{-1}$, or $\mathbf{g}_2^{-1}$. For all $p \in j\mathbb{R}$, we obtain

$$\Delta P(s_2, s_L) = \left| \frac{s_2 - \overline{s_L}}{1 - s_2 s_L} \right| = \left| \frac{\mathbf{g}_2(s_G) - \overline{s_L}}{1 - \mathbf{g}_2(s_G) s_L} \right|$$

$$= \left| \frac{s_G - \mathbf{g}_2^{-1}(\overline{s_L})}{1 - s_G \overline{\mathbf{g}_2^{-1}(\overline{s_L})}} \right| = \Delta P(s_G, \overline{\mathbf{g}_2^{-1}(\overline{s_L})}).$$

Then $\Delta P(s_2, s_L) = \Delta P(s_G, s_1)$, provided we can show $s_1 = \overline{\mathbf{g}_2^{-1}(\overline{s_L})}$. In terms of the chain matrices, this requires us to show

$$s_1 = \mathcal{G}(\Theta_1; s_L) = \overline{\mathcal{G}(\Theta_2^{-1}; \overline{s_L})} = \mathcal{G}(\overline{\Theta_2^{-1}}; s_L).$$

This equality will follow if we can show $\Theta_1 \sim \overline{\Theta_2^{-1}}$ or that

$$\Theta_1 \sim \begin{bmatrix} -1 & s_{11}/\det[S] \\ -s_{22}/\det[S] & 1/\det[S] \end{bmatrix} \sim \begin{bmatrix} -1 & \overline{s_{22}} \\ -\overline{s_{11}} & \overline{\det[S]} \end{bmatrix} \sim \overline{\Theta_2^{-1}}.$$

Because $S(p)$ is inner, $\det[S]$ is inner so that $\overline{\det[S]} = 1/\det[S]$ on $j\mathbb{R}$. Also, on $j\mathbb{R}$, $S(p)$ is unitary so that

$$S^{-1} = \frac{1}{\det[S]} \begin{bmatrix} s_{22} & -s_{12} \\ -s_{21} & s_{11} \end{bmatrix} = \begin{bmatrix} \overline{s_{11}} & \overline{s_{12}} \\ \overline{s_{21}} & \overline{s_{22}} \end{bmatrix}.$$

Then, $\overline{s_{22}} = s_{11}/\det[S]$ and $\overline{s_{11}} = s_{22}/\det[S]$. Thus, $\Theta_1 \sim \overline{\Theta_2^{-1}}$ so that $s_1 = g_2^{-1}(\overline{s_L})$ or that the LFT law holds. By Lemma 4.3, the LFT laws give the TGP laws.

Appendix C. Proof of Theorem 6.1

Let $C(\mathbf{T}, \mathbb{C}^{N \times N})$ denote the continuous functions on the unit circle $\mathbf{T}$. Let $\mathcal{R}_M^L$ denote those rational functions $g^{-1}(q)H(q)$ in $C(\mathbf{T}, \mathbb{C}^{N \times N})$ where $g(q)$ and $H(q)$ are polynomials with degrees $\partial[g] \leq M$ and $\partial[H] \leq L$. The Existence Theorem [9, page 154] shows that $\mathcal{R}_M^L$ is a boundedly compact subset of $C(\mathbf{T}, \mathbb{C}^{N \times N})$. Lemma 3.3 shows the Cayley transform preserves compactness. Thus, $\mathcal{R}_M^L \circ \mathbf{c}$ is a boundedly compact subset of $1 \dotplus C(j\mathbb{R}, \mathbb{C}^{N \times N})$. By Lemma 3.1, $U^+(N)$ is a closed subset of $L^\infty(j\mathbb{R}, \mathbb{C}^{N \times N})$. The intersection of a closed and bounded set with a boundedly compact set is compact. Thus, $U^+(N) \cap \mathcal{R}_M^L \circ \mathbf{c}$ is a compact subset of $1 \dotplus C(j\mathbb{R}, \mathbb{C}^{N \times N})$. We claim that $U^+(N, d) = U^+(N) \cap \mathcal{R}_d^d \circ \mathbf{c}$. Observe $\mathcal{R}_d^d \circ \mathbf{c}$ consists of all rational functions with the degree of the numerator and denominator not exceeding d and that are also continuous on $j\mathbb{R}$, including the point at infinity. If $S \in U^+(N) \cap \mathcal{R}_d^d \circ \mathbf{c}$, then $\deg_{\mathrm{SM}}[S] \leq d$. This forces S into $U^+(N, d)$. Consequently, $U^+(N, d) \supseteq U^+(N) \cap \mathcal{R}_d^d \circ \mathbf{c}$. For the converse, suppose $S \in U^+(N, d)$. By Corollary 6.1, $S \in \mathcal{A}_1(\mathbb{C}_+, \mathbb{C}^{N \times N})$ and thus forces S into $\mathcal{R}_d^d \circ \mathbf{c}$. Thus, $U^+(N, d) \subseteq U^+(N) \cap \mathcal{R}_d^d \circ \mathbf{c}$ and equality must hold. Thus, $U^+(N, d)$ is compact.

Appendix D. Proof of Theorem 5.5

We start by remarking upon the disk with strict inequalities:

$$D(c, r) := \{\phi \in L^\infty(j\mathbb{R}) : |\phi(j\omega) - c(j\omega)| < r(j\omega) \quad \text{a.e.}\}.$$

First, $D(c, r)$ need not be open. For example, $D(0, 1)$ contains the open unit ball and is contained in its closure:

$$BL^\infty(j\mathbb{R}) \subset D(0, 1) \subset \bar{B}L^\infty(j\mathbb{R}).$$

However,

$$\phi(j\omega) := \frac{\omega}{1+|\omega|}$$

belongs to $D(0,1)$ but with $\|\phi\|_\infty = 1$, there is no neighborhood of ϕ that is contained in the open unit ball.

Second, consider what the strict inequalities mean for those $\gamma : L^\infty(j\mathbb{R}) \to \mathbb{R}$ that are continuous with sublevel sets

$$[\gamma \le \alpha] = \bar{D}(c_\alpha, r_\alpha).$$

We cannot claim that $[\gamma < \alpha]$ is $D(c_\alpha, r_\alpha)$. Instead, $[\gamma < \alpha]$ is an *open set* contained by $D(c_\alpha, r_\alpha)$. In this regard, the following result gives us some control of the strict inequality.

THEOREM D.1. *Let c, $r \in L^\infty(j\mathbb{R})$. Assume $r^{-1} \in L^\infty(j\mathbb{R})$. Let V be any nonempty open subset of $L^\infty(j\mathbb{R})$ such that $V \subseteq D(c,r)$. For any $\phi \in V$,*

$$\|r^{-1}(\phi - c)\|_\infty < 1.$$

PROOF. For any $\phi \in V$, the openness of V implies there is an $\varepsilon > 0$ such that

$$\phi + \varepsilon BL^\infty(j\mathbb{R}) \subset V.$$

Consider the particular element of the open ball:

$$\Delta\phi := \varepsilon' \times \text{sgn}(\phi - c)\frac{r}{\|r\|_\infty},$$

where $0 < \varepsilon' < \varepsilon$ and

$$\text{sgn}(z) := \begin{cases} z/|z| & \text{if } z \ne 0, \\ 0 & \text{if } z = 0. \end{cases}$$

Then $\phi + \Delta\phi \in D(c,r)$ so that

$$r > |\phi + \Delta\phi - c| = |\phi - c| + \varepsilon'\frac{r}{\|r\|_\infty} \qquad \text{a.e.}$$

Divide by r and take the norm to get

$$1 \ge \|r^{-1}(\phi - c)\|_\infty + \varepsilon'\|r\|_\infty^{-1},$$

or that $1 > \|r^{-1}(\phi - c)\|_\infty$. To complete the argument, we need to demonstrate that the preceding argument is not vacuous. That is, $D(c,r)$ does indeed contain an open set. Because r does not "pinch off", $0 < \|r\|_{-\infty}$. Choose any $0 < \eta < \|r\|_{-\infty}$. For any $\phi \in BL^\infty(j\mathbb{R})$

$$\|(\eta\phi + c) - c\|_\infty \le \eta < r \qquad \text{a.e.}$$

Thus, the open set $c + \eta BL^\infty(j\mathbb{R})$ is contained in $D(c,r)$. □

PROOF OF THEOREM 5.5. There always holds

$$\rho_{\bar{B}\mathcal{A}_1} := \inf\{\|\Delta P(s_2, s_L)\|_\infty : s_2 \in \bar{B}\mathcal{A}_1(\mathbb{C}_+)\}$$
$$\geq \min\{\|\Delta P(s_2, s_L)\|_\infty : s_2 \in \bar{B}H^\infty(\mathbb{C}_+)\} = \rho_{\bar{B}H^\infty}.$$

Suppose the inequality is strict. Then there is an $s_2 \in \bar{B}H^\infty(\mathbb{C}_+)$ such that

$$\rho_{\bar{B}\mathcal{A}_1} > \|\Delta P(s_2, s_L)\|_\infty. \qquad (D\text{–}1)$$

By Lemma 4.6, the mapping $\Delta\rho(s_2) := \|\Delta P(s_2, s_L)\|_\infty$ is a continuous function on $\bar{B}L^\infty(j\mathbb{R})$. Consequently, $[\Delta\rho < \rho_{\bar{B}\mathcal{A}_1}]$ is open with

$$[\Delta\rho < \rho_{\bar{B}\mathcal{A}_1}] \subset D(k_{\mathcal{A}}, r_{\mathcal{A}}),$$

where the center function and radius functions are

$$k_{\mathcal{A}} := \bar{s}_L \frac{1 - \rho_{\bar{B}\mathcal{A}_1}^2}{1 - \rho_{\bar{B}\mathcal{A}_1}^2 |s_L|^2}, \quad r_{\mathcal{A}} := \rho_{\bar{B}\mathcal{A}_1} \frac{1 - |s_L|^2}{1 - \rho_{\bar{B}\mathcal{A}_1}^2 |s_L|^2}.$$

Let $r_{\mathcal{A}}$ have spectral factorization $r_{\mathcal{A}} = |q_{\mathcal{A}}|$. By Theorem D.1,

$$\|q_{\mathcal{A}}^{-1} k_{\mathcal{A}} - q_{\mathcal{A}}^{-1} s_2\|_\infty < 1.$$

If we assume that $q_{\mathcal{A}}^{-1} k_{\mathcal{A}} \in 1 \dotplus C_0(j\mathbb{R})$, Theorem 5.2 forces equality:

$$1 > \|q_{\mathcal{A}}^{-1} k_{\mathcal{A}} - H^\infty(\mathbb{C}_+)\|_\infty = \|q_{\mathcal{A}}^{-1} k_{\mathcal{A}} - \mathcal{A}_1(\mathbb{C}_+)\|_\infty.$$

The equality lets us select $s_{\mathcal{A}} \in \mathcal{A}_1(\mathbb{C}_+)$ that satisfies

$$1 - \varepsilon_0 > \|q_{\mathcal{A}}^{-1}(k_{\mathcal{A}} - s_{\mathcal{A}})\|_\infty,$$

for some $1 > \varepsilon_0 > 0$. This forces the pointwise result:

$$(1 - \varepsilon_0) r_{\mathcal{A}} \geq |k_{\mathcal{A}} - s_{\mathcal{A}}| \qquad \text{a.e.}$$

With some effort, we will show that this pointwise equality implies

$$\Delta\rho(s_{\mathcal{A}}) < \rho_{\bar{B}\mathcal{A}_1}.$$

This contradiction implies that Equation D–1 cannot be true or that the inequality $\rho_{\bar{B}\mathcal{A}_1} \geq \rho_{\bar{B}H^\infty}$ cannot be strict.

To start this demonstration, we first prove $q_{\mathcal{A}}^{-1} k_{\mathcal{A}}$ is continuous. Because s_L belongs to the open unit ball of the disk algebra, both $k_{\mathcal{A}}$ and $r_{\mathcal{A}}$ belong to $1 \dotplus C_0(j\mathbb{R})$. Thus, it remains to prove that $q_{\mathcal{A}}^{-1}$ is continuous. Lemma 3.3 gives that $R_{\mathcal{A}} = r_{\mathcal{A}} \circ \mathbf{c}^{-1}$ belongs to $C(\mathbf{T})$. Ignore the trivial case when $\rho_{\bar{B}\mathcal{A}_1} = 0$. Because

$$R_{\mathcal{A}} \geq \rho_{\bar{B}\mathcal{A}_1}(1 - \|s_L\|_\infty^2) > 0$$

it follows that $\log(R_{\mathcal{A}}) \in C(\mathbf{T})$ and defines the outer function [18, page 24]:

$$Q_{\mathcal{A}}(z) := \exp\left(\frac{1}{2\pi} \int_0^{2\pi} \frac{e^{jt} + z}{e^{jt} - z} \log(R_{\mathcal{A}}(e^{jt})) dt\right) \in \mathcal{A}(\mathbf{D}).$$

Lemma 3.3 gives that $q_{\mathcal{A}} = Q_{\mathcal{A}} \circ \mathbf{c} \in \mathcal{A}_1(\mathbb{C}_+)$ and is also an outer function. Because $q_{\mathcal{A}}$ is an outer function $q_{\mathcal{A}}^{-1} \in \mathcal{A}_1(\mathbb{C}_+)$. Thus, a spectral factorization exists in the disk algebra.

To continue, define for $\varepsilon \in [0, \varepsilon_0]$,

$$\rho(\varepsilon) := (1 - \varepsilon)\rho_{\bar{B}\mathcal{A}_1}.$$

Define

$$k_\varepsilon := \bar{s}_L \frac{1 - \rho(\varepsilon)^2}{1 - \rho(\varepsilon)^2 |s_L|^2}, \qquad r_\varepsilon := \rho_\rho(\varepsilon) \frac{1 - |s_L|^2}{1 - \rho(\varepsilon)^2 |s_L|^2}.$$

In $L^\infty(j\mathbb{R})$, $k_\varepsilon \to k_{\mathcal{A}}$ and $r_\varepsilon \to r_{\mathcal{A}}$ as $\varepsilon \to 0$. Then

$$|s_{\mathcal{A}} - k_\varepsilon| \le |s_{\mathcal{A}} - k_{\mathcal{A}}| + |k_{\mathcal{A}} - k_\varepsilon|$$
$$\le (1 - \varepsilon_0) r_{\mathcal{A}} + |k_{\mathcal{A}} - k_\varepsilon| \le (1 - \varepsilon_0) r_\varepsilon + |r_{\mathcal{A}} - r_\varepsilon| + |k_{\mathcal{A}} - k_\varepsilon|.$$

Because the last two terms are bounded as $\mathcal{O}[\varepsilon]$,

$$|s_{\mathcal{A}} - k_\varepsilon| \le r_\varepsilon - \varepsilon_0 r_\varepsilon + \mathcal{O}[\varepsilon].$$

Because $r_{\mathcal{A}}$ is uniformly positive, and r_ε converges to $r_{\mathcal{A}}$, the last two terms are uniformly negative for all $\varepsilon > 0$ sufficiently small. This puts

$$s_{\mathcal{A}} \in \bar{D}(k_\varepsilon, r_\varepsilon) \iff \Delta\rho(s_{\mathcal{A}}) < (1 - \varepsilon)\rho_{\bar{B}\mathcal{A}_1}. \qquad \square$$

References

[1] J. C. Allen and David F. Schwartz, *User's guide to antenna impedance models and datasets*, SPAWAR TN **1791**, 1998.

[2] Hongming An, B. K. J. C. Nauwelaers, and A. R. Van de Capelle, "Broadband microstrip antenna design with the simplified real frequency technique", *IEEE Transactions on Antennas and Propagation* **42**:2 (1994).

[3] H. Baher, *Synthesis of electrical networks*, Wiley, New York, 1984.

[4] Norman Balabanian and Theodore A. Bickart, *Linear network theory*, Matrix Publishers, Beaverton (OR), 1981.

[5] Lennart Carleson and Sigvard Jacobs, "Best uniform approximation by analytic functions", *Arkiv før Matematik* **10** (1972), 219–229.

[6] Joseph J. Carr, *Practical antenna handbook*, Tab Books, Blue Ridge Summit (PA), 1989.

[7] Michael de la Chapelle, "Computer-aided analysis and design of microwave fiber-optic links", *Microwave Journal* **32**:9 (1989).

[8] Nan-Cheng Chen, H. C. Su, and K. L. Wong "Analysis of a broadband slot-coupled dielectric-coated hemispherical dielectric resonator antenna", *Microwave and Optical Technology Letters* **8**:1 (1995).

[9] E. W. Cheney, *Approximation theory*, Chelsea, New York, 1982.

[10] Man-Duen Choi, "Positive semidefinite biquadratic forms", *Linear Alg. Appl.* **12** (1975), 95–100.

[11] Kenneth R. Cioffi, "Broad-band distributed amplifier impedance-matching techniques", *IEEE Transactions on Microwave Theory and Techniques* **37**:12 (1989).

[12] Eva Decker, "On the boundary behavior of singular inner functions", *Michigan Math. J.* **41**:3 (1994), 547–562.

[13] R. G. Douglas, *Banach algebra techniques in operator theory*, Academic Press, New York, 1972.

[14] R. G. Douglas and J. W. Helton, "The precise theoretical limits of causal Darlington synthesis", *IEEE Transactions on Circuit Theory*, CT-20, Number 3 (1973), 327.

[15] R. G. Douglas and J. W. Helton, "Inner dilations of analytic matrix functions and Darlington synthesis", *Acta Sci. Math. (Szeged)*, **43** (1973), 61–67.

[16] Janusz A. Dobrowolski and Wojciech Ostrowski *Computer-aided analysis, modeling, and design of microwave networks*, Artech House, Boston (MA), 1996.

[17] Nelson Dunford and Jacob T. Schwartz, *Linear Operators*, Part I, Interscience, New York, 1967.

[18] Peter L. Duren, *Theory of H^p spaces*, Academic Press, New York, 1970.

[19] J. B. Garnett, *Bounded analytic functions*, Academic Press, New York, 1981.

[20] Kazimierz Geobel and Simeon Reich *Uniform convexity, hyperbolic geometry, and nonexpansive mappings*, Marcel Dekker, New York, 1984.

[21] Guillermo Gonzalez, *Microwave transistor amplifiers*, 2nd edition, Prentice Hall, Upper Saddle River (NJ), 1997.

[22] Anthony N. Gerkis, "Broadband impedance matching using the real frequency network synthesis technique", *Applied Microwave and Wireless* (1998).

[23] A. Ghiasi and A. Gopinath, "Novel wide-bandwidth matching technique for laser diodes", *IEEE Transactions on Microwave Theory and Techniques* **38**:5 (1990), 673–675.

[24] Charles L. Goldsmith and Brad Kanack, Broad-band reactive matching of high-speed directly modulated laser diodes, *IEEE Microwave and Guided Wave Letters* **3**:9 (1993), 336–338.

[25] Martin Hasler and Jacques Neirynck, *Electric filters*, Artech House, Dedham (MA), 1986.

[26] Roger Helkey, J. C. Twichell, and Charles Cox, "A down-conversion optical link with RF gain", *J. Lightwave Technology* **15**:5 (1997).

[27] Henry Helson, *Harmonic analysis*, Addison-Wesley, Reading (MA), 1983.

[28] J. William Helton, "Broadbanding: gain equalization directly from data", *IEEE Transactions on Circuits and Systems*, CAS-28, Number 12 (1981), 1125–1137.

[29] J. William Helton, "Non-Euclidean functional analysis and electronics", *Bull. Amer. Math. Soc.* **7**:1 (1982), 1–64.

[30] J. William Helton, "A systematic theory of worst-case optimization in the frequency domain: high-frequency amplifiers", *IEEE ISCAS*, Newport Beach (CA), 1983.

[31] J. William Helton, [1987] *Operator theory, analytic functions, matrices, and electrical engineering*, CBMS Regional Conference Series **68**, Amer. Math. Soc., Providence, 1987.

[32] J. William Helton and Orlando Merino, *Classical control using H^∞ methods*, SIAM, Philadelphia, 1998.

[33] William Hintzman, "Best uniform approximations via annihilating measures", *Bull. Amer. Math. Soc.* **76** (1975), 1062–1066.

[34] William Hintzman, "On the existence of best analytic approximations", *Journal of Approximation Theory* **14** (1975), 20–22.

[35] K. Hoffman, *Banach spaces of analytic functions*, Prentice-Hall, 1962.

[36] Stephan A. Ivanov, [1995] "Application of the planar model to the analysis and design of the Y-junction strip-line circulator", *IEEE Transactions on Microwave Theory and Techniques* **43**:6 (1995).

[37] Taisuke Iwai, S. Ohara, H. Yamada, Y. Yamaguchi, K. Imanishi, and K. Joshin, "High efficiency and high linearity InGaP/GaAs HBT power amplifiers: matching techniques of source and load impedance to improve phase distortion and linearity", *IEEE Transactions on Electron Devices*, **45**:6 (1998).

[38] V. E. Katsnelson and B. Kirstein, "On the theory of matrix-valued functions belonging to the Smirnov class", in *Topics in Interpolation Theory*, edited by H. Dym, Birkhäuser, Basel, 1997.

[39] Paul Koosis, *Introduction to H_p spaces*, Cambridge University Press, Cambridge, 1980.

[40] Brian J. Markey, Dilip K. Paul, Rajender Razdan, Benjamin A. Pontano, and Niloy K. Dutta, "Impedance-matched optical link for C-band satellite applications", *IEEE Transactions on Antennas and Propagation* **43**:9 (1995), 960–965.

[41] Wen C. Masters, Second H-Infinity Program Review and Workshop, Office of Naval Research, 1999.

[42] Z. Nehari, "On bounded bilinear forms", *Annals of Mathematics*, **15**:1 (1957), 153–162.

[43] Ruth Onn, Allan O. Steinhardt, and Adam W. Bojanczyk, "The hyperbolic singular value decomposition and applications", *IEEE Transactions on Signal Processing*, **39**:7 (1991), 1575–1588.

[44] David M. Pozar, *Microwave engineering*, third edition, Prentice-Hall, Upper Saddle River (NJ), 1998.

[45] Vladimir V. Peller and Sergei R. Treil "Approximation by analytic matrix functions: the four block problem", preprint, 1999.

[46] Marvin Rosenblum and James Rovnyak, *Hardy classes and operator theory*, Oxford University Press, New York, 1985.

[47] Walter Rudin, *Functional analysis*, McGraw-Hill, New York, 1973.

[48] Walter Rudin, *Real and complex analysis*, McGraw-Hill, New York, 1974.

[49] David F. Schwartz and J. C. Allen, "H^∞ approximation with point constraints applied to impedance estimation", *Circuits, Systems, & Signal Processing* **16**:5 (1997), 507–522.

[50] Abraham A. Ungar, "The hyperbolic Pythagorean theorem, in the Poincaré disk model of hyperbolic geometry", *Amer. Math. Monthly* **108**:8 (1999), 759–763.

[51] H. P. Westman, (editor), *Reference data for radio engineers*, 5th edition, Howard W. Sams, New York, 1970.

[52] M. Ronald Wohlers, *Lumped and distributed passive networks*, Academic Press, New York, 1969.

[53] Dante C. Youla, "A tutorial exposition of some key network-theoretic ideas underlying classical insertion-loss filter design", *Proceedings of the IEEE* **59**:5 (1971), 760–799.

[54] Dante C. Youla, F. Winter, S. U. Pillai, "A new study of the problem of compatible impedances", *International Journal Circuit Theory and Applications* **25** (1997), 541–560.

[55] Paul Young, *Electronic communication techniques*, 4th edition, Prentice-Hall, Upper Saddle River (NJ), 1999.

[56] Nicholas Young, *An introduction to Hilbert space*, Cambridge University Press, Cambridge, 1988.

[57] Eberhard Zeidler, *Nonlinear functional analysis and its applications*, vol. III, Springer, New York, 1985.

[58] Kehe Zhu, *Operator theory in function spaces*, Dekker, New York, 1990.

JEFFERY C. ALLEN
SPAWAR SYSTEM CENTER
SAN DIEGO, CA 92152-5000

DENNIS M. HEALY, JR.
DEPARTMENT OF MATHEMATICS
UNIVERSITY OF MARYLAND
COLLEGE PARK, MD 20742-4015
UNITED STATES
  dhealy@math.umd.edu

Modern Signal Processing
MSRI Publications
Volume **46**, 2003

Engineering Applications of the Motion-Group Fourier Transform

GREGORY S. CHIRIKJIAN AND YUNFENG WANG

ABSTRACT. We review a number of engineering problems that can be posed or solved using Fourier transforms for the groups of rigid-body motions of the plane or three-dimensional space. Mathematically and computationally these problems can be divided into two classes: (1) physical problems that are described as degenerate diffusions on motion groups; (2) enumeration problems in which fast Fourier transforms are used to efficiently compute motion-group convolutions. We examine engineering problems including the analysis of noise in optical communication systems, the allowable positions and orientations reachable with a robot arm, and the statistical mechanics of polymer chains. In all of these cases, concepts from non-commutative harmonic analysis are put to use in addressing real-world problems, thus rendering them tractable.

1. Introduction

Noncommutative harmonic analysis is a beautiful and powerful area of pure mathematics that has connections to analysis, algebra, geometry, and the theory of algorithms. Unfortunately, it is also an area that is almost unknown to engineers. In our research group, we have addressed a number of seemingly intractable "real-world" engineering problems that are easily modeled and/or solved using techniques of noncommutative harmonic analysis. In particular, we have addressed physical/mechanical problems that are described well as functions or processes on the rotation and rigid-body-motion groups. The interactions and evolution of these functions are described using group-theoretic convolutions and diffusion equations, respectively. In this paper we provide a survey of some of these applications and show how computational harmonic analysis on motion groups is used.

The group of rigid-body motions, denoted as $SE(N)$ (shorthand for "special Euclidean" group in N-dimensional space), is a unimodular semidirect product group, and general methods for constructing unitary representations of such Lie groups have been known for some time (see [1; 25; 35], for example). In the past 40 years, the representation theory and harmonic analysis for the Euclidean groups have been developed in the pure mathematics and mathematical physics literature. The study of matrix elements of irreducible unitary representation of SE(3) was initiated by N. Vilenkin [39; 40] in 1957 (some particular matrix elements are also given in [41]). The most complete study of $\widetilde{\mathrm{SE}}(3)$ (the universal covering group of SE(3)) with application to the harmonic analysis was given by W. Miller in [28]. The representations of SE(3) were also studied in [16; 36; 37]. In recent works, fast Fourier transforms for SE(2) and SE(3) have been proposed [24], and an operational calculus has been constructed [5].

However, despite the considerable progress in mathematical developments of the representation theory of SE(3), these achievements have not yet been widely incorporated in engineering and applied fields. In work summarized here we try to fill this gap. A more detailed treatment of numerous applications can be found in [6].

In Section 2 we review the representation theory of SE(2), give the matrix elements of the irreducible unitary representations and review the definition of the Fourier transform for SE(2). We also review operational properties of the Fourier transform. We do not go into the intricate details of the Fourier transform for SE(3), as those are provided in the references described above and they add little to the understanding of how to apply noncommutative harmonic analysis to real-world problems. Sections 3, 4 and 5 are devoted to application areas: coherent optical communications, robotics, and polymer statistical mechanics, respectively.

2. Fourier Analysis of Motion

In this section we review the basic definitions and properties of the Euclidean motion groups. Our emphasis is on the motion group of the plane, but most of the concepts extend in a natural way to three-dimensional space. See [6] for a complete treatment.

2.1. Euclidean motion group. The Euclidean motion group, SE(N), is the semidirect product of $\mathbb{R}^N$ with the special orthogonal group, SO(N). We denote elements of SE(N) as $g = (\boldsymbol{a}, A) \in \mathrm{SE}(N)$ where $A \in \mathrm{SO}(N)$ and $\boldsymbol{a} \in \mathbb{R}^N$. The identity element is $e = (0, I)$ where I is the $N \times N$ identity matrix. For any $g = (\boldsymbol{a}, A)$ and $h = (\boldsymbol{r}, R) \in \mathrm{SE}(N)$, the group law is written as $g \circ h = (\boldsymbol{a} + A\boldsymbol{r}, AR)$, and $g^{-1} = (-A^T \boldsymbol{a}, A^T)$. Any $g = (\boldsymbol{a}, A) \in \mathrm{SE}(N)$ acts transitively on a position $\boldsymbol{x} \in \mathbb{R}^N$ as

$$g \cdot \boldsymbol{x} = A\boldsymbol{x} + \boldsymbol{a}.$$

That is, position vector $\boldsymbol{x}$ is rigidly moved by rotation followed by a translation.

Often in the engineering literature, no distinction is made between a *motion*, g, and the result of that motion acting on the identity element (called a *pose* or *reference frame*). Hence, we interchangeably use the words "motion" and "frame" when referring to elements of SE(N).

It is convenient to think of an element of SE(N) as an $(N + 1) \times (N + 1)$ matrix of the form:

$$g = \begin{pmatrix} A & a \\ 0^T & 1 \end{pmatrix}.$$

In the engineering literature, matrices with this kind of structure are called *homogeneous transforms*.

For example, each element of SE(2) can be parameterized using polar coordinates as:

$$g(r, \theta, \phi) = \begin{pmatrix} \cos\phi & -\sin\phi & r\cos\theta \\ \sin\phi & \cos\phi & r\sin\theta \\ 0 & 0 & 1 \end{pmatrix},$$

where $r \geq 0$ is the magnitude of translation. SE(2) is a 3-dimensional manifold much like $\mathbb{R}^3$. We can integrate over SE(2) using the volume element $d(g(r, \theta, \phi)) = (4\pi^2)^{-1} r \, dr \, d\theta \, d\phi$. This volume element is bi-invariant in the sense that it does not change under left and right shifts by any fixed element $h \in$ SE(2):

$$d(h \circ g) = d(g \circ h) = d(g).$$

Bi-invariant volume elements exist for SE(N) for $N = 2, 3, 4, \ldots$. A group with bi-invariant volume element is called a *unimodular* group.

The Lie group SE(2) has an associated Lie algebra $se(2)$. Physically, elements of SE(2) describe finite motions in the plane, whereas elements of $se(2)$ represent infinitesimal motions. Since SE(2) is a three-dimensional Lie group, there are three independent directions along which any infinitesimal motion can be decomposed. The vector space of all such motions relative to the identity element $e \in$ SE(2) together with the matrix commutator operation defines $se(2)$. As with any vector space, we can choose an appropriate basis. One such basis for the Lie algebra $se(2)$ consists of the following three matrices:

$$X_1 = \begin{pmatrix} 0 & 0 & 1 \\ 0 & 0 & 0 \\ 0 & 0 & 0 \end{pmatrix}; \quad X_2 = \begin{pmatrix} 0 & 0 & 0 \\ 0 & 0 & 1 \\ 0 & 0 & 0 \end{pmatrix}; \quad X_3 = \begin{pmatrix} 0 & -1 & 0 \\ 1 & 0 & 0 \\ 0 & 0 & 0 \end{pmatrix}.$$

The following one-parameter motions are obtained by exponentiating the above basis elements of $se(2)$:

$$g_1(t) = \exp(tX_1) = \begin{pmatrix} 1 & 0 & t \\ 0 & 1 & 0 \\ 0 & 0 & 1 \end{pmatrix};$$

$$g_2(t) = \exp(tX_2) = \begin{pmatrix} 1 & 0 & 0 \\ 0 & 1 & t \\ 0 & 0 & 1 \end{pmatrix};$$

$$g_3(t) = \exp(tX_3) = \begin{pmatrix} \cos t & -\sin t & 0 \\ \sin t & \cos t & 0 \\ 0 & 0 & 1 \end{pmatrix}.$$

For the purposes of the current discussion, we can take as a definition of $se(2)$ the vector space spanned by any linear combination of X_1, X_2, and X_3. The exponential mapping

$$\exp : se(2) \to \mathrm{SE}(2)$$

is well-defined for every element of $se(2)$ and is invertible except at a set of measure zero in $\mathrm{SE}(2)$.

Any rigid-body motion in the plane can be expressed as an appropriate combination of these three basic motions. For example, $g = g_1(x)g_2(y)g_3(\phi)$.

2.2. Differential operators on $\mathrm{SE}(2)$. The way to take partial derivatives of a function of motion is to evaluate

$$\tilde{X}_i^R f \triangleq \frac{d}{dt} f(g \circ \exp(tX_i))|_{t=0}, \qquad \tilde{X}_i^L f \triangleq \frac{d}{dt} f(\exp(tX_i) \circ g)|_{t=0}.$$

(In our notation, R means that the exponential appears on the right, and L means that it appears on the left. This means that $\tilde{X}_i^R$ is invariant under left shifts, while $\tilde{X}_i^L$ is invariant under right shifts. Our notation is different than others in the mathematics literature where the superscript denotes the invariance of the vector field formed by the concatenation of these derivatives.) Explicitly, we find the differential operators $\tilde{X}_i^R$ in polar coordinates to be [6]

$$\tilde{X}_1^R = \cos(\phi - \theta)\frac{\partial}{\partial r} + \frac{\sin(\phi - \theta)}{r}\frac{\partial}{\partial \theta},$$

$$\tilde{X}_2^R = -\sin(\phi - \theta)\frac{\partial}{\partial r} + \frac{\cos(\phi - \theta)}{r}\frac{\partial}{\partial \theta},$$

$$\tilde{X}_3^R = \frac{\partial}{\partial \phi},$$

and in Cartesian coordinates to be

$$\tilde{X}_1^R = \cos\phi\frac{\partial}{\partial x} - \sin\phi\frac{\partial}{\partial y}, \quad \tilde{X}_2^R = \sin\phi\frac{\partial}{\partial x} + \cos\phi\frac{\partial}{\partial y}, \quad \tilde{X}_3^R = \frac{\partial}{\partial \phi}.$$

The differential operators $\tilde{X}_i^L$ in polar coordinates are

$$\tilde{X}_1^L = \cos\theta\frac{\partial}{\partial r} - \frac{\sin\theta}{r}\frac{\partial}{\partial \theta}, \quad \tilde{X}_2^L = \sin\theta\frac{\partial}{\partial r} + \frac{\cos\theta}{r}\frac{\partial}{\partial \theta}, \quad \tilde{X}_3^L = \frac{\partial}{\partial \phi} + \frac{\partial}{\partial \theta}.$$

2.3. Fourier analysis on $\mathrm{SE}(2)$. The Fourier transform, $\mathcal{F}$, of a function of motion, $f(g)$ where $g \in \mathrm{SE}(N)$, is an infinite-dimensional matrix defined as [6]:

$$\mathcal{F}(f) = \hat{f}(p) = \int_G f(g)U(g^{-1}, p)\, d(g)$$

where $U(g,p)$ is an infinite dimensional matrix function with the property that $U(g_1 \circ g_2, p) = U(g_1, p)U(g_2, p)$. This kind of matrix is called a *matrix representation* of SE(N). It has the property that it converts convolutions on SE(N) into matrix products:

$$\mathcal{F}(f_1 * f_2) = \mathcal{F}(f_2)\mathcal{F}(f_1).$$

In the case when $N = 2$, the original function is reconstructed as

$$\mathcal{F}^{-1}(\hat{f}) = f(g) = \int_0^\infty \operatorname{trace}(\hat{f}(p)U(g,p))p\,dp,$$

and the matrix elements of $U(g,p)$ are expressed explicitly as [6]:

$$u_{mn}(g(r,\theta,\phi),p) = j^{n-m}e^{-j[n\phi+(m-n)\theta]}J_{n-m}(p\,r)$$

where $J_\nu(x)$ is the νth order Bessel function and $j = \sqrt{-1}$. This inverse transform can be written in terms of elements as

$$f(g) = \sum_{m,n\in\mathbb{Z}} \int_0^\infty \hat{f}_{mn}u_{nm}(g,p)p\,dp. \tag{2-1}$$

In analogy with the classical Fourier transform, which converts derivatives of functions of position into algebraic operations in Fourier space, there are operational properties for the motion-group Fourier transform.

By the definition of the SE(2)-Fourier transform $\mathcal{F}$ and operators $\tilde{X}_i^R$ and $\tilde{X}_i^L$, we can write the Fourier transform of the derivatives of a function of motion as

$$\mathcal{F}[\tilde{X}_i^R f] = \tilde{u}(X_i, p)\hat{f}(p), \qquad \mathcal{F}[\tilde{X}_i^L f] = -\hat{f}(p)\tilde{u}(X_i, p),$$

where

$$\tilde{u}(X_i, p) \triangleq \frac{d}{dt}U(\exp(tX_i), p)\bigg|_{t=0}.$$

Explicitly,

$$u_{mn}(\exp(tX_1), p) = j^{n-m}J_{m-n}(pt).$$

We know that

$$\frac{d}{dx}J_m(x) = \tfrac{1}{2}[J_{m-1}(x) - J_{m+1}(x)]$$

and

$$J_{m-n}(0) = \begin{cases} 1 & \text{for } m-n = 0, \\ 0 & \text{for } m-n \neq 0. \end{cases}$$

Hence,

$$\tilde{u}_{mn}(X_1, p) = \frac{d}{dt}u_{mn}(\exp(tX_1), p)\bigg|_{t=0} = -\frac{jp}{2}(\delta_{m,n+1} + \delta_{m,n-1}).$$

Likewise,

$$u_{mn}(\exp(tX_2), p) = j^{n-m}e^{-j(n-m)\pi/2}J_{m-n}(pt) = J_{m-n}(pt),$$

and so

$$\tilde{u}_{mn}(X_2, p) = \frac{d}{dt} u_{mn}(\exp(tX_2), p)\Big|_{t=0}$$

$$= \frac{p}{2}(J_{m-n-1}(0) - J_{m-n+1}(0)) = \frac{p}{2}(\delta_{m,n+1} - \delta_{m,n-1}).$$

Similarly, we find

$$u_{mn}(\exp(tX_3), p) = e^{-jmt}\delta_{m,n}$$

and

$$\tilde{u}_{mn}(X_3, p) = \frac{d}{dt} u_{mn}(\exp(tX_3), p)\Big|_{t=0} = -jm\delta_{m,n}.$$

Fast Fourier transforms for SE(2) and SE(3) have been outlined in [6; 24]. Operational properties for SE(3) which are analogous to those presented here for SE(2) can be found in [5; 6]. Subsequent sections in this paper describe various applications of motion-group Fourier analysis to problems in engineering.

3. Phase Noise in Coherent Optical Communications

In optical communications, laser light is used to transmit information along fiber optic cables. There are several methods that are used to transmit and detect information within the light. Coherent detection (in contrast to direct detection) is a method that has the ability to detect the phase, frequency, amplitude and polarization of the incident light signal . Therefore, information can be transmitted via phase, frequency, amplitude, or polarization modulation. However, the phase of the light emitted from a semiconductor laser exhibits random fluctuations due to spontaneous emissions in the laser cavity [19]. This phenomenon is commonly referred to as *phase noise*. Phase noise puts strong limitations on the performance of coherent communication systems. Evaluating the influence of phase noise is essential in system design and optimization and has been studied extensively in the literature [10; 12]. Analytical models that describe the relationship between phase noise and the filtered signal are found in [2; 11]. In particular, the Fokker–Planck approach represents the most rigorous description of phase noise effects [13; 14]. To better apply this approach to system design and optimization, an efficient and powerful computational tool is necessary. In this section, we describe one such tool that is based on the motion-group Fourier transform. Readers unfamiliar with the technical terms used below are referred to [21]. The discussion in the following paragraph provides a context for this particular engineering application, but the value of noncommutative harmonic analysis in this context is solely due to its ability to solve equation (3–1).

Let $s(t)$ be the input signal to a bandpass filter which is corrupted by phase noise. Using the equivalent baseband representation and normalizing it to unit amplitude, this signal can be written as [14]

$$s(t) = e^{j\phi(t)}$$

where $\phi(t)$ is the phase noise, usually modeled as a Brownian motion process. The function $h(t)$ is the impulse response of the bandpass filter. The output of the bandpass filter is denoted $z(t)$. Let us represent $z(t)$ through its real and imaginary parts:

$$z(t) = x(t) + jy(t) = r(t)e^{j\theta(t)}.$$

The 3-D Fokker–Planck equation defining the probability density function (pdf) of $z(t)$ is derived as [2; 45]:

$$\frac{\partial f}{\partial t} = -h(t)\cos\phi\frac{\partial f}{\partial x} - h(t)\sin\phi\frac{\partial f}{\partial y} + \frac{D}{2}\frac{\partial^2 f}{\partial \phi^2} \qquad (3\text{--}1)$$

with initial condition $f(x, y, \phi; 0) = \delta(x)\delta(y)\delta(\phi)$, where δ being the Dirac delta function. The parameter D is related to the laser line width Δv by $D = 2\pi\Delta v$. Having an efficient method for solving equation (3–1) is of great importance in the design of filters.

A number of papers have attempted to solve the above equations using a variety of techniques including series expansions, numerical methods based on discretizing the domain, and analytical methods [42; 45]. However, all of them are based on classical partial differential equation solution techniques.

In our work, we present a new method for solving these methods using harmonic analysis on groups. These techniques reduce the above Fokker–Planck equations to systems of linear ordinary differential equations with constant or time-varying coefficients in a generalized Fourier space. The solution to this system of equations in generalized Fourier space is simply a matrix exponential for the case of constant coefficients. A usable solution is then generated via the generalized Fourier inversion formula.

Using the differential operators defined on the motion group, the 3-D Fokker–Planck equation in (3–1) can be rewritten as

$$\frac{\partial f}{\partial t} = \left(-h(t)\tilde{X}_2^R + \frac{D}{2}(\tilde{X}_3^R)^2\right)f. \qquad (3\text{--}2)$$

This equation describes a kind of process that evolves on the group of rigid-body motions SE(2). Applying the motion-group Fourier transform to (3–2), we can convert it to an infinite system of linear ordinary differential equations:

$$\frac{d\hat{f}}{dt} = A(t)\hat{f}. \qquad (3\text{--}3)$$

For equation (3–2), the matrix is

$$A(t) = -h(t)\tilde{u}(X_2, p) + \frac{D}{2}\left(\tilde{u}(X_3, p)\right)^2$$

and its elements are

$$A(t)_{mn} = -h(t)\frac{p}{2}(\delta_{m,n+1} - \delta_{m,n-1}) - \frac{D}{2}m^2\delta_{m,n}.$$

Numerical methods such as Runge–Kutta integration can be applied to easily solve the truncated version of this system. In the case when $h(t)$ is a constant, then A is a constant matrix and the solution to the resulting linear time-invariant system can be written in closed form as

$$\hat{f}(p;t) = \exp(At)$$

with the initial condition that $\hat{f}(p;0)$ is the infinite-dimensional identity matrix. In practice we truncate A at finite dimension, then exponentiate.

Once we get the solution to (3–3), we can then substitute it into the Fourier inversion formula for the motion group in (2–1) to recover the pdf $f(g;t)$ of $z(t)$. To get the pdf $f(r,\theta;t)$ is just an integration with respect to ϕ as

$$f(r,\theta;t) = \frac{1}{2\pi}\int_0^{2\pi} f(g;t)d\phi = \sum_{n\in\mathbb{Z}} j^{-n}e^{-jn\theta}\int_0^\infty \hat{f}_{0,n}J_{-n}(p\,r)p\,dp. \qquad (3\text{–}4)$$

Integrating equation (3–4) over θ will give us the marginal pdf of $|z(t)|$ as:

$$f(r;t) = \int_0^\infty \hat{f}_{0,0}(p)J_0(p\,r)p\,dp. \qquad (3\text{–}5)$$

Using our method, we can get a simple and compact expression for the marginal pdf for the output of the bandpass filter given in (3–5).

For details and numerical results generated using this approach, see [43].

4. Robotics

A robotic manipulator arm is a device used to position and orient objects in space. The set of all reachable positions and orientations is called the workspace of the arm. A robot arm that can attain only a finite number of different states is called a discretely-actuated manipulator. For such manipulators, it is a combinatorially explosive problem to enumerate by brute force all possible states for arms that have a high degree of articulation. The function that describes the relative density of reachable positions and orientations in the workspace (called a *workspace density function*) has been shown to be an important quantity in planning the motions of these manipulator arms [4]. This function is denoted as $f(g;L)$ where $g \in \mathrm{SE}(N)$, and L is the length of the arm.

Noncommutative harmonic analysis enters in this problem as a way to reduce this complexity. It was shown in [4] that the workspace density function $f(g;L_1+L_2)$ for two concatenated manipulator segments with length L_1 and L_2 is the motion-group convolution

$$f(g;L_1 + L_2) = f(g;L_1) * f(g;L_2) = \int_G f(h;L_1)f(h^{-1}\circ g;L_2)\,dh, \qquad (4\text{–}1)$$

where h is a dummy variable of integration and dh is the bi-invariant (Haar) measure for $\mathrm{SE}(N)$. That is, given two short arms with known workspace densities, we can generate the workspace density of the long arm generated by stacking one short arm on the other using equation (4–1). In order to perform these convolutions efficiently, the concept of FFTs for the motion groups was studied in [6].

In the rest of this section, we discuss an alternative method for generating manipulator workspace density functions that does not explicitly compute convolutions. Instead, it relies on the same kinds of degenerate diffusions we have seen already in the context of phase noise.

4.1. Inspiration of the algorithm. Consider a discretely-actuated serial manipulator which consists of concatenated segments called modules. Suppose that each module can reach 16 different states. The workspace of this manipulator with 2 modules, 3 modules and 4 modules can be generated by brute force enumeration because 16^2, 16^3, and 16^4 are not terribly huge numbers. It is easy to imagine that the size of the workspace will spread out with the increment of modules. This enlargement of the workspace is just like the diffusion produced by a drop of ink spreading in a cup of water. Inspired by this observation, we view the workspace of a manipulator as something that grows/evolves from a single point source at the base as the length of the manipulator increases from zero. The workspace is generated after the manipulator grows to full length.

4.2. Implementation of the algorithm. With this analogy, we then need to determine what kind of diffusion equation is suitable to model this process. We get such an equation by realizing that some characteristics of manipulators are similar to those of polymer chains like DNA.

During our study of conformational statistics in polymer science, we derived a diffusion-type equation defined on the motion group [7]. This equation describes the probability density function of the position and orientation of the distal end of a stiff macromolecule chain relative to its proximal end. By involving parameters which indicate the kinematic properties of a manipulator into this equation, we can modify it to the diffusion-type equation describing the evolution of the workspace density function. It is written explicitly as

$$\frac{\partial f}{\partial L} = \left(\alpha \tilde{X}_1^R + \beta (\tilde{X}_1^R)^2 + \tilde{X}_3^R + \varepsilon (\tilde{X}_3^R)^2 \right) f. \qquad (4\text{--}2)$$

Here f stands for the workspace density function, and L is the manipulator length. The differential operators $\tilde{X}_1^R$ and $\tilde{X}_3^R$ are those defined on SE(2) given earlier. Parameters β, ε and α describe the kinematic properties of manipulators. We define these kinematic properties as flexibility, extensibility and the degree of asymmetry. The parameter β describes the flexibility of a manipulator in the sense of how much a segment of the manipulator can bend per unit length. A larger value of β means that the manipulator can bend a lot. The parameter ε describes the extensibility of a manipulator in the sense of how much a manipulator can extend along its backbone direction. A larger value of ε means that the manipulator can extend a lot. The parameter α describes the asymmetry in how the manipulator bends. When $\alpha = 0$, the manipulator can reach left and right with equal ease. When $\alpha < 0$, there is a preference for bending to the left, and when $\alpha > 0$ there is a preference for bending to the right. Since α, β, and ε are qualitative descriptions of the kinematic properties of a manipulator, they are not directly measurable.

This simple three-parameter model qualitatively captures the behavior that has been observed in numerical simulations of workspace densities of discretely-actuated variable-geometry truss manipulators [23]. Clearly, equation (4–2) can be solved in the same way as the phase-noise equation. We have done this in [43].

5. Statistical Mechanics of Macromolecules

In this section, we show how certain quantities of interest in polymer physics can be generated numerically using Euclidean-group convolutions. We also show how for wormlike polymer chains, a partial differential equation governs a process that evolves on the motion group and describes the diffusion of end-to-end position and orientation. This equation can be solved using the SE(3)-Fourier transform in a manner very similar to the way the phase-noise Fokker–Planck was addressed in Section 3. This builds on classical works in polymer theory such as [8; 15; 20; 22; 34; 44].

5.1. Mass density, frame density, and Euclidean group convolutions.
In statistical mechanical theories of polymer physics, it is essential to compute ensemble properties of polymer chains averaged over all of their possible conformations [9; 27]. Noncommutative harmonic analysis provides a tool for computing probability densities used in these averages.

In this subsection we review three statistical properties of macromolecular ensembles. These are: (1) The ensemble mass density for the whole chain $\rho(\boldsymbol{x})$, which is generated by imagining that one end of the chain is held fixed and a cloud is generated by all possible conformations of the chain superimposed on each other; (2) The ensemble tip frame density $f(g)$ (where g is the frame of reference of the distal end of the chain relative to the fixed proximal end); (3) The function $\mu(g, \boldsymbol{x})$, which is the ensemble mass density of all configurations which grow from the identity frame fixed to one end of the chain and terminate at the relative frame g at the other end. Figures that describe these quantities can be found in [3].

The functions ρ, f, and μ are related to each other. Given $\mu(g, \boldsymbol{x})$, the ensemble mass density is calculated by adding the contribution of each μ for each different end position and orientation:

$$\rho(\boldsymbol{x}) = \int_G \mu(g, \boldsymbol{x}) \, dg. \qquad (5\text{--}1)$$

This integration is written as being over all motions of the end of the chain, but only frames g in the support of μ contribute to the integral. Here G is shorthand for SE(3) and dg denotes the invariant integration measure for SE(3).

In an analogous way, it is not difficult to see that integrating the $\boldsymbol{x}$-dependence out of μ provides the total mass of configurations of the chain starting at frame e and terminating at frame g. Since each chain has mass M, this means that the frame density $f(g)$ is related to $\mu(g, \boldsymbol{x})$ as:

$$f(g) = \frac{1}{M} \int_{\mathbb{R}^3} \mu(g, \boldsymbol{x}) d\boldsymbol{x}. \tag{5-2}$$

We note the total number of frames attained by one end of the chain relative to the other is

$$F = \int_G f(g) \, dg.$$

It then follows that

$$\int_{\mathbb{R}^3} \rho(\boldsymbol{x}) d\boldsymbol{x} = F \cdot M.$$

If the functions $\rho(\boldsymbol{x})$ and $f(g)$ are known for the whole chain then a number of important thermodynamic and mechanical properties of the polymer can be determined [6].

We can divide the chain into P segments that are short enough to allow brute force enumeration calculation of $\rho_i(\boldsymbol{x})$ and $f_i(g)$ for $i = 1, \ldots, P$, where g is the *relative* frame of reference of the distal end of the segment with respect to the proximal one. For a homogeneous chain, such as polyethylene, these functions are the same for each value of $i = 1, \ldots, P$.

In the general case of a heterogeneous chain, we can calculate the functions $\rho_{i,i+1}(\boldsymbol{x})$, $f_{i,i+1}(g)$, and $\mu_{i,i+1}(g, \vec{x})$ for the concatenation of segments i and $i+1$ from those of segments i and $i+1$ separately in the following way:

$$\rho_{i,i+1}(\boldsymbol{x}) = F_{i+1}\rho_i(\boldsymbol{x}) + \int_G f_i(h)\rho_{i+1}(h^{-1} \circ \boldsymbol{x}) \, dh, \tag{5-3}$$

$$f_{i,i+1}(g) = (f_i * f_{i+1})(g) = \int_G f_i(h)f_{i+1}(h^{-1} \circ g) \, dh. \tag{5-4}$$

and

$$\mu_{i,i+1}(g, \vec{x}) = \int_G \left(\mu_i(h, \vec{x})f_{i+1}(h^{-1} \circ g) + f_i(h)\mu_{i+1}(h^{-1} \circ g, h^{-1} \circ \vec{x}) \right) \, dh. \tag{5-5}$$

In these expressions $h \in G = \mathrm{SE}(3)$ is a dummy variable of integration. The meaning of equation (5–3) is that the mass density of the ensemble of all conformations of two concatenated chain segments results from two contributions. The first is the mass density of all the conformations of the lower segment (weighted by the number of different upper segments it can carry, which is $F_{i+1} = \int_G f_{i+1} \, dg$). The second contribution results from rotating and translating the mass density of the ensemble of the upper segment, and adding the contribution at each of these poses (positions and orientations). This contribution is weighted by the number of frames that the distal end of the lower segment can attain relative to its base. Mathematically $L(h)\rho_{i+1}(\boldsymbol{x}) = \rho_{i+1}(h^{-1} \circ \boldsymbol{x})$ is a left-shift operation which geometrically has the significance of rigidly translating and rotating the function $\rho_{i+1}(\boldsymbol{x})$ by the transformation h. The weight $f_i(h)\,dh$ is the number of configurations of the ith segment terminating at frame of reference h.

The meaning of equation (5–4) is that the distribution of frames of reference at the terminal end of the concatenation of segments i and $i+1$ is the group-theoretical *convolution* of the frame densities of the terminal ends of each of the two segments relative to their respective bases. This equation holds for exactly the same reason why equation (4–1) does in the context of robot arms.

Equation (5–5) says that there are two contributions to $\mu_{i,i+1}(g,\vec{x})$. The first comes from adding up all the contributions due to each $\mu_i(h,\vec{x})$. This is weighted by the number of upper segment conformations with distal ends that reach the frame g given that their base is at frame h. The second comes from adding up all shifted (translated and rotated) copies of $\mu_{i+1}(g,\vec{x})$, where the shifting is performed by the lower distribution, and the sum is weighted by the number of distinct configurations of the lower segment that terminate at h. This number is $f_i(h)\,dh$.

Equations (5–3), (5–4) and (5–5) can be iterated as described in [3; 6].

5.2. Statistics of stiff molecules as solutions to PDEs on SO(3) and SE(3).

Experimental measurements of the stiffness constants of DNA and other stiff (or semi-flexible) macromolecules have been reported in a number of papers, as well as the statistical mechanics of such molecules. See [17; 26; 29; 30; 31; 32; 33; 38], for example.

The stiffness and chirality (how helical the molecule is) can be described with parameters D_{lk} and d_l for $l, k = 1, 2, 3$. In particular, D_{lk} are the elements of the inverse of the stiffness matrix. When a force is applied, these constants determine how easily one end of the molecule deflects from the helical shape that it assumes when no forces act on it. The parameters d_l describe the helical shape of an undeformed molecule with flexibility described by D_{lk}. These parameters are described in detail in [7].

Degenerate diffusion equations describing the evolution of position and orientation of frames of reference attached to points on the chain at different values of length, L, have been derived [6; 43]. These equations incorporate stiffness and chirality information and are written in terms of SE(3) differential operators as

$$\left(\frac{\partial}{\partial L} - \frac{1}{2}\sum_{k,l=1}^{3} D_{lk}\tilde{X}_l^R\tilde{X}_k^R - \sum_{l=1}^{3} d_l\tilde{X}_l^R + \tilde{X}_6^R\right)f = 0. \qquad (5\text{–}6)$$

The initial conditions are $f(\boldsymbol{a}, A; 0) = \delta(\boldsymbol{a})\delta(A)$ where $g = (\boldsymbol{a}, A)$.

This equation has been solved using the operational properties of the SE(3) Fourier transform in [5; 6; 43].

6. Conclusions

This paper has reviewed a number of applications of harmonic analysis on the motion groups. This illustrates the power of noncommutative harmonic analysis, and its potential as a computational and analytical tool for solving real-world problems. We hope that this review will stimulate interest among others working in the field of noncommutative harmonic analysis to apply these methods to problems in engineering, and we hope that those in the engineering sciences will appreciate noncommutative harmonic analysis for the powerful tool that it is.

Acknowledgments

This material is based upon work supported by the National Science Foundation under Grant IIS-0098382. Any opinions, findings, and conclusions or recommendations expressed in this material are those of the authors and do not necessarily reflect the views of the National Science Foundation.

References

[1] L. Auslander and C. C. Moore, *Unitary representations of solvable Lie groups*, Mem. Amer. Math. Soc. **62**, AMS, 1966.

[2] D. J. Bond, "The statistical properties of phase noise", *Br. Telecom. Technol. J.* **7**:4 (Oct 1989), 12–17.

[3] G. S. Chirikjian, "Conformational statistics of macromolecules using generalized convolution", *Comp. Theor. Polymer Science* **11** (Feb 2001), 143–153.

[4] G. S. Chirikjian and I. Ebert-Uphoff, "Numerical convolution on the Euclidean group with applications to workspace generation", *IEEE Transactions on Robotics and Automation* **14**:1 (Feb 1998), 123–136.

[5] G. S. Chirikjian and A. B. Kyatkin, "An operational calculus for the Euclidean motion group: applications in robotics and polymer science", *J. Fourier Analysis and Applications* **6**:6 (2000), 583–606.

[6] G. S. Chirikjian and A. B. Kyatkin, *Engineering applications of noncommutative harmonic analysis*, CRC Press, 2000.

[7] G. S. Chirikjian and Y. F. Wang, "Conformational statistics of stiff macromolecules as solutions to PDEs on the rotation and motion groups", *Physical Review E* **62**:2 (Jul 2000), 880–892.

[8] H. E. Daniels, "The statistical theory of stiff chains", *Proc. Roy. Soc. Edinburgh* **A63** (1952), 290–311.

[9] P. J. Flory, *Statistical mechanics of chain molecules*, Wiley, 1969 (reprinted Hanser, Munich, 1989).

[10] G. J. Foschini, L. J. Greenstein and G. Vannucci, "Noncoherent detection of coherent lightwave signals corrupted by phase noise", *IEEE Trans. on Communications* **36** (Mar 1988), 306–314.

[11] G. J. Foschini, G. Vannucci and L. J. Greenstein, "Envelope statistics for filtered optical signals corrupted by phase noise", *IEEE Trans. on Communications* **37**:12 (Dec 1989), 1293–1302.

[12] I. Garrett and G. Jacobsen, "Possibilities for coherent optical communication systems using lasers with large phase noise", *Br. Telecom Technol J.* **7**:4 (Oct 1989), 5–11.

[13] I. Garrett and G. Jacobsen, G., "Phase noise in weakly coherent systems", *IEEE Proc.*, **136J** (Jun 1989), 159–165.

[14] I. Garrett, D. J. Bond, J. B. Waite, D. S. L. Lettis and G. Jacobsen, "Impact of phase noise in weakly coherent systems: a new and accurate approach", *Journal of Lightwave Technology*, **8**:3 (Mar 1990), 329–337.

[15] W. Gobush, H. Yamakawa, W. H. Stockmayer, W. S. Magee, "Statistical mechanics of wormlike chains, I: asymptotic behavior", *J. Chem. Phys.* **57**:7 (Oct 1972), 2839–2843.

[16] D. Gurarie, *Symmetry and laplacians: introduction to harmonic analysis, group representations and applications*, Elsevier, 1992.

[17] P. J. Hagerman, "Analysis of the ring-closure probabilities of isotropic wormlike chains: application to duplex DNA", *Biopolymers* **24** (1985), 1881–1897.

[18] Z. Haijun and O. Zhong-can, "Bending and twisting elasticity: A revised Marko-Siggia model on DNA chirality", *Physical Review E* **58**:4 (Oct 1998), 4816–4819.

[19] C. H. Henry, "Theory of linewidth of semiconductor lasers", *IEEE J. Quantum Electron* **QE-18** (Feb 1982), 259–264.

[20] J. J. Hermans and R. Ullman, "The statistics of stiff chains, with applications to light scattering", *Physica* **18**:11 (1952), 951–971.

[21] G. Jacobsen, *Noise in digital optical transmission system*, The Artech House Library, London, 1994.

[22] O. Kratky and G. Porod, "Röntgenuntersuchung Gelöster Fadenmoleküle", *Recueil des Travaux Chimiques des Pays-Bas* **68**:12 (1949), 1106–1122.

[23] A. B. Kyatkin and G. S. Chirikjian, "Synthesis of binary manipulators using the Fourier transform on the Euclidean group",*ASME J. Mechanical Design* **121** (Mar 1999), 9–14.

[24] A. B. Kyatkin and G. S. Chirikjian, "Algorithms for fast convolutions on motion groups", *Applied and Computational Harmonic Analysis* **9** (Sep 2000), 220–241.

[25] G. W. Mackey, *Induced representations of groups and quantum mechanics*, Benjamin, New York and Amsterdam, 1968.

[26] J. F. Marko, E. D. Siggia, "Bending and twisting elasticity of DNA", *Macromolecules* **27** (1994), 981–988.

[27] W. L. Mattice and U. W. Suter, *Conformational theory of large molecules: the rotational isomeric state model in macromolecular systems*, Wiley, New York, 1994.

[28] W. Miller Jr., *Lie theory and special functions*, Academic Press, New York, 1968; see also (by the same author) "Some applications of the representation theory of the Euclidean group in three-space", *Commun. Pure Appl. Math.*, **17**, 527–540, 1964.

[29] R. P. Mondescu and M. Muthukumar, "Brownian motion and polymer statistics on certain curved manifolds", *Physical Review E* **57**:4 (Apr 1998), 4411–4419.

[30] J. D. Moroz and P. Nelson, "Torsional directed walks, entropic elasticity, and DNA twist stiffness", *Proc. Nat. Acad. Sci. USA* **94**:26 (1997), 14418–14422.

[31] J. D. Moroz and P. Nelson, "Entropic elasticity of twist-storing polymers", *Macromolecules* **31**:18 (1998), 6333–6347.

[32] P. Nelson, "New measurements of DNA twist elasticity", *Biophysical Journal* **74**:5 (1998), 2501–2503.

[33] T. Odijk, "Physics of tightly curved semiflexible polymer chains", *Macromolecules* **26** (1993), 6897–6902.

[34] G. Porod, "X-ray and light scattering by chain molecules in solution", *J. Polymer Science* **10**:2 (1953), 157–166.

[35] L. Pukanszky, "Unitary Representations of Solvable Lie Groups", *Ann. Sci. Ecol. Norm. Sup.* **4**:4, pp.457–608, 1971.

[36] J. S. Rno, "Harmonic analysis on the Euclidean group in three-space, I, II", *J. Math. Phys.*, **26** (1985), 675–677, 2186–2188.

[37] J. Talman, *Special functions*, Benjamin, Amsterdam, 1968.

[38] D. Thirumalai and B.-Y. Ha, "Statistical mechanics of semiflexible chains: a mean field variational approach", pp. 1–35 in *Theoretical and Mathematical Models in Polymer Research*, edited by A. Grosberg, Academic Press, 1998.

[39] N. J. Vilenkin, "Bessel functions and representations of the group of Euclidean motions", *Uspehi Mat. Nauk.*, 11:3 (1956), 69–112 (in Russian).

[40] N. J. Vilenkin, E. L. Akim and A. A. Levin, "The matrix elements of irreducible unitary representations of the group of Euclidean three-dimensional space motions and their properties", *Dokl. Akad. Nauk SSSR* 112 (1957), 987–989 (in Russian).

[41] N. J. Vilenkin, and A. U. Klimyk, *Representation of Lie group and special functions*, 3 vol., Kluwer, 1991.

[42] J. B. Waite and D. S. L. Lettis, "Calculation of the properties of phase noise in coherent optical receivers", *Br. Telecom. Technol. J.* **7**:4 (Oct 1989), 18–26.

[43] Y. F. Wang, *Applications of diffusion processes in robotics, optical communications and polymer science*, Ph.D. Dissertation, Johns Hopkins University, 2001.

[44] H. Yamakawa, *Helical wormlike chains in polymer solutions*, Springer, Berlin, 1997.

[45] X. Zhang, "Analytically solving the Fokker–Planck equation for the statistical characterization of the phase noise in envelope detection", *Journal of Lightwave Technology*, **13**:8 (Aug 1995), 1787–1794.

GREGORY S. CHIRIKJIAN
DEPARTMENT OF MECHANICAL ENGINEERING
JOHNS HOPKINS UNIVERSITY
BALTIMORE, MD 21218
UNITED STATES
gregc@jhu.edu

YUNFENG WANG
DEPARTMENT OF ENGINEERING
THE COLLEGE OF NEW JERSEY
EWING, NJ 08534
UNITED STATES
jwang@tcnj.edu

Modern Signal Processing
MSRI Publications
Volume **46**, 2003

Fast X-Ray and Beamlet Transforms for Three-Dimensional Data

DAVID L. DONOHO AND OFER LEVI

ABSTRACT. Three-dimensional volumetric data are becoming increasingly available in a wide range of scientific and technical disciplines. With the right tools, we can expect such data to yield valuable insights about many important phenomena in our three-dimensional world.

In this paper, we develop tools for the analysis of 3-D data which may contain structures built from lines, line segments, and filaments. These tools come in two main forms: (a) Monoscale: the X-ray transform, offering the collection of line integrals along a wide range of lines running through the image — at all different orientations and positions; and (b) Multiscale: the (3-D) beamlet transform, offering the collection of line integrals along line segments which, in addition to ranging through a wide collection of locations and positions, also occupy a wide range of scales.

We describe different strategies for computing these transforms and several basic applications, for example in finding faint structures buried in noisy data.

1. Introduction

In field after field, we are currently seeing new initiatives aimed at gathering large high-resolution three-dimensional datasets. While three-dimensional data have always been crucial to understanding the physical world we live in, this transition to ubiquitous 3-D data gathering seems novel. The driving force is undoubtedly the pervasive influence of increasing storage capacity and computer processing power, which affects our ability to create new 3-D measurement instruments, but which also makes it possible to analyze the massive volumes of data that inevitably result when 3-D data are being gathered.

Keywords: 3-D volumetric (raster-scan) data, 3-D x-ray transform, 3-D beamlet transform, line segment extraction, curve extraction, object extraction, linogram, slant stack, shearing, planogram.

Work partially supported by AFOSR MURI 95–P49620–96–1–0028, by NSF grants DMS 98–72890 (KDI), and by DARPA ACMP BAA 98-04.

As examples of such ongoing developments we can mention: Extragalactic Astronomy [50], where large-scale galaxy catalogs are being developed; Biological Imaging, where methods like single-particle electron microscopy and tomographic electron microscopy directly give 3-D data about structure of biological interest at the cellular level and below[45; 26]; and Experimental Particle Physics, where 3-D detectors lead to new types of experiments and new data analysis questions [22].

In this paper we describe tools which will be helpful for analyzing 3-D data when the features of interest are concentrated on lines, line segments, curves, and filaments. Such features can be contrasted to datasets where the objects of interest might be blobs or pointlike objects, or where the objects of interest might be sheets or planar objects. Effectively, we are classifying objects by their dimensionality; and for this paper the underlying objects of interest are of dimension 1 in R^3.

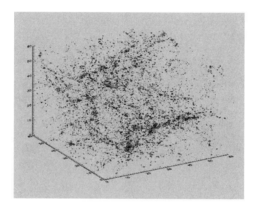

Figure 1. A simulated large-scale galaxy distribution. (Courtesy of Anatoly Klypin.)

1.1. Background motivation. As an example where such concerns arise, consider an exciting current development in extragalactic astronomy: the compilation and publication of the Sloan Digital Sky Survey, a catalog of galaxies which spans an order of magnitude greater scale than previous catalogs and which contains an order of magnitude more data.

The catalog is thought to be massive enough and detailed enough to shed considerable new light on the processes underlying the formation of matter and galaxies. It will be particularly interesting (for us) to better understand the filamentary and sheetlike structure in the large-scale galaxy distribution. This structure reflects gravitational processes which cause the matter in the universe to collapse from an initially fully three-dimensional scatter into a scatter concentrated on lower-dimensional structures [41; 25; 49; 48].

Figure 1 illustrates a point cloud dataset obtained from a simulation of galaxy formation. Even cursory visual inspection suggests the presence of filaments and perhaps sheets in the distribution of matter. Of course, this is artificial data. Similar figures can be prepared for real datasets such as the Las Campanas catalog, and, in the future, the Sloan Digital Sky Survey. To the eye, the simulated and real datasets will look similar. But can one say more? Can one rigorously compare the quantitative properties of real and simulated data? Existing techniques, based on two-point correlation functions, seem to provide only very weak ability to discriminate between various point configurations [41; 25].

This is a challenging problem, and we expect that it can be attacked using the methods suggested in this paper. These methods should be able to quantify the extent and nature of filamentary structure in such datasets, and to provide invariants to allow detailed comparisons of point clouds. While we do not have space to develop such a specific application in detail in this paper, we hope to briefly convey here to the reader a sense of the relevance of our methods.

What we will develop in this paper is a set of tools for digital 3-D data which implement the *X-Ray transform* and related transforms. For analysis of continuum functions $f(x, y, z)$ with $(x, y, z) \in \mathbf{R}^3$, the *X*-ray transform takes the form

$$(Xf)(L) = \int_L f(p)dp,$$

where L is a line in R^3, and p is a variable indexing points in the line; hence the mapping $f \mapsto Xf$ contains within it all line integrals of f.

It seems intuitively clear that the X-ray transform and related tools should be relevant to the analysis of data containing filamentary structure. For example, it seems that in integrating along any line which matches a filament closely over a long segment, we will get an unusually large coefficient, while on lines that miss filaments we will get small coefficients, and so the spread of coefficients across lines may reflect the presence of filaments.

This sort of intuitive thinking resembles what on a more formal level would be called the principle of matched filtering in signal detection theory. That principle says that to detect a signal in noisy data, when the signal is at unknown location but has a known signature template, we should integrate the noisy data against the signature template shifted to all locations where the signal may be residing. Now filaments intuitively resemble lines, so integration along lines is a kind of intuitive matched filtering for filaments. Once this is said, it becomes clear that one wants more than just integrating along lines, because filamentarity can be a relatively local property, while lines are global objects. As filaments might resemble lines only over moderate-length line segments, one might find it more informative to compare them with templates of line integrals over *line segments* at all lengths, locations, and orientations. Such segments may do a better job of matching templates built from fragments of the filament.

Hence, in addition to the X-ray transform, we also consider in this paper a multiscale digital X-ray transform which we call the beamlet transform. As defined here, the beamlet transform is designed for data in a digital $n \times n \times n$ array. Its intent is to offer multiscale, multiorientation line integration.

1.2. Connection to 2-D beamlets. Our point of view is an adaptation to the 3-D setting of the viewpoint of Donoho and Huo, who in [21] have considered beamlet analysis of 2-D images. They have shown that beamlets are connected with various image processing problems ranging from curve detection to image segmentation. In their classification, there are several levels to 2-D beamlet analysis:

- *Beamlet dictionary:* a special collection of line segments, deployed across orientations, locations, and scales in 2-D, to sample these in an efficient and complete manner.
- *Beamlet transform:* the result of obtaining line integrals of the image along all the beamlets.
- *Beamlet graph:* a graph structure underlying the 2-D beamlet dictionary which expresses notions of adjacency of beamlets. Network flow algorithms can use this graph to explore the space of curves in images very efficiently. Multiscale chains of 2-D beamlets can be expressed naturally as connected paths in the beamlet graph.
- *Beamlet algorithms:* algorithms for image processing which exploit the beamlet transform and perhaps also the beamlet graph.

They have built a wide collection of tools to operationalize this type of analysis for 2-D images. These are available over the internet [1; 2]. In the BeamLab environment, one can, for example, assemble the various components in the above picture to extract filaments from noisy data. This involves calculating beamlet transforms of the noisy data, using the resulting coefficient pyramid as input to processing algorithms which are organized around the beamlet graph and which use various graph-theoretical optimization procedures to find paths in the beamlet graph which optimize a statistical goodness-of-match criterion.

Exactly the same classification can be made in three dimensions, and very similar libraries of tools and algorithms can be built. Finally, many of the same applications from the two-dimensional case are relevant in 3-D. Our goal in this paper is to build the very basic components of this picture: describing the X-ray and beamlet transforms that we work with, the resulting beamlet pyramids, and a few resulting beamlet algorithms that are easy to implement in this framework. Unfortunately, in this paper we are unable to explore all the analogous beamlet-based algorithms — such as the algorithms for extracting filaments from noisy data using shortest-path and related algorithms in the beamlet graph. We simply scratch the surface.

1.3. Contents. The contents of the paper are as follows:

- Section 2 offers a discussion of two different systems of lines in 3-D, one system enumerating all line segments connecting pairs of voxel corners on the faces of the digital cube, and one system enumerating all possible slopes and intercepts.
- Section 3 discusses the construction of beamlets as a multiscale system based on these systems of lines, and some properties of such systems. The most important pair of properties being (a) the low cardinality of the system: it has $O(n^4)$ elements as opposed to the $O(n^6)$ cardinality of the system of all multiscale line segments, while (b) it is possible to express each line segment in terms of a short chain of $O(\log(n))$ beamlets.
- Section 4 discusses two digital X-ray transform algorithms based on the vertex-pairs family of lines.
- Section 5 discusses transform algorithms based on the slope-intercept family of lines.
- Section 6 exhibits some performance comparisons
- Section 7 offers some basic examples of X-ray analysis and synthesis.
- Section 8 discusses directions for future work.

2. Systems of Lines in 3-D

To implement a digital X-ray transform one needs to define structured families of digital lines. We use two specific systems here, which we call the vertex-pair system and the slope-intercept system. Alternative viewpoints on 'digital geometry' and 'discrete lines' are described in [33; 34].

2.1. Vertex-pair systems. Take an $n \times n \times n$ cube of unit volume voxels, and call the set of vertices V the voxel corners which are not interior to the cube. These vertices occur on the faces on the data cube, and there are about $6(n+1)^2$ such vertices. For an illustration, see Figure 2.

To keep track of vertices, we label them by the face they belong to $1 \leq f \leq 6$ and by the coordinates $[k_1, k_2]$ within the face.

Now consider the collection of all line segments generated by taking distinct pairs of vertices in V. This includes many 'global scale lines' crossing the cube from one face to another, at voxel-level resolution. In particular it does not contain any line segments with endpoints strictly inside the cube.

The set has roughly $18n^4$ elements, which can be usefully indexed by the *pair of faces* (f_1, f_2) they connect and the coordinates $[k_1^1, k_2^1]$, $[k_1^2, k_2^2]$ of the endpoints on those faces. There are 15 such face-pairs involving distinct faces, and we can uniquely specify a line by picking any such face-pair and any pair of coordinate pairs obeying $k_i^j \in \{0, 1, 2, \ldots n\}$.

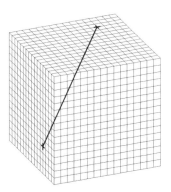

Figure 2. The vertices associated with the data cube are the voxel corners on the surface; a digital line indicated in red, with endpoints at vertices indicated in green.

2.2. Slope-intercept systems. We now consider a different family of lines, defined not by the endpoints, but by a parametrization. For this family, it is best to change the origin of the coordinate system so that the data cube becomes an $n \times n \times n$ collection of cubes with center of mass at $(0,0,0)$. Hence, for (x, y, z) in the data cube we have $|x|, |y|, |z| \leq n/2$. We can consider three kinds of lines: *x-driven, y-driven, and z-driven*, depending on which axis provides the shallowest slopes. An x-driven line takes the form

$$z = s_z x + t_z, \quad y = s_y x + t_y$$

with slopes s_z, s_y, and intercepts t_z and t_y. Here the slopes $|s_z|, |s_y| \leq 1$. y- and z-driven lines are defined with an interchange of roles between x and y or z, as the case may be.

We will consider the family of lines generated by this, where the slopes and intercepts run through an equispaced family:

$$s_x, s_y, s_z \in \{2\ell/n : \ell = -n/2, \ldots, n/2-1\}, \qquad t_x, t_y, t_z \in \{\ell : -n+1, \ldots, n-1\}.$$

3. Multiscale Systems: Beamlets

The systems of line segments we have just defined consist of *global scale* segments beginning and ending on faces of the cube. For analysis of fragments of lines and curves, it is useful to have access to line segments which begin and end well inside the cube and whose length is adjustable so that there are line segments of all lengths between voxel scale and global scale.

A seemingly natural candidate for such a collection is the family of *all* line segments between any voxel corner and any other voxel corner. For later use, we call such segments *3-D beams*. This set is expressive — it approximates any line segment we may be interested in to within less than the diameter of one voxel.

On the other hand, the set of all such beams can be of huge cardinality — with $O(n^3)$ choices for both endpoints, we get $O(n^6)$ 3-D beams — so that it is clearly infeasible to use the collection of 3-D beams as a basic data structure even for $n = 64$. Note that digital 3-D imagery is becoming available with $n = 2048$ from Resolution Sciences, Inc., Corte Madera, CA, and many important applications involve the analysis of volumetric images that contain filamentary objects such as blood vessel networks or fibers in a paper. For such datasets it seems natural to use beams-based analysis tools, however, working with $O(n^6)$ storage would be prohibitive.

The challenge, then, is to develop a *reduced-cardinality* substitute for the collection of 3-D beams, but one which is nevertheless expressive, in that it can be used for many of the same purposes as 3-D beams. Throughout this section we will be working in the context of vertex-pair systems of lines.

3.1. The beamlet system. A dyadic interval $D(j,k)$ satisfies $D(j,k) = [k/2^j, (k+1)/2^j] \subset [0,1]$ where k is an integer between 0 and 2^j; it has length 2^{-j}. A dyadic cube $C(k_1, k_2, k_3, j) \subset [0,1]^3$ is the direct product of dyadic intervals

$$[k_1/2^j, (k_1+1)/2^j] \otimes [k_2/2^j, (k_2+1)/2^j] \otimes [k_3/2^j, (k_3+1)/2^j]$$

where $0 \leq k_1, k_2, k_3 < 2^j$ for an integer $j \geq 0$. Such cubes can be viewed as descended from the unit cube $C(0,0,0,0) = [0,1]^3$ by recursive partitioning. Hence, the splitting $C(0,0,0,0)$ in half along each axis $D(j,k_1) \otimes D(j,k_2) \otimes D(j,k_3)$ yields the eight cubes $C(k_1, k_2, k_3, 1)$ where $k_i \in \{0,1\}$, splitting those in half along each axis we get the 64 subcubes $C(k_1, k_2, k_3, 2)$ where $k_i \in \{0,1,2,3\}$, and if we decompose the unit cube into n^3 voxels using a uniform n-by-n-by-n grid with $n = 2^J$ dyadic, then the individual voxels are the n^3 cells $C(k_1, k_2, k_3, J)$, $0 \leq k_1, k_2, k_3 < n$.

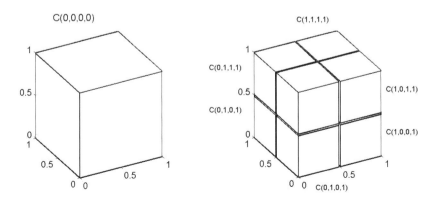

Figure 3. Dyadic cubes.

Associated to each dyadic cube we can build a system of lines based on vertex pairs. For a dyadic cube $Q = C(k_1, k_2, k_3, j)$ tiled by voxels of side $1/n$ for a dyadic $n = 2^J$ with $J > j$, let $V_n(Q)$ be the set of voxel corners on the faces of Q and let $B_n(Q)$ be the collection of all line segments generated by vertex-pairs from $V_n(Q)$.

DEFINITION 1. We call $B_n(Q)$ the set of *3-D beamlets* associated to the cube Q. Taking the collection of all dyadic cubes at all dyadic scales $0 \leq j \leq J$, and all beamlets generated by all these cubes, the *3-D beamlet dictionary* is the union of all the beamlet sets of all dyadic subcubes of the unit cube, and we denote this set by B_n.

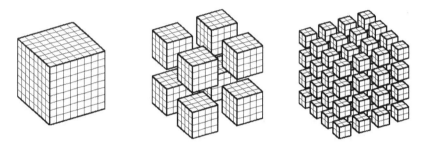

Figure 4. Vertices on dyadic cubes are always just the points on the faces of the cubes.

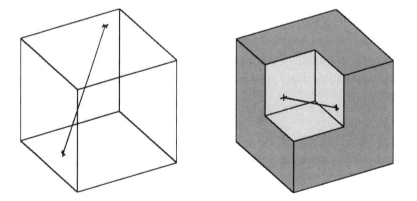

Figure 5. Examples of beamlets at two different scales: (a) scale 0 (coarsest scale); (b) scale 1 (next finer scale).

This dictionary of line segments has three desirable properties.

- It is a *multi-scale* structure: it consists of line segments occupying a range of scales, locations, and orientations.
- It has *controlled cardinality*: there are only $O(n^4)$ 3-D beamlets, as compared to $O(n^6)$ beams.

- It is *expressive*: a small number of beamlets can be chained together to approximately represent any beam.

The first property is obvious: the multi-scale, multi-orientation, multi- location nature has been obtained as a direct result of the construction.

To show the second property, we compute the cardinality of B_n. By assumption, our voxel size $1/n$ has $n = 2^J$, so there are $J + 1$ scales of dyadic cubes. Of course for any scale $0 \le j \le J$ there are 2^{3j} dyadic cubes of scale j; each of these dyadic cubes contains $2^{3(J-j)}$ voxels, approximately $6 \times 2^{2(J-j)}$ boundary vertices, and therefore $18 \times 2^{4(J-j)}$ 3-D beamlets.

The total number of 3-D beamlets at scale j is the number of dyadic cubes at scale j, times the number of beamlets of a dyadic cube at scale j, which gives $18 \times 2^{4J-j}$. Summing for all scales gives a total of approximately $36 \times 2^{4J} = O(n^4)$ elements total.

We will now turn to our third claim — that the collection of 3-D beamlets is expressive. To develop our support for this claim, we will first introduce some additional terminology and make some simple observations, and then state and prove a formal result.

3.2. Decompositions of beams into chains of beamlets. In decomposing a dyadic cube Q at scale j into its 8 disjoint dyadic subcubes at scale $j + 1$, we call those subcubes the children of Q, and say that Q is their parent. We also say that 2 dyadic cubes are siblings if they have the same parent. Terms such as descendants and ancestors have the obvious meanings. In this terminology, except at the coarsest and finest scales, all dyadic subcubes have 8 children, 7 siblings and 1 parent. The data cube has neither parents nor siblings and the individual voxels don't have children. We can view the inheritance structure of the set of dyadic cubes as a balanced tree where each node corresponds to a dyadic cube, the data cube corresponds to the root and the voxel cubes are the leaves. The depth of a node is simply the scale parameter j of the corresponding cube $C(k_1, k_2, k_3, j)$.

The dividing planes of a dyadic cube are the 3 planes that divide the cube into its 8 children; we refer to them as the x-divider, y-divider and z-divider. For example the x-divider of $C(0, 0, 0, 0)$ is the plane $\{(1/2, y, z) : 0 \le y, z \le 1\}$, the y-divider is $\{(x, 1/2, z) : 0 \le x, z \le 1\}$, and the z-divider is $\{(x, y, 1/2) : 0 \le x, y \le 1\}$.

We now make a remark about beamlets of data cubes at different dyadic n. Suppose we have two data cubes of sizes $n_1 = 2^{j_1}$ and $n_2 = 2^{j_2}$, and suppose that $n_2 > n_1$. Viewing the two data cubes as filling out the same volume $[0, 1]^3$, consider the beamlets in each system associated with a common dyadic cube $C(k_1, k_2, k_3, j)$, $0 \le j \le j_1 < j_2$. The collection of beamlets associated with the n_2-based system has a finer resolution than those associated with the n_2-based system; indeed every beamlet in the B_{n_1} also occurs in the B_{n_2}. Hence, in a natural sense, the beamlet families refine, and have a natural limit, B_∞,

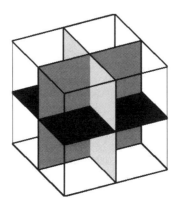

Figure 6. Dividing planes of a cube.

say. B_∞, of course, is the collection of all line segments in $[0,1]^3$ with both endpoints on the boundary of some dyadic cube. We will call members of this family the *continuum beamlets*, as opposed to the members of some B_n, which are *discrete beamlets*. Every discrete beamlet is also a continuum beamlet, but not the reverse.

LEMMA 1. Divide a continuum beamlet associated to a dyadic cube Q into the components lying in each of the child subcubes. There are either one, two, three or four distinct components, and these are continuum beamlets.

PROOF. Traverse the beamlet starting from one endpoint headed toward the other. If you travel through more than one subcube along the way, then at any crossing from one cube to another, you will have to penetrate one of the x-, y-, or z-dividers. You can cross each such dividing plane at most once, and so there can be at most 4 different subcubes traversed.   □

THEOREM 1. Each line segment lying inside the unit cube can be approximated by a connected chain of m discrete beamlets in B_n where the Hausdorff distance from the chain to the beam is at most $1/n$ and where the number of links m in the chain is bounded above by $6 log_2(n)$.

PROOF. Consider the arbitrary line segment ℓ inside the unit cube with endpoints v_1 and v_2 that are not necessary voxel corners. We can approximate ℓ with a beam b by replacing each endpoint with the closest voxel corner. Since the $\sqrt{3}/(2n)$ neighborhood of any point inside the unit cube must include a vertex, the Hausdorff distance between ℓ and b is bounded by $\sqrt{3}/(2n)$.

We now decompose the beam b into a minimal cardinality chain of connected continuum beamlets, by a recursive algorithm which starts with a line segment, and at each stage breaks it into a chain of continuum beamlets, with remainders on the ends, to which the process is recursively applied.

In detail, this works as follows. If b is already a continuum beamlet for $C(0,0,0,0)$ we are done; otherwise, b can be decomposed into a chain of (at most

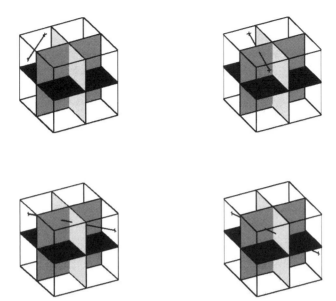

Figure 7. Decomposition of several beamlets into continuum beamlets at next finer scale, indicating cases which can occur.

four) segments based on crossings of b with the 3 dividing planes of $C(0,0,0,0)$. The interior segments of this chain all have endpoints on the dividing planes and hence are all continuum beamlets for the cubes at scale $j = 1$. We go to work on the remaining segments. Either endmost segment of the chain might be a continuum beamlet for the associated dyadic cube at scale $j = 1$; if so, we are done with that segment; if not, we decompose the segment into its components lying in the children dyadic cubes at scale $j = 2$. Again, the internal segments of this chain will be continuum beamlets, and additionally, at least one of the two endmost segments will be a continuum beamlet. If both endmost segments are continuum beamlets, then we are done. If not, take the segment which is not a beamlet and break it into its crossings with the dividing planes of the enclosing dyadic cube. Continue in this way until we reach the finest level, where, by hypothesis, we obtain a segment which has an endpoint in common with the original beam b. Since b is a beam, it ends in a vertex corner, and since the segment arose from earlier stages of the algorithm, the other endpoint is on the boundary of a dyadic cube. Hence the segment is a continuum beamlet and we are done.

Let's upperbound the number of beamlets generated by this algorithm. Assume always that we never fortuitously get an end segments to be a beamlet when it is not mandated by the above comments. So we have 2 continuum beamlets at the 1st scale and we are left with 2 segments to replace by 2 chains of discrete beamlets at finer scales. In the worst case, each of the segments when decomposed at the next scale, generates 3 continuum beamlets and 1 non-beamlet.

Continuing to the finest scale, in which the dyadic cubes are the individual vox-els, we can have at most 2 beamlets in the chain at the finest scale. So in the worst case our chain will include 2 continuum beamlets at the 1st scale, 2 at the finest scale and 6 at any other scale $2, 3, ..., J - 1$, So we get a maximum total of $2 + 6(J - 1) + 2 = 6J - 2$ continuum beamlets needed to represent any line segment in the unit cube.

We now take the multiscale chain of beamlets and approximate it by a chain of discrete beamlets. The point is that the Hausdorff distance between line segments is upperbounded by the distance between corresponding endpoints. Now both endpoints of any continuum beamlet in B_∞ lie on certain voxel faces. Hence they lie within a $1/(\sqrt{2}n)$ neighborhood of some voxel corner. Hence any continuum beamlet in B_∞ can be approximated by a discrete beamlet in B_n within a Hausdorff distance of $1/(\sqrt{2}n)$. Notice that there may be several choices of such approximants; we can make the choice of approximant consistently from one beamlet to the next to maintain chain connectivity if we like.

So we get a maximum total of $6J - 2$ connected beamlets needed to ap-proximate any line segment in the unit cube to within a Hausdorff distance of $\max\{\sqrt{3}/(2n), 1/(\sqrt{2}n)\} < 1/n$. $\qquad\square$

The fact that arbitrary line segments can be approximated by relatively few beamlets implies that *every smooth curve can be approximated by relatively few beamlets*.

To see this, notice that a smooth curve can be approximated to within distance $1/m^2$ by a chain about m line segments — this is a simple application of calculus. But then, approximating each line segment in the chain by its own chain of $6\log(n)$ beamlets, we get approximation within distance $1/m^2 + 1/n$ by $O(\log(n) \cdot m)$ beamlets. Moreover, we can set up the process so that the individual chains of beamlets form a single unbroken chain. Compare also [17, Lemma 2.2, Corollary 2.3, Lemma 3.2].

4. Vertex-Pairs Transform Algorithms

Let $v = (k_1, k_2, k_3)$ be a voxel index, where $0 \le k_i < n$ and let $I(v)$ be the corresponding voxel intensities of a 3D digital image. Let $f(x)$ be the function on R^3 that represents the data cube by piecewise constant interpolation — i.e. the value $f(x) = I(v)$ when $x \in v$.

DEFINITION 2. For each line segment $b \in B_n$, let $\gamma_b(\cdot)$ correspond to the unit speed path traversing b.

The discrete X-ray transform based on global-scale vertex-pairs lines is defined as follows. With $B_n([0, 1])^3$ denoting the collection of vertex-pairs line segments of associated to the cube $[0, 1]^3$,

$$X_I(b) = \int f(\gamma_b(\ell)) \, d\ell, \quad b \in B_n([0, 1])^3.$$

The beamlet transform based on multiscale vertex-pairs lines is the collection of all multiscale line integrals

$$T_I(b) = \int f(\gamma_b(\ell)) \, d\ell, \quad b \in B_n.$$

4.1. Direct evaluation. There is an obvious algorithm for computing beamlet/ X-ray coefficients: one at a time, simply compute the sums underlying the defining integrals. This algorithm steps systematically through the beamlet dictionary using the indexing method we described above, identifies the voxels on the path γ_b for each beamlet, visits each voxel and forms a sum weighting the voxel value with the arc length of γ_b in that voxel.

In detail, the sum we are referring to works as follows. Let $Q(v)$ denote the cube representing voxel v and γ_b the curve traversing b

$$T_I(b) = \sum I(v) \, \text{Length}(\gamma_b \cap Q(v)).$$

Hence, defining weights $w_b(v) = \text{Length}(\gamma_b(l) \cap Q(v))$ as the arc lengths of the corresponding fragments, one simply needs the sum $\sum_v w_b(v) I(v)$.

Of course, most voxels are not involved in this sum; one only wants to involve the voxels where $w_b > 0$. The straightforward way to do this, explicitly following the curve γ_b from voxel to voxel and calculating the arc length of the fragment of curve within the voxel, is inelegant and bulky. A far better way to do this is to identify three equispaced sequences and then merge them. Those sequences are: (1) the intersections of γ_b with the parallel planes $x = k_1/n$; (2) the intersections with the planes $y = k_2/n$; and (3) the intersections with the planes $z = k_3/n$. Each of these collections of intersections is equispaced and easy to calculate. It is also very easy to merge them in the order they would be encountered in a traverse of the beamlet in definite order. This merger produces the sequence of intersections that would be encountered if we pedantically tracked the progress of the beamlet voxel-by-voxel. The weights $w_b(v)$ are just the distances between successive points.

The complexity of this algorithm is rather stiff: on an $n \times n \times n$ voxel array there are order $O(n^4)$ beamlets to follow, and most of the sums require $O(n)$ flops, so the whole algorithm requires $O(n^5)$ flops in general. Experimental studies will be described below.

4.2. Two-scale recursion. There is an asymptotically much faster algorithm for 3-D X-ray and beamlet transforms, based on an idea which has been well-established in the two-dimensional case; see articles of Brandt and Dym [12], by Götze and Druckenmiller [29], and by Brady [9], or the discussion in [21].

The basis for the algorithm is the divide and conquer principle. As depicted in Figure 7, and proven in Lemma 1, each 3-D continuum beamlet can be decomposed into 2, 3, or 4 continuum beamlets at the next finer scale:

$$b = \bigcup_i b_i \tag{4-1}$$

It follows that

$$\int f(\gamma_b(\ell))d\ell = \sum_i \int f(\gamma_{b_i}(\ell))d\ell.$$

This suggests that we build an algorithm on this principle, so that for $b \in B_n$ we identify several b_i associated to the child dyadic cubes of b, getting the formula

$$T_I(b) = \sum_i T_I(b_i).$$

Hence, if we could compute all the beamlet coefficients at the finest scale, we could then use this principle to work systematically from fine scales to coarse scales, and produce all the beamlet coefficients as a result.

The computational complexity of this fine-to-coarse strategy is obviously very favorable: it is bounded by $4B_n$ flops, since each coefficient's computation requires at most 4 additions. So we get an $O(n^4)$ rather than $O(n^5)$ algorithm.

There is a conceptual problem with implementing this principle, since in general, the decomposition of a discrete beamlet in B_n into its fragments at the next finer scale (as we have seen) produces continuum beamlets, i.e. the b_i are in general only in B_∞, and not B_n. Hence it is not really the case that the terms $T_I(b_i)$ are available from finer scale computations. To deal with this, one uses approximation, identifying discrete beamlets $\hat{b}_i$ which are 'near' the continuum beamlets, and approximates the $T_I(b_i)$ by combinations of 'nearby' $T_I(\hat{b}_i)$.

Hence, in the end, we get favorable computational complexity for an approximately correct answer. We also get one very large advantage: instead of computing just a single X-ray transform, it computes all the scales of the multiscale beamlet transform in one pass. In other words: it costs the same to compute all scales or to compute just the coarsest scale.

As we have described it, there are no parameters to 'play with' to control the accuracy, at perhaps greater computational expense. What to do if we want high accuracy? Staying within this framework, we can obtain higher precision by oversampling. We create an $N \times N \times N$ data cube, where $N = 2^e n$ where e is an oversampling parameter (e.g. e=3), fill the values from the original data cube by interpolation (e.g. piecewise constant interpolation), run the two-scale algorithm for B_N, and then keep only the coefficients associated to $b \in B_N \cap B_n$. The complexity goes up as 2^{4e}.

5. Slope-Intercept Transform Algorithms

We now develop two algorithms for X-ray transform based on the slope-angle family of lines described in Section 2.2. Both are decidedly more sophisticated than the vertex-pairs algorithms, which brings both benefits and costs.

5.1. The slant stack/shearing algorithm. The first algorithm we describe adapts a fast algorithm for the X-ray transform in dimension 2, using this as an 'engine', and repeatedly applying it to obtain a fast algorithm for the X-ray transform in dimension 3.

5.1.1. Slant Stack The fast slant stack algorithm has been developed by Averbuch et al. (2001) [6] as way to rapidly calculate all line integrals along lines in 2-dimensional slope/angle form; i.e. either x-driven 2-dimensional lines of the form

$$y = sx + t, \ -n/2 \le x < n/2;$$

where $s = k/n$ for $-n \le k < n$ and where $-n \le t < n$ or y-driven 2-dimensional lines of the form

$$x = sy + t, \ -n/2 \le y < n/2,$$

where s and t run through the same discrete ranges. The algorithm is approximate, because it does not exactly compute the voxel-level definition of X-ray coefficient assumed in Section 3 above (involving sums of voxel values times arc lengths). Instead, it computes exactly the appropriate sums deriving from so-called sinc-interpolation filters. For the set of x-driven lines we have

$$SlantStack(y = sx + t, I) = \sum_{u=-n/2}^{n/2-1} \tilde{I}(u, su + z),$$

where I is a 2D discrete array and $\tilde{I}$ is its 2D sinc interpolant. The transform for the y-driven lines is defined in a similar fashion with the roles of x and y interchanged. The algorithm can obtain approximate line integrals along all lines of these two forms in $O(n^2 \log(n))$ flops, which is excellent considering that the number of pixels is $O(n^2)$. It is achieved by using a discrete Projection-Slice theorem that relates the Slant Stack coefficients and the 2D Fourier coefficients. To be more specific, we are able to calculate the slant stack coefficients by first calculating the 2D Fourier Transform of I on a pseudopolar grid (see Figure 8) and then applying a series of 1-D inverse FFTs along radial lines. Each application of the 1-D inverse FFT yields a vector of coefficients that correspond to the slant-stack transform of I along a family of parallel lines.

Figure 9 shows backprojections of different delta sequences, each concentrated at a single point in the coefficient space and corresponding to a choice of slope-intercept pair. The panels show the 2-D arrays of weights involved in the coefficient computation. Summing with these weights is approximately the same as exactly summing along lines of given slope/intercept.

As Averbuch et al. point out, the fast slant stack belongs to a group of algorithms developed over the years in synthetic aperture radar by Lawton [40] and in medical imaging by Pasciak [44] and by Edholm and Herman [24], where it is called the Linogram. The Linogram has been exploited systematically for more than ten years in connection with many problems of medical imaging, including

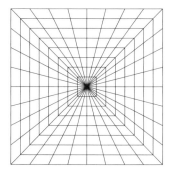

Figure 8. The Pseudopolar Grid is constructed from concentric squares $n = 8$ are converted into data at the intersections of concentric squares and lines radiating from the origin with equispaced slopes.

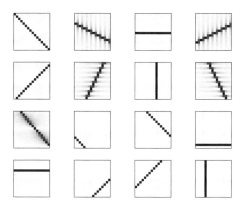

Figure 9. 2D Slant Stack Lines.

cone-beam and fan-beam tomography, which concern image reconstruction from subsets of the X-ray transform. In a 3-D context the most closely related work in medical imaging concerns the *planogram*; see [38; 39], and our discussion in Section 10.5 below. The terminology 'slant stack' comes from seismology, where this type of transform, with different algorithms, has been in use since the 1970's [15].

5.1.2. Overall Strategy We can use the slant stack to build a 3-D X-ray transform by grouping together lines into subfamilies which live in a common plane. We then extract that plane from the data cube and apply the slant stack to that plane, rapidly obtaining integrals along all lines in that plane. We ignore for the moment the question of how to extract planes from digital data when the planes are not oriented along the coordinate axes.

In detail, our strategy works as follows. Suppose we want to get transform coefficients corresponding to x-driven 3-D lines, i.e. lines obeying

$$y = s_y x + t_y, \quad z = s_z x + t_z.$$

Within the family of all n^4 lines of this type, consider the subfamily $\mathcal{L}_{xz,n}(s_z, t_z)$ of all lines with a fixed value of (s_z, t_z) and a variable value of (s_y, t_y). Such lines all lie in the plane $P_{xz}(s_z, t_z)$ of (x, y, z) with (x, y) arbitrary, $z = s_z x + t_z$. We can consider this set of lines as taking all x-driven 2-D lines in the (x, y) plane and then 'tilting' the plane to obey the equation $z = s_z x + t_z$. Our intention is to extract this plane, sampling it as a function of x and y, and use the slant stack to evaluate all the line integrals for all the x-driven lines in that plane, thereby obtaining all the integrals in $\mathcal{L}_{xz,n}(s_z, t_z)$ at once, and to repeat this for other families, working systematically through values of s_z and t_z.

Some of these subfamilies with constant intercept t and varying slope s are depicted in Figure 10.

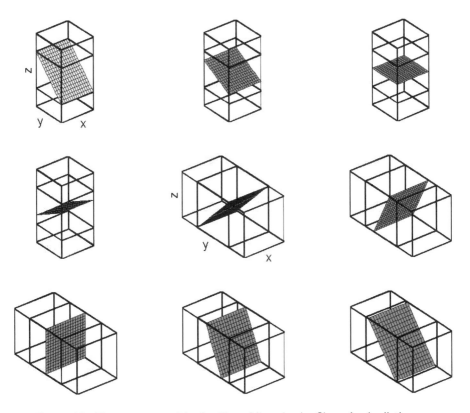

Figure 10. Planes generated by families of lines in the Slope-Angle dictionary; subpanels indicate various choices of slope.

In the end, then, our coordinate system for lines has one slope and one inter-cept to specify a plane and one slope and one intercept to specify a line within[*] the plane.

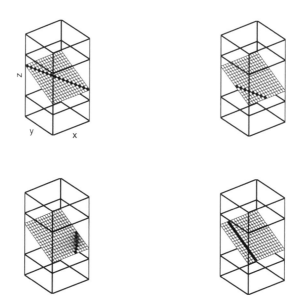

Figure 11. Lines selected from planes via slope-intercept indexing.

5.1.3. 3-D Shearing

To carry out this strategy, we need to extract data lying in a general 2-D plane within a digital 3-D array.

We make a simple observation: to extract from the function $f(x, y, z)$ defined on the full cube its restriction to the plane with $z = s_z x + t_z$, and x, y varying, we simply create a new function $f'(x, y, z)$ defined by

$$f'(x, y, z) = f(x, y, z - s_z x - t_z)$$

for x, y, z varying throughout $[0, 1]^3$, with f taken as vanishing at arguments outside the unit cube. We then take $g(x, y) = f'(x, y, 0)$ as our extracted plane. The idea is illustrated in Figure 12.

In order to apply this idea to the case of digital arrays $I(x, y, z)$ defined on a discrete grid, note that, in general, $z - s_z x - t_z$ will not be an integer even when z and x are, and so the expression $I(x, y, z - s_z x - t_z)$ is not defined; one needs to make sense of this quantity somehow. At this point we invoke the notion of *shearing of digital images* as discussed, for example, in [54; 6]. Given a 2-D $n \times n$ image $I(x, y)$ where $-n/2 \leq x, y < n/2$, we define the shearing of y as a function x at slope s, $Sh_{xy}^{(s)}$, according to

$$(Sh_{xy}^{(s)} I)(x, y) = I_2(x, y - sx).$$

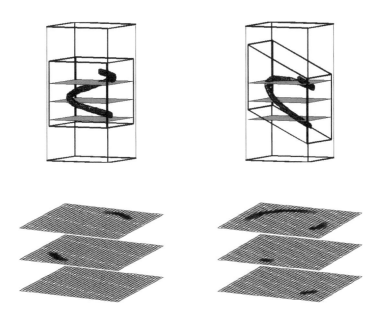

Figure 12. Shearing and slicing a 3D image. Extracting horizontal slices of a sheared 3-D image is the same as extracting slanted slices of the original image.

In words, the image is shifted vertically in each column x =constant, with the shift varying from one column to the next in an x-dependent way. Here $I_2(x, y)$ is an image which has been interpolated in the vertical direction so that the second argument can be a general real number and not just an integer. Specifically,

$$I_2(x, u) = \sum_v \phi_n(u - v)I(x, v),$$

where ϕ_n is an interpolation kernel — a continuous function of a real variable obeying $\phi_n(0) = 1$, $\phi_n(k) = 0$ for $k \neq 0$. The shearing of x as a function of y works similarly, with

$$(Sh_{yx}^{(s)}I)(x, y) = I_1(x - sy, y),$$

with

$$I_1(u, y) = \sum_v \phi_n(u - v)I(v, y).$$

We define a shearing operator for a 3-D data cube by applying a 2-D operator systematically to each 2-D planes in a family of parallel planes normal to one of the coordinate axes. Thus, if we speak of shearing in z as a function of x, we mean

$$Sh_{xz}^{(s)}I(x, y, z) = I_3(x, y, z - sx).$$

What shearing does is map a family of tilted parallel planes into a plane normal to one of the coordinate axes. In the above example, data along the plane $z = sx + t$ is mapped onto the plane $z = t$. Figure 12 illustrates the process graphically, exaggerating the process, by allowing pieces of the original image to be sheared out of the original data volume. In fact those pieces 'moving out' of the data volume get 'chopped away' in actual computations.

5.1.4. The Algorithm Armed with this tool, we define the slant stack based X-ray transform algorithm as follows, giving details only for a part of the computation. The algorithm works separately with x-driven, y-driven, and z-driven lines. The procedure for x-driven lines is as follows:

- for each slope s_z
    - Shear z as a function of x with slope s_z, producing the 3-D voxel array I_{xz,s_z}.
    - for each intercept t_z
        * Extract the 2-D image $I_{s_z,t_z}(x,y) = I_{xz,s_z}(x,y,t_z)$.
        * Calculate the 2-D X-ray transform of this image, obtaining an array of coefficients $X(s_y, t_y)$, and storing these in the array $X_3('x', s_y, t_y, s_z, t_z)$.
    - end for
- end for

The procedure is analogous for y- and z- driven lines.

The lines generated by this algorithm are as illustrated in Figure 11.

The time complexity of this algorithm is $O(n^4 \log(n))$. Indeed, the cost of the 2-D slant-stack algorithm is order $n^2 \log(n)$ (see [6]), and this must be applied order n^2 times, one for each member of $\mathcal{L}_{xz,n}(s_z, t_z)$

5.2. Compatibility with cache memory. A particularly nice property of this algorithm is that it is *cache-aware* , i.e. it is very well-organized for use with modern hierarchical memory computers [32]. In currently dominant computer architectures, main memory is accessed at a speed which can be an order of magnitude slower than the cache memory on the CPU chip. As a result, other things being equal, an algorithm runs much faster if it operates as follows:

- Load n items from main memory into the cache
- Work intensively to compute n results
- Send the n results out to main memory

Here the idea is that the main computations involve relatively small blocks of data that can be kept in cache all at once, are referred to many times while in the fast cache memory, saving dramatically on main memory accesses.

The Slant-Stack/Shearing algorithm we have described above has exactly this form. In fact it can be decomposed in steps, every one of which can be conceptualized as follows:

- Load n items from main memory into the cache
- Do some combination of:

- Compute an n-point forward FFT ; or
- Compute an n-point inverse FFT ; or
- Perform elementwise transformation on the n-vector;

• Send the n results out to main memory

Thus the 2-D slant stack and the 3-D data shearing operations can all be decomposed into steps of this form. For example, data shearing requires computing sums of the form $I'(x, y, z) = \sum_u \phi(z - sx - u)I(x, y, u)$. For each fixed (x, y), we take the n numbers $(I(x, y, u) : u = -n/2, ..., n/2 - 1)$, take their 1-D FFT along the last slice, multiply the FFT by a series of appropriate coefficients, and then take their inverse 1-D. The story for the slant stack is similar, but far more complicated. A typical step in that algorithm involves the 2-D FFT, which is obtained by applying order $2n$ 1-D FFT's, once along each row and once along each column. For more details see comments in [6].

It is also worth remarking that several modern CPU architectures offer FFT *in silico*, so that the FFT step in the above decomposition runs without any memory accesses for instruction fetches. Such architectures (which include the G4 processor running on Apple Macintosh and IBM RS/6000) are even more favorable towards this algorithm.

As a result of this cache- and CPU-favorable organization the observed behavior of this algorithm is far more favorable than what asymptotic theory would suggest. The vertex-pairs algorithms of the previous section sit at the opposite extreme; since those algorithms involve summing data values along lines, and the indices of those values are scattered throughout the linear storage allocated to the data cube, those algorithms appear to be performing essentially random access to memory; hence such algorithms run at the memory access speed rather than the cache speed. In some circumstances those algorithms can even run more slowly still, since cache misses can cost considerably more than one memory access, and random accesses can cause large numbers of cache misses. These remarks are in line with behavior we will observe empirically below.

5.3. Frequency domain algorithm. Mathematical analysis shows that the 3-D X-ray transform of a continuum function $f(x, y, z)$ can be obtained from the Fourier transform [51; 47]. This frequency-domain approach requires coordinatizing planes through the origin in frequency space by

$$\mathcal{P}_{\mathbf{u}_1, \mathbf{u}_2} = \{\xi = \mathbf{u}_1 \xi_1 + \mathbf{u}_2 \xi_2\}$$

extracting sections of the Fourier transform along such planes,

$$\hat{g}(\xi_1, \xi_2) = \hat{f}(\mathbf{u}_1 \xi_1 + \mathbf{u}_2 \xi_2),$$

and then taking the inverse Fourier transform of those sections:

$$g = \mathcal{F}^{-1}\hat{g}.$$

The resulting function g gives the X-ray transform for lines

$$g(x_1, x_2) = \int f(x_1 \mathbf{v}_1 + x_2 \mathbf{v}_2 + t \mathbf{v}_3) dt,$$

with an appropriate orthobasis $(\mathbf{v}_1, \mathbf{v}_2, \mathbf{v}_3)$.

To carry this out with digital data would require developing a method to efficiently extract many planes through the origin of the Fourier transform cube, and then perform 2-D inverse FFT's of the data in those planes. But how to rapidly extract a rich selection of planes through the origin? (The problem initially sounds similar to the problem encountered in the previous section, but recall that the set of planes needed there were families of parallel planes, not families of planes through the origin.

Our approach is as follows. Pick a fixed preferred coordinate axis, x, say. Pick a subordinate axis, z, say. In each constant-y slice, do a two-dimensional shearing of the FT data, shearing z as a function of x at fixed slope s_z. In effect, we have tilted the data cube, so that slices normal to the z-axis in the sheared volume correspond to tilted planar slices in the original volume. So now take each y-z plane, and apply idea of Cartesian-to-pseudopolar conversion as described in [6]. This uses interpolation to convert a planar Cartesian grid into a new point set consisting of n lines through the origin at various angles, and equispaced samples along each line. This conversion being done for each plane with x fixed, then, grouping the data in a given line through the origin across all x values produces a plane; see Figure 13. We then take a 2-D inverse transform of the data in this plane.

The computational complexity of the method goes as follows. $O(n^3 \log(n))$ operations are required for transforming from the original space domain to the frequency domain; $O(n^2 \log(n))$ work for each conversion of a Cartesian plane to

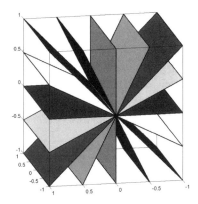

Figure 13. Selecting planes through the origin. Performing cartesian-to-pseudo-polar conversion in the yz plane and then gathering all the data for one radial line across different values of x produces a series of planes through the origin.

pseudopolar coordinates, giving $O(n^3 \log(n))$ work to convert a whole stack of parallel planes in this way; $O(n^3 \log(n))$ work to shear the array as a function of the preferred coordinate; and $3n$ such shearings need to be performed. Overall, we get $O(n^4)$ coefficients in $O(n^4 \log(n))$ flops.

We have not pursued this method in detail, for one reason: *it is mathematically equivalent to the slant-stack-and-shearing algorithm*, providing exactly the same results (assuming exact arithmetic). This is a consequence of the projection-slice theorem for the slant stack transform proved in [6].

6. Performance Measures

We now consider two key measures of performance of the fast algorithms just defined: accuracy and timing.

6.1. Accuracy of two-scale recursion. To estimate the accuracy of the two-scale recursion algorithm, we considered a 16^3 array and compared coefficients from two-scale approximation with direct evaluation. We computed the average error for the different scales and applied the algorithms both to a 3-D image that contains a single beamlet and to a 3-D image that contains randomly distributed ones in a sea of zero, chose so that both 3D images has the same $l2$ norm. The table below shows that the coefficients obtained from the two-scale recursion are significantly different from those of direct evaluation.

Analyze Single Beamlet		Analyze Random Scatter	
scale	relative error	scale	relative error
0	0.117	0	0.056
1	0.107	1	0.061
2	0.076	0	0.048
3	1.5×10^{-17}	3	3.7×10^{-17}

One way to understand this phenomenon is to look at what the coefficients are measuring by studying the *equivalent kernels* for those coefficients. Let T^1 be the linear transform on I corresponding to the exact evaluation of the line integrals and let T^2 be the linear transform corresponding to the two-scale recursion algorithm. Apply the adjoint of each transform to a coefficient-space vector with a one in one position and a zero in other positions, getting

$$w_b^j = (T^j)' \delta^b, \quad j = 1, 2. \tag{6-1}$$

Each w_b^j lives in image-space—i.e., it is indexed by voxels v, and the entries $w_b(v)$ indicate the weights such that $T_I[b] = \sum_v I(v) w_b(v)$. In essence this 'is' the beamlet we are using in that beamlet transform. For later use: we call the operation of calculating w_b that of 'backprojection', because we are going back from coefficient space to image space. This usage is consistent with usage of the term in the tomographic literature, i.e. [47; 15].

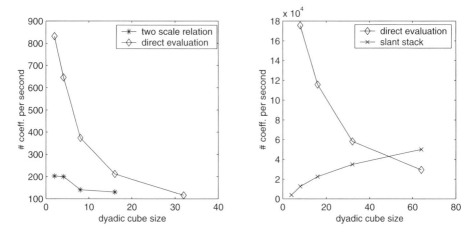

Figure 14. Timing comparison.

6.2. Timing comparison. The defining feature of 3-D processing is the massive volume of data involved and the attendant long execution times for even basic tasks. So the burning issue is: how do the algorithms perform in terms of CPU time to complete the task? The display in Figure 14 below shows that both the direct evaluation and the two scale recursion methods slow down dramatically as n increases — one expects a $1/n^{5/3}$ or $1/n^{4/3}$ scaling law to be evident in this display, and in rough terms, the display is entirely consistent with that law. The surprising thing in this display is the *improvement* in performance of the slant stack with increasing n. This seeming anomaly is best interpreted in terms of the cache-awareness of the slant stack algorithm. The slant stack algorithm becomes more and more immune to cache misses as n increases (at least in the range we are studying), and so the number of cache misses per coefficient drops lower and lower for this algorithm, while this effect is totally absent for the direct evaluation and two-scale recursion algorithm.

7. Examples of X-Ray Transforms

We now give a few examples of the X-ray transform based on the slant stack method.

7.1. Synthesis. While we have not discussed it at length, the adjoint of the X-ray transform is a very useful operator; for each variant of the X-ray transform that we have discussed, the corresponding adjoint can be computed using ideas very similar to those which allowed to compute the transform itself, and with comparable computational complexity. Just as the X-ray transform takes voxel arrays into X-ray coefficient arrays, the adjoint transform takes X-ray coefficient arrays into voxel arrays.

We have already mentioned, near (6–1) above, that when the adjoint operator is applied to a coefficient array filled with zeros except for a one in a single slot, the result is a voxel array. This array contains the weights $w_b(v)$ underlying the corresponding X-ray transform coefficient. In formal mathematical language this is the Riesz representer of the b-th coefficient. Intuitively, the representer should have its nonzero weights all concentrated on or near the corresponding 'geometrically correct' line.

To check this, we depict in Figure 15 representers of four different X-ray coefficients. Evidently, these are geometrically correct.

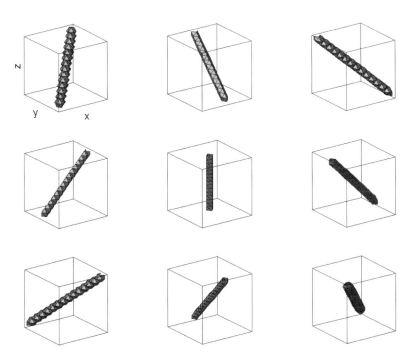

Figure 15. Representers of several X-ray coefficients.

It is also worth considering what happens if we apply the adjoint to coefficient vectors which are ones in various regions and zeros elsewhere in coefficient space. Intuitively, the result should be a bundle of lines. Depending on the span of the region in slope and intercept, the result might be simply like a thick rod (if only intercepts are varying) or like a dumbbell (if only slopes are varying). To check this, we depict in Figure 16 backprojection of six different region indicators. With a little reflection, we can see that these are geometrically correct.

It is of interest to consider backprojection of more interesting coefficient arrays, such as wavelets with vanishing moments. We have done so and will discuss the results elsewhere.

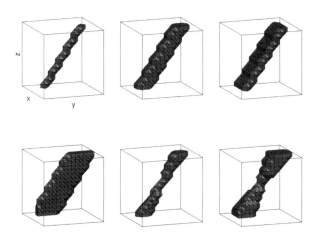

Figure 16. X-ray back-projections of various rectangles in coefficient space.
Note that if the rectangle involves intercepts only, the backprojection is rectangular (until cut off by cube boundary). If the rectangle involves slopes, the
backprojection is dumbbell-shaped (see lower right)

7.2. Analysis. Now that we have the ability to generate linelike objects in 3-D
via backprojection from the X-ray domain, we can conveniently investigate the
properties of X-ray analysis.

Consider the example given in Figure 17. A beam is generated by backprojection as in the previous section. It is then analyzed according to the X-ray
transform. If the X-ray transform were orthogonal, then we would see perfect
concentration of the transform in coefficient space, at precisely the location of the
spike used to generate the beam. However, the transform is not orthogonal, and
what we see is a concentration — but not perfect concentration — in coefficient
space near the location of the true generator.

Also, if the transform were orthogonal, the rearranged sorted coefficients
would have a single nonzero coefficient. As the figure shows, the coefficients
decay linearly on a semilog plot, indicating power-law decay. The lower right
subpanel shows the decay of the wavelet-X-ray coefficients that are computed by
applying a four dimensional periodic orthogonal wavelet transform to the X-ray
coefficients. As expected, the decay is much faster than the decay of the X-ray
coefficients.

8. Application: Detecting Fragments of a Helix

We now sketch briefly an application of beamlets to detecting fragments of
a helix buried in noise. We suppose that we observe a cube of noisy 3-D data,
and that, possibly, the data contains (buried in noise) a filamentary object. By
'filamentary object' we mean the kind of situation depicted in Figure 18. A series
of pixels overlapping a nonstraight curve is highlighted there, and we imagine

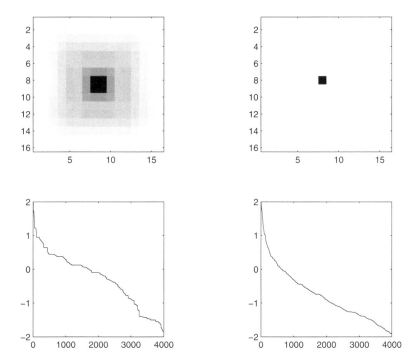

Figure 17. X-Ray analysis of a beam. (a) The X-ray transform sliced in the constant-intercept plane. (b) The X-ray transform sliced in the constant-slope plane. (c) The sizes of sorted X-ray coefficients. (d) The sizes of sorted wavelet-X-ray coefficients.

that, when such an object is 'present' in our data, that a constant multiple of that 3-D template is added to a pure noise data cube.

Figure 18. A noiseless helix.

When this is done, we have a situation that is hard to depict graphically, since one cannot 'see through' such a noisy cube. By this we mean the following: to visualize such a data cube, it seems that we have just two rendering options. We can view the cube as opaque, render only the surface, and then we certainly will not see what's going on inside the cube. Or we can view the cube as transparent, in which case, when each voxel is assigned a gray value based on the corresponding data value, we see a very uniformly gray object.

Being stymied by the task of 3-D visualization of the noisy cube, we instead display some 2-D slices of the cube; see the rightmost panel of Figure 19. For comparison, we also display the same slices of the noiseless helix. The key point to take away from this figure is that the noise level is so bad that the presence of the helical object would likely not be visible in any slice through the data volume.

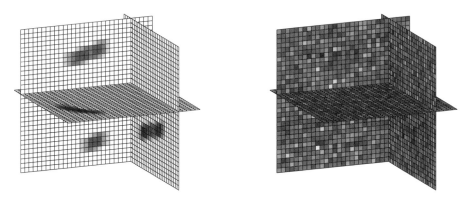

Figure 19. Three orthogonal slices through (a) a noiseless helix; (b) the noisy data volume.

Here is a simple idea for detecting a noisy helix: *beamlet thresholding.* We simply take the beamlet transform, normalize each empirical beamlet coefficient by dividing by the length of the beamlet, and then identify beamlet coefficients (if any) that are unusually large compared to what one would expect if we were in a noise-only situation.

Figure 20 shows the results of applying such a procedure to the noisy data example of Figures 18-19. The extreme right subpanel shows the beamlets that were found to have significant coefficients. The center panel shows the result of backprojecting those significant beamlets; a rough approximation to the filament (far left) has been recovered.

9. Application: A Frame of Linelike Elements

We also briefly sketch an application in using the X-ray transform for data representation. As we have seen in Section 7.1, the backprojection of a delta sequence in X-ray coefficient space is a line-like element. We have so far interpreted this as meaning that the X-ray transform defines an *analysis* of data

Figure 20. A noiseless helix, a reconstruction from noisy data obtained by backprojecting coefficients exceeding threshold, and a depiction of the beamlets associated to significant coefficients.

via line-like elements. But it may also be interpreted as saying that backprojection from coefficient space defines a synthesis operator, which, for the 'right' coefficient array, can synthesize a volumetric image from linelike elements.

The trick is to find the 'right' coefficient array to synthesize a given desired object. This can be conceptually challenging because the X-ray transform is overdetermining, giving order n^4 coefficients for an order n^3 data cube. Iterative methods for solving large-scale linear systems can be tried, but will probably be ineffective, owing to the large spread in singular values of the X-ray operator.

There is a way to modify the (slant-stack/shearing) X-ray transform to produce something that has reasonably controlled spread of the singular values. This uses the fact, as described in Averbuch et al. [6], that there is an effective preconditioner for the 2-D slant stack operator S (say), such that the preconditioned operator $\tilde{S}$ obeys

$$c_0\|I\|_2 \leq \|\tilde{S}I\|_2 \leq c_1\|I\|_2.$$

Here $c_1/c_0 < 1.1$. Hence, the transform from 2-d images to their coefficients is almost norm-preserving. In effect, $\tilde{S}$ performs a kind of fractional differentiation of the image before applying S. If, in following the construction of the X-ray transform that was laid out in Section 5.1, we simply replace each invocation of S by $\tilde{S}$. Then effectively, the transform coefficients, grouped together in the families $\mathcal{L}_{xz,n}(s_z, t_z)$ have in each such group, roughly the same norm as the data in the corresponding plane $\mathcal{P}_{xz,n}(s_z, t_z)$, say of the data cube. For each fixed slope s_z, the family of planes $\mathcal{P}_{xz,n}(s_z, t_z)$ with different intercepts t_z, fill out the whole data cube, and so the norms of all these planes, combined together by a sum of squares, gives the squared norm of the whole data cube. It follows that the transform of a volumetric image $I(x, y, z)$ should yield a coefficient array with ℓ^2 norm roughly proportional to the ℓ^2 norm of the array I.

DEFINITION 3. The preconditioned X-ray transform $\tilde{X}$ is the result of following the prescription for Section 5.1 to build an X-ray transform, only using the preconditioned slant stack rather than the slant stack.

We should note that in the theory of the continuum X-ray transform [51], there is the notion of *X-ray isometry*, which preserves the L^2 norm while mapping from physical space to line space. This can be viewed as applying the X-ray transform to a fractional differentiation of the object f, rendering the whole system an isometry. The preconditioned digital X-ray operator $\tilde{X}$ we have just described is a digital analog, although it does not provide a precise isometry.

Standard facts in linear algebra (e.g. [28; 30]) imply that, because the output norm $\|\tilde{X}I\|_2$ is (roughly) proportional to the input norm $\|I\|_2$, iterative algorithms (relaxation, conjugate gradients, etc.) should be able to efficiently solve equations $\tilde{X}I = y$.

The X-ray transform is highly redundant (as it maps n^3 arrays into $O(n^4)$ arrays). As a way to obtain greater sparsity, one might consider applying an orthogonal wavelet transform to the X-ray coefficients. This will preserve the norm of the coefficients, while it may compress the energy into a few large coefficients. The transform is (naturally) 4-dimensional, but as the display in Figure 17 suggests, our concern is more to compress in the slope variable where the analysis of a beam is spread out, rather than in the intercept variables, where the analysis of a beam is already compressed.

DEFINITION 4. The wavelet-compressed X-ray transform $\widetilde{WX}$ is the result of applying an orthogonal 4-D wavelet transform to the preconditioned X-ray transform.

Label the coefficient indices in the wavelet-compressed X-ray transform domain as $\lambda \in \Lambda$, and let the entries in $\widetilde{WX}$ be labeled $\alpha = (\alpha_\lambda)$; they are the wavelet-compressed preconditioned X-ray coefficients.

It turns out that one can reconstruct the original image I from its coefficients α. As the wavelet transform is norm-preserving, the map $I \mapsto \widetilde{WX}I$ is proportional to an almost norm-preserving transform, and hence one can go back from coefficient space to image space, using iterative linear algebra. Call this generalized inverse (linear) transformation $\widetilde{WX}^\dagger$. Then certainly $I = \widetilde{WX}^\dagger \alpha$.

This can be put in a more interesting form. The result of applying this generalized inverse transform to a delta coefficient sequence $\delta_{\lambda_0}(\lambda)$ spiking at coefficient index λ_0 (say) provides a volumetric object $\phi_{\lambda_0}(v)$. Hence we may write

$$I = \sum_\lambda \alpha_\lambda \phi_\lambda.$$

The object ϕ_λ is a *frame element*, and we have thus defined a *frame of linelike elements* in 3-space. Emmanuel Candès in personal correspondence has called such things *tubelets*, although we are reluctant to settle on that name for now (tubes being flexible rather than straight and rigid).

In [16] a similar construction has been applied in the continuum case: a wavelet tight frame has been applied to the X-ray isometry to form a linelike frame in the continuum $\mathbf{R}^3$.

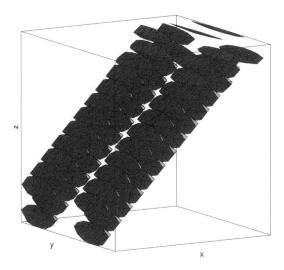

Figure 21. A frame element.

This construction is also reminiscent of the construction of ridgelets for representation of continuous functions in 2-D [14]. Indeed, orthonormal ridgelets can be viewed as the application of orthogonal wavelet transform to the Radon isometry [18]. In [19] a construction paralleling the one suggested here has been carried out for 2-D digital data.

10. Discussion

We finish up with a few loose ends.

10.1. Availability. The figures in this paper can be reproduced by code which is part of the beamlab package. Point your web browser to http://www-stat.stanford.edu/~beamlab to obtain the software. The software has the ability to reproduce all the figures in this paper and has been produced consistent with the philosophy of reproducible research.

10.2. In practice. There are of course many variations on the above schemes, but we have restrained ourselves from discussing them here, even when they are variations we find practically useful, in order to keep things simple. A few examples:

- We find it very useful to work with an alternative vertex-pair dictionary, where the vertices of beamlets are not at corners of boundary voxels for a dyadic cube, but instead at midpoints of boundary faces of boundary voxels.
- We find it useful to work with slight variations of the slant stack defined in [6], where the angular spacing of lines is chosen differently than in that paper.

Rather than burden the reader with such details, we suggest merely that the interested reader study the released software.

10.3. Beamlet algorithms. As mentioned in the introduction, in this paper we have not been able to describe the use of the graph structure of the beamlets in which two beamlets are connected in the graph *if and only if* they have an endpoint in common. In all the examples above, each beamlet is treated independently of other beamlets. As we showed earlier, every smooth curve can be efficiently approximated by relatively few beamlets in a connected chain. In order to take advantage of this fact we must use some mechanism for examining different beamlet chains. The graph structure affords us such a mechanism.

This structure can be useful because there are some low complexity, network-flow based procedures [43; 27] that allow one to optimize over all paths through a graph. Such paths in the beamlet graph correspond to connected chains of beamlets. When applied in the multiscale graph provided by 2-D beamlets, these algorithms were found in [21] to have interesting applications in detecting filaments and segmenting data in 2-D. One expects that the same ideas will prove useful in 3-D.

10.4. Connections with particle physics. In a series of interesting papers spanning both 2-D and 3-D applications, David Horn and collaborators Halina Abramovicz and Gideon Dror have found several ways to deploy line-based systems in data analysis and detector construction[4; 5; 22]. Most relevant to our work here is the paper [22] which describes a linelike system of feature detectors for analysis of data from 3-D particle physics detectors. Professor Horn has pointed out to us, and we agree, that such methods are very powerful in the right settings, and that the main thing holding back widespread deployment of such methods is the immense size of the number of lines needed to give a comprehensive analysis of 3-D data.

10.5. Connections with tomography and medical imaging. The field of medical imaging is rapidly developing these days, and particularly in the last few years, 3-D tomography has become a 'hot topic', with several major conferences and workshops. What is the connection of this work to ongoing work in medical imaging?

Obviously, the X-ray transform, as we have defined it, is closely connected to problems of medical imaging, which certainly obtain line integrals in 3-space and aim to use these to reconstruct the object of interest.

However, the layout of our X-ray transform is (seemingly) rather different than current medical scanners. Such scanners are designed according to physical and economic constraints which place various constraints on the line integrals which can be observed by the system. In contrast, we have only computational constraints and we seek to represent a very wide range of line integrals in our approach. For example, in an X-ray system, a source is located at a fixed point, and can send out beams in a cone, and the line integrals can be measured by a receiving device (film or other) on a planar surface. One obtains many line integrals, but they all have one endpoint in common. In a PET system, events in the specimen generate are detected by pairs of detectors collinear with the event. One obtains, by summing detector-pair counts over time, an estimated line integral. The collection of integrals is limited by the geometry of the detector arrays.

Essentially, in the vertex-pairs transform, we contemplate a situation that would be analogous, in PET tomography, to having cubical room, with arrays of detectors lining the walls, floor, and ceiling, and with all pairs of detectors corresponding to lines which can be observed by the system. In (physical) X-ray tomography, our notion of X-ray transform would correspond to a system where there is a 'source wall' and the rest of the surfaces were 'receivers', with the specimen or patients being studied oriented successively standing, prone, facing and in profile to the 'source wall'. The (omnidirectional) X-ray source would be located for a sequence of exposures at each point of an array on the source wall (say).

Neither situation is quite what medical imaging experts mean when they say 3-D tomography. For the last ten years or so, there has been a considerable body of work on so called cone-beam reconstruction in 3-D physical X-ray tomography; see [47; 35]. In an example of such a setting [47], a source is located at a fixed point, the specimen is mounted on a turntable in front of a screen, and an exposure is made by generating radiation, which travels through the specimen and the line integral is recorded by a rectangular array at the the screen. This is repeated for each orientation of the turntable. This would be the equivalent of observing the X-ray transform only for those lines which originate on a specific circle in the $z = 0$ plane, and is considerably less coverage than what we envisage.

In PET imaging there are now so-called 'fully 3-D scanners', such as the CTI ECAT EXACT HR+ described in [46]. This scanner comprises 32 circular detector rings with 288 detectors each, allowing for a total of 77×10^6 lines. While this is starting to exhibit some of the features of our system, with very large numbers of beams, the detectors are only sensitive to lines occurring within a cone of opening less than 30 degrees. The closest 3-D imaging device to our setting appears to be the fully 3-D PET system described in [37; 38; 39] where two parallel planar detector arrays provide the ability to gather data on all pairs of lines joining a point in one detector plane to a point in the other plane. In [38] a mathematical analysis of this system has suggested the relevance of the linogram (known as slant stack throughout our article) to the fully 3-D problem, without explicitly defining the algorithm suggested here. Without doubt, ongoing developments in 3-D PET can be expected to exhibit many similarities to the work in this paper, although it will be couched in a different language and aimed at different purposes.

Another set of applications in medical imaging, to interactive navigation of 3-D data, is described in [10], based on supporting tools [9; 11; 55] which are reminiscent of the two-scale recursive algorithm for the beamlet transform.

10.6. Visibility We conclude with a more speculative connection. Suppose we have 3-D voxel data which are binary, with a '1' indicating occupied and a '0' indicating unoccupied. Then a beam which hits only '0' voxels is 'clear', whereas a beam which hits some '1' voxels is 'occluded'. Question: can we rapidly tell whether a beam is 'clear' or 'occluded', for a more or less random beam?

The question seems to call for rapid calculation of line integrals along every possible line segment. Obviously, if we proceed in the 'obvious' way, the algorithmic cost of answering a such a query is order n, since there are line segments containing order n voxels.

Note that, if we precompute the beamlet transform, we can approximately *answer any query about the clarity of a beam* in order $O(\log(n))$ operations. Indeed the beam can written as a chain of beamlets, and we merely have to examine all those beamlet coefficients checking that they are all zero. There are only $O(\log(n))$ coefficients to check, from Theorem 1 above.

We can also rapidly determine *the maximum distance we can go along a ray before becoming occluded.* That is, suppose we are at a given point and might want to travel in a fixed direction. How far can we go before hitting something?

To answer this, consider the the segment starting at our fixed point and heading in the given direction until it reaches the boundary of the data cube — we obviously wouldn't want to go out of the data cube, because we don't have information about what lies there. Take the segment and decompose into beamlets. Now check that all the beamlets are 'clear', i.e. have beamlet coefficients zero. If any are not clear, go to the occluded beamlet closest to the origin, and divide it into its (at most four) children at the next level. If any are not clear, go to the occluded beamlet closest to the origin, and, once again, divide it into its (at most four) children at the next level. Continuing in this way, we soon reach the finest level, and determine the closest occlusion along that beam. The algorithm takes $O(\log(n))$ operations, assuming the beamlet transform has been precomputed.

This allows for rapid computation of what might be called safety graphs, where for each possible heading one might consider taking from a given point, one obtains the distance one can go without collision. The cost is proportional to #headings $\times \log(n)$, which seems to be quite reasonable.

Traditional visibility analysis [23] assumes far more about the occluding objects (e.g. polyhedral structure); perhaps our approach would be more useful when occlusion is very complicated and arises in natural systems subject to direct voxelwise observation.

Acknowledgments

Thanks to Amir Averbuch, Achi Brandt, Emmanuel Candès, Raphy Coifman, David Horn, Peter Jones, Xiaoming Huo, Boaz Shaanan, Jean-Luc Starck, Arne Stoschek and Leonid Yaroslavsky for helpful comments, preprints, and references. Donoho would like to thank the Sackler Institute of Tel Aviv University, and both authors would like to thank the Mathematics and Computer Science departments of Tel Aviv University, for their hospitality during the pursuit of this research.

References

[1] http://www.isye.gatech.edu/~xiaoming/beamlab.

[2] http://www-stat.stanford.edu/~beamlab, http://www.beamlab.org.

[3] http://www-stat.stanford.edu/~wavelab.

[4] H. Abramowicz, D. Horn, U. Naftali, and C. Sahar-Pikielny, "An orientation selective neural network and its application to cosmic muon identification", *Nucl. Instr. Meth. Phys. Res.* A378 (1996), 305–311.

[5] H. Abramowicz, D. Horn, U. Naftali, and C. Sahar-Pikielny, "An orientation selective neural network for pattern identification in particle detectors", pp. 925–931 in *Advances in neural information processing systems* **9**, edited by M. C. Mozer, M. J. Jordan and T. Petsche, MIT Press 1997.

[6] A. Averbuch, R. Coifman, D. Donoho, M. Israeli, and Y. Shkolnisky, "Fast Slant Stack: A notion of Radon transform for data in a cartesian grid which is rapidly computible, algebraically exact, geometrically faithful and invertible", to appear in *SIAM J. Sci. Comput.*.

[7] J. R. Bond, L. Kofman and D. Pogosyan, "How filaments of galaxies are woven into the cosmic web", *Nature* **380**:6575 (April 1996), 603–606.

[8] R. K. Ahuja, T. L. Magnanti, and J. B. Orlin, *Network flows: theory, algorithms, and applications*, Prentice-Hall, 1993.

[9] M. L. Brady, "A fast discrete approximation algorithm for the Radon transform", *SIAM J. Computing* **27**:1 (February 1998), 107–19.

[10] M. Brady, W. Higgins, K. Ramaswamy and R. Srinivasan, "Interactive navigation inside 3D radiological images", pp. 33–40 in *Proc. Biomedical Visualization '95*, Atlanta, GA, IEEE Comp. Sci Press, Loas Alamitos CA, 1995.

[11] M. Brady and W. Yong, "Fast parallel discrete approximation algorithms for the Radon transform", pp. 91–99 in *Proc. 4th ACM Symp. Parallel Algorithms and Architectures*, ACM, New York, 1992.

[12] A. Brandt and J. Dym, "Fast calculation of multiple line integrals", *SIAM J. Sci. Comput.* **20**:4 (1999), 1417–1429.

[13] E. Sharon, A. Brandt, and R Basri, "Fast multiscale image segmentation", pp. 70–77 in *Proceedings IEEE Conference on Computer Vision and Pattern Recognition*, vol. 1, 2000.

[14] E. Candès and D. Donoho, "Ridgelets: the key to high-dimensional intermittency?", *Phil. Trans. R. Soc. Lond. A.* **357** (1999), 2495–2509.

[15] S. R. Deans, *The Radon transform and some of its applications*, Krieger Publishing, Malabar (FL), 1993.

[16] D. L. Donoho, "Tight frames of k-plane ridgelets and the problem of representing d-dimensional singularities in $\mathbf{R}^n$", *Proc. Nat. Acad. Sci. USA* **96** (1999), 1828–1833.

[17] D. L. Donoho, "Wedgelets: nearly minimax estimation of edges", *Ann. Stat.* **27**:3 (1999), 859–897.

[18] D. L. Donoho, "Orthonormal ridgelets and linear singularities", *Siam J. Math Anal.* **31**:5 (2000), 1062–1099.

[19] D. L. Donoho and Georgina Flesia, "Digital ridgelet transform based on true ridge functions", to appear in *Beyond wavelets*, edited by J. Schmeidler and G. V. Welland, Academic Press, 2002.

[20] D. Donoho and X. Huo, "Beamlet pyramids: a new form of multiresolution analysis, suited for extracting lines, curves, and objects from very noisy image data", in *Proceedings of SPIE*, volume 4119, July 2000.

[21] D. L. Donoho and Xiaoming Huo, "Beamlets and multiscale image analysis", pp. 149–196 in *Multiscale and multiresolution methods*, edited by T. J. Barth and T. F. Chan and R. Haimes, Lecture Notes in Computational Science and Engineering **20**, Springer, 2001.

[22] Gideon Dror, Halina Abramowicz and David Horn, "Vertex identification in high energy physics experiments", pp. 868–874 *Advances in Neural Information Processing Systems* **11**, edited by M. S. Kearns, S. A. Solla, and D. A. Cohn, MIT Press, Cambridge (MA), 1999.

[23] Frédo Durand, "A multidisciplinary survey of visibility: notes of ACM Siggraph Course on Visibility, Problems, Techniques, and Applications", July 2000. http://graphics.lcs.mit.edu/~fredo/PUBLI/surv.pdf.

[24] P. Edholm and G. T. Herman, "Linograms in image reconstruction from projections", *IEEE Trans. Medical Imaging*, **MI-6**:4 (1987), 301–307.

[25] A. Fairall, *Large-scale structures in the universe*, Chichester, West Sussex, 1998.

[26] J. Frank (editor), *Electron tomography, three-dimensional imaging with the transmission electron microscope*, Kluwer/Plenum, 1992.

[27] D. Geiger, A. Gupta, L. A. Costa, and J. Vlontzos, "Dynamic programming for detecting, tracking and matching deformable contours", *IEEE Trans. on Pattern Analysis and Machine Intelligence* **17**:3 (1995), 294–302.

[28] G. Golub and C. van Loan, *Matrix computations*, Johns Hopkins University Press, Baltimore, 1983.

[29] W. A. Götze and H. J. Druckmüller, "A fast digital Radon transform — an efficient means for evaluating the Hough transform", *Pattern Recognition* **28**:12 (1995), 1985–1992.

[30] A. Greenbaum, *Iterative methods for solving linear systems*, SIAM, Philadelphia, 1997.

[31] L. Guibas, J. Hershberger, D. Leven, M. Sharir, and R. Tarjan, "Linear time algorithms for visibility and shortest path problems inside triangulated simple polygons", *Algorithmica* **2** (1987), 209–233.

[32] J. L. Hennessy and D. A. Patterson, pp. 373–427 in *Computer architecture: a quantitative approach*, newblock Morgan Kaufmann, San Francisco, 1996.

[33] G. T. Herman, *Geometry of digital spaces*, Birkhäuser, 1998.

[34] G. T. Herman and A. Kuba, *Discrete tomography: foundations, algorithms and applications.* Birkhäuser, 1999.

[35] G. T. Herman and Jayaram K. Udupa, *3D imaging in medicine*, 2nd Edition, CRC Press, 1999.

[36] X. Huo, *Sparse image representation via combined transforms*, PhD thesis, Stanford, August 1999.

[37] C. A. Johnson, J. Seidel, R. E. Carson, W. R. Gandler, A. Sofer , M. V. Green, and M. E. Daube-Witherspoon, "Evaluation of 3D reconstruction algorithms for a small animal PET camera", *IEEE Trans. Nucl. Sci.* 1996.

[38] P. E. Kinahan, D. Brasse, M. Defrise. R. Clackdoyle, C. Comtat, C. Michel and X. Liu, "Fully 3-D iterative reconstruction of planogram data", in *Proc. Sixth International Meeting on Fully Three-Dimensional Image Reconstruction in Radiology and Nuclear Medicine*, Asilomar (CA), October 2001.

[39] D. Brasse, P. E. Kinahan, R. Clackdoyle, C. Comtat, M. Defrise and D. W. Townsend, "Fast fully 3D image reconstruction using planograms", paper 15–207 in *Proc. 2000 IEEE Nuclear Science and Medical Imaging Symposium*.

[40] W. Lawton, "A new polar Fourier transform for computer-aided tomography and spotlight synthetic aperture radar", *IEEE Trans. Acoustics Speech Signal Process.* **36**:6 (1988), 931–933.

[41] V. J. Martinez and E. Saar, *Statistics of the galaxy distribution*, Chapman and Hall, 2001.

[42] D. Marr, *Vision : a computational investigation into the human representation and processing of visual information*, W. H. Freeman, San Francisco, 1982.

[43] U. Montanari, "On the optimal detection of curves in noisy pictures", *Comm. ACM* **14**:5 (1971), 335–345.

[44] J. E. Pasciak, "A note on the Fourier algorithm for image reconstruction", Preprint AMD 896, Applied Mathematics Department, Brookhaven National Laboratory (Upton, NY), 1981.

[45] James B. Pawley (editor), *Handbook of biological confocal microscopy*, 2nd edition, Kluwer, 1997.

[46] Jinyi Qi, Richard M. Leahy, Chinghan Hsu, Thomas H. Farquhar, and Simon R. Cherry, "Fully 3D Bayesian image reconstruction for the ECAT EXACT HR+ 1", *IEEE Trans. Nucl. Sci.*, 1997.

[47] A. G. Ramm and A. I. Katsevich, *The Radon transform and local tomography*, CRC Press, Boca Raton (FL), 1996.

[48] B. S. Sathyaprakash, V. Sahni, and S. F. Shandarin, "Emergence of filamentary structure in cosmological gravitational clustering" *Astrophys. J. Lett.* **462**:1 (1996), L5–8.

[49] W. C. Saslaw, *The distribution of the galaxies: gravitational clustering in cosmology*, Cambridge University Press, Cambridge 2000.

[50] Sloan Digital Sky Survey Website: http://www.sdss.org/.

[51] D. C. Solmon, "The X-ray transform", *J. Math. Anal. Appl.* **56** (1976), 61–83.

[52] J.-L. Starck, F. Murtagh, and A. Bijaoui, *Image processing and data analysis*, Cambridge University Press, 1998.

[53] Unattributed, "Imaging system automates volumetric microanalysis", *Vision Systems Design*, Technology Trends Section, June 2001.

[54] M. Unser, P. Thévenaz and L. Yaroslavsky, "Convolution-based interpolation for fast, high-quality rotation of images", *IEEE Trans. on Image Proc.*, **4**:10 (1995), 1371–1381.

[55] T.-K. Wu and M. Brady, "Parallel approximate computation of projection for animated volume-rendered displays", pp. 61–66 in *Proc. 1993 Parallel Rendering Symp.*, 1993.

DAVID L. DONOHO
DEPARTMENT OF STATISTICS
STANFORD UNIVERSITY
SEQUOIA HALL
STANFORD, CA 94305
UNITED STATES
    donoho@stat.stanford.edu

OFER LEVI
SCIENTIFIC COMPUTING AND COMPUTATIONAL MATHEMATICS
STANFORD UNIVERSITY
GATES 2B
STANFORD, CA 94305
UNITED STATES
    levi@sccm.stanford.edu

Modern Signal Processing
MSRI Publications
Volume **46**, 2003

Fourier Analysis and Phylogenetic Trees

STEVEN N. EVANS

ABSTRACT. We give an overview of phylogenetic invariants: a technique for reconstructing evolutionary family trees from DNA sequence data. This method is useful in practice and is based on a number of simple ideas from elementary group theory, probability, linear algebra, and commutative algebra.

1. Introduction

Phylogeny is the branch of biology that seeks to reconstruct evolutionary family trees. Such reconstruction can take place at various scales. For example, we could attempt to build the family tree for various present day indigenous populations in the Americas and Asia in order to glean information about the possible course of migration of humans into the Americas. At the level of species, we could seek to determine whether modern humans are more closely related to chimpanzees or to gorillas. Ultimately, we would like to be able to reconstruct the entire "tree of life" that describes the course of evolution leading to all present day species. Because the status of the "leaves" on which we wish to build a tree differs from instance to instance, biologists use the general term *taxa* (singular *taxon*) for the leaves in a general phylogenetic problem.

For example, for 4 taxa, we might seek to decide whether the tree

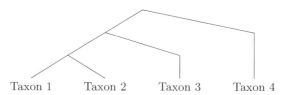

$$\text{Taxon 1} \qquad \text{Taxon 2} \qquad \text{Taxon 3} \qquad \text{Taxon 4}$$

Mathematics Subject Classification: Primary: 62P10, 13P10. Secondary: 68Q40, 20K01.

Keywords: invariant, phylogeny, DNA, genome, tree, discrete Fourier analysis, algebraic variety, elimination ideal, free module.

Research supported in part by NSF grant DMS-0071468.

or the tree

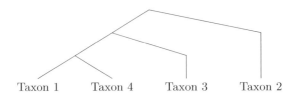

Taxon 1   Taxon 4   Taxon 3   Taxon 2

describes the course of evolution. In such trees:

- the arrow of time is down the page,
- paths down through the tree represent *lineages* (*lines of descent*),
- any point on a lineage corresponds to a point of time in the life of some ancestor of a taxon,
- vertices other than leaves represent times at which lineages diverge,
- the root corresponds to the most recent common ancestor of all the taxa.

Phylogenetic reconstruction has a long history. Classically, reconstruction was based on the observation and measurement of morphological similarities between taxa with the the possible adjunction of similar evidence from the fossil record; and these methods continue to be used. However, with the recent explosion in technology for sequencing large pieces of a genome rapidly and cheaply, reconstruction from the huge amounts of readily available DNA sequence data is now by far the most commonly used technique. Moreover, reconstruction from DNA sequence data has the added attraction that it can operate fairly automatically on quite well-defined digital data sets that fit into the framework of classical statistics, rather than proceeding from a somewhat ill-defined mix of qualitative and quantitative data with the need for expert oversight to adjust for difficulties such as morphological similarity due to convergent evolution.

There is a substantial literature on both the mathematics behind various approaches to phylogenetic reconstruction and the algorithmic issues that arise when we try to implement these approaches with large amounts of data and large numbers of taxa. We won't attempt to survey this literature or provide a complete bibliography. Rather, these lecture notes are devoted to some of the mathematics behind one particular approach: that of *phylogenetic invariants*. Not only is this technique of practical utility, but it requires a nice combination of elementary group theory, probability, linear algebra, and commutative algebra.

The outline of the rest of these notes is as follows. Section 2 begins with a discussion of the sort of DNA sequence data that are used for phylogenetic reconstruction and how these data are pre-processed using sequence alignment techniques. We then describe a very general class of "Markov random field" models that incorporate arbitrary mechanisms for nucleotide substitution and a dependence structure for the nucleotides exhibited by the taxa that mirrors the phylogenetic tree. Section 3 introduces 3 restricted classes of substitution mechanisms that are commonly used in the literature: the Jukes-Cantor model and the 2- and 3-parameter Kimura models. We observe in Section 4 that standard statistical techniques such as maximum likelihood are still computationally very demanding for infering phylogenies even for such restricted models and we propose the alternative approach of phylogenetic invariants. We point out in Sections 5 and 6 that an underlying group structure is present in the restricted substitution models and develop the Fourier analysis that is necessary for exploiting this group structure to construct and recognise invariants.

Section 7 is a warm-up that uses these algebraic tools to exhibit an invariant for a particular tree. The ideas in this section are then generalised in Section 8 to characterise the class of all invariants for an arbitrary tree. Finally, we determine the "dimension" of the space of invariants for an arbitrary tree in Section 9 and show in Section 10 that different trees have different invariants, with the "dimension" of the class of distinguishing invariants depending in a simple manner on the difference between the two trees.

2. Data and General Models

We assume that reader is familiar with the basic notion of the hereditary information of organisms being carried by DNA molecules that consist of two linked chains built from an alphabet of four *nucleotides* and twisted around each other in a double helix, and, moreover, that such a molecule can be described by listing the sequence of the nucleotides encountered along one of the chains using the letters A for adenine, G for guanine, C for cytosine, T for thymine. A lively and entertaining guide to the fundamentals is [GW91].

The totality of the DNA in any somatic cell constitutes the genome of the individual. The genomes of different individuals differ. As evolution occurs, one nucleotide is substituted for another, segments of DNA are deleted, and new segments are inserted.

Sequence alignment is a procedure that attempts to provide algorithms that takes DNA sequences from several taxa, line up "common positions" at which substitutions may or may not have occurred, and determine where deletions and insertions have occurred in certain sequences relative to the others. For example, an alignment of two taxa might produce an output such as the following:

$$\text{Taxon 1} \quad \ldots \text{A G T A A C T} \ldots$$
$$\text{Taxon 2} \quad \ldots \text{A T} * * * \text{C A} \ldots$$

Reading from left to right: both taxa have an A in the "same" position, the next position is common to both taxa but Taxon 1 has a G there whereas Taxon 2 has a T, then (due to insertions or deletions) there is a stretch of 3 positions that are present in the genome of Taxon 1 but not present in the genome of Taxon 2 *etc.* There are many approaches to deriving such alignments, and a discussion of them is outside the scope of these notes. A good introduction to some of the mathematical issues is [Wat95].

Our basic data are DNA sequences for each of our taxa that have been pre-processed in some suitable way to align them. For simplicity, we suppose that we are dealing with segments where there have been no insertions or deletions, so all the taxa share the same common positions and differences between nucleotides at these positions are due to substitutions.

The standard statistical paradigm dictates (in very broad terms) how we should go about taking these data and producing inferences about the phylogeny connecting our taxa. Firstly, we should begin with a probability model that incorporates the possible trees as a "parameter" along with other parameters that describe the mechanism by which substitutions occur relative to such a tree. Secondly, we should determine the choice of parameters (in particular, the choice of tree) that best fits the observed sequence data according to some criterion.

A standard assumption in the literature is that the behaviour at widely separated positions on the genome is statistically independent. With this assumption, the modelling problem reduces to one of modelling the nucleotide observed at a given position.

In order to describe the general class of single position models typically used in the literature, it is easiest to begin by imagining that we can observe not only the nucleotides for the taxa but also those for the unobserved intermediates represented by the interior vertices of the tree. (For simplicity, let us refer to the taxa and the intermediates as "individuals" for the moment.) Two individuals share the same lineage up to their most recent common ancestor and so the processes such as mutation leading to substitution act on the genomes of their common ancestors in the same way up until the split in lineages that occurs at the most recent common ancestor. After the split in lineages, it is a reasonable first approximation to assume that the random mechanisms by which substitutions occur are operating independently on the genomes of the ancestors that are no longer shared. Mathematically, this translates into an assumption that that the nucleotides exhibited by two individuals are conditionally independent given the nucleotide exhibited by their most recent common ancestor. Equivalently, the nucleotides exhibited by two individuals are conditionally independent given the nucleotide exhibited by *any* individual on the path that connects the two individuals in the tree.

For example, consider the tree

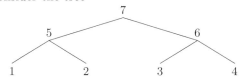

with four taxa. Letting Y_i denote the nucleotide exhibited by individual i, we have, for example, that

- Y_1 and Y_2 are conditionally independent given Y_5,

- the pair (Y_1, Y_2) are conditionally independent of the pair (Y_3, Y_4) given any one of Y_5, Y_6, or Y_7.

Because of this dependence structure, a joint probability such as

$$\mathbb{P}\{Y_1 = A, Y_2 = A, Y_3 = G, Y_4 = C, Y_5 = T, Y_6 = T, Y_7 = A\}$$

can be computed as

$$\mathbb{P}\{Y_7 = A\} \times \mathbb{P}\{Y_5 = T \mid Y_7 = A\} \times \mathbb{P}\{Y_6 = T \mid Y_7 = A\} \times \mathbb{P}\{Y_1 = A \mid Y_5 = T\}$$
$$\times \mathbb{P}\{Y_2 = A \mid Y_5 = T\} \times \mathbb{P}\{Y_3 = G \mid Y_6 = T\} \times \mathbb{P}\{Y_4 = C \mid Y_6 = T\}.$$

Thus, for a given tree, the joint probabilities of the individuals exhibiting a particular set of nucleotides are determined by the vector of 4 unconditional probabilities for the root individual and the 4×4 matrices of conditional probabilities for each edge.

Given such a model for the nucleotides exhibited by all the individuals (taxa and intermediates), we obtain a model for the nucleotides exhibited by the taxa by taking the marginal probability distribution for the taxa. Operationally, this just means that we sum over the possibilities for the intermediates.

For example, suppose that we have the tree

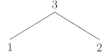

with two taxa. Then, for example,

$$\begin{aligned}
\mathbb{P}\{Y_1 = A, Y_2 = G\} &= \mathbb{P}\{Y_1 = A, Y_2 = G, Y_3 = A\} + \mathbb{P}\{Y_1 = A, Y_2 = G, Y_3 = G\} \\
&\quad + \mathbb{P}\{Y_1 = A, Y_2 = G, Y_3 = C\} + \mathbb{P}\{Y_1 = A, Y_2 = G, Y_3 = T\} \\
&= \mathbb{P}\{Y_3 = A\}\mathbb{P}\{Y_1 = A \mid Y_3 = A\}\mathbb{P}\{Y_2 = G \mid Y_3 = A\} \\
&\quad + \mathbb{P}\{Y_3 = G\} \times \mathbb{P}\{Y_1 = A \mid Y_3 = G\} \times \mathbb{P}\{Y_2 = G \mid Y_3 = G\} \\
&\quad + \mathbb{P}\{Y_3 = C\} \times \mathbb{P}\{Y_1 = A \mid Y_3 = C\} \times \mathbb{P}\{Y_2 = G \mid Y_3 = C\} \\
&\quad + \mathbb{P}\{Y_3 = T\} \times \mathbb{P}\{Y_1 = A \mid Y_3 = T\} \times \mathbb{P}\{Y_2 = G \mid Y_3 = T\}.
\end{aligned}$$

We now introduce some notation to describe in full generality the sort of model we have just outlined.

Let $\mathbf{T}$ be a finite rooted tree. Write ρ for the root of $\mathbf{T}$, $\mathbf{V}$ for the set of vertices of $\mathbf{T}$, and $\mathbf{L} \subset \mathbf{V}$ for the set of leaves. We regard $\mathbf{T}$ as a directed graph with edge directions leading away from the root. The elements of $\mathbf{L}$ correspond to the taxa, the tree $\mathbf{T}$ is the phylogenetic tree for the taxa, and the elements of $\mathbf{V} \backslash \mathbf{L}$ correspond to ancestors alive at times when the lineages of taxa diverge. It is convenient to enumerate $\mathbf{L}$ as $(l_1, \ldots, l_m)$ and $\mathbf{V}$ as $(v_1, \ldots, v_n)$, with the convention that $l_j = v_j$ for $j = 1, \ldots, m$ and $\rho = v_n$.

Each vertex $v \in \mathbf{V}$ other than the root ρ has a a *father* $\sigma(v)$ (that is, there is a unique $\sigma(v) \in \mathbf{V}$ such that the directed edge $(\sigma(v), v)$ is in the rooted tree

T.) If v_α and v_ω are two vertices such that there exist vertices $v_\beta, v_\gamma \ldots, v_\xi$ with $\sigma(v_\beta) = v_\alpha$, $\sigma(v_\gamma) = v_\beta$, $\ldots, \sigma(v_\omega) = v_\xi$ (that is, there is a directed path in **T** from α to ω), then we say that v_ω is a descendent of v_α or that v_α is an ancestor of v_ω and we write $v_\alpha \leq v_\omega$ or $v_\omega \geq v_\alpha$. Note that a vertex is its own ancestor and its own descendent. The *outdegree* outdeg(u) of $u \in \mathbf{V}$ is the number of *children* of u, that is, the number of $v \in \mathbf{V}$ such that $u = \sigma(v)$. To avoid degeneracies we always suppose that outdeg(v) ≥ 2 for all $v \in \mathbf{V}\backslash\mathbf{L}$. (Note: Terms such as "father" and "child" are just standard terminology from the theory of trees and don't have any biological significance — an edge in our tree may correspond to thousands of actual generations.)

Let π be a probability distribution on $\{A, G, C, T\}$ — the *root distribution*, The probability $\pi(B)$ is the probability that the common ancestor at the root exhibits nucleotide B. For each vertex $v \in \mathbf{V}\backslash\{\rho\}$, let $P^{(v)}$ be a stochastic matrix on $\{A, G, C, T\}$ (that is, the rows of $P^{(v)}$ are probability distributions on $\{A, G, C, T\}$.) We refer to $P^{(v)}$ as the *substitution matrix* associated with the edge $(\sigma(v), v)$. The entry $P^{(v)}(B', B'')$ is the conditional probability that the individual at vertex v exhibits nucleotide B'' given that the individual at vertex $\sigma(v)$ exhibits nucleotide $B' \in \{A, G, C, T\}$.

Define a probability distribution μ on $\{A, G, C, T\}^{\mathbf{V}}$ by setting

$$\mu((B_v)_{v \in \mathbf{V}}) := \pi(B_\rho) \prod_{v \in \mathbf{V}\backslash\{\rho\}} P^{(v)}(B_{\sigma(v)}, B_v).$$

The distribution μ is the joint distribution of the nucleotides exhibited by all of the individuals in the tree, both the taxa and the unobserved ancestors. The induced marginal distribution on $\{A, G, C, T\}^{\mathbf{L}}$ is

$$p((B_\ell)_{\ell \in \mathbf{L}}) := \sum_{v \in \mathbf{V}\backslash\mathbf{L}} \sum_{B_v} \mu\big(((B_v)_{v \in \mathbf{V}\backslash\mathbf{L}}, (B_\ell)_{\ell \in \mathbf{L}})\big),$$

where each of the dummy variables B_v, $v \in \mathbf{V}\backslash\mathbf{L}$, is summed over the set $\{A, G, C, T\}$. The distribution p is the joint distribution of the nucleotides exhibited by the taxa.

With this model in hand, we could try to make inferences from sequence data using standard statistical techniques. For example, we could apply the method of maximum likelihood where we determine the choice of the parameters **T**, π, and $P^{(v)}$, $v \in \mathbf{V}\backslash\{\rho\}$, that makes the probability of the observed data greatest. (As we discussed above, we would need to observe the nucleotides at several positions and assume they were independent and governed by the same single-position model.) Maximum likelihood is known to have various optimality properties when we have large numbers of data, but unless we have just a few taxa there are a huge number of parameters over which we have to optimise and implementing maximum likelihood directly is numerically infeasible. There are various approaches to overcoming these difficulties — for instance, we can maximise likelihoods 4 taxa at a time and hope to fit the subtrees inferred in this manner into one overall tree for all the taxa. Another approach is to constrain the substitution matrices in some way and hope that the extra structure this introduces makes the inferential problem easier to solve (while still retaining some degree of biological plausibility.) That is the approach we will follow starting in the next section.

3. More Specific Models

The general model for the observed nucleotides outlined in the Section 2 allows the substitution matrices to be arbitrary. As we discussed in the Section 2, there are practical reasons for constraining the form of these matrices.

The substitution matrix $P^{(v)}$ represents the cumulative effect of the substitutions that occur between the times that the individuals associated with $\sigma(v)$ and v were alive. In order to arrive at a reasonable form for $P^{(v)}$, it is profitable to think about how we would go about modelling the dynamics of this substitution process.

The most natural and tractable dynamics are (time-homogeneous) Markovian ones. That is, if the position currently exhibits a certain nucleotide, B' say, then (independently of the past) the nucleotide changes at rate $r(B', B'')$ to some other nucleotide B''. More formally, if the position currently exhibits nucleotide B', then:

- independently of the past, the probability that the elapsed time until a change occurs is greater than t is $\exp(-\sum_{B''} r(B', B'') t)$,
- independently of how long it takes until a change occurs, the probability that it is to B'' is proportional to $r(B', B'')$.

There are obvious caveats in the use of such Markov chain models. Certain positions on the genome can't be altered without serious consequences for the viability of the organism, and so a model that allows substitution to occur in a completely random fashion is not appropriate at such positions. However, if we look at positions that are not associated with regions of the genome that have an identifiable function, then it is somewhat difficult to recognise two positions as being the "same" in two different individuals for the purposes of alignment. Some care is therefore necessary in practice to find positions that can be aligned but are such that a Markov chain model is plausible.

The simplest Markov chain model for nucleotide substitution is the Jukes-Cantor model [JC69; Ney71] in which $r(B', B'')$ is the same for all B', B''. Under this model, the distribution of the amount of time spent at a nucleotide before a change occurs does not depend on the nucleotide and all 3 choices of the new nucleotide are equally likely when a change occurs.

Biochemically, the nucleotides fall into two families: the *purines* (adenine and guanine) and the *pyrimidines* (cytosine and thymine). Substitutions within a family are called *transitions*, and they have a different biochemical status to substitutions between families, which are called *transversions*. Kimura [Kim80] proposed a model that recognised this distinction by assigning a common rate to all the transversions and possibly different common rate to all the transitions. We can represent the rates schematically as follows:

$$
\begin{array}{ccc}
A & \longleftrightarrow & C \\
\updownarrow & \times & \updownarrow \\
G & \longleftrightarrow & T
\end{array}
$$

The solid arrows represent transitions and the dashed arrows represent transversions. There are two rate parameters, $\alpha, \beta > 0$, say, such that $r(B', B'') = \alpha$ if B' and B'' are connected by a solid arrow, and $r(B', B'') = \beta$ if B' and B'' are connected by a dashed arrow.

Later, Kimura [Kim81] introduced a generalisation of this model with the following rate structure:

Now there are 3 types of arrows (solid, dashed, and double) and 3 corresponding rate parameters ($\alpha, \beta, \gamma > 0$, say.) For example, if the current nucleotide is A then, independently of the past, the probability that it takes longer than time t until a change is $\exp(-(\alpha+\beta+\gamma)t)$ and, independently of how long it takes until a change, the change is to G with probability $\alpha/(\alpha+\beta+\gamma)$, to C with probability $\beta/(\alpha + \beta + \gamma)$, and to T with probability $\gamma/(\alpha + \beta + \gamma)$. There does not appear to be a convincing biological rationale for this model with $\beta \neq \gamma$. However, the extra parameter allows some more flexibility in fitting to data. Moreover, the analysis of the three-parameter model is no more difficult than that of the two-parameter one, and is even somewhat clearer from an expository point of view. We refer the reader to [ES93; EZ98] for the changes that are necessary in what follows when dealing with the one- and two-parameter models.

Probabilists usually record the rates for a Markov chain as an *infinitesimal generator matrix*. For example, the infinitesimal generator for the three-parameter Kimura model is

$$
Q = \begin{array}{c} \\ A \\ G \\ C \\ T \end{array}
\begin{array}{cccc}
A & G & C & T \\
\left(\begin{array}{cccc}
-(\alpha + \beta + \gamma) & \alpha & \beta & \gamma \\
\alpha & -(\alpha + \beta + \gamma) & \gamma & \beta \\
\beta & \gamma & -(\alpha + \beta + \gamma) & \alpha \\
\gamma & \beta & \alpha & -(\alpha + \beta + \gamma)
\end{array}\right).
\end{array}
$$

The infinitesimal generator is more than just an accounting device: for any $s, t \geq 0$ the entry in row B' and column B'' of the matrix

$$\exp(tQ) = I + tQ + \frac{t^2}{2!}Q^2 + \frac{t^3}{3!}Q^3 + \cdots$$

gives the conditional probability that nucleotide B'' will be exhibited at time $s + t$ given that nucleotide B' is exhibited at time s.

Because the matrix Q is symmetric, $\exp(tQ)$ can be computed using the spectral theorem once the eigenvalues and eigenvectors of Q have been computed. This is straightforward for Q, but we won't go into the details. Also, the diagonalisation follows easily using the Fourier ideas of Section 6. As an example, the conditional probability that nucleotide A will be exhibited at time $s + t$ given that nucleotide A is exhibited at time s is

$$\tfrac{1}{4}\big(1 + \exp(-2t(\alpha + \gamma)) + \exp(-2t(\beta + \gamma)) + \exp(-2t(\alpha + \beta))\big),$$

and the the conditional probability that nucleotide G will be exhibited at time $s + t$ given that nucleotide A is exhibited at time s is

$$\tfrac{1}{4}\big(1 - \exp(-2t(\alpha + \gamma)) + \exp(-2t(\beta + \gamma)) - \exp(-2t(\alpha + \beta))\big).$$

Both of these probabilities converge to $\tfrac{1}{4}$ as $t \to \infty$: of course, we expect from the symmetries of the Markov chain that if it evolves for a long time, then it will converge towards an equilibrium distribution in which all nucleotides are equally likely to be exhibited.

It is clear without computing $\exp(tQ)$ explicitly that this matrix is of the form

$$
\begin{array}{c}
\begin{array}{cccc}
A & G & C & T
\end{array} \\
\begin{array}{c} A \\ G \\ C \\ T \end{array}
\left(
\begin{array}{cccc}
w & x & y & z \\
x & w & z & y \\
y & z & w & x \\
z & y & x & w
\end{array}
\right),
\end{array}
$$

where $0 \leq w, x, y, z \leq 1$. Not all such matrices are given by $\exp(tQ)$ for a suitable choice of α, β, γ, t. However, we suppose *from now on* that each substitution matrix $P^{(v)}$ is of this somewhat more general form for some w, x, y, z (that can vary with v.) Thus, once a tree $\mathbf{T}$ with m leaves and n vertices is fixed, there are $3n$ independent parameters in the model: 3 for the root distribution π and 3 for each of the $n - 1$ substitution matrices. Note that each of the 4^m model probabilities $p((B_\ell)_{\ell \in \mathbf{L}})$, $(B_\ell)_{\ell \in \mathbf{L}} \in \{A, G, C, T\}^{\mathbf{L}}$ is a polynomial in these $3n$ variables.

4. Making Inferences

From the development in Sections 2 and 3, we have a model for the joint probability of the taxa exhibiting a particular set of nucleotides. For more than a small number of taxa, this model still has too many parameters for us to apply maximum likelihood. Moreover, maximum likelihood necessarily estimates all the numerical parameters in the model, even though the tree parameter is typically the one that is of most interest.

An alternative approach to estimating the tree that does not involve directly estimating the numerical parameters was suggested in [CF87] and [Lak87]. The ideas behind this approach is as follows. For a given tree $\mathbf{T}$, the model probabilities $p((B_\ell)_{\ell \in \mathbf{L}})$, $(B_\ell)_{\ell \in \mathbf{L}} \in \{A, G, C, T\}^{\mathbf{L}}$, have a specific functional form in terms of the numerical parameters defining the root distribution and the substitution matrices (indeed, the model probabilities are polynomials in these variables.) This should constrain the model probabilities to lie on some lower dimensional surface in $\mathbb{R}^{\mathbf{L}}$. Rather than represent this surface *explicitly* as the range of a vector of polynomials, we could try to characterise the surface *implicitly* as a subset of a locus of points in $\mathbb{R}^{\mathbf{L}}$ that are common zeroes of a family of polynomials. That is, we want to represent the surface as a subset of an *algebraic variety*.

Because we assuming that the same model (with the same numerical substitution mechanism parameters) governs each position in our data set and that the behaviour at different positions is independent, the strong law of large numbers gives that the quantities $p((B_\ell)_{\ell \in \mathbf{L}})$, $(B_\ell)_{\ell \in \mathbf{L}} \in \{A, G, C, T\}^{\mathbf{L}}$, can be consistently estimated in a model-free way by computing the proportion of positions in our data set at which Taxon 1 exhibits nucleotide B_1, Taxon 2 exhibits nucleotide B_2, *etc.* Call these estimates $\hat{p}((B_\ell)_{\ell \in \mathbf{L}})$, $(B_\ell)_{\ell \in \mathbf{L}} \in \{A, G, C, T\}^{\mathbf{L}}$, so that $\hat{p}((B_\ell)_{\ell \in \mathbf{L}})$ will be close to $p((B_\ell)_{\ell \in \mathbf{L}})$ with high probability when we observe a sufficient number of different positions to have enough independent identically distributed data points for the strong law of large numbers to kick in.

We hope that the varieties for two different trees (say, Tree I and Tree II) have a "small" intersection and so a "generic" point on the variety for one tree will not be a common zero of the polynomials defining the variety for the other tree. That is, we hope that we can find a polynomial f such that $f(p((B_\ell)_{\ell \in \mathbf{L}})) = 0$ for all choices of substitution mechanism parameters for Tree I whereas $f(p((B_\ell)_{\ell \in \mathbf{L}})) \neq 0$ for all but a "small" set of choices of substitution mechanism parameters for Tree II. If this is the case, then $f(\hat{p}((B_\ell)_{\ell \in \mathbf{L}}))$ should be close to zero (that is, "zero up to random error") if Tree I is the correct tree regardless of the numerical parameters in the model, whereas this quantity should be "significantly nonzero" if Tree II is the correct tree unless we have been particularly unfortunate and the numerical parameters are such that the vector $p((B_\ell)_{\ell \in \mathbf{L}})$ happens to lie on the intersection of the varieties for the two trees.

The polynomials that are zero on the algebraic variety associated with a tree are called the *(phylogenetic) invariants* of the model. Note that the set of invariants has the structure of an *ideal* in the ring of polynomials in the model probabilities: the sum of two invariants is an invariant and the product of an invariant with an arbitrary polynomial is an invariant.

In order to use the invariant idea to reconstruct phylogenetic trees we need to address the following questions:

i) How do we recognize when a polynomial is an invariant?
ii) How do we find a generating set for the ideal of invariants (and how big is such a set)?
iii) Do different trees have different invariants?
iv) How do we determine whether a vector of polynomials applied to estimates of the model probabilities is "zero up to random error" or "significantly nonzero"?

In principle, questions (i) and (ii) can be answered using general theory from computational commutative algebra. There is an algorithm using Gröbner bases that solves the *implicitization problem* of finding a generating set for the ideal of polynomials that are 0 on a general parametrically given algebraic variety (see [CLO92].) Unfortunately, this algorithm appears to be computationally infeasible for the size of problem that occurs for even a modest number of taxa. Other methods adapted to our particular problem are therefore necessary, and this is what we study in these notes. Along the way, we answer question (iii) and even establish how many algebraically independent invariants there are that distinguish between two trees. We don't deal with the more statistical question (iv) in these notes.

5. Some Group Structure

We begin with a step that may seem somewhat bizarre at first, but pays off handsomely. Consider the *Klein 4-group* $\mathbb{Z}_2 \oplus \mathbb{Z}_2$ consisting of the elements $\{(0,0),(0,1),(1,0),(1,1)\}$ equipped with the group operation of coordinatewise addition modulo 2. The addition table for $\mathbb{Z}_2 \oplus \mathbb{Z}_2$ is thus

$$
\begin{array}{c|cccc}
+ & (0,0) & (0,1) & (1,0) & (1,1) \\
\hline
(0,0) & (0,0) & (0,1) & (1,0) & (1,1) \\
(0,1) & (0,1) & (0,0) & (1,1) & (1,0) \\
(1,0) & (1,0) & (1,1) & (0,0) & (0,1) \\
(1,1) & (1,1) & (1,0) & (0,1) & (0,0)
\end{array}.
$$

Identify the nucleotides $\{A, G, C, T\}$ with the elements of $\mathbb{Z}_2 \oplus \mathbb{Z}_2$ as follows: $A \leftrightarrow (0,0)$, $G \leftrightarrow (0,1)$, $C \leftrightarrow (1,0)$, and $T \leftrightarrow (1,1)$. This turns $\mathbb{G} := \{A, G, C, T\}$ into a group with the addition table

$$
\begin{array}{c|cccc}
+ & A & G & C & T \\
\hline
A & A & G & C & T \\
G & G & A & T & C \\
C & C & T & A & G \\
T & T & C & G & A
\end{array}.
$$

Suppose that X and Y are two $\mathbb{G}$-valued random variables such that the conditional distribution of Y given X is described by the matrix

$$
\begin{array}{cc}
 & \begin{array}{cccc} A & G & C & T \end{array} \\
\begin{array}{c} A \\ G \\ C \\ T \end{array} &
\left(\begin{array}{cccc}
w & x & y & z \\
x & w & z & y \\
y & z & w & x \\
z & y & x & w
\end{array} \right).
\end{array}
$$

Note that $\mathbb{P}\{Y = B'' \,|\, X = B'\}$ only depends on the pair of nucleotides (B', B'') through the difference $B'' - B'$. It follows easily from this that the joint distribution of the pair (X, Y) is same as that of the pair $(X, X + Z)$, where $\mathbb{P}\{Z = A\} = w$, $\mathbb{P}\{Z = G\} = x$, $\mathbb{P}\{Z = C\} = y$, $\mathbb{P}\{Z = T\} = z$, and Z is independent of X.

The model that we described in Section 3 had an arbitrary root distribution π and substitution matrices $P^{(v)}$ that satisfy $P^{(v)}(B', B'') = q^{(v)}(B'' - B')$ for some probability distribution $q^{(v)}$ on $\mathbb{G}$. Repeatedly applying the observation of the previous paragraph shows that if if $(Z_v)_{v \in \mathbf{V}}$ is a vector of independent $\mathbb{G}$-valued random variables, with Z_ρ having distribution π, and Z_v, $v \in \mathbf{V} \setminus \{\rho\}$, having distribution $q^{(v)}$, then the $\mathbb{G}$-valued random variables

$$ Y_\ell := \sum_{v \le \ell} Z_v, \ \ell \in \mathbf{L}, $$

have joint distribution

$$ \mathbb{P}\{Y_1 = B_1, \ldots, Y_m = B_m\} = p((B_\ell)_{\ell \in \mathbf{L}}). $$

That is, by suitable addition of independent $\mathbb{G}$-valued "weights," we can construct a vector of random variables having the same joint distribution as the nucleotides exhibited by the taxa. For example, for the tree

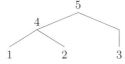

the construction is

$$
\begin{array}{rcccccc}
Y_1 & = & Z_1 & & + & Z_4 & + & Z_5 \\
Y_2 & = & & Z_2 & + & Z_4 & + & Z_5 \\
Y_3 & = & & Z_3 & & & + & Z_5
\end{array}
$$

6. A Little Fourier Analysis

We've seen that the model of Section 3 can be represented in terms of sums of indpendent random variables taking values in a finite, Abelian group. Probabilists have known for a long time that Fourier analysis is a very powerful technique for handling such sums. In this section we'll review some basic facts about Fourier analysis for an arbitrary finite, Abelian group $(\mathbb{H}, +)$.

Let $\mathbb{T} = \{z \in \mathbb{C} : |z| = 1\}$ denote the unit circle in the complex plane, and regard $\mathbb{T}$ as an Abelian group with the group operation being ordinary complex multiplication. The *characters* of $\mathbb{H}$ are the group homomorphisms mapping $\mathbb{H}$ into $\mathbb{T}$. That is, $\chi : \mathbb{H} \to \mathbb{T}$ is a character if $\chi(h_1 + h_2) = \chi(h_1)\chi(h_2)$ for all $h_1, h_2 \in \mathbb{G}$. The characters form an Abelian group under the operation of pointwise multiplication of functions. This group is called the *dual group* of $\mathbb{H}$ and is denoted by $\hat{\mathbb{H}}$. The groups $\mathbb{H}$ and $\hat{\mathbb{H}}$ are isomorphic. Given $h \in \mathbb{H}$ and $\chi \in \hat{\mathbb{H}}$, write $\langle h, \chi \rangle$ for $\chi(h)$.

The elements of $\mathbb{H}$ form an orthogonal basis for the space of functions from $\mathbb{H}$ to $\mathbb{C}$. Given a function $f : \mathbb{H} \to \mathbb{C}$, the *Fourier transform* of f is the function $\hat{f} : \hat{\mathbb{H}} \to \mathbb{C}$ given by

$$\hat{f}(\chi) = \sum_{h \in \mathbb{H}} f(h)\langle h, \chi \rangle.$$

A function can be recovered from its Fourier transform via *Fourier inversion*:

$$f(h) = \frac{1}{\#\mathbb{H}} \sum_{\chi \in \hat{\mathbb{H}}} \hat{f}(\chi)\overline{\langle h, \chi \rangle}.$$

Given two finite, Abelian groups $\mathbb{H}'$ and $\mathbb{H}''$, the dual of the product group $\mathbb{H}'' \oplus \mathbb{H}''$ is isomorphic to $\widehat{\mathbb{H}'} \oplus \widehat{\mathbb{H}''}$ via the identification

$$\langle (h', h''), (\chi', \chi'') \rangle = \langle h', \chi' \rangle \times \langle h'', \chi'' \rangle.$$

One may write $\hat{\mathbb{G}} = \{1, \phi, \psi, \phi\psi\}$, where the following table gives the values of $\langle g, \chi \rangle$ for $g \in \mathbb{G}$ and $\chi \in \hat{\mathbb{G}}$:

$$\begin{array}{c}
\begin{array}{cccc}
(0,0) & (0,1) & (1,0) & (1,1)
\end{array} \\
\begin{array}{c}
1 \\ \phi \\ \psi \\ \phi\psi
\end{array}
\left(\begin{array}{cccc}
1 & 1 & 1 & 1 \\
1 & -1 & 1 & -1 \\
1 & 1 & -1 & -1 \\
1 & -1 & -1 & 1
\end{array}\right).
\end{array}$$

The *characteristic function* of a $\mathbb{H}$-valued random variable X is the Fourier transform of its probability mass function:

$$\xi(\chi) = \sum_{h \in \mathbb{H}} \mathbb{P}\{X = h\}\langle h, \chi \rangle = \mathbb{E}\left[\langle X, \chi \rangle\right]$$

(here, following the usual convention in probability theory, $\langle X, \chi \rangle$ is the random variable obtained by composing the random variable X with the function $\langle \cdot, \chi \rangle$.) The probability mass function of X can be recovered from its Fourier transform by Fourier inversion:

$$\mathbb{P}\{X = h\} = \frac{1}{\#\mathbb{H}} \sum_{\chi \in \hat{\mathbb{H}}} \xi(\chi)\overline{\langle h, \chi \rangle}.$$

Finally, note that if X' and X'' are independent $\mathbb{H}$-valued random variables, then

$$\mathbb{E}[\langle X' + X'', \chi \rangle] = \mathbb{E}[\langle X', \chi \rangle \langle X'', \chi \rangle] = \mathbb{E}[\langle X', \chi \rangle]\,\mathbb{E}[\langle X'', \chi \rangle].$$

That is, the characteristic function of $X'+X''$ is the product of the characteristic functions of X' and X''.

7. Finding an Invariant

Let's begin by seeing how the observations of Sections 5 and 6 can be used to find an invariant for an instance of the model of Section 3.

Consider the tree

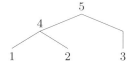

with the associated model for the nucleotides Y_1, Y_2, Y_3 exhibited by the taxa written in terms of independent $\mathbb{G}$-valued random variables $Z_1, \ldots, Z_5$ as follows:

$$
\begin{aligned}
Y_1 &= Z_1 && + Z_4 + Z_5 \\
Y_2 &= \ Z_2 && + Z_4 + Z_5 \\
Y_3 &= \ Z_3 && \ + Z_5
\end{aligned}
$$

Using the results of Section 6 and the notation given there for for the characters of $\mathbb{G}$ we have

$$
\begin{aligned}
\mathbb{E}[\langle Y_1, \phi \rangle \langle Y_2, \phi \rangle \langle Y_3, \psi \rangle] \\
= \mathbb{E}[\langle Z_1, \phi \rangle \langle Z_4, \phi \rangle \langle Z_5, \phi \rangle \langle Z_2, \phi \rangle \langle Z_4, \phi \rangle \langle Z_5, \phi \rangle \langle Z_3, \psi \rangle \langle Z_5, \psi \rangle] \\
= \mathbb{E}[\langle Z_1, \phi \rangle] \times \mathbb{E}[\langle Z_2, \phi \rangle] \times \mathbb{E}[\langle Z_3, \psi \rangle] \times \mathbb{E}[\langle Z_4, \phi^2 \rangle] \times \mathbb{E}[\langle Z_5, \phi^2 \psi \rangle] \\
= \mathbb{E}[\langle Z_1, \phi \rangle] \times \mathbb{E}[\langle Z_2, \phi \rangle] \times \mathbb{E}[\langle Z_3, \psi \rangle] \times \mathbb{E}[\langle Z_5, \psi \rangle].
\end{aligned}
$$

A similar argument shows that

$$\mathbb{E}[\langle Y_1, \phi \rangle \langle Y_2, \phi \rangle]\,\mathbb{E}[\langle Y_3, \psi \rangle] = \mathbb{E}[\langle Z_1, \phi \rangle]\,\mathbb{E}[\langle Z_2, \phi \rangle]\,\mathbb{E}[\langle Z_3, \psi \rangle]\,\mathbb{E}[\langle Z_5, \psi \rangle].$$

Thus

$$\mathbb{E}[\langle Y_1, \phi \rangle \langle Y_2, \phi \rangle \langle Y_3, \psi \rangle] - \mathbb{E}[\langle Y_1, \phi \rangle \langle Y_2, \phi \rangle]\,\mathbb{E}[\langle Y_3, \psi \rangle] = 0.$$

Writing all of the expectations in the last equation as sums in terms of the model probabilities $p((B_\ell)_{\ell \in \mathbf{L}})$ gives a polynomial in the model probabilities of total degree 2 that is satisfied for all choices of the numerical parameters defining the root distribution and the substitution matrices. Thus we have found an invariant for this tree.

Now consider the tree

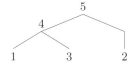

with the associated model for the nucleotides Y_1, Y_2, Y_3 exhibited by the taxa written in terms of independent $\mathbb{G}$-valued random variables $Z_1, \ldots, Z_5$ as follows:

$$
\begin{aligned}
Y_1 &= Z_1 &&&&+& Z_4 &+& Z_5 \\
Y_2 &= & Z_2 &&&+& &+& Z_5 \\
Y_3 &= & & Z_3 && & Z_4 &+& Z_5
\end{aligned}
$$

Now

$$
\mathbb{E}[\langle Y_1, \phi \rangle \langle Y_2, \phi \rangle \langle Y_3, \psi \rangle] - \mathbb{E}[\langle Y_1, \phi \rangle \langle Y_2, \phi \rangle] \, \mathbb{E}[\langle Y_3, \psi \rangle]
$$

$$
= \mathbb{E}[\langle Z_1, \phi \rangle] \, \mathbb{E}[\langle Z_2, \phi \rangle] \, \mathbb{E}[\langle Z_3, \psi \rangle] \, \mathbb{E}[\langle Z_4, \phi\psi \rangle] \, \mathbb{E}[\langle Z_5, \psi \rangle]
$$

$$
- \ \mathbb{E}[\langle Z_1, \phi \rangle] \, \mathbb{E}[\langle Z_2, \phi \rangle] \, \mathbb{E}[\langle Z_3, \psi \rangle] \, \mathbb{E}[\langle Z_4, \phi \rangle] \, \mathbb{E}[\langle Z_4, \psi \rangle] \, \mathbb{E}[\langle Z_5, \psi \rangle]
$$

$$
= \mathbb{E}[\langle Z_1, \phi \rangle] \, \mathbb{E}[\langle Z_2, \phi \rangle] \, \mathbb{E}[\langle Z_3, \psi \rangle]
$$

$$
\times \big(\mathbb{E}[\langle Z_4, \phi\psi \rangle] - \mathbb{E}[\langle Z_4, \phi \rangle] \, \mathbb{E}[\langle Z_4, \psi \rangle] \big) \mathbb{E}[\langle Z_5, \psi \rangle].
$$

It is not hard to show that that the vector

$$
\big(\mathbb{E}[\langle Z_4, \phi \rangle], \mathbb{E}[\langle Z_4, \psi \rangle], \mathbb{E}[\langle Z_4, \phi\psi \rangle] \big)
$$

ranges over a subset of $\mathbb{R}^3$ with nonempty interior as the distribution of Z_4 ranges over the set of possible distributions on $\mathbb{G}$. Thus

$$
\mathbb{E}[\langle Z_4, \phi\psi \rangle] - \mathbb{E}[\langle Z_4, \phi \rangle] \, \mathbb{E}[\langle Z_4, \psi \rangle]
$$

is certainly not identically 0 and the invariant we found for the previous tree is not an invariant for this tree.

8. Finding All Invariants

The examples studied in Section 7 indicate how we should proceed to find all the invariants for a general tree. The ideas that we describe in this section were developed in [ES93].

We call a vector $(\chi_{\ell_1}, \ldots, \chi_{\ell_m}) \in \hat{\mathbb{G}}^m$ an *allocation of characters to leaves*. Such an allocation of characters to leaves induces an *allocation of characters to vertices* $(\chi_{v_1}, \ldots, \chi_{v_n}) \in \hat{\mathbb{G}}^n$ as follows. The character χ_v is the product of the χ_ℓ for all leaves ℓ that are descendents of v, that is,

$$
\chi_v := \prod_{\ell \geq v} \chi_\ell.
$$

In particular, if $v = v_i$ is a leaf (and hence the leaf ℓ_i by our numbering convention), then $\chi_{v_i} = \chi_{\ell_i}$.

Let

$$
\{(\chi_{i,1}, \ldots, \chi_{i,n}), \, i = 1, \ldots, 4^m\}
$$

be an enumeration of the various allocations of characters to vertices induced by the 4^m different allocations of characters to leaves. Define $3n$ vectors $\{\mathbf{x}_{v,\theta} = (x_{v,\theta}^{(1)}, \ldots, x_{v,\theta}^{(4^m)}), v \in \mathbf{V}, \theta = \phi, \psi, \phi\psi\}$ of dimension 4^m by setting

$$x_{v_j,\theta}^{(i)} := \begin{cases} 1 & \text{if } \chi_{i,j} = \theta, \\ 0 & \text{otherwise}, \end{cases}$$

for $i = 1, \ldots, 4^m$, $j = 1, \ldots, n$ and $\theta \in \{\phi, \psi, \phi\psi\}$.

Write $\mathcal{R}(\mathbf{T})$ for the free $\mathbb{Z}$-module generated by the set $\{\mathbf{x}_{v,\theta} : v \in \mathbf{V}, \theta = \phi, \psi, \phi\psi\}$. That is, $\mathcal{R}(\mathbf{T})$ is the collection of integer vectors of dimension 4^m consisting of $\mathbb{Z}$-linear combinations of the $\mathbf{x}_{v,\theta}$. Set

$$\mathcal{N}(\mathbf{T}) := \left\{ a \in \mathbb{Z}^{4^m} : \sum_{i=1}^{4^m} a_i x_{v,\theta}^{(i)} = 0, \ v \in \mathbf{V}, \ \theta = \phi, \psi, \phi\psi \right\},$$

so that $\mathbb{Z}^{4^m} = \mathcal{R}(\mathbf{T}) \oplus \mathcal{N}(\mathbf{T})$.

For $a \in \mathbb{Z}^{4^m}$, the polynomial

$$\prod_{\{i:a_i \geq 0\}} \left(\mathbb{E}\left[\prod_{j=1}^m \langle Y_j, \chi_{i,j} \rangle \right] \right)^{a_i} - \prod_{\{i:a_i \leq 0\}} \left(\mathbb{E}\left[\prod_{j=1}^m \langle Y_j, \chi_{i,j} \rangle \right] \right)^{-a_i}$$

$$= \prod_{\{i:a_i \geq 0\}} \left(\sum_{(B_1,\ldots,B_m) \in \mathbb{G}^m} \prod_{j=1}^m \langle B_j, \chi_{i,j} \rangle p(B_1, \ldots, B_m) \right)^{a_i}$$

$$- \prod_{\{i:a_i \leq 0\}} \left(\sum_{(B_1,\ldots,B_m) \in \mathbb{G}^m} \prod_{j=1}^m \langle B_j, \chi_{i,j} \rangle p(B_1, \ldots, B_m) \right)^{-a_i}$$

is an invariant if and only if $a \in \mathcal{N}(\mathbf{T})$. It is shown in [ES93] that this is the only game in town: all invariants arise from algebraic combinations and rearrangements of these basic invariants.

Indeed, it is shown in [ES93] that if $\{(a_{1,r}, \ldots, a_{4^m,r}), r = 1, \ldots, \operatorname{rank} \mathcal{N}(\mathbf{T})\}$ is a $\mathbb{Z}$-basis for the free $\mathbb{Z}$-module $\mathcal{N}(\mathbf{T})$, then the set of polynomials of the form

$$\prod_{\{i:a_{i,r} \geq 0\}} \left(\mathbb{E}\left[\prod_{j=1}^m \langle Y_j, \chi_{i,j} \rangle \right] \right)^{a_{i,r}} - \prod_{\{i:a_{i,r} \leq 0\}} \left(\mathbb{E}\left[\prod_{j=1}^m \langle Y_j, \chi_{i,j} \rangle \right] \right)^{-a_{i,r}}$$

generates the ideal of invariants but no subset thereof does. Finding a $\mathbb{Z}$-basis for $\mathcal{N}(\mathbf{T})$ is just elementary linear algebra — we are simply finding a basis for the null space of an integer-valued matrix — and can be done using Gaussian elimination.

9. How Many Invariants Are There?

Given our tree $\mathbf{T}$ with m leaves (taxa) and n vertices in total, we have 4^m model probabilities $p((B_\ell)_{\ell \in \mathbf{L}})$ that arise as polynomials in $3n$ "free parameters" — 3 free parameters for the root distribution and 3 free parameters for each of the substitution matrices. A naive "degrees of freedom" argument would suggest that there should, in some sense, be $4^m - 3n$ independent relations between the model probabilities. We verify this numerology in this section by showing that $\operatorname{rank} \mathcal{R}(\mathbf{T}) = 3n$, and hence $\operatorname{rank} \mathcal{N}(\mathbf{T}) = 4^m - 3n$. This and related results were presented in [EZ98], but our proof here is quite different.

Let $\mathbf{X}$ denote the $4^m \times 3n$ matrix with columns indexed by $\mathbf{V} \times \{\phi, \psi, \phi\psi\}$ that has the column corresponding to (v, θ), given by $\mathbf{x}_{v,\theta}$. We need to show that the matrix $\mathbf{X}$ has (real) rank $3n$, and this is equivalent to showing that the associated $3n \times 3n$ Gram matrix $\mathbf{X}^t \mathbf{X}$ has full rank (see 0.4.6(d) of [HJ85].)

The entry of $\mathbf{X}^t \mathbf{X}$ with indices $((v^*, \theta^*), (v^{**}, \theta^{**}))$, $v^*, v^{**} \in \mathbf{V}$, $\theta^*, \theta^{**} \in \{\phi, \psi, \phi\psi\}$, is the usual scalar product of $\mathbf{x}_{v^*, \theta^*}$ with $\mathbf{x}_{v^{**}, \theta^{**}}$, which is just the number of assignments of characters to leaves that assign θ^* to v^* and θ^{**} to v^{**}. We can compute this number of assignments as follows.

If $v^* = v^{**}$ and $\theta^* = \theta^{**}$, then it is clear by symmetry that this entry is 4^{m-1}, whereas if $v^* = v^{**}$ and $\theta^* \neq \theta^{**}$, then this entry is obviously 0.

Consider now the case where $v^* \neq v^{**}$, so that the collection of leaves descended from v^* is not the same as the collection of leaves descended from v^{**}. We claim that the entry of $\mathbf{X}^t \mathbf{X}$ with indices $((v^*, \theta^*), (v^{**}, \theta^{**}))$ is 4^{m-2}. To see this, write $\mathbf{L}^*$ and $\mathbf{L}^{**}$ for the leaves descended from v^* and v^{**}, respectively. Suppose first that $\mathbf{L}^{**} \subsetneq \mathbf{L}^*$. If we have an assignment of characters to leaves that assigns the characters η^* to v^* and η^{**} to v^{**}, then replacing the character assigned to some $\ell^* \in \mathbf{L}^* \backslash \mathbf{L}^{**}$ from χ^* (say) to $\rho^* \rho^{**} \eta^* \chi^*$ and replacing the character assigned to some $\ell^{**} \in \mathbf{L}^{**}$ from χ^{**} (say) to $\rho^{**} \eta^{**} \chi^{**}$ gives a new assignment of characters to leaves that assigns ρ^* to v^* and ρ^{**} to v^{**}. It follows that number of assignments of characters to leaves that assign θ^* to v^* and θ^{**} to v^{**} is indeed 4^{m-2} when $\mathbf{L}^{**} \subsetneq \mathbf{L}^*$. A symmetric argument argument handles the case $\mathbf{L}^* \subsetneq \mathbf{L}^{**}$, and we leave this to the reader.

We conclude that $\mathbf{X}^t \mathbf{X}$ can be partitioned into 3×3 blocks so that the blocks down the diagonal are all of the form

$$\begin{pmatrix} 4^{m-1} & 0 & 0 \\ 0 & 4^{m-1} & 0 \\ 0 & 0 & 4^{m-1} \end{pmatrix},$$

while the off-diagonal blocks are all of the form

$$\begin{pmatrix} 4^{m-2} & 4^{m-2} & 4^{m-2} \\ 4^{m-2} & 4^{m-2} & 4^{m-2} \\ 4^{m-2} & 4^{m-2} & 4^{m-2} \end{pmatrix}.$$

Now

$$\mathbf{X}^t \mathbf{X} = 4^{m-2}(\mathbf{D} + \mathbf{1}\mathbf{1}^t),$$

where $\mathbf{1}$ is the (column) vector with all entries equal to 1 and $\mathbf{D}$ is a matrix partitioned into 3×3 blocks with the blocks down the diagonal all of the form

$$\begin{pmatrix} 3 & -1 & -1 \\ -1 & 3 & -1 \\ -1 & -1 & 3 \end{pmatrix},$$

and the off-diagonal blocks all zero. Note that $\mathbf{D}$ is invertible with inverse a partitioned matrix that has blocks down the diagonal all of the form

$$\begin{pmatrix} \frac{1}{2} & \frac{1}{4} & \frac{1}{4} \\ \frac{1}{4} & \frac{1}{2} & \frac{1}{4} \\ \frac{1}{4} & \frac{1}{4} & \frac{1}{2} \end{pmatrix},$$

and the off-diagonal blocks all zero. A standard result on inverses of small rank perturbations (see 0.7.4 of [HJ85]) gives that $\mathbf{X}^t\mathbf{X}$ is indeed invertible (and hence full rank), with inverse

$$4^{-(m-2)}\left(\mathbf{D}^{-1} - \frac{1}{1 + \mathbf{1}^t\mathbf{D}^{-1}\mathbf{1}}\mathbf{D}^{-1}\mathbf{1}\mathbf{1}^t\mathbf{D}^{-1}\right) = 4^{-(m-2)}\left(\mathbf{D}^{-1} - \frac{1}{1 + 3n}\mathbf{1}\mathbf{1}^t\right).$$

10. How Well Do Invariants Distinguish Between Trees?

The last question remaining from Section 4 is, "Do different trees have different invariants?" The answer is "Yes." This follows from Theorem 10 in [SSE93]. We give a different proof which actually establishes "how many" independent invariants distinguish between two different trees.

We begin by making explicit the natural notion of equivalence for trees with labelled leaves. We say that two trees $\mathbf{T}'$ and $\mathbf{T}''$ with the same set $\mathbf{L}$ of leaves are *identical* if there is a bijection τ from the set of vertices $\mathbf{V}'$ of $\mathbf{T}'$ to the set of vertices $\mathbf{V}''$ of $\mathbf{T}''$ such that $\tau(\ell) = \ell$ for each leaf $\ell \in \mathbf{L}$ and $u \in \mathbf{V}'$ is the father of $v \in \mathbf{V}'$ in $\mathbf{T}'$ if and only if $\tau(u) \in \mathbf{V}''$ is the father of $\tau(v) \in \mathbf{V}''$ in $\mathbf{T}''$. This is equivalent to requiring that $\tau(\ell) = \ell$ for each leaf $\ell \in \mathbf{L}$ and $u \in \mathbf{V}'$ is the ancestor of $v \in \mathbf{V}'$ in $\mathbf{T}'$ if and only if $\tau(u) \in \mathbf{V}''$ is the ancestor of $\tau(v) \in \mathbf{V}''$ in $\mathbf{T}''$. It is not hard to see that two trees $\mathbf{T}'$ and $\mathbf{T}''$ with the same set $\mathbf{L}$ of leaves are identical if and only if for each $v' \in \mathbf{V}'$ the set of leaves descended from v' is equal to the set of leaves descended from some $v'' \in \mathbf{V}''$ and vice-versa.

Given two trees $\mathbf{T}'$ and $\mathbf{T}''$ with the same set $\mathbf{L}$ of leaves, write $\nu(\mathbf{T}', \mathbf{T}'')$ for the number of vertices v'' of $\mathbf{T}''$ such that the collection of leaves descended from v'' is not the collection of leaves descended from any vertex of $\mathbf{T}'$. If $\mathbf{T}'$ and $\mathbf{T}''$ are not identical, then either $\nu(\mathbf{T}', \mathbf{T}'') > 0$ or $\nu(\mathbf{T}'', \mathbf{T}') > 0$. We claim that the rank of the free $\mathbb{Z}$-module $\mathcal{N}(\mathbf{T}') \cap \mathcal{R}(\mathbf{T}'')$ is $3\nu(\mathbf{T}', \mathbf{T}'')$. That is, there are $3\nu(\mathbf{T}', \mathbf{T}'')$ algebraically independent invariants for the tree $\mathbf{T}'$ that are not invariants for the tree $\mathbf{T}''$, and similarly with the roles of $\mathbf{T}'$ and $\mathbf{T}''$ interchanged.

To establish this claim, first note that

$$\text{rank}\,(\mathcal{N}(\mathbf{T}') \cap \mathcal{R}(\mathbf{T}'')) = \text{rank}\,(\mathcal{R}(\mathbf{T}'')) - \text{rank}\,(\mathcal{R}(\mathbf{T}') \cap \mathcal{R}(\mathbf{T}''))$$
$$= \text{rank}\,(\mathcal{R}(\mathbf{T}') + \mathcal{R}(\mathbf{T}'')) - \text{rank}\,(\mathcal{R}(\mathbf{T}')).$$

Write $\mathbf{V}'$ and $\mathbf{V}''$ for the vertices of $\mathbf{T}'$ and $\mathbf{T}''$, respectively, and let $\tilde{\mathbf{V}}''$ denote the set of vertices v'' of $\mathbf{T}''$ such that the collection of leaves descended from v'' is not the collection of leaves descended from any vertex of $\mathbf{T}'$. Hence $|\tilde{V}''| = \nu(\mathbf{T}', \mathbf{T}'')$. Of course, if $v'' \in \mathbf{V}'' \backslash \tilde{\mathbf{V}}''$, then there is a vertex $v' \in \mathbf{V}'$ such that the assignment of characters to v' and v'' for each assignment of characters to leaves are the same, and hence the vector $\mathbf{x}_{v',\theta}$ (calculated for $\mathbf{T}'$) is the same as the vector $\mathbf{x}_{v'',\theta}$ (calculated for $\mathbf{T}''$.) The claim will thus follow if we can show that the vectors

$$\{\mathbf{x}_{v',\theta} : v' \in \mathbf{V}', \, \theta = \phi, \psi, \phi\psi\} \cup \{\mathbf{x}_{v'',\theta} : v'' \in \tilde{\mathbf{V}}'', \, \theta = \phi, \psi, \phi\psi\}$$

are linearly independent over the integers (equivalently, over the reals.)

Let $\mathbf{X}$ denote the $4^m \times 3(|\mathbf{V}'| + |\tilde{\mathbf{V}}''|)$ matrix obtained by putting together all these vectors — say indexing the columns by $(\mathbf{V}' \cup \tilde{\mathbf{V}}'') \times \{\phi, \psi, \phi\psi\}$ and making the column corresponding to (v, θ) equal to $\mathbf{x}_{v,\theta}$, for $v \in \mathbf{V}'$ or $v \in \tilde{\mathbf{V}}''$. We need to show that $\mathbf{X}$ has (real) rank $3(|\mathbf{V}'| + |\tilde{\mathbf{V}}''|)$, and this is equivalent to showing that the associated $3(|\mathbf{V}'| + |\tilde{\mathbf{V}}''|) \times 3(|\mathbf{V}'| + |\tilde{\mathbf{V}}''|)$ Gram matrix $\mathbf{X}^t\mathbf{X}$ has full rank. An argument very similar to that in Section 9 completes the proof.

References

[CF87] J. A. Cavender and J. Felsenstein. Invariants of phylogenies in a simple case with discrete states. *J. Classification*, 4:57–71, 1987.

[CLO92] D. Cox, J. Little, and D. O'Shea. *Ideals, varieties, and algorithms : an introduction to computational algebraic geometry and commutative algebra*. New York : Springer-Verlag, 1992.

[ES93] S. N. Evans and T. P. Speed. Invariants of some probability models used in phylogenetic inference. *Ann. Statist.*, 21:355–377, 1993.

[EZ98] S. N. Evans and X. Zhou. Constructing and counting phylogenetic invariants. *J. Comput. Biol.*, 5:713–724, 1998.

[GW91] Larry Gonick and Mark Wheelis. *The cartoon guide to genetics*. Harper Perennial, New York, updated edition, 1991.

[HJ85] R. A. Horn and C. R. Johnson. *Matrix analysis*. Cambridge University Press, Cambridge, 1985.

[JC69] T. H. Jukes and C. Cantor. Evolution of protein molecules. In H. N. Munro, editor, *Mammalian Protein Metabolism*, pages 21–132. New York: Academic Press, 1969.

[Kim80] M. Kimura. A simple method for estimating evolutionary rates of base substitution through comparative studies of nucleotide sequences. *J. Mol. Evol.*, 16:111–120, 1980.

[Kim81] M. Kimura. Estimation of evolutionary sequences between homologous nucleotide sequences. *Proc. Natl. Acad. Sci. USA*, 78:454–458, 1981.

[Lak87] J. A. Lake. A rate-independent technique for analysis of nucleic acid sequences: evolutionary parsimony. *Mol. Biol. Evol.*, 4:167–191, 1987.

[Ney71] J. Neyman. Molecular studies of evolution: A source of novel statistical problems. In S. S. Gupta and J. Yackel, editors, *Statistical Decision Theory and Related Topics*, pages 1–27. New York: Academic Press, 1971.

[SSE93] L. A. Székely, M. A. Steel, and P. L. Erdős. Fourier calculus on evolutionary trees. *Adv. in Appl. Math.*, 14(2):200–210, 1993.

[Wat95] Michael S. Waterman. *Introduction to computational biology : maps, sequences and genomes*. Chapman & Hall, London, New York, 1995.

STEVEN N. EVANS
DEPARTMENT OF STATISTICS #3860
UNIVERSITY OF CALIFORNIA AT BERKELEY
367 EVANS HALL
BERKELEY, CA 94720-3860
UNITED STATES
evans@stat.Berkeley.EDU

Modern Signal Processing
MSRI Publications
Volume **46**, 2003

Diffuse Tomography as a Source of Challenging Nonlinear Inverse Problems for a General Class of Networks

F. ALBERTO GRÜNBAUM

ABSTRACT. Diffuse tomography refers to the use of probes in the infrared part of the energy spectrum to obtain images of highly scattering media. There are important potential medical applications and a host of difficult mathematical issues in connection with this highly nonlinear inverse problem. Taking into account scattering gives a problem with many more unknowns, as well as pieces of data, than in the simpler linearized situation. The aim of this paper is to show that in some very simplified discrete model, reckoning with scattering gives an inversion problem whose solution can be reduced to that of a *finite* number of linear inversion problems. We see here that at least for the model in question, the proportion of variables that can be solved for is higher in the nonlinear case than in the linear one. We also notice that this gives a highly nontrivial problem in what can be called *network tomography*.

1. Introduction

Optical, or *diffuse*, tomography, refers to the use of low energy probes to obtain images of highly scattering media.

The main motivation for this line of work is, at present, the use of an infrared laser to obtain images of diagnostic value. There is a proposal to use this in neonatal clinics to measure oxygen content in the brains of premature babies as well as in the case of repeated mammography. With the discovery of highly specific markers that respond well in the optical or infrared region there are many potential applications of this emerging area; see [A1; A2].

There are a number of physically reasonable models that have been used in the formulation of the associated direct and inverse problems. These models are based on some approximation to a wave propagation model, such as the so-called *diffusion approximation*, or a transport equation model resulting in some type of linear Boltzmann equation. See [A1; A2; D; NW] for recent surveys of work

The author was supported in part by NSF Grant # FD99711151.

in this area. These papers give a detailed description of the physically relevant formulations that different authors have considered.

Our Markov chain formulation, going back to [G1; GP1; SGKZ], is different from those contained in these papers. We model the evolution of a photon as it moves through tissue by means of a Markov chain. At any (discrete) instant of time a photon occupies one of the states of the chain. These states are meant to represent a discretization of phase space, i.e. they encode position as well as velocity of a photon at a given time. The chain has three kinds of states: incoming states (which are meant to represent source positions surrounding the object of interest), hidden states (which are meant to represent the positions and velocities of photons inside the tissue) and finally, outgoing states(which represent detectors surrounding the object). We should also add an absorbing state at the center of each pixel to indicate that a photon "entering the pixel" can die in it. Instead of adding these extra states we simply do not assume that the sum of the one-step transition probabilities from a state should add to one. The difference between one and this sum is the probability of being absorbed into the pixel in question when coming into it from the corresponding state.

The direct problem would consist of determining different "input-output" quantities once the one-step transition probability matrix of our Markov chain has been given.

The resulting inverse problem amounts to reconstructing the one-step transition probability matrix for our Markov chain (with three kinds of states) from boundary measurements. This model is too simple and too general to faithfully reflect the physics of diffuse tomography but could be of interest in other set-ups. It gives a difficult class of *nonlinear* inverse problems for a certain *general class of networks* with a complex pattern of connections which are motivated by the diffuse tomography picture.

Since our model is the result of a discretization both in the positions occupied by a photon as well as the direction in which it is moving, the states will be indicated below by arrows placed at the boundaries of each pixel and pointing in one of four possible directions. One of the smallest cases of interest in dimension two is this:

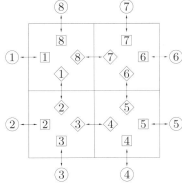

This simple model features four pixels, eight source positions, eight detector positions as well as eight hidden states. In this figure, incoming states are labeled by numbers enclosed in squares, outgoing states are labeled by numbers enclosed in circles, and hidden states are labeled by numbers enclosed in diamonds. The possible one step transitions are indicated in the next section, whereas the figure below displays (by means of arrows, as explained earlier) *only* the eight states of each kind.

In [G4] a discussion can be found of the corresponding smallest case in dimension three, where pixels are replaced by voxels and we have six different directions for our states.

The physics, or what is left of it, is best compressed into a *multiterminal network* where the nodes are the states of our Markov chain and the oriented edges indicate one-step transitions (with unknown probabilities) between the corresponding nodes. This is what a probabilist would call a state diagram.

As an example, here is the network corresponding to the physical model shown on the previous page (for clarity, when two nodes are joined by two opposite edges, we draw a single edge with arrows at both ends):

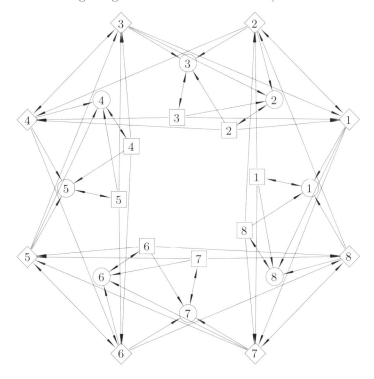

Notice that there is an underlying linear dynamics governed by the (unknown) one-step transition probability matrix of our Markov chain, but the inversion problem of interest is still nonlinear.

A remarkable feature of this simple model is that, at least for systems arising from very coarse tomographic discretizations, it gives an exactly solvable system of nonlinear equations, i.e., a certain number of unknowns are expressible in terms of the data and a number of free parameters. The advantages of this rather uncommon situation are clear: for instance it is possible to go beyond iterative methods of solution, which are very common for nonlinear problems.

In both the two-dimensional and three-dimensional situations we can consider as data the *photon count for a source-detector pair* which is defined as the probability that a photon that started at the source in question emerges at the detector in question regardless of the number of steps involved. If we assume that every one-step transition takes one unit of time we can consider the *time-of-flight* as a random variable associated to each incoming-outgoing pair. The photon count is the moment of order zero of this collection of random variables.

In Section 2 we see how far one can go using only the moment of order zero of time of flight. Section 3 considers the situation when we also use a small part of the information contained in the first moment of this collection of random variables. Section 4 deals with the issue of dealing with those variables that cannot be solved from the data. Finally Section 5 alludes to the fact that this same machinery can be applied in the non-physical situation when the dimension is neither two nor three but arbitrary.

It is also instructive in each case to consider the *standard tomographic* linear problem when scattering is completely ignored and a photon can only be absorbed in a pixel or continue in its straight-line trajectory. In this case each one of the four pixels, conveniently labeled $(1,1)$, $(1,2)$, $(2,1)$ and $(2,2)$ as the entries of a 2×2 matrix, is characterized by one parameter, its absorption probability.

The results regarding the ratio between the number of variables we can solve for and the total number of unknowns for each one of these scenarios are given below.

In the two-dimensional case, using four pixels (see figure on page 138) there are three situations:

(1) The linear one where scattering is ignored, gives a problem with 4 unknowns and 4 pieces of data, of which only three are independent and allows one to solve for 3 out of 4 unknowns.
(2) The general model discussed above (as in [GP1; GP2]) allows one to solve for 48 out of a total of 64 unknowns, leaving the ratio of $\frac{3}{4}$ unchanged.
(3) The use of time-of-flight information, which is discussed in Section 4, as well as in [G3], [GM1] gives a slightly better ratio, namely $\frac{56}{64} = \frac{7}{8}$.

When this comparison is done in dimension three, with a total of eight voxels, we get three situations:

(1) The linear version of the problem (scattering being ruled out) gives a system of 12 equations in 8 unknowns which can be solved for 7 of them in terms of one arbitrary parameter, giving a ratio of $\frac{7}{8}$.

(2) The general model (discussed in Sections 2 and 3) yields a system of 576 nonlinear equations in 288 variables that can be solved for 240 of them, with a ratio of $\frac{240}{288} = \frac{5}{6}$.

(3) The use of time-of-flight information (discussed in Section 4) raises the ratio to $\frac{264}{288} = \frac{11}{12}$. This shows that the consideration of a fully nonlinear problem can (in some sense) lead to a better determined problem than the corresponding linearized one.

We do not consider here the important issues of the difficulty in solving these systems or the sensitivity to errors of the corresponding problem.

For a very nice and up-to-date discussion of work in this area one can see [A1], [A2], [D], [NW]. These papers give a detailed description of the physically relevant formulations that different authors have considered. For an early reference in the area of *network tomography* see [V]. For similar problems in an area of great practical interest see the recent article [CHNY].

Remark This is an appropriate place to mention an oversight in [G4]. The labeling of the states given in the introduction to that paper does not correspond to the one used in [G4, Section 3]. The labeling used in the introduction to [G4] represents an improvement over the one used in [G4, Section 3]. The results in [G4] are correct, but some of the inversion formulas are unduly complicated since they are written down using a more complicated labeling scheme. When we use the labeling given in the introduction to [G4] we can reduce the entire problem to a set of equivalent linear ones, obviating the last nonlinear step in [G4]. This is reported in [GM2].

2. General Framework and Some Results

The one-step transition probability matrix P is naturally broken up into blocks that connect different types of states. We denote by P_{IO} the block dealing with a one-step transition from an arbitrary incoming state to an arbitrary outgoing state. P_{HH} denotes the corresponding block connecting hidden to hidden states, P_{IH} the one connecting incoming to hidden states and finally P_{HO} accounts for one-step transitions between hidden and outgoing states. For completeness we give these matrices below.

$$
P_{HH} = \begin{pmatrix}
0 & \text{N11S} & 0 & 0 & 0 & 0 & \text{N11E} & 0 \\
\text{S21N} & 0 & 0 & \text{S21E} & 0 & 0 & 0 & 0 \\
\text{W21N} & 0 & 0 & \text{W21E} & 0 & 0 & 0 & 0 \\
0 & 0 & \text{E22W} & 0 & 0 & \text{E22N} & 0 & 0 \\
0 & 0 & \text{S22W} & 0 & 0 & \text{S22N} & 0 & 0 \\
0 & 0 & 0 & 0 & \text{N12S} & 0 & 0 & \text{N12W} \\
0 & 0 & 0 & 0 & \text{E12S} & 0 & 0 & \text{E12W} \\
0 & \text{W11S} & 0 & 0 & 0 & 0 & \text{W11E} & 0
\end{pmatrix} ;
$$

$$P_{HO} = \begin{pmatrix} \text{N11W} & 0 & 0 & 0 & 0 & 0 & 0 & \text{N11N} \\ 0 & \text{S21W} & \text{S21S} & 0 & 0 & 0 & 0 & 0 \\ 0 & \text{W21W} & \text{W21S} & 0 & 0 & 0 & 0 & 0 \\ 0 & 0 & 0 & \text{E22S} & \text{E22E} & 0 & 0 & 0 \\ 0 & 0 & 0 & \text{S22S} & \text{S22E} & 0 & 0 & 0 \\ 0 & 0 & 0 & 0 & 0 & \text{N12E} & \text{N12N} & 0 \\ 0 & 0 & 0 & 0 & 0 & \text{E12E} & \text{E12N} & 0 \\ \text{W11W} & 0 & 0 & 0 & 0 & 0 & 0 & \text{W11N} \end{pmatrix};$$

$$P_{IH} = \begin{pmatrix} 0 & \text{E11S} & 0 & 0 & 0 & 0 & \text{E11E} & 0 \\ \text{E21N} & 0 & 0 & \text{E21E} & 0 & 0 & 0 & 0 \\ \text{N21N} & 0 & 0 & \text{N21E} & 0 & 0 & 0 & 0 \\ 0 & 0 & \text{N22W} & 0 & 0 & \text{N22N} & 0 & 0 \\ 0 & 0 & \text{W22W} & 0 & 0 & \text{W22N} & 0 & 0 \\ 0 & 0 & 0 & 0 & \text{W12S} & 0 & 0 & \text{W12W} \\ 0 & 0 & 0 & 0 & \text{S12S} & 0 & 0 & \text{S12W} \\ 0 & \text{S11S} & 0 & 0 & 0 & 0 & \text{S11E} & 0 \end{pmatrix};$$

$$P_{IO} = \begin{pmatrix} \text{E11W} & 0 & 0 & 0 & 0 & 0 & 0 & \text{E11N} \\ 0 & \text{E21W} & \text{E21S} & 0 & 0 & 0 & 0 & 0 \\ 0 & \text{N21W} & \text{N21S} & 0 & 0 & 0 & 0 & 0 \\ 0 & 0 & 0 & \text{N22S} & \text{N22E} & 0 & 0 & 0 \\ 0 & 0 & 0 & \text{W22S} & \text{W22E} & 0 & 0 & 0 \\ 0 & 0 & 0 & 0 & 0 & \text{W12E} & \text{W12N} & 0 \\ 0 & 0 & 0 & 0 & 0 & \text{S12E} & \text{S12N} & 0 \\ \text{S11W} & 0 & 0 & 0 & 0 & 0 & 0 & \text{S11N} \end{pmatrix}.$$

The choice of names for the variables in P is meant to indicate the corresponding transitions, for instance N11S means that we enter pixel $(1,1)$ going north and exit it going south. It is convenient to refer to the figure on page 138 at this point.

Just as in [GP1], [GP2] we find it convenient to introduce matrices A, X, Y, W by means of

$$A = P_{HO}^{-1},$$
$$P_{IO} = XA^{-1}, \quad P_{HH} = A^{-1}W, \quad P_{IH} = XA^{-1}W - Y.$$

The transformation, for a given P_{HO}, from the matrices P_{HH}, P_{IO}, P_{IH} to the matrices W, X, Y was introduced by S. Patch in [P3]. Notice that from A, X, W and Y it is possible to recover (in that order) the matrices P_{HO}, P_{IO}, P_{HH} and, finally, P_{IH}.

One advantage of introducing these matrices is that the input-output relation

$$Q_{IO} = P_{IO} + P_{IH}(I - P_{HH})^{-1}P_{HO}$$

can be rewritten, by multiplying both sides first by A on the right and then by $(I - A^{-1}W)$ on the right again, in the form

$$Q_{IO}(A - W) = X - Y.$$

In [GP1], [GP2] we exploited the block structure of the matrices A, W, X, Y to show that once Q_{IO} is given then A is arbitrary. After choosing A, it is then possible to derive explicit formulas for X, Y and W.

In the three-dimensional case the situation is a bit better, although the equations that we have to handle are naturally harder to deal with. We find that the matrix A can no longer be picked arbitrarily but only $2/3$ of it is arbitrary. This means that using *photon count* alone it is possible to express 24 of the 72 entries in the matrix A in terms of the data and 48 free parameters in A. By the *photon count* matrix we refer to the matrix whose entries are given by the probabilities that a photon that starts at a given source position would emerge from the tissue at a specified detector position. For details consult [G4] and [GM2].

3. Using the First Moment of Time-of-Flight

Now we go beyond the photon count and consider the first moment of the time-of- flight. As observed in the introduction the moment of order zero of this collection of random variables (one for each source-detector pair) gives the photon count matrix Q_{IO}.

If we denote the expression

$$P_{IH}(I - P_{HH})^{-2}P_{HO}$$

by R, we have:

LEMMA. The first moment of the "time-of-flight" can be expressed as

$$Q_{IO} + R.$$

PROOF. Start from the observation that the j-th moment of the time of flight is given by

$$Q_{IO}^{(j)} = P_{IO} + \sum_{k=0}^{\infty} P_{IH}P_{HH}^k P_{HO}(k+2)^j. \tag{3-1}$$

In particular, if $j = 0$ we recover (after an appropriate summation of the corresponding geometric series) the expression for $Q_{IO} \equiv Q_{IO}^{(0)}$ given in Section 2. We will return to this expression later in this section.

For $j = 1$ we get

$$
\begin{aligned}
Q_{IO}^{(1)} &= P_{IO} + 2P_{IH}(I - P_{HH})^{-1}P_{HO} + P_{IH}P_{HH}(I - P_{HH})^{-2}P_{HO} \\
&= Q_{IO}^{(0)} + P_{IH}(I - P_{HH})^{-2}[I - P_{HH} + P_{HH}]P_{HO} \\
&= Q_{IO}^{(0)} + R. \qquad \square
\end{aligned}
$$

Since Q_{IO} is taken as data we can consider R as the extra information provided by the expected value of time of flight.

Observe now that we have the relation

$$Q_{IO}A - X(A) = R(A - W(A)).$$

This follows, for instance, by noticing that each side of this identity is given by $P_{IH}(I - P_{HH})^{-1}$.

In the two-dimensional case ([GP2; GM1]) this concludes the job since we can use some of the entries of the matrix R to determine the ratios among eight pairs of the entries in A. Explicit formulas are given in [GM1].

The three-dimensional case has been given a first treatment in [G4]. By using the labeling mentioned in the introduction to that paper it is possible to obtain explicit formulas similar to those mentioned above. For details see [GM2].

It is very important to notice that in *either dimension* the entire problem of determining the blocks in P admits a natural "gauge transformation" given exactly by a diagonal matrix D. Consider the transformation that goes from a given set of blocks, to a new one given by the relations

$$\tilde{P}_{IO} = P_{IO},$$
$$\tilde{P}_{IH} = P_{IH}D^{-1},$$
$$\tilde{P}_{HH} = DP_{HH}D^{-1},$$
$$\tilde{P}_{HO} = DP_{HO}.$$

Notice that this gauge transformation preserves the required block structure of all the matrices in question. Moreover the probability of going from an arbitrary incoming state to an arbitrary outgoing state in m steps, given by the matrix P_{IO} if $m = 1$ and by $P_{IH}P_{HH}^{m-2}P_{HO}$ if $m \geq 2$, is clearly invariant under the transformation mentioned above. It follows then by referring to (3–1) for the j-th moment of the time of flight distribution that this is not affected by this gauge.

In conclusion, we have shown that the zeroth and first moments of the time-of-flight distribution determine the matrix P up to the choice of the arbitrary diagonal matrix D introduced above.

4. Taking into Account a Physical Model

An important question remains: how should the values of the 24 free parameters be picked (or the 8 free parameters in dimension two)? A similar question was discussed in [GP2] where we considered the effect of imposing on our very general model the assumption of "microscopic reversibility", i.e., a one-step transition from a state (of our Markov chain) given by the vector **v** to a state given by the vector **w** has the same probability as a transition from the sates given by the vectors −**w** and −**v** respectively. On the other hand, in [G2], [GZ] we considered the case of isotropic scattering. Each one of these cases leads to a dramatic reduction in the number of free parameters.

It is tempting to make some of these simplifying assumptions at the very *beginning* of the process, thereby reducing the number of unknowns. Experience seems to indicate that the possibility of reducing the *already nonlinear* system of equations to a linear one is greatly enhanced by making use of these assumptions at the end of the process.

5. A Network Tomography Problem for the Hypercube

The two-dimensional and three-dimensional problems discussed above have a firm foundation in diffuse tomography. It is however possible to go to higher dimensions and consider the corresponding *d- dimensional hypercube* and the network that goes along with it. By using the techniques in [GM1] and [GM2] it is possible to see that by measuring the first two moments (zeroth and first) of time-of-flight we can determine everything explicitly up to a total of $d\, 2^d$ free parameters. This happens to be the dimension of the gauge that appears at the end of Section 3, and thus this result is optimal. Details will appear in [GM3].

Acknowledgments. We thank the editors for useful suggestions on ways to improve the presentation.

References

[A1] S. Arridge, "Optical tomography in medical imaging", *Inverse Problems* **15** (1999), R41–R93.

[A2] S. Arridge and J. C. Hebden, "Optical imaging in medicine, II: Modelling and reconstruction", *Phys. Med. Biol.* **42** (1997), 841–853.

[D] O. Dorn, "A transport-backtransport method for optical tomography", *Inverse Problems* **14** (1998), 1107–1130.

[G1] F. A. Grünbaum, "Tomography with diffusion", pp. 16–21 in *Inverse Problems in Action*, edited by P. C. Sabatier, Springer, Berlin.

[G2] F. A. Grünbaum, "Diffuse tomography: the isotropic case", *Inverse Problems* **8** (1992), 409–419.

[G3] F. A. Grünbaum, "Diffuse tomography: using time-of-flight information in a two-dimensional model", *Int. J. Imaging Technology* **11** (2001), 283–286.

[G4] F. A. Grünbaum, "A nonlinear inverse problem inspired by three-dimensional diffuse tomography", *Inverse Problems* **17** (2001), 1907–1922.

[GM1] F. A. Grünbaum and L. Matusevich, "Explicit inversion formulas for a model in diffuse tomography", *Adv. Appl. Math.* **29** (2002), 172–183.

[GM2] F. A. Grünbaum and L. Matusevich, "A nonlinear inverse problem inspired by 3-dimensional diffuse tomography", *Int. J. Imaging Technology* **12** (2002), 198–203.

[GM3] F. A. Grünbaum and L. Matusevich, "A network tomography problem related to the hypercube", in preparation.

[GP1] F. A. Grünbaum and S. Patch, "The use of Grassmann identities for inversion of a general model in diffuse tomography", in *Proceedings of the Lapland Conference on Inverse Problems*, Saariselka, Finland, June 1992.

[GP2] F. A. Grünbaum and S. Patch, "Simplification of a general model in diffuse tomography", pp. 744–754 in *Inverse problems in scattering and imaging*, edited by M. A. Fiddy, Proc. SPIE **176**, 1992.

[GP3] F. A. Grünbaum and S. Patch, "How many parameters can one solve for in diffuse tomography?", in *Proceedings of the IMA Workshop on Inverse Problems in Waves and Scattering*, March 1995.

[GZ] F. A. Grünbaum and J. Zubelli, "Diffuse tomography: computational aspects of the isotropic case", *Inverse Problems* **8** (1992), 421–433.

[NW] F. Natterer and F. Wubbeling, *Mathematical methods in image reconstruction*, SIAM Monographs on Mathematical Modeling and Computation, SIAM, Philadelphia, 2001.

[P1] S. Patch, "Recursive recovery of a family of Markov transition probabilities from boundary value data", *J. Math. Phys.* **36**:7 (July 1995), 3395–3412.

[P2] S. Patch, "A recursive algorithm for diffuse planar tomography", Chapter 20 in *Discrete Tomography: Foundations, Algorithms, and Applications*, edited by G. Herman and A. Kuba, Birkhäuser, Boston, 1999.

[P3] S. Patch, "Recursive recovery of Markov transition probabilities from boundary value data", Ph.D. thesis, UC Berkeley, 1994.

[SGKZ] J. Singer, F. A. Grünbaum, P. Kohn and J. Zubelli, "Image reconstruction of the interior of bodies that diffuse radiation", *Science* **248** (1990), 990–993.

[V] J. Vardi, "Network tomography: estimating source-destination traffic intensities from link data", *J. Amer. Stat. Assoc.*, **91** (1996), 365–377.

[CHNY] M. Coates, A. Hero, R. Nowak and B. Yu, "Internet tomography", *Signal Processing Magazine*, **19**:3 (2002), 47–65.

F. ALBERTO GRÜNBAUM
DEPARTMENT OF MATHEMATICS
UNIVERSITY OF CALIFORNIA
BERKELEY, CA 94720
UNITED STATES
grunbaum@math.berkeley.edu

Modern Signal Processing
MSRI Publications
Volume **46**, 2003

An Invitation to Matrix-Valued Spherical Functions: Linearization of Products in the Case of Complex Projective Space $P_2(\mathbb{C})$

F. ALBERTO GRÜNBAUM, INÉS PACHARONI, AND JUAN TIRAO

ABSTRACT. The classical (scalar-valued) theory of spherical functions, put forward by Cartan and others, unifies under one roof a number of examples that were very well-known before the theory was formulated. These examples include special functions such as like Jacobi polynomials, Bessel functions, Laguerre polynomials, Hermite polynomials, Legendre functions, which had been workhorses in many areas of mathematical physics before the appearance of a unifying theory. These and other functions have found interesting applications in signal processing, including specific areas such as medical imaging.

The theory of matrix-valued spherical functions is a natural extension of the well-known scalar-valued theory. Its historical development, however, is different: in this case the theory has gone ahead of the examples. The purpose of this article is to point to some examples and to interest readers in this new aspect in the world of special functions.

We close with a remark connecting the functions described here with the theory of matrix-valued orthogonal polynomials.

1. Introduction and Statement of Results

The theory of matrix-valued spherical functions (see [GV; T]) gives a natural extension of the well-known theory for the scalar-valued case, see [He]. We start with a few remarks about the scalar-valued case.

The classical (scalar-valued) theory of spherical functions (put forward by Cartan and others after him) allows one to unify under one roof a number of examples that were very well known before the theory was formulated. These examples include many special functions like Jacobi polynomials, Bessel functions, Laguerre polynomials, Hermite polynomials, Legendre functions, etc.

This paper is partially supported by NSF grants FD9971151 and 1-443964-21160 and by CON-ICET grant PIP 655-98.

All these functions had "proved themselves" as the work-horse in many areas of mathematical physics before the appearance of a unifying theory. Many of these functions have found interesting applications in signal processing in general as well as in very specific areas like medical imaging. It suffices to recall, for instance, that Cormack's approach [C] — for which he got the 1979 Nobel Prize in Medicine, along with G. Hounsfield — was based on classical orthogonal polynomials and that the work of Hammaker and Solmon [HS] as well as that of Logan and Shepp [LS] is based on the use of Chebychev polynomials.

The crucial property here is the fact that these functions satisfy the integral equation that characterizes spherical functions of a homogeneous space. For a review on some of these topics the reader can either look at some of the specialized books on the subject such as [He] or start from a more introductory approach as that given in either [DMcK] and [T1, vol. I].

This integral equation is actually satisfied by all Gegenbauer polynomials and not only those corresponding to symmetric spaces. This point is fully exploited in [DG] where this property is put to use to show that different weight functions can be used in carrying out the usual tomographic operations of projection and backprojection. This works well for parallel beam tomography but has never been made to work for fan beam tomography because of a lack of an underlying group theoretical formulation in this case. For a number of issues in this area, including a number of open problems, see [G2].

For a variety of other applications of spherical functions one can look at [DMcK; T1].

We now come to the main issue in this article.

The situation with the matrix-valued extension of this theory is entirely different. In this case the theory has gone ahead of the examples and, in fact, to the best of our knowledge, the first examples involving nonscalar matrices have been given recently in [GPT1; GPT2; GPT3]. For scalar-valued instances of nontrivial type, see [HeSc].

The issue of how useful these functions may turn out to be as a tool in areas like geometry, mathematical physics, or signal processing in the broad sense is still open. From a historical perspective one could argue, rather tautologically, that the usefulness of the classical spherical functions rests on the many interesting properties they all share. With that goal in mind, it is natural to try to give a glimpse at these new objects and to illustrate some of their properties. The rather mixed character of the audience attending these lectures gives us an extra incentive to make this material accessible to people that might normally not look in the specialized literature.

The purpose of this contribution is thus to present very briefly the essentials of the theory and to describe one example in some detail. This is not the appropriate place for a complete description, and we refer the interested reader to the papers [GPT1; GPT2; GPT3].

We hope to pique the curiosity of some readers by exploring the extent to which the property of "positive linearization of products" holds in the case of the spherical functions associated to $P_2(\mathbb{C})$. This result has been important in the scalar case, including its use in the proof of the Bieberbach conjecture, see [AAR]. The property in question is illustrated well by considering the case of Legendre polynomials: the product of any two such is expressed as a linear combination involving other Legendre polynomials with degrees ranging from the absolute value of the difference to the sum of the degrees of the two factors involved. Moreover, the coefficients in this expansion are positive.

We should stress that the intriguing property described here is one enjoyed by a *matrix-valued function* put together from different spherical functions of a given type. In the classical *scalar-valued* case these two notions agree and the warning is not needed. This combination of spherical functions has already been seen, see [GPT1; GPT2; GPT3] to enjoy a natural form of the *bispectral property*. For an introduction to this expanding subject we could consult, for instance, [DG1; G12]. The roots of this problem are too long to trace in this short paper, but the reader may want to take a look at [S1]. For off-shoots that have yet to be explored further one can also see [G13; G15]. The short version of the story is that some remarkably useful *algebraic* properties that have surfaced first in signal processing and which one would like to extend and better understand have a long series of connections with other parts of mathematics. For a collection of problems arising in this area see [HK].

The issue of linearization of products, without insisting on any positivity results, plays (in the scalar-valued case) an important role in fairly successful applications of mathematics. For example, the issue of expressing the product of spherical harmonics of different degrees as a sum of spherical harmonics plays a substantial role in both theoretical and practical algorithms for the harmonic analysis of functions on the sphere. For some developments in this area see [DH] as well as [KMHR].

In the context of quantum mechanics this discussion is the backbone of the *addition rule for angular momenta* as can be seen in any textbook on the subject.

In the last section we make a brief remark connecting the functions described here with the theory of matrix-valued orthogonal polynomials, as developed for instance in [D] and [DVA].

2. Matrix-Valued Spherical Functions

Let G be a locally compact unimodular group and let K be a compact subgroup of G. Let $\hat{K}$ denote the set of all equivalence classes of complex finite dimensional irreducible representations of K; for each $\delta \in \hat{K}$, let ξ_δ denote the character of δ, $d(\delta)$ the degree of δ, i.e. the dimension of any representation in the class δ, and $\chi_\delta = d(\delta)\xi_\delta$.

Given a homogeneous space G/K a zonal spherical function ([He]) φ on G is a continuous complex valued function which satisfies $\varphi(e) = 1$ and

$$\varphi(x)\varphi(y) = \int_K \varphi(xky)\,dk \qquad\qquad x, y \in G. \qquad (2\text{--}1)$$

The following definition gives a fruitful generalization of this concept.

DEFINITION 2.1 [T; GV]. A spherical function Φ on G of type $\delta \in \hat{K}$ is a continuous function on G with values in $\operatorname{End}(V)$ such that

(i) $\Phi(e)$ equals I, the identity transformation.
(ii) $\Phi(x)\Phi(y) = \int_K \chi_\delta(k^{-1})\Phi(xky)\,dk$, for all $x, y \in G$.

The connection with differential equations of the group G comes from the property below.

Let $D(G)^K$ denote the algebra of all left invariant differential operators on G which are also invariant under all right translation by elements in K. If (V, π) is a finite dimensional irreducible representation of K in the equivalence class $\delta \in \hat{K}$, a spherical function on G of type δ is characterized by:

(i) $\Phi : G \longrightarrow \operatorname{End}(V)$ is analytic.
(ii) $\Phi(k_1 g k_2) = \pi(k_1)\Phi(g)\pi(k_2)$, for all $k_1, k_2 \in K$, $g \in G$, and $\Phi(e) = I$.
(iii) $[D\Phi](g) = \Phi(g)[D\Phi](e)$, for all $D \in D(G)^K$, $g \in G$.

We will be interested in the specific example given by the complex projective plane. This can be realized as the homogeneous space G/K, where $G = \operatorname{SU}(3)$ and $K = \operatorname{S}(\operatorname{U}(2) \times \operatorname{U}(1))$. In this case iii) above can be replaced by: $[\Delta_2 \Phi](g) = \lambda_2 \Phi(g)$, $[\Delta_3 \Phi](g) = \lambda_3 \Phi(g)$ for all $g \in G$ and for some $\lambda_2, \lambda_3 \in \mathbb{C}$. Here Δ_2 and Δ_3 are two algebraically independent generators of the polynomial algebra $D(G)^G$ of all differential operators on G which are invariant under left and right multiplication by elements in G.

The set $\hat{K}$ can be identified with the set $\mathbb{Z} \times \mathbb{Z}_{\geq 0}$. If $k = \begin{pmatrix} A & 0 \\ 0 & a \end{pmatrix}$, with $A \in \operatorname{U}(2)$ and $a = (\det A)^{-1}$, then

$$\pi(k) = \pi_{n,l}(A) = (\det A)^n\, A^l,$$

where A^l denotes the l-symmetric power of A, defines an irreducible representation of K in the class $(n, l) \in \mathbb{Z} \times \mathbb{Z}_{\geq 0}$.

For simplicity we restrict ourselves in this brief presentation to the case $n \geq 0$. The paper [GPT1] deals with the general case. The representation $\pi_{n,l}$ of $\operatorname{U}(2)$ extends to a unique holomorphic multiplicative map of $\operatorname{M}(2, \mathbb{C})$ into $\operatorname{End}(V_\pi)$, which we shall still denote by $\pi_{n,l}$. For any $g \in \operatorname{M}(3, \mathbb{C})$, we shall denote by $A(g)$ the left upper 2×2 block of g, i.e.

$$A(g) = \begin{pmatrix} g_{11} & g_{12} \\ g_{21} & g_{22} \end{pmatrix}.$$

For any $\pi = \pi_{(n,l)}$ with $n \geq 0$ let $\Phi_\pi : G \longrightarrow \text{End}(V_\pi)$ be defined by

$$\Phi_\pi(g) = \Phi_{n,l}(g) = \pi_{n,l}(A(g)).$$

It happens that Φ_π is a spherical function of type (n, l), one that will play a very important role in the construction of *all* the remaining spherical functions of the same type.

Consider the open set

$$\mathcal{A} = \{\, g \in G : \det A(g) \neq 0 \,\}.$$

The group $G = \text{SU}(3)$ acts in a natural way in the complex projective plane $P_2(\mathbb{C})$. This action is transitive and K is the isotropy subgroup of the point $(0, 0, 1) \in P_2(\mathbb{C})$. Therefore $P_2(\mathbb{C}) = G/K$. We shall identify the complex plane $\mathbb{C}^2$ with the affine plane $\{\, (x, y, 1) \in P_2(\mathbb{C}) : (x, y) \in \mathbb{C}^2 \,\}$.

The canonical projection $p : G \longrightarrow P_2(\mathbb{C})$ maps the open dense subset $\mathcal{A}$ onto the affine plane $\mathbb{C}^2$. Observe that $\mathcal{A}$ is stable by left and right multiplication by elements in K.

To determine all spherical functions $\Phi : G \longrightarrow \text{End}(V_\pi)$ of type $\pi = \pi_{n,l}$, we use the function Φ_π introduced above in the following way: in the open set $\mathcal{A}$ we define a function H by

$$H(g) = \Phi(g)\,\Phi_\pi(g)^{-1},$$

where Φ is suppose to be a spherical function of type π. Then H satisfies:

(i) $H(e) = I$.
(ii) $H(gk) = H(g)$, for all $g \in \mathcal{A}, k \in K$.
(iii) $H(kg) = \pi(k)H(g)\pi(k^{-1})$, for all $g \in \mathcal{A}, k \in K$.

Property ii) says that H may be considered as a function on $\mathbb{C}^2$.

The fact that Φ is an eigenfunction of Δ_2 and Δ_3 makes H into an eigenfunction of certain differential operators D and E on $\mathbb{C}^2$.

We are interested in considering the differential operators D and E applied to a function $H \in C^\infty(\mathbb{C}^2) \otimes \text{End}(V_\pi)$ such that $H(kp) = \pi(k)H(p)\pi(k)^{-1}$, for all $k \in K$ and p in the affine complex plane $\mathbb{C}^2$. This property of H allows us to find ordinary differential operators $\tilde{D}$ and $\tilde{E}$ defined on the interval $(0, \infty)$ such that

$$(D\,H)(r, 0) = (\tilde{D}\tilde{H})(r), \qquad (E\,H)(r, 0) = (\tilde{E}\tilde{H})(r),$$

where $\tilde{H}(r) = H(r, 0)$.

Introduce the variable $t = (1 + r^2)^{-1}$, which converts the operators $\tilde{D}$ and $\tilde{E}$ into new operators D and E.

The functions $\tilde{H}$ turn out to be diagonalizable. Thus, in an appropriate basis of V_π, we can write $\tilde{H}(r) = H(t) = (h_0(t), \dots, h_l(t))$.

We find it very convenient to introduce two integer parameters w, k subject to the following three inequalities: $0 \leq w$, $0 \leq k \leq l$, which give a very convenient parametrization of the irreducible spherical functions of type (n, l). In fact, for each pair (l, n), there are a total of $l + 1$ *families* of matrix-valued functions of t and w. In this instance these matrices are diagonal and one can put these diagonals together into a *full matrix-valued function* as we will do in the next two sections. It appears that this function, which coincides with the usual spherical function in the scalar case, enjoys some interesting properties.

The reader can consult [GPT1] to find a fairly detailed description of the entries that make up the matrices mentioned up to now. A flavor of the results is given by the following statement.

For a given $l \geq 0$, the spherical functions corresponding to the pair (l, n) have components that are expressed in terms of generalized hypergeometric functions of the form $_{p+2}F_{p+1}$, namely

$$_{p+2}F_{p+1}\left(\begin{array}{c} a, b, s_1 + 1, \ldots, s_p + 1 \\ c, s_1, s_2, \ldots, s_p \end{array}; t\right) = \sum_{j=0}^{\infty} \frac{(a)_j (b)_j}{j!(c)_j}(1 + d_1 j + \cdots + d_p j^p)t^j.$$

3. The Bispectral Property

For given nonnegative integers n, l and w consider the matrix whose rows are given by the vectors $H(t)$ corresponding to the values $k = 0, 1, 2, \ldots, l$ discussed above. Denote the corresponding matrix by

$$\Phi(w, t).$$

As a function of t, $\Phi(w, t)$ satisfies two differential equations

$$D\Phi(w, t)^t = \Phi(w, t)^t \Lambda, \quad E\Phi(w, t)^t = \Phi(w, t)^t M .$$

Here Λ and M are diagonal matrices with

$$\Lambda(i, i) = -w(w + n + i + l + 1) - (i - 1)(n + i),$$
$$M(i, i) = \Lambda(i, i)(n - l + 3i - 3) - 3(i - 1)(l - i + 2)(n + i),$$

for $1 \leq i \leq l + 1$; D and E are the differential operators introduced earlier. Moreover we have

THEOREM 3.1. *There exist matrices* A_w, B_w, C_w, *independent of* t, *such that*

$$A_w \Phi(w - 1, t) + B_w \Phi(w, t) + C_w \Phi(w + 1, t) = t\Phi(w, t) .$$

The matrices A_w and C_w consist of two diagonals each and B_w is tridiagonal. Assume, for convenience, that these vectors are normalized in such a way that for $t = 1$ the matrix $\Phi(w, 1)$ consists of all ones.

For details on these matrices as well as for a full proof of this statement, which was conjectured in [GPT1], the reader can consult [GPT2] and [PT].

4. Linearization of Products

The property in question states that the product of members of certain families of (scalar-valued) orthogonal polynomials is given by an expansion of the form

$$P_i P_j = \sum_{k=|j-i|}^{j+i} a_k P_k$$

and that the coefficients in the expansion are all nonnegative.

For a nice and detailed account of the situation in the scalar case, see for instance [A], [S]. Very important contributions on these and related matters are [G] and [K].

It is important to note that the property in question is not true for all families of orthogonal polynomials, in fact it is not even true for all Jacobi polynomials $P_w^{(\alpha,\beta)}$, *normalized by the condition* $P_w^{(\alpha,\beta)}(1)$ *positive*. For our purpose it is important to recall that nonnegativity is satisfied if $\alpha \geq \beta$ and $\alpha + \beta \geq 1$.

The case $l = 0$, $n > 1$.

From [GPT1] we know that when $l = 0$ and $n \geq 0$ the appropriate eigenfunctions (without the standard normalization) are given by

$$\Phi(w,t) = {}_2F_1\left(\begin{matrix} -w, \; w+n+2 \\ n+1 \end{matrix}; t\right).$$

This means that with the usual convention that the Jacobi polynomials are positive for $t = 1$ we are dealing with the family

$$P_w^{(1,n)}(t).$$

If $n = 0$ or $n = 1$ the family $P_w^{(1,n)}$ meets the sufficient conditions for nonnegativity given above. For $n = 0$ the coefficients a_k are all strictly positive; in the case $n = 1$ the coefficients $a_{|i-j|+2k}$, are strictly positive while the coefficients $a_{|i-j|+k}$, k odd, are zero, as the example below illustrates.

We now turn our attention to the case $n > 1$.

CONJECTURE 4.1. *For n an integer larger than one, the coefficients in the expansion for the product $P_i P_j$ above alternate in sign.*

This conjecture is backed up by extensive experiments, one of which is shown below. It deals with the case of w (that is, i and j) equal to 3 and 4. Richard Askey supplied a proof of this conjecture. This gives us a new chance to thank him for many years of encouragement and help.

The product of the (scalar-valued, and properly normalized) functions $\Phi(3,t)$ and $\Phi(4,t)$ is given by the expansion

$$\Phi(3,t)\Phi(4,t) = a_1\Phi(1,t) + a_2\Phi(2,t) + a_3\Phi(3,t) + a_4\Phi(4,t)$$
$$+ a_5\Phi(5,t) + a_6\Phi(6,t) + a_7\Phi(7,t),$$

with coefficients given by the expressions

$$a_1 = \frac{(n+2)(n+3)(n+4)}{(n+8)(n+9)(n+10)},$$

$$a_2 = -\frac{6(n-1)(n+3)(n+4)(n+6)^2}{(n+7)(n+8)(n+9)(n+10)(n+11)},$$

$$a_3 = \frac{3(n+4)(n+5)(7n^3+52n^2+67n+162)}{(n+7)(n+9)(n+10)(n+11)(n+12)},$$

$$a_4 = -\frac{4(n-1)(n+6)(11n^3+123n^2+436n+648)}{(n+8)(n+9)(n+11)(n+12)(n+13)},$$

$$a_5 = \frac{3(n+5)(n+6)(n+7)(19n^3+155n^2+162n+504)}{(n+8)(n+9)(n+10)(n+11)(n+13)(n+14)},$$

$$a_6 = -\frac{42(n-1)(n+5)(n+6)^2(n+7)(n+8)}{(n+9)(n+10)(n+11)(n+12)(n+13)(n+15)},$$

$$a_7 = \frac{14(n+5)(n+6)^2(n+7)^2(n+8)}{(n+10)(n+11)(n+12)(n+13)(n+14)(n+15)}.$$

This shows that even in the scalar-valued case, as soon as we are dealing with nonclassical spherical functions we encounter an interesting sign alternating property that is quite different from the more familiar case. Here and below we see that things become different once n is an integer larger than one.

Now we explore the picture in the case of general l.

The case $l > 0$, $n > 1$

CONJECTURE 4.2. *If $i \leq j$ then the product of $\Phi(i,t)$ and $\Phi(j,t)$ allows for a (unique) expansion of the form*

$$\Phi(i,t)\Phi(j,t) = \sum_{k=\min\{j-i-l,0\}}^{j+i+l} A_k\Phi(k,t).$$

Here the coefficients A_k are matrices and the matrix-valued function $\Phi(w,t)$ is the one introduced in Section 3. This conjecture holds for all nonnegative n and is well known for $l = 0$ and $n = 0$.

In the case of $l = 0$ we obtain the usual range in the expansion coefficients ranging from $j-i$ to $j+i$ as in the case of addition of angular momenta. For larger values of l we see that *extra* terms appear at each end of the expansion.

CONJECTURE 4.3. *If $i < j$ then the coefficients A_k in the expansion*

$$\Phi(i,t)\Phi(j,t) = \sum_{k=\min\{j-i-l,0\}}^{j+i+l} A_k\Phi(k,t).$$

with k in the range j − i, j + i have what we propose to call "the hook alternating property."

We will explain this conjecture by displaying one example. First notice that we exclude those coefficients that are not in the *traditional* or *usual* range discussed above.

At this point it may be appropriate in the name of *truth in advertisement* to admit that we have no concrete evidence of the significance of the property alluded to above and displayed towards the end of the paper. We trust that the reader will find the property cute and intriguing. It would be very disappointing if nobody were to find some use for it.

The results illustrated below have been checked for many values of $l > 0$, but are displayed here for $l = 1$ only.

Recall that from [GPT1] the rows that make up the matrix-valued function $H(t, w)$ are given as follows: the first row is obtained from the column vector

$$H(t) = \left(\begin{array}{c} \left(1 - \dfrac{\lambda}{n+1}\right) {}_3F_2\left(\begin{array}{cc} -w, & w+n+3, & \lambda-n \\ & n+2, & \lambda-n-1 \end{array}; t \right) \\ {}_2F_1\left(\begin{array}{cc} -w, & w+n+3 \\ & n+1 \end{array}; t \right) \end{array} \right)$$

with

$$\lambda = -w(w+n+3)$$

and the second row comes from the column vector

$$H(t) = \left(\begin{array}{c} {}_2F_1\left(\begin{array}{cc} -w, & w+n+4 \\ & n+2 \end{array}; t \right) \\ -(n+1)\, {}_3F_2\left(\begin{array}{cc} -w-1, & w+n+3, & \lambda \\ & n+1, & \lambda-1 \end{array}; t \right) \end{array} \right)$$

with

$$\lambda = -w(w+n+4) - n - 2.$$

The product of the matrices $\Phi(2, t)$ and $\Phi(6, t)$ is given by the expansion

$$\Phi(2,t)\Phi(6,t) = A_3\Phi(3,t) + A_4\Phi(4,t) + A_5\Phi(5,t) + A_6\Phi(6,t)$$
$$+ A_7\Phi(7,t) + A_8\Phi(8,t) + A_9\Phi(9,t),$$

where

$$A_3 = \left(\begin{array}{cc} 0 & 0 \\ 0 & \dfrac{16(n+4)(n+5)(n+6)^2(n+7)^2}{(n+11)(n+12)(n+13)(n+14)(n+15)(n+16)} \end{array} \right);$$

$$A_4 = \left(\begin{array}{cc} L_{11} & L_{12} \\ L_{21} & L_{22} \end{array} \right) \text{ with}$$

$$L_{11} = \frac{15(n+5)^2(n+6)(n+8)}{2(n+12)(n+13)(n+14)(n+15)},$$

$$L_{12} = \frac{5(n+5)(n+6)(4\,n^2+55\,n+216)}{6(n+13)(n+14)(n+15)(n+16)},$$

$$L_{21} = \frac{(n+5)(n+6)(n+7)(8\,n^2+153\,n+724)}{2(n+12)(n+13)(n+14)(n+15)(n+16)},$$

$$L_{22} = -\frac{5(n+6)(n+7)(248\,n^4+4665\,n^3+27202\,n^2+45137\,n-23252)}{12(n+11)(n+13)(n+14)(n+15)(n+16)(n+17)};$$

$$A_5 = \begin{pmatrix} M_{11} & M_{12} \\ M_{21} & M_{22} \end{pmatrix} \text{ with}$$

$$M_{11} = -\frac{(n+5)(n+6)(185\,n^3+3284\,n^2+15732\,n+10368)}{6(n+7)(n+12)(n+14)(n+15)(n+16)},$$

$$M_{12} = -\frac{(n+5)(85\,n^4+1817\,n^3+11380\,n^2+7072\,n-93460)}{7(n+7)(n+13)(n+15)(n+16)(n+17)},$$

$$M_{21} = -\frac{(n+6)^2(170\,n^4+4735\,n^3+42068\,n^2+99767\,n-168628)}{12(n+7)(n+12)(n+14)(n+15)(n+16)(n+17)},$$

$$M_{22} = \frac{\begin{array}{c}4327\,n^7+163698\,n^6+2480127\,n^5+19091004\,n^4+78090428\,n^3\\+163454544\,n^2+172290528\,n+132098688\end{array}}{14(n+7)(n+12)(n+13)(n+15)(n+16)(n+17)(n+18)};$$

$$A_6 = \begin{pmatrix} N_{11} & N_{12} \\ N_{21} & N_{22} \end{pmatrix} \text{ with}$$

$$N_{11} = \frac{2(193\,n^5+5832\,n^4+65284\,n^3+328884\,n^2+727621\,n+634422)}{7(n+8)(n+13)(n+14)(n+16)(n+17)},$$

$$N_{12} = \frac{171\,n^5+4729\,n^4+45764\,n^3+188570\,n^2+442336\,n+1133640}{8(n+8)(n+14)(n+15)(n+17)(n+18)},$$

$$N_{21} = \frac{171\,n^6+7071\,n^5+116213\,n^4+959879\,n^3+4245034\,n^2+10640548\,n+15755112}{7(n+8)(n+13)(n+14)(n+16)(n+17)(n+18)},$$

$$N_{22} = -\frac{\begin{array}{c}4269\,n^7+169934\,n^6+2677678\,n^5+21066480\,n^4+85737209\,n^3\\+169428298\,n^2+129986220\,n-46794888\end{array}}{8(n+8)(n+13)(n+14)(n+15)(n+17)(n+18)(n+19)};$$

$$A_7 = \begin{pmatrix} P_{11} & P_{12} \\ P_{21} & P_{22} \end{pmatrix} \text{ with}$$

$$P_{11} = -\frac{3(n+5)(129\,n^4 + 3710\,n^3 + 36430\,n^2 + 129960\,n + 76536)}{8(n+9)(n+14)(n+15)(n+16)(n+18)},$$

$$P_{12} = -\frac{(n+5)(n+10)(57\,n^3 + 917\,n^2 + 2274\,n - 11268)}{3(n+9)(n+15)(n+16)(n+17)(n+19)},$$

$$P_{21} = \frac{-3(57\,n^6 + 2505\,n^5 + 44489\,n^4 + 389955\,n^3 + 1576582\,n^2 + 1465908\,n - 4434696)}{8(n+9)(n+14)(n+15)(n+16)(n+18)(n+19)},$$

$$P_{22} = \frac{\begin{array}{c} 2(n+10)(829\,n^6 + 27979\,n^5 + 352571\,n^4 + 2024521\,n^3 \\ + 5197384\,n^2 + 5712396\,n + 5004720) \end{array}}{3(n+9)(n+14)(n+15)(n+16)(n+17)(n+19)(n+20)};$$

$$A_8 = \begin{pmatrix} Q_{11} & Q_{12} \\ Q_{21} & Q_{22} \end{pmatrix} \text{ with}$$

$$Q_{11} = \frac{5(n+5)(n+6)(21\,n^2 + 401\,n + 1920)}{6(n+15)(n+16)(n+17)(n+18)},$$

$$Q_{12} = \frac{15(n+5)(n+6)(n+8)(n+11)}{2(n+16)(n+17)(n+18)(n+19)},$$

$$Q_{21} = \frac{5(n+6)(10\,n^4 + 329\,n^3 + 4942\,n^2 + 36611\,n + 96300)}{6(n+15)(n+16)(n+17)(n+18)(n+20)},$$

$$Q_{22} = -\frac{3(n+6)(n+11)(430\,n^4 + 9773\,n^3 + 67728\,n^2 + 129129\,n - 59220)}{4(n+15)(n+16)(n+17)(n+18)(n+19)(n+21)};$$

$$A_9 = \begin{pmatrix} 0 & 0 \\ T_{21} & T_{22} \end{pmatrix} \text{ with}$$

$$T_{21} = \frac{99(n+4)(n+6)(n+7)(n+10)}{4(n+16)(n+17)(n+18)(n+19)(n+20)},$$

$$T_{22} = \frac{165(n+4)(n+6)(n+7)(n+8)(n+10)(n+12)}{2(n+16)(n+17)(n+18)(n+19)(n+20)(n+21)}.$$

Notice that if we concentrate our attention on the coefficients within the *traditional* range we see that the first matrix A_4 has its first *hook* made up of positive entries, the second hook (which in this example consists of only one entry) has negative signs. The second matrix A_5 has its first hook negative, the second hook positive. The third matrix A_6 repeats the behavior of the first one, the fourth one A_7 imitates the second one, and so on.

Extensive experimentation shows that this *double alternating property* holds for values of l greater than zero. For coefficient matrices in the traditional expansion range, the first matrix has its first hook positive, the second one negative, the third positive, etc. The second matrix has the same alternating pattern of signs for the hooks but its first hook is negative. The third matrix imitates the first, etc.

The following picture captures the phenomenon described above for n larger than one and when the index k is in the traditional range.

$$
\begin{array}{lll}
+++\cdots+ & \quad ---\cdots- & \\
+--\cdots- & \quad -++\cdots+ & \\
+-+\cdots+ & \quad -+-\cdots- & \\
+-+ & \quad -+- & \text{etc.}\\
\vdots\ \vdots\ \vdots & \quad \vdots\ \vdots\ \vdots & \\
+-+ & \quad -+- &
\end{array}
$$

5. The Relation with Matrix-Valued Orthogonal Polynomials

We close the paper remarking, once again, that our matrix-valued spherical functions are orthogonal with respect to a nice inner product and have polynomial entries. Yet, they do not fit directly into the existing theory of matrix-valued orthogonal polynomials as given for instance in [D] and [DVA].

It is however possible to establish such a connection: define the matrix-valued function $\Psi(j, t)$ by means of the relation

$$\Phi(j, t) = \Psi(j, t)\Phi(0, t).$$

It is now a direct consequence of the definitions that the family $\Psi(j, t)$ satisfies all the standard requirements in [DVA] and not only satisfies a three term recursion relation but also $\Psi(j, t)^t$ satisfies a fixed differential equation with matrix coefficients and only the "eigenvalue matrix" depends on j. In other words the family $\Psi(j, t)$ meets all the conditions given at the beginning of Section 3 and meets also the conditions of the standard theory in [DVA] giving an example of a *classical family of matrix-valued orthogonal polynomials*. In particular, the coefficients in the differential operator D (obtained by conjugation from the one in [GPT1]) are matrix polynomials of degree going with the order of differentiation. For a nice introduction to this circle of ideas, see the pioneering work in [D].

Acknowledgments. We are much indebted to the editors for suggesting a number of places where the exposition could be improved. Grünbaum acknowledges a useful conversation with A. Duran that steered him in the direction to Section 5 above.

References

[A] R. Askey, *Orthogonal polynomials and special functions,* SIAM, (1975).

[AAR] G. Andrews, R. Askey and R. Roy, *Special functions,* Encyclopedia of Mathematics and its applications, Cambridge University Press, 1999.

[C] A. Cormack, "Representation of a function by its line integrals, with some radiological applications I", J. Appl. Physics **34** (1963), 2722–2727.

[D] A. Duran, "Matrix inner product having a matrix symmetric second order differential operators", Rocky Mountain Journal of Mathematics **27**:2 (1997).

[DG] M. E. Davison and F. A. Grünbaum, "Tomographic reconstructions with arbitrary directions", Comm. Pure and Appl. Math. **34** (1981), 77–120.

[DH] J. Driscoll and D. Healy, Jr., "Computing Fourier transforms and convolutions on the 2-sphere", Advances in Applied Mathematics **15** (1994), 202–250.

[DMcK] H. Dym and H. P. McKean, Jr., *Fourier series and integrals,* Academic Press.

[DVA] A. Duran and W. Van Assche, "Orthogonal matrix polynomials and higher order recurrence relations", Linear algebra and its applications **219** (1995), 261–280.

[G] G. Gasper, "Positive sums of the classical orthogonal polynomials", SIAM J. Math. Anal. **8** (1977), 423–447.

[G2] F. A. Grünbaum, "Backprojections in tomography, spherical functions and addition formulas: a few challenges", pp. 143–152 in *Inverse problems, image analysis, and medical imaging,* Contemporary Mathematics **313**, edited by M. Z. Nashed and O. Scherzer, Amer. Math. Soc., Providence, 2002.

[GPT1] F. A. Grünbaum, I. Pacharoni and J. A. Tirao, "Matrix valued spherical functions associated to the complex projective plane", J. Functional Analysis **188** (2002) 350–441.

[GPT2] F. A. Grünbaum, I. Pacharoni and J. Tirao, "A matrix valued solution to Bochner's problem", J. Physics A Math. Gen. **34** (2001), 10647–10656.

[GPT3] F. A. Grünbaum, I. Pacharoni and J. A. Tirao, "Matrix valued spherical functions associated to the three dimensional hyperbolic space", Int. J. Math. **13**:7 (2002), 727–784.

[GV] R. Gangolli and V. S. Varadarajan, *Harmonic analysis of spherical functions on real reductive groups,* Ergebnisse der Mathematik **101**, Springer, Berlin, 1988.

[DG1] J. Duistermaat and F. A. Grünbaum, *"Differential equations in the spectral parameter",* Commun. Math. Phys. **103** (1986), 177–240.

[G12] F. A. Grünbaum, *"Time-band limiting and the bispectral problem",* Comm. Pure Appl. Math. **47** (1994), 307–328.

[G13] F. A. Grünbaum, *"A new property of reproducing kernels of classical orthogonal polynomials",* J. Math. Anal. Applic. **95** (1983), 491–500.

[G15] F. A. Grünbaum, *"Some explorations into the mystery of band and time limiting",* Adv. Appl. Math. **13** (1992), 328–349.

[HS] Ch. Hamaker and D. Solmon, "The angles between the null-spaces of X-rays", J. Math. Anal. Appl. **62** (1978), 1–23.

[HK] J. Harnad and A. Kasman (editors), *The bispectral problem,* CRM proceedings and lectures notes **14**, Amer. Math. Soc., Providence, 1998.

[HeSc] G. Heckman and H. Schlicktkrull, *Harmonic analysis and special functions on symmetric spaces,* Perspective in mathematics **16**, Academic Press, San Diego, 1994.

[He] S. Helgason, *Groups and geometric analysis,* Mathematical Surveys and Monographs **83**, Amer. Math. Soc., Providence, 2000

[K] T. Koornwinder, "Positivity proofs for linearization and connection coefficients of orthogonal polynomials satisfying an addition formula", J. London Math. Society **18**:2 (1978), 101–114.

[KMHR] P. Kostelec, D. Maslen, D. Healy, Jr. and D. Rockmore, "Computational harmonic analysis for tensor fields on the two-sphere", J. Comput. Phys. **162** (2000), 514–535.

[LS] B. Logan and L. Shepp, "Optimal reconstruction of a function from its projections", Duke Math. J. (1975), 645–659.

[PT] I. Pacharoni and J. A. Tirao, "Three term recursion relation for functions associated to the complex projective plane", to appear in Mathematical Physics, Analysis and Geometry, 2003.

[S] R. Szwarc, "Orthogonal polynomials and a discrete boundary value problem, II", Siam J. Math. Anal. **23** (1992), 965–969.

[S1] D. Slepian, *"Some comments on Fourier analysis, uncertainty and Modeling"*, SIAM Review **25**:3 (July 1983).

[T1] A. Terras, *Harmonic analysis on symmetric spaces and applications*, 2 vol., Springer, NY, 1985 and 1988.

[T] J. Tirao, "Spherical functions", Rev. Unión Matem. Argentina **28** (1977), 75–98.

F. ALBERTO GRÜNBAUM
DEPARTAMENT OF MATHEMATICS
UNIVERSITY OF CALIFORNIA
BERKELEY CA 94720
   grunbaum@math.berkeley.edu

INÉS PACHARONI
CIEM-FaMAF
UNIVERSIDAD NACIONAL DE CÓRDOBA
CÓRDOBA 5000
ARGENTINA
   pacharon@mate.uncor.edu

JUAN TIRAO
CIEM-FaMAF
UNIVERSIDAD NACIONAL DE CÓRDOBA
CÓRDOBA 5000
ARGENTINA
   tirao@mate.uncor.edu

Modern Signal Processing
MSRI Publications
Volume **46**, 2003

Image Registration for MRI

PETER J. KOSTELEC AND SENTHIL PERIASWAMY

ABSTRACT. To *register* two images means to align them so that common
features overlap and differences — for example, a tumor that has grown —
are readily apparent. Being able to easily spot differences between two
images is obviously very important in applications. This paper is an introduction to image registration as applied to medical imaging. We first define
image registration, breaking the problem down into its constituent component. We then discuss various techniques, reflecting different choices that
can be made in developing an image registration technique. We conclude
with a brief discussion.

1. Introduction

1.1. Background. To *register* two images means to *align* them, so that common features overlap and differences, should there be any, between the two are
emphasized and readily visible to the naked eye. We refer to the process of
aligning two images as *image registration*.

There are a host of clinical applications requiring image registration. For
example, one would like to compare two Computed Tomography (CT) scans
of a patient, taken say six months ago and yesterday, and identify differences
between the two, e.g., the growth of a tumor during the intervening six months
(Figure 1). One could also want to align Positron Emission Tomography (PET)
data to an MR image, so as to help identify the anatomic location of certain
mental activation [43]. And one may want to register lung surfaces in chest
Computed Tomography (CT) scans for lung cancer screening [7]. While all
of these identifications can be done in the radiologist's head, the possibility
always exists that small, but critical, features could be missed. Also, beyond
identification itself, the extent of alignment required could provide important
quantitative information, e.g., how much a tumor's volume has changed.

Kostelec's work is supported in part by NSF BCS Award 9978116, AFOSR under award
F49620-00-1-0280, and NIH grants PO1 CA80139. Periaswamy's work is supported in part
by NSF Grants EIA-98-02068 and IIS-99-83806.

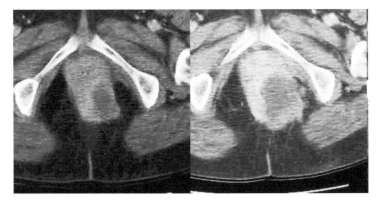

Figure 1. Two CT images showing a pelvic tumor's growth over time. The grayscale has been adjusted so as to make the tumor, the darker gray area within the mass in the center of each image, more readily visible. In actuality, it is barely darker than the background tissue.

When registering images, we are determining a geometric transformation which aligns one image to fit another. For a number of reasons, simple image subtraction does not work. MR image volumes are acquired one slice at a time. When comparing a six month old MR volume with one acquired yesterday, chances are that the slices (or "imaging planes") from the two volumes are not parallel. As a result, the perspectives would be different. By this, we mean the following. Consider a right cylindrical cone. A plane slicing through the cone, parallel to its base, forms a circle. If the slice is slightly off parallel, an ellipse results. In terms of human anatomy, a circular feature in the first slice appears as an ellipse in the second. In the case of mammography, tissue is compressed differently from one exam to the next. Other architectural distortions are possible. Since the body is an elastic structure, how it is oriented in gravity induces a variety of non-rigid deformations. These are just some of the reasons why simple image subtraction does not work.

For the neuroscientist doing research in functional Magnetic Resonance Imaging (fMRI), the ability to accurately align image volumes is of vital importance. Their results acutely depend on accurate registration. To provide a brief background, to "do" fMRI means to attempt to determine which parts of the brain are active in response to some given stimulus. For instance, the human subject, in the MR scanner, would be asked to perform some task, e.g., finger-tap at regular intervals, or attend to a particular instrument while listening to a piece of music [20], or count the number of occurrences of a particular color when shown a collection of colored squares [8]. As the subject performs the task, the researcher effectively takes 3-D MR movies of the subject's brain. The goal is to identify those parts of the brain responsible for processing the information the

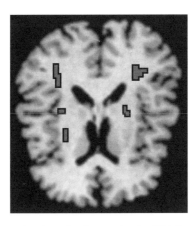

Figure 2. fMRI. By registering the frames in the MR "movie" and performing statistical analyses, the researcher can identify the active part(s) of the brain by finding those pixels whose intensities change most in response to the given stimulus. The active pixels are usually false-coloured in some fashion, to make them more obvious, similar to those shown in this figure.

stimulus provides. The researcher's hope of accomplishing this is based on the Blood Oxygenation Level Dependent (BOLD) hypothesis (see [6]).

The BOLD hypothesis roughly states that the parts of the brain that process information, in response to some stimulus, need more oxygen than those parts which do not. Changes in the blood oxygen level manifest themselves as changes in the strength of the MR signal. This is what the researcher attempts to detect and measure. The challenge lies in the fact that the changes in signal strength are very small, on the order of only a few percent greater than background noise [5]. And to make matters worse, the subject, despite their noblest intentions, cannot help but move at least ever so slightly during the experiment. So, before useful analysis can begin, the signal strength must be maximized.

This is accomplished by task repetition, i.e., having the subjects repeat the task over and over again. Then all the image volumes are registered *within* each subject. Assuming gaussian noise, adding the registered images will strengthen the elusive signal. Statistical analyses are done within subject, and then combined across all subjects. This is the usual order of events [18].

1.2. What's inside this paper. This will be a whirlwind, and by no means exhaustive, tour of image registration for MRI. We will briefly touch upon a few of the many and varied techniques used to register MR images. Note that the survey articles by Brown [11] and Van den Elsen [38] are excellent sources for more in-depth discussion of image registration, the problem and the techniques. Our purpose here, within this paper, is to whet the reader's appetite, to stimulate her interest in this very important image processing challenge, a challenge which has a host of applications, both in medical imaging and beyond.

The paper is organized as follows. We first give some background and establish a theoretical framework that will provide a means of defining the critical components involved in image registration. This will enable us to identify those issues which need to be addressed when performing image registration. This will be followed by examples of various registration techniques, explained at varying depths. The methods presented are not meant to represent any sort of definitive list. We want to point out to the reader just some of the techniques which exist, so that they can appreciate how difficult the problem of image registration is, as well as how varied the solutions can be. We close with a brief discussion.

Acknowledgments. We thank Daniel Rockmore and Dennis Healy for inviting us to participate in the MSRI Summer Graduate Program in Modern Signal Processing, June 2001. We also thank Digger 'The Boy' Rockmore for helpful discussions, and for granting us the use of his image in this paper.

2. Theory

Suppose we have two brain MR images, taken of the same subject, but at different times, say, six months ago and yesterday. We need to align the six month old image, which we will call the *source image*, with the one acquired yesterday, the *target image*. (These terms will be used throughout this paper.) A tumor has been previously identified, and the radiologist would like to determine how much the tumor has grown during the six weeks. Instead of trying to "eyeball it," the two images would enable an quantitative estimate of the growth rate. How do we proceed?

Do we assume that a simple rigid motion will suffice? Determining the correct rotation and translation parameters is, as we will see later, a relatively quick and straightforward process. However, if non-linear deformations have occurred within the brain (which, as described in Sec. 1.1, is likely for any number of reasons), applying a rigid motion model in this situation will not produce an optimal alignment. So probably some sort of non-rigid or elastic model would be more appropriate.

Are we looking to perform a global alignment, or a local one? That is, will the same transformation, e.g., affine, rigid body, be applied to the entire image, or should we instead employ a local model of sorts, where different parts of the image/volume are moved in different, though smoothly connected, ways?

Should the method we use depend on active participation by the radiologist, to help "prime" or "guide" the method so that accurate alignment is achieved? Or do we instead want the technique to be completely automated and free of human intervention?

Wow, that's a lot of questions we have to think about, and answer, too. How do we begin? To tackle the alignment problem, we had first better *organize* it.

2.1. The four components. The multitude of challenges inherent in performing image registration can be better addressed by distilling the problem into four distinctive components [11].

I. The feature space. Before registering two images, we must decide exactly *what* it is that will be registered. The type of algorithm developed depends critically on the *features* chosen. And when you think about it, there are alot of features from which to choose. Will we work with the raw pixel intensities themselves? Or perhaps the edges and contours of the images? If we have volumetric data, perhaps we should use the surface the volume defines, as in a 3-D brain scan? We could have the user identify features common to both images, with the intent to aligning those landmarks. Then again, if we wish to align images of different modalities, say MRI with PET, then perhaps statistical properties of the images that would be optimal for our purpose. So you see, the *feature space* we choose will really drive the algorithm we develop.

II. The search space. When one says, "I want to align these two images," what is one really saying? That is, what is the rigorous form of the sentence? The two images can be considered samples of two (unknown), compact, real-valued functions, $f(\mathbf{x})$, $g(\mathbf{x})$, defined on $\mathbb{R}^n$ (where n is 2 or 3). To align the images means we wish to find a transformation $T(\mathbf{x})$ such that $f(\mathbf{x}) = g(T(\mathbf{x}))$ for all $\mathbf{x}$. Fine. So what kind of transformation are we willing to consider? This is the *Search Space* we need to define.

For example, you can consider the simple rigid body transformations, rotation plus translation. Or, if you would like to account for differences in scale, you may instead decide to search for the best affine transformation. But both of these transformations are global in some respect, and you may want to do something more localized or *elastic*, and transform different parts of the image by differing amounts, e.g., to account for non-uniform deformations. Your decision here will very much influence the nature of the registration algorithm.

III. The search strategy. Suppose we have chosen our Search Space. We select a transformation $T_0(\mathbf{x})$ and try it. Based on the results of $T_0(\mathbf{x})$, how should we choose the next transformation, $T_1(\mathbf{x})$, to try? There are any number of ways: Linear Programming techniques; a relaxation method; some sort of energy minimization.

IV. The similarity metric. This ties in with the Search Strategy. When comparing the new transformation with the old, we need to quantify the differences between the geometrically transformed source image with the target image. That is, we need to measure how well $f(\mathbf{x})$ compares with $g(T(\mathbf{x}))$. Using mean-squared error might be the suitable choice. Or perhaps correlation is the key. Our choice will depend on many factors, such as whether or not the two images are of the same modality.

So once these choices are made, our search for an optimal transformation, one that aligns the source image with the target, continues until we find one that makes us happy.

3. A Potpourri of Methods

Given the content in Section 2, the reader can well believe that there are a multitude of registration methods possible, each resulting from a particular choice of feature and search spaces, search strategy, and similarity metric But always bear in mind that there is no single *right* registration algorithm. Each technique has its own strengths and weaknesses. It all depends on what *you* want.

Very broadly speaking, registration techniques may be divided into two categories, *rigid* and *nonrigid*. Some examples of Rigid registration techniques include: Principal Axes [2], Correlation-based methods [12], Cubic B-Splines [37], and Procrustes [19; 34]. For Non-Rigid techniques, there are Spline Warps [9], Viscous Fluid Models [13], and Optic Flow Fields [30].

The survey articles [11; 38] mentioned previously go into some of these techniques in greater depth. Now, to begin our "If it's Tuesday, this must be Belgium" tour of MR image registration techniques.

3.1. Principal Axes. We begin with the Principal Axes algorithm (e.g., see [2]). To summarize its properties, based on the classification scheme of Section 2.1, the feature space the algorithm acts upon effectively consists of the features of the images, such as edges, corners, and the like. The search space consists of global translations and rotations. The search strategy is not so much a "search," as we are finding the closed formed solution based on the eigenvalue decomposition of a certain covariance matrix. The similarity metric is the variance of the projection of the feature's location vector onto the principal axis.

The algorithm is based on the straightforward and powerful observation that the head is shaped like an ellipse/ellipsoid (depending on the dimension). For purposes of image registration, the critical features of an ellipse are its center of mass, and principal orientations, i.e., major and minor axes. Using these properties, one can derive a straightforward alignment algorithm which can automatically and quickly determine a rotation + translation that aligns the source image to the target.

Let I denote the 2-D array representing an image, with pixel intensity $I(x, y)$ at location (x, y). The center of mass, or centroid, is

$$\hat{x} = \frac{\sum_{x,y} x\, I(x, y)}{\sum_{x,y} I(x, y)} \qquad \hat{y} = \frac{\sum_{x,y} y\, I(x, y)}{\sum_{x,y} I(x, y)}.$$

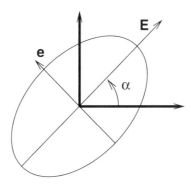

Figure 3. Principal axes. The eigenvectors $\mathbf{E}$ and $\mathbf{e}$, corresponding to the largest and smallest eigenvalues, respectively, indicate the directions of the major and minor axes, respectively.

With the centroid in hand, we form the covariance matrix

$$\mathbf{C} = \begin{pmatrix} c_{11} & c_{12} \\ c_{21} & c_{22} \end{pmatrix},$$

where

$$c_{11} = \sum_{x,y} (x - \hat{x})^2 \, I(x, y),$$

$$c_{22} = \sum_{x,y} (y - \hat{y})^2 \, I(x, y),$$

$$c_{12} = \sum_{x,y} (x - \hat{x})(y - \hat{y}) \, I(x, y),$$

$$c_{21} = c_{12}.$$

The eigenvectors of $\mathbf{C}$ corresponding to the largest and smallest eigenvalues indicate the direction of the major and minor axes of the ellipse, respectively. See Figure 3.

The principal axes algorithm may be described as follows. First, calculate the centroid, and eigenvectors of the source and target images via an eigenvalue decomposition of the covariance matrices. Next, align the centers of mass via a translation. Next, for each image determine the angle α (Figure 3) the maximal eigenvector forms with the horizontal axis, and rotate the test image about its center by the difference in angles. The images are now aligned.

Figure 4 shows the procedure in action. In this example, the target image is a rotated version of the source image, with a small block missing. Subtracting the target from the aligned source renders the missing data quite apparent.

While the principal axes algorithm is easy to implement, it does have the shortcoming that it is sensitive to missing data. As an exaggerated example, suppose the target MR image covers the entire head, while the source MR image has only the top half, say from the eyes on up. In this case, the anatomical

Source   Target   Difference

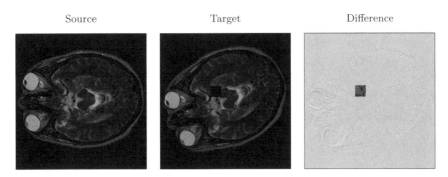

Figure 4. Principal axes: aligning axial images. The difference between the aligned source and target images is easily apparent in the far right panel.

feature located at the centroid of the source image will differ from the anatomical feature located at the centroid of the target. However, be that as it may, one can certainly use the algorithm to provide a coarse approximation to "truth." That is, one may use rotation + translation parameters as "seed" values for more accurate methods.

3.2. Fourier-based correlation. Fourier-based Correlation is another method for performing rigid alignment of images. The feature space it uses consists of all the pixels in the image, and its search space covers all global translations and rotations. (It can also be used to find local translations and rotations [31].) As the name implies, the search strategy are the *closed form* Fourier-based methods, and the similarity metric is correlation, and its variants, e.g., phase only correlation [12]. As with Principal Axes, it is an automatic procedure by which two images may be rigidly aligned. Furthermore, it is an efficient algorithm, courtesy of the FFT [12].

The algorithm may be described as follows. Let $f(x,y)$ and $g(x,y)$ denote the source and target images, respectively. Uppercase letters will denote the function's Fourier transform (FT):

$$f(x,y) \overset{\text{FT}}{\Longleftrightarrow} F(\omega_x, \omega_y), \qquad g(x,y) \overset{\text{FT}}{\Longleftrightarrow} G(\omega_x, \omega_y).$$

To clarify, (x,y) denote coordinates in the spatial domain, and (ω_x, ω_y) denote coordinates in the frequency domain. Suppose the source and target are related by a translation (a,b) and rotation θ:

$$f(x,y) = g\big((x\cos\theta + y\sin\theta) - a, \, (-x\sin\theta + y\cos\theta) - b\big).$$

Then, using properties of the Fourier transform, we have

$$F(\omega_x, \omega_y) = e^{-i(a\,\omega_x + b\,\omega_y)} G(\omega_x\cos\theta + \omega_y\sin\theta, \, -\omega_x\sin\theta + \omega_y\cos\theta).$$

By taking norms and obtaining the power spectrum, all evidence of translation by (a,b) has disappeared:

$$\big|F(\omega_x,\omega_y)\big|^2 = \big|G(\omega_x\cos\theta + \omega_y\sin\theta, \, -\omega_x\sin\theta + \omega_y\cos\theta)\big|^2.$$

Power Spectrum

cartesian coordinates   polar coordinates

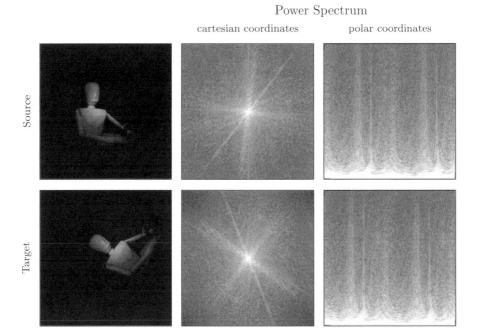

Figure 5. By considering the power spectra, translations vanish. Furthermore, in polar coordinates, rotations become translations.

Note that rotating $g(x, y)$ by θ in the spatial domain is equivalent to rotating $|G(\omega_x, \omega_y)|^2$ by that amount in the frequency domain. By switching to polar coordinates (setting $x = r \cos \psi$, $y = r \sin \psi$), we have

$$|F(r, \psi)|^2 = |G(r, \psi - \theta)|^2$$

and hence rotation in the cartesian plane becomes translation in the polar plane. See Figure 5.

We are now in a position to give an outline for the Fourier-based correlation method of image registration:

1. Take the discrete Fourier transform of the source image $f(x)$ and target image $g(x)$.

2. Next, send the power spectra to polar coordinates land:

$$|F(r, \psi)|^2 = |G(r, \psi - \theta)|^2.$$

3. Use your favourite correlation technique to determine the rotation angle. (Note that this is strictly a *translation* problem.) And then rotate the source image (which is in the spatial domain) by that amount.

4. Use your favourite correlation to now determine the translation amount in the spatial domain, between the (so far) only-rotated source image, and the target image.

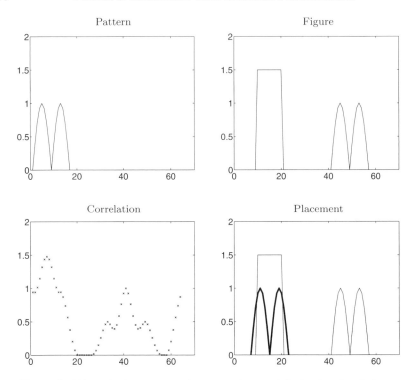

Figure 6. We seek the pattern, shown on the top left, in the signal shown on the top right. In the lower left, we plot the correlation values. The location of the maximum value should indicate the location of the pattern within the signal, but as we see in the lower right figure, placing the pattern, drawn in a thick line, at this "maximum" location is incorrect.

Given how easy and direct the algorithm is, it would come as a surprise if there were *not* any caveats associated with it.

In practice, the source and target images are probably not exactly identical. This could easily result in multiple peaks, which means that the maximum peak may not be the correct one. This phenomenon is illustrated in Figure 6. Therefore, when using correlation to determine the proper rotation and translation parameters, several potential sets of parameters, e.g., corresponding to the 4 largest correlation peaks, need to be tried. The best (in some sense, e.g., least-squares) is the value you choose. Secondly, the images certainly should be of the same modality. Registering an MR with a PET image probably won't work at all!

But on the bright side, along with computation efficiency, one can apply the technique to subregions of images and "glue" the results together. For example, one can divide the images into quarters, determine rotation and translation parameters for each, all independent of each other, and then smoothly apply these four sets of parameters, to encompass a complete (and non-rigid) registration of the source to target image [31]. Also, as with Principal Axes, Fourier-based correlation may be used to achieve coarse registrations, as starting points for fancier methods.

3.3. Procrustes algorithm. The Procrustes Algorithm [19; 34] is an image registration algorithm that depends on the active participation of the user. It does have as its inspiration a rather colourful character from Greek mythology. Especially for this reason, we feel compelled to briefly mention it.

It is a "one size fits all" algorithm: one image is compelled to fit another. The name is most appropriate for this algorithm. Procrustes is a character from Greek mythology. He was an innkeeper who guaranteed all his beds were the correct length for his guests. "The top of your head will be at precisely the top edge of the bed. Similarly the soles of your feet will be at the bottom edge." And for his (unfortunate) guests of varying heights, they were. Procrustes would employ some rather gruesome measures to make his claim true. Ouch.

As already mentioned, the algorithm depends on human intervention. Quite simply, the user identifies common features or *landmarks* in the images (so this is the feature space) and, by rigid rotation and translation (the search space), forces a registration that respects these landmarks. In a perfect world, to determine the proper rotation and translation parameters, three pairs of landmarks would suffice. The rotation parameters place the images in the same orientation, the translation parameters, well, translate the images into alignment.

But we do not inhabit a perfect world. The slightest variation in distance between any homologous pair represents an error in landmark identification which cannot be reconciled with rigid body motions. And so we need to compromise. (Procrustes would have difficulty understanding this. While his enthusiasm for achieving a perfect fit is admirable, it could result in some uncomfortable side effects for the patients.) Lacking a perfect match, the similarity metric employed is instead the mean squared distance between homologous landmarks when computing the six rigid body parameters. The search strategy is to minimize via least-squares.

The good news is that this can be accomplished efficiently. A closed form solution exists, in fact. However, the not so good news is that it depends on the accurate identification of landmarks. If you say that the anatomical feature at Point A_1 in source image A really corresponds with the anatomical feature at Point B_1 in the target image B, you had better be right. And being right takes time, especially since the slightest deviation is a source of error.

3.4. AIR: automated image registration. AIR is a sophisticated and powerful image registration algorithm. Developed by Woods et al [41; 42; 43], the feature space it uses consists of all the pixels in the image, and the search space consists of up to fifth-order polynomials in spatial coordinates x, y (and z, if 3-D), involving as many as 168 parameters. The goal is to define a single, global transformation. We outline some of AIR's characteristics:

- AIR is a fully automated algorithm.
- Unlike the algorithms so far discussed, AIR can be used in *multi-modal* situations.
- AIR does not depend on landmark identification.
- AIR uses overall *similarity* between images.
- AIR is iterative.

It is a robust and versatile algorithm. The fact that AIR software is publicly available [1] has only added to its widespread use.

AIR is based on the following assumption. If two images, acquired the same way (i.e., same modality) are perfectly aligned, then the *ratio* of one image to another, on a pixel by pixel basis, ought to be fairly uniform across voxels. If registration is not spot on correct, then there would be a substantial degree of nonuniformity in ratios. Ergo, to register the two images, compute the standard deviation of the ratio, and *minimize it*. This error function is called the "ratio of image uniformity", or RIU. The algorithm's search strategy is based on gradient descent, and the similarity metric is actually a normalized version of the RIU between the two volumes. An iterative procedure is used to minimize the normalized RIU in which the registration parameters (three rotation and three translation terms) with the largest partial derivative is adjusted in each iteration [41].

Since we are dealing with ratios and not pixel intensities themselves, it is this idea of using the ratios to register images which provides us with the flexibility to align images of different modalities.

Suppose we are in the situation where we want to align an MR to a PET image. On the face of it, the ratios will not be uniform across the images. Different tissue types will have different ratios. However, and this is key, *within* a given tissue type, the ratio ought to be fairly uniform when the images are registered. Therefore, what you want to do is maximize the uniformity within the tissue type, where the tissue-typing is based on the MRI voxel intensity. This requires two modifications of the original algorithm [43]. First, one has to manually edit the scalp, skull and meninges from the MR image since these features are not present in the PET image. The second modification consists of first performing a histogram matching. Denote the two images to be histogram matched as $f_1(\cdot)$ and $f_2(\cdot)$, and $c_2(\cdot)$ as the sampled cumulative distribution function of image $f_2(\cdot)$. The histogram of $f_2(\cdot)$ is made to match that of $f_1(\cdot)$ by mapping each pixel $f_1(x, y)$ to $c_2(f_1(x, y))$, between the MR and PET images (with 256 bins), followed by a segmentation of the images according to the 256 bin values. Each of the segmented MR and PET images (with corresponding bin values) are then registered separately.

In terms of implementation, both the within-modality and cross-modality versions of the algorithm, the registration is performed on sub-sampled images, in decreasing order of sub-sampling.

There are a number of things to keep in mind. AIR's global approach implies the transformation will be consistent throughout the entire image volume. However, this does introduce the possibility of obtaining an unstable transformation, especially near the image boundaries. And small and/or local perturbations may result in disproportionate changes in the global transformation. And the AIR algorithm is also computationally intensive. It is not easy, after all, to minimize the standard deviation of the ratios. However, the algorithm does perform well with noisy data [36].

3.5. Mutual information based techniques. Mutual Information [39] is an error metric (or similarity metric) used in image registration based on ideas from Information Theory. Mutual Information uses the pixel intensities themselves. The strategy is this: minimize the information content of the *difference image*, i.e., the content of target-source.

Consider Figure 7. The particular example is a bit of a cheat, but it illustrates the point. In the top row we have two axial images. They are the source

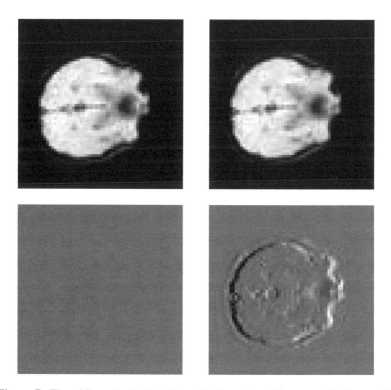

Figure 7. The philosophy behind Mutual Information. The source is the top left image, and the target is the top right. The difference image between the aligned source and target (lower left) looks nearly completely blank. Some structure might be vaguely visible, but not nearly as much as the difference image resulting translating the aligned source by 1 pixel (lower right).

and target images. The image on the lower left is the difference between the aligned source and target. Since the pixel intensities of the source and target are nearly identical, the difference image is basically blank. Now suppose we take the aligned source and translate it by one pixel. In the resulting difference image, the boundary of the skull is quite obvious. Whereas in the first difference image one has to "hunt" for features (and fail to find any), in the second we do not. Features stand out. So, in a sense, the second difference image has more information than that first: we see a shape. Mutual Information wants that difference image to have as little information as possible.

To go a little further, let us begin with the question: how well does one image explain, or "predict", another? We use a joint probability distribution. Let $p(a,b)$ denote the probability that a pixel value a in the source and b in the target occurs, for all a and b. We estimate the joint probability distribution by making a joint histogram of pixel values. When two images are in alignment, the corresponding anatomical area overlap, and hence there are lots of high values. In misalignment, anatomical areas are mixed up, e.g., brain over skin, and this results in a somewhat more dispersed joint histogram. See Figures 8 and 9.

What we want to do is make the "crispiest" joint probability distribution possible. Let $I(A,B)$ denote the *Mutual Information* of two images A and B. This can be defined in terms of the entropies (i.e., "How dispersed is the joint probability distribution?") $H(A)$, $H(B)$ and $H(A,B)$:

$$I(A,B) = H(A)+H(B)-H(A,B) = \sum_{x\in A,\, y\in B} p(x,y)\log_2\left(\frac{p(x,y)}{p(x)p(y)}\right).$$

Therefore, to *maximize* their mutual information $I(A,B)$, to get image A to tell us as much as possible about B, we need to *minimize* the entropy $H(A,B)$. The reader is encouraged to read the seminal paper by Viola et al. [39] for further information regarding exactly how the entropy $H(A,B)$ is minimized. In brief, [39] use a stochastic analog of the gradient descent technique to maximize $I(A,B)$, after first approximating the derivatives of the mutual information error measure. In order to obtain these derivatives, the probability density functions are approximated by a sum of Gaussians using the Parzen-window method [16] (after this approximation, the derivatives can be obtained analytically). The geometric distortion model used is global affine. In general, the various implementations differ in the minimization technique. For example, Collignon et al. [14] use Powell's method for the minimization.

In the final analysis, we find that Mutual Information is quite good in multimodal situations. However, it is computationally very expensive, as well as being sensitive to the how the interpolation is done, e.g., the minimum found may not be the correct/optimal one.

A functional image   Perfect alignment

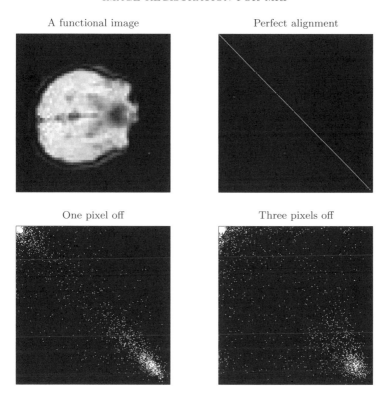

One pixel off   Three pixels off

Figure 8. Joint histograms of identical source and target images. No registration is necessary to align them. The resulting joint histogram is a diagonal line. Translating by 1 pixel significantly disperses the diagonal (lower left), and by 3 pixels, further still (lower right).

3.6. Optic flow fields. This registration technique [30] borrows tools from differential flow estimation. The underlying philosophical principle of the algorithm is that we want to *flow* from the source to the target. Think of an air bubble that is rising to the surface of a lake. The bubble's surface smoothly bends and flexes this way and that as it floats upward. The source and target images are two snapshots taken of the rising bubble. Starting from the two snapshots, the algorithm determines the deformations that occur when going from source to target. The source image is the bubble at $t = 0$, and the target image is the bubble at $t = 1$. What happened between 0 and 1 ?

The highlights of this technique are:

- The technique based on differential flow estimation.
- Idea: Want to *flow* from the source image to reference image.
- The procedure is fully automated.
- Uses an affine model.
- Allows for intensity variations between the source and target images.

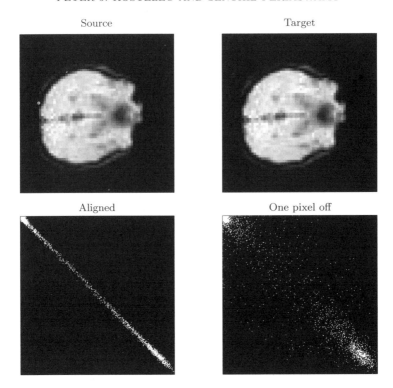

Figure 9. Joint histograms of different source and target images. While not strictly a diagonal line, the joint histogram of the aligned source and target images is relatively narrow (lower left). Translating by one pixel significantly disperses the diagonal (lower right).

Full details and results of the algorithm may be found in [30]. Since the model is very straightforward, we will delve a little deeper into this algorithm than we have so far with the previous algorithms discussed. It can be considered as an example of how, beginning with basic principles, a registration technique is born.

Our starting point is the general form of a 2-D affine transformation:

$$\begin{bmatrix} x_1 \\ y_1 \end{bmatrix} = \begin{bmatrix} m_1 & m_2 \\ m_3 & m_4 \end{bmatrix} \begin{bmatrix} x \\ y \end{bmatrix} + \begin{bmatrix} m_5 \\ m_6 \end{bmatrix}$$

where x, y denote spatial coordinates in the source image and x_1, y_1 denote spatial coordinates in the target. Depending on the values m_1, m_2, m_3 and m_4, certain well known geometric transformations can result (see Figure 10).

Now recall our description at the beginning of this section, that of a bubble rising through the water. We took two snapshots, one at $t = 0$, and one at $t = 1$, of the *same bubble*. Hence it is reasonable to have a single function, with temporal variable t, represent the bubble at time t.

With this in mind, let $f(x, y, t)$, $f(\hat{x}, \hat{y}, t-1)$ represent the source and target images, respectively. To further simplify the model, at least for the moment, we

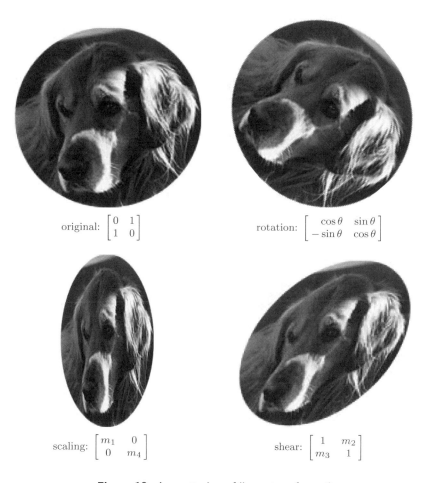

original: $\begin{bmatrix} 0 & 1 \\ 1 & 0 \end{bmatrix}$ rotation: $\begin{bmatrix} \cos\theta & \sin\theta \\ -\sin\theta & \cos\theta \end{bmatrix}$

scaling: $\begin{bmatrix} m_1 & 0 \\ 0 & m_4 \end{bmatrix}$ shear: $\begin{bmatrix} 1 & m_2 \\ m_3 & 1 \end{bmatrix}$

Figure 10. A smattering of linear transformations.

will make the "Brightness-Constancy" assumption: identical anatomical features in both images will have the same pixel intensity. That is, we are not allowing for the possibility that, say, the left eye in the MR source image to be brighter or darker than the left eye in the MR target image. Before tackling more difficult issues later, we want to ensure that only an affine transformation, and nothing else, is required to mold the source into the target.

Using the notation we have just introduced (which we will slightly abuse now), we have the situation:

$$f(x, y, t) = f(m_1 x + m_2 y + m_5, \ m_3 x + m_4 y + m_6, \ t - 1) \qquad (3\text{--}1)$$

We use a least squares approach to estimate the parameters $\vec{m} = (m_1 \ldots m_6)^T$ in (3–1). Now the function we *really* want to minimize is:

$$E(\vec{m}) = \sum_{x,y \in \Omega} \left(f(x,y,t) - f(m_1 x + m_2 y + m_5,\ m_3 x + m_4 y + m_6,\ t-1) \right)^2 \quad (3\text{–}2)$$

where Ω denotes the region of interest. However, the fact that $E(\vec{m})$ is not linear means that minimizing will be tricky. So we take an easy way out and instead take its truncated, first-order Taylor series expansion. Letting

$$k = f_t + x f_x + y f_y,$$
$$\vec{c} = (x f_x \quad y f_x \quad x f_y \quad y f_y \quad f_x \quad f_y)^T, \quad (3\text{–}3)$$

where the subscripts denote partial derivatives, we eventually arrive at this much more reasonable error function:

$$E(\vec{m}) = \sum_{x,y \in \Omega} \left(k - \vec{c}^T \vec{m} \right)^2. \quad (3\text{–}4)$$

To minimize (3–4), we differentiate with respect to $\vec{m}$:

$$\frac{dE}{d\vec{m}} = \sum_{\Omega} -2\vec{c} \left(k - \vec{c}^T \vec{m} \right),$$

set equal to 0, and solve for the model parameters to obtain:

$$\vec{m} = \left(\sum_{\Omega} \vec{c}\,\vec{c}^T \right)^{-1} \left(\sum_{\Omega} \vec{c} k \right). \quad (3\text{–}5)$$

And lo! we have determined $\vec{m}$. However, there is a caveat. We are assuming that the 6×6 matrix $\left(\sum_{\Omega} \vec{c}\,\vec{c}^T \right)$ in (3–5) is, in fact, invertible. We can usually guarantee this by making sure that the spatial region Ω is large enough to have sufficient image content, e.g., we would want some "interesting" features in Ω like edges, and not simply a "bland" area. The parameters $\vec{m}$ are for the region Ω.

In terms of actually implementation, the parameters $\vec{m}$ are estimated locally, for different spatial neighborhoods. By applying this algorithm in a multi-scale fashion, it is possible to capture large motions. (See [30] for details.) This is illustrated in Figure 11, in the case where the target image is a synthetically warped version of the source image.

Editorial. As an aside, we mention that doing an experiment such as this, registering an image with a warped version of itself is not altogether silly. If an algorithm being developed fails in an ideal test case such as this, chances are very good that it will fail for genuinely different images. However, to make a "fair" ideal test, the method of warping the image should be independent of the registration method. For example, if the registration algorithm is to determine an affine transform, do not warp the image using an affine transform. Use some other method, e.g., apply Bookstein's thin-plate splines [9].

Source   Target   Registered result

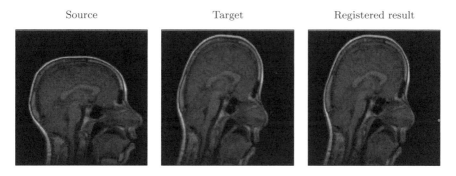

Figure 11. Flowing from source to target: An "ideal" experiment.

The optic flow model can next be modified to account for differences of contrast and brightness between the two images with the addition of two new parameters, m_7 for contrast, and m_8 for brightness. The new version of (3–1) is

$$m_7 f(x, y, t) + m_8 = f(m_1 x + m_2 y + m_5, m_3 x + m_4 y + m_6, t - 1). \qquad (3\text{–}6)$$

We are also assuming that, in addition to the affine parameters, the brightness and contrast parameters are constant within small spatial neighborhoods.

Minimizing the least squares error as before, using a first-order Taylor series expansion, gives a solution identical in form to (3–5) except that this time

$$\begin{aligned} k &= f_t - f + x f_x + y f_y, \\ \vec{c} &= (x f_x \quad y f_x \quad x f_y \quad y f_y \quad f_x \quad f_y \quad -f \quad -1)^T; \end{aligned} \qquad (3\text{–}7)$$

compare equations (3–3).

Now, we have been working under the assumption that the affine and contrast/brightness parameters are constant within some small spatial neighborhood. This introduces two conflicting conditions.

Recall $\left(\sum_\Omega \vec{c}\,\vec{c}^T\right)$. This matrix needs to have an inverse. As was mentioned earlier, this can be arranged by considering a large enough region Ω, i.e., a region with sufficient image content. However, the larger the area, the *less* likely it is that the brightness constancy assumption holds. Think about it: image content can be edges, and edges can have very different intensities, when compared with surrounding tissue.

Fortunately, the model can be modified one more time. Instead of a single error function (3–4), we can instead consider the sum of *two* errors:

$$E(\vec{m}) = E_b(\vec{m}) + E_s(\vec{m}) \qquad (3\text{–}8)$$

where

$$E_b(\vec{m}) = \left(k - \vec{c}^T \vec{m}\right)^2$$

Source   Target   Registered result

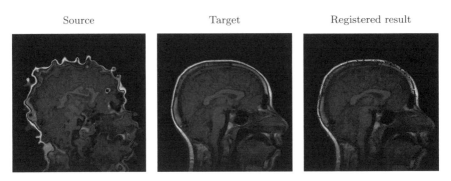

Figure 12. Registering an excessively distorted source image to a target image.

with k and $\vec{c}$ defined as in (3–7) and (**??**), and

$$E_s(\vec{m}) = \sum_{i=1}^{8} \lambda_i \left(\left(\frac{\partial m_i}{\partial x} \right)^2 + \left(\frac{\partial m_i}{\partial y} \right)^2 \right),$$

where λ_i is a positive constant, set by the user, that weights the smoothness constraint imposed on m_i.

As before, one works with Taylor series expansions of (3–8), but things become a little more complicated. Complete details of how to work with (3–8), as well with generalizations to 3-D, may be found in [30]. Some results are shown in Figures 12-13.

4. Conclusion

We have presented a whirlwind introduction to image registration for MRI. After providing a theoretical framework by which the problem is defined, we presented, in no particular order, a number of different algorithms. We then provided a more detailed discussion of an algorithm based on the idea of optic flow fields.

Our intent in this paper was to illustrate how the problem of image registration can have a wide variety of very dissimilar solutions. And there exist many more techniques than those presented here. For example, image features that some of these methods depend upon include surfaces [28; 15; 17], edges [27; 21], and contours [26; 35]. There are also methods based on B-splines [37; 22; 33], thin-plate splines [9; 10], and low-frequency discrete cosine basis functions [3; 4].

There are many survey articles the reader may wish to read, to learn more about medical image registration, In addition to those cited earlier ([11; 38]), we also call attention to [25; 24; 23; 40]. The simple existence of so many techniques provides more than sufficient support for the thesis that there are many paths to the One Truth: perfect image alignment.

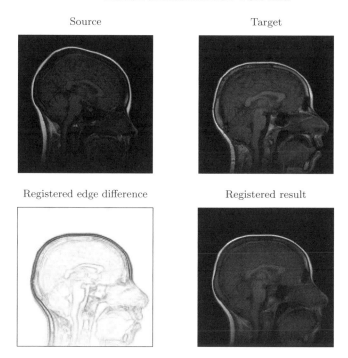

Figure 13. Registering two different clinical images. The lower left image shows how the edges of the registered source compare with the target's edges. The lower right image shows the registered source itself, after it has undergone both geometric *and* intensity-correction transformations.

References

[1] The homepage for the AIR ("Automated Image Registration") software package is http://bishopw.loni.ucla.edu/AIR5/.

[2] N. Alpert, J. Bradshaw, D. Kennedy, and J. Correia, The principal axes transformation: a method for image registration, *J. Nuclear Medicine* **31** (1990), 1717–1722.

[3] J. Ashburner and K. J. Friston, Multimodal image coregistration and partitioning: a unified framework, *NeuroImage* **6**:3 (1997), 209–217.

[4] J. Ashburner, P. Neelin, D. L. Collins, A. C. Evans and K. J. Friston, Incorporating prior knowledge into image registration, *NeuroImage* **6** (1997), 344–352.

[5] Peter A. Bandettini, Eric C. Wong, R. Scott Hinks, Ronald S. Tikofsky, and James S. Hyde, Time course EPI of human brain function during task activation, *Magnetic Resonance in Medicine* **25** (1992), 390–397.

[6] P. A. Bandettini, E. C. Wong, J. R. Binder, S. M. Rao, A. Jesmanowicz, E. Aaron, T. Lowry, H. Forster, R. S. Hinks, J. S. Hyde, Functional MRI using the BOLD approach: Dynamics and data analysis techniques, pp. 335–349 in *Perfusion and Diffusion: Magnetic Resonance Imaging*, edited by D. LeBihan and B. Rosen, Raven Press, New York, 1995.

[7] M. Betke, H. Hong, and J. P. Ko, Automatic 3D registration of lung surfaces in computed tomography scans, pp. 725–733 *Fourth International Conference on Medical*

Image Computing and Computer-Assisted Intervention, Utrecht, The Netherlands, October 2001.

[8] Amanda Bischoff-Grethe, Shawnette M. Proper, Hui Mao, Karen A. Daniels, and Gregory S. Berns, Conscious and unconscious processing of nonverbal predictability in Wernicke's Area, *Journal of Neuroscience* **20**:5 (March 2000), 1975–1981.

[9] F. L. Bookstein, Principal Warps: Thin-plate splines and the decomposition of deformations, *IEEE Transactions on Pattern Analysis and Machine Intelligence*, **11**:6 (June 1989), 567–585.

[10] F. L. Bookstein, Thing-plate splines and the atlas problem for biomedical images, *Information Processing in Medical Imaging*, July 1991, 326–342.

[11] Leslie G. Brown, A Survey of Image Registration Techniques, *ACM Computing Surveys*, **24**:4 (December 1992), 325–376.

[12] E. D. Castro and C. Morandi, Registration of translated and rotated images using finite Fourier transforms, *IEEE Trans. Pattern Anal. Mach. Intell.*, **PAMI-9** (1987), 700–703.

[13] G.E. Christensen, R.D. Rabbit, and M.I. Miller, A deformable neuroanatomy textbook based on viscous fluid mechanics, pp. 211–216 in *Proceedings of the 1993 Conference on Information Sciences and Systems*, Johns Hopkins University, March 1995.

[14] A. Collignon and F. Maes and D. Delaere and D. Vandermeulen, P. Suetens and G. Marchal, Automated multimodality image registration using information theory, pp. 263–274 in *Information Processing in Medical Imaging*, edited by Y. Bizais, C. Barillot, and R. Di Paolo, Kluwer, Dordrecht, 1995.

[15] A. M. Dale, B. Fischl, and M. I. Sereno, Cortical surface-based analysis, I: Segmentation and surface reconstruction, *NeuroImage* **9**:2 (Feb 1999), 179–194.

[16] R. O. Duda and P.E. Hart, *Pattern classification and scene analysis*, Wiley, New York, 1973.

[17] B. Fischl, M. I. Sereno, and A. M. Dale, Cortical surface-based analysis, II: Inflation, flattening, and a surface-based coordinate system, *NeuroImage* **9**:2 (Feb. 1999), 195–207.

[18] R. S. J. Frackowiak, K. J. Friston, C. D. Frith, R. J. Dolan, and J. C. Mazziotta, *Human Brain Function*, Academic Press, San Diego, 1997.

[19] J. R. Hurley and R. B. Cattell, The PROCRUSTES program: Producing direct rotation to test a hypothesized factor structure, *Behav. Sci.* **7** (1962), 258–262.

[20] P. Janata, B. Tillman, and J. J. Bharucha, Listening to polyphonic music recruits domain-general attention and working memory circuits, *Cognitive, Affective, and Behavioral Neuroscience*, **2**:2 (2002), 121–140.

[21] W. S. Kerwin and C. Yuan, Active edge maps for medical image registration, pp. 516–526 in *Proceedings of SPIE – The International Society for Optical Engineering*, July 2001.

[22] P. J. Kostelec, J. B. Weaver, and D. M. Healy, Jr., Multiresolution Elastic Image Registration, *Medical Physics*, **25**:9 (1998), 1593–1604.

[23] H. Lester and S. Arridge, A Survey of Hierarchical Non-linear Medical Imaging Registration, *Pattern Recognition* **32**:1 (1999), 129–149.

[24] J. B. Antoine Maintz and Max A. Viergever, A Survey of Medical Image Registration, *Medical Image Analysis* **2**:1 (1998), 1–36.

[25] C. R. Maurer Jr. and J. M. Fitzpatrick, A Review of Medical Image Registration, chapter in *Interactive Image-Guided Neurosurgery*, American Association of Neurological Surgeons, Park Ridge, IL, 1993.

[26] G. Medioni and R. Nevatia, Matching images using linear features, *IEEE Trans. Pattern Anal. Mach. Intell.* **6**:6 (Nov. 1984), 675–685.

[27] M. L. Nack, Rectification and registration of digital images and the effect of cloud detection, pp. 12–23 in *Machine Processing of Remotely Sensed Data*, West Lafayette, IN, June 1977.

[28] C. A. Pelizarri, G. T. Y. Chen, D. R. Spelbring, R. R. Weichselbaum, and C. T. Chen, Accurate three-dimensional registration of CT, PET and/or MR images of the brain, *J. Computer Assisted Tomography*, **13**:1 (1989), 20–26.

[29] Senthil Periaswamy, www.cs.dartmouth.edu/~sp.

[30] Senthil Periaswamy and Hany Farid, Elastic registration in the presence of intensity variations, to appear in *IEEE Transactions in Medical Imaging*.

[31] S. Periaswamy, J. B. Weaver, D. M. Healy, Jr., and P. J. Kostelec, Automated multiscale elastic image registration using correlation, pp. 828–838 in *Proceedings of the SPIE – The International Society for Optical Engineering* **3661**, 1999.

[32] William K. Pratt, *Digital signal processing*, Wiley, New York, 1991.

[33] D. Rueckert, L. I. Sonoda, C. Hayes, D. L. G. Hill, M. O. Leach, and D. J. Hawkes, Non-rigid registration using free-form deformations: Application to breast MR images, *IEEE Trans. Medical Imaging*, **18**:8 (August 1999), 712–721.

[34] P. H. Schonemann, A generalized solution of the orthogonal Procrustes problem, *Psychometrika*, **31**:1 (1966), 1–10.

[35] Wen-Shiang V. Shih, Wei-Chung Lin, and Chin-Tu Chen, Contour-model-guided nonlinear deformation model for intersubject image registration, pp. 611–620 in *Proceedings of SPIE - The International Society for Optical Engineering* **3034**, April 1997.

[36] Arthur W. Toga and John C. Mazziotta (eds.), *Brain mapping: the methods*, Academic Press, San Diego, 1996.

[37] M. Unser, A. Aldroubi and C. Gerfen, A multiresolution image registration procedure using spline pyramids, pp. 160–170 *Proceedings of the SPIE – Mathematical Imaging: Wavelets and Applications in Signal and Image Processing* **2034**, 1993.

[38] P. A. Van den Elsen, E. J. D. Pol, M. A. Viergever, Medical Image Matching - a review with classification, *IEEE Engineering in Medicine and Biology* **12**:1 (1993), 26–39,

[39] P. Viola and W. M. Wells, III, Alignment by maximization of mutual information, pp. 16–23 in *International Conf. on Computer Vision*, IEEE Computer Society Press, 1995.

[40] J. West, J. Fitzpatrick, M. Wang, B. Dawant, C. Maurer, R. Kessler, and R. Maciunas, Comparison and evaluation of retrospective intermodality image registration techniques, pp. 332–347 *Proceedings of the SPIE - The International Society for Optical Engineering*, Newport Beach, CA., 1996.

[41] R. P. Woods, S. R. Cherry, and J. C. Mazziotta, Rapid automated algorithm for alignment and reslicing PET images, *J. Computer Assisted Tomography* **16** (1992), 620–633.

[42] R. P. Woods, S. T. Grafton, C. J. Holmes, S. R. Cherry, and J. C. Mazziotta, Automated image registration, I: General methods and intrasubject, intramodality validation, *J. Computer Assisted Tomography* **22** (1998), 141–154.

[43] R. P. Woods, J. C. Mazziotta, and S. R. Cherry, MRI-PET registration with automated algorithm, *J. Comp. Assisted Tomography*, **17**:4 (1993) 536–546.

PETER J. KOSTELEC
DEPARTMENT OF MATHEMATICS
DARTMOUTH COLLEGE
HANOVER, NH 03755
UNITED STATES
geelong@cs.dartmouth.edu

SENTHIL PERIASWAMY
DEPARTMENT OF COMPUTER SCIENCE
DARTMOUTH COLLEGE
HANOVER, NH 03755
UNITED STATES
sp@cs.dartmouth.edu

Modern Signal Processing
MSRI Publications
Volume **46**, 2003

Image Compression:
The Mathematics of JPEG 2000

JIN LI

ABSTRACT. We briefly review the mathematics in the coding engine of
JPEG 2000, a state-of-the-art image compression system. We focus in
depth on the transform, entropy coding and bitstream assembler modules.
Our goal is to present a general overview of the mathematics underlying a
state of the art scalable image compression technology.

1. Introduction

Data compression is a process that creates a compact data representation
from a raw data source, usually with an end goal of facilitating storage or transmission. Broadly speaking, compression takes two forms, either *lossless* or *lossy*,
depending on whether or not it is possible to reconstruct exactly the original
datastream from its compressed version. For example, a data stream that consists of long runs of 0s and 1s (such as that generated by a black and white
fax) would possibly benefit from simple *run-length encoding*, a lossless technique
replacing the original datastream by a sequence of counts of the lengths of the
alternating substrings of 0s and 1s. Lossless compression is necessary for situations in which changing a single bit can have catastrophic effects, such as in
machine code of a computer program.

While it might seem as though we should always demand lossless compression, there are in fact many venues where exact reproduction is unnecessary. In
particular, media compression, which we define to be the compression of image, audio, or video files, presents an excellent opportunity for lossy techniques.
For example, not one among us would be able to distinguish between two images
which differ in only one of the 2^{29} bits in a typical 1024×1024 color image. Thus
distortion is tolerable in media compression, and it is the content, rather than

Keywords: Image compression, JPEG 2000, transform, wavelet, entropy coder, subbitplane
entropy coder, bitstream assembler.

the exact bits, that is of paramount importance. Moroever, the size of the original media is usually very large, so that it is essential to achieve a considerably high *compression ratio* (defined to be the ratio of the size of the original data file to the size of its compressed version). This is achieved by taking advantage of *psychophysics* (say by ignoring less perceptible details of the media) and by the use of *entropy coding*, the exploitation of various information redundancies that may exist in the source data.

Conventional media compression solutions focus on a static or one-time form of compression — i.e., the compressed bitstream provides a static representation of the source data that makes possible a unique reconstruction of the source, whose characteristics are quantified by a compression ratio determined at the time of encoding. Implicit in this approach is the notion of a "one shoe fits all" technique, an outcome that would appear to be variance with the multiplicity of reconstruction platforms upon which the media will ultimately reside. Often, different applications may have different requirements for the compression ratio as well as tolerating various levels of compression distortion. A publishing application may require a compression scheme with very little distortion, while a web application may tolerate relatively large distortion in exchange for smaller compressed media.

Recently *scalable compression* has emerged as a category of media compression algorithms capable of trading between compression ratio and distortion *after* generating an initially compressed *master bitstream*. Subsets of the master then may be extracted to form particular *application bitstreams* which may exhibit a variety of compression ratios. (I.e., working from the master bitstream we can achieve a range of compressions, with the concomitant ability to reconstruct coarse to fine scale characteristics.) With scalable compression, compressed media can be tailored effortlessly for applications with vastly different compression ratio and quality requirements, a property which is particularly valuable in media storage and transmission.

In what follows, we restrict our attention to image compression, in particular, focusing on the *JPEG 2000 image compression standard*, and thereby illustrate the mathematical underpinnings of a modern scalable media compression algorithm. The paper is organized as follows. The basic concepts of the scalable image compression and its applications are discussed in Section 2. JPEG 2000 and its development history are briefly reviewed in Section 3. The transform, quantization, entropy coding, and bitstream assembler modules are examined in detail in Sections 4 to 7. Readers interested in further details may refer to [1; 2; 3].

2. Image Compression

Digital images are used every day. A digital image is essentially a 2D data array $x(i,j)$, where i and j index the row and column of the data array, and

$x(i,j)$ is referred to as a pixel. Gray-scale images assign to each pixel a single scalar intensity value G, whereas color images traditionally assign to each pixel a *color vector* (R, G, B), which represent the intensity of the red, green, and blue components, respectively. Because it is the content of the digital image that matters, the underlying 2D data array may undergo big changes while still conveying the content to the user with little or no perceptible distortion. An example is shown in Figure 1. On the left the classic image processing test case *Lena* is shown as a 512×512 grey-scale image. To the right of the original are several applications, each showing different sorts of compression. The first application illustrates the use of *subsampling* in order to fit a smaller image (in this case 256×256). The second application uses JPEG (the predecessor to JPEG 2000) to compress the image to a bitstream, and then decode the bitstream back to an image of size 512×512. Although in each case the underlying 2D data array is changed tremendously, the primary content of the image remains intelligible.

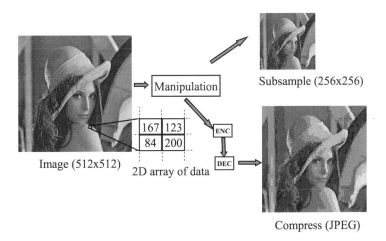

Figure 1. Souce digital image and compressions.

Each of the applications above results in a reduction in the amount of source image data. In this paper, we focus our attention on JPEG 2000, which is a next generation image compression standard. JPEG 2000 distinguishes itself from older generations of compression standards not only by virtue of its higher compression ratios, but also by its many new functionalities. The most noticeable among them is its scalability. From a compressed JPEG 2000 bitstream, it is possible to extract a subset of the bitstream that decodes to an image of variable quality and resolution (inversely correlated with its accompanying compression ratio), and/or variable spatial locality.

Scalable image compression has important applications in image storage and delivery. Consider the application of digital photography. Presently, digital cameras all use non-scalable image compression technologies, mainly JPEG. A camera with a fixed amount of the memory can accommodate a small number of high quality, high-resolution images, or a large number of low quality, low-resolution images. Unfortunately, the image quality and resolution must be determined before shooting the photos. This leads to the often painful trade-off between removing old photos to make space for new exciting shots, and shooting new photos of poorer quality and resolution. Scalable image compression makes possible the adjustment of image quality and resolution *after* the photo is shot, so that instead, the original digital photos always can be shot at the highest possible quality and resolution, and when the camera memory is filled to capacity, the compressed bitstream of existing shots may be truncated to smaller size to leave room for the upcoming shots. This need not be accomplished in a uniform fashion, with some photos kept with reduced resolution and quality, while others retain high resolution and quality. By dynamically trading between the number of images and the image quality, the use of precious camera memory is apportioned wisely.

Web browsing provides another important application of scalable image compression. As the resolution of digital cameras and digital scanners continues to increase, high-resolution digital imagery becomes a reality. While it is a pleasure to view a high-resolution image, for much of our web viewing we'd trade the resolution for speed of delivery. In the absence of scalable image compression technology it is common practice to generate multiple copies of the compressed bitstream, varying the spatial region, resolution and compression ratio, and put all copies on a web server in order to accommodate a variety of network situations. The multiple copies of a fixed media source file can cause data management headaches and waste valuable server space. Scalable compression techniques allow a single scalable master bitstream of the compressed image on the server to serve all purposes. During image browsing, the user may specify a region of interest (ROI) with a certain spatial and resolution constraint. The browser then only downloads a subset of the compressed media bitstream covering the current ROI, and the download can be performed in a progressive fashion so that a coarse view of the ROI can be rendered very quickly and then gradually refined as more and more bits arrive. Therefore, with scalable image compression, it is possible to browse large images quickly and on demand (see e.g., the Vmedia project [25]).

3. JPEG 2000

3.1. History. JPEG 2000 is the successor to JPEG. The acronym JPEG stands for Joint Photographic Experts Group. This is a group of image processing experts, nominated by national standard bodies and major companies to work to produce standards for continuous tone image coding. The official title of the committee is "ISO/IEC JTC1/SC29 Working Group 1", which often appears in the reference document. The JPEG members select a DCT based image compression algorithm in 1988, and while the original JPEG was quite successful, it became clear in the early 1990s that new wavelet-based image compression schemes such as CREW (compression with reversible embedded wavelets) [5] and EZW (embedded zerotree wavelets) [6] were surpassing JPEG in both performance and available features, such as scalability. It was time to begin to rethink the industry standard in order to incorporate these new mathematical advances.

Based on industrial demand, the JPEG 2000 research and development effort was initiated in 1996. A call for technical contributions was issued in March 1997 [17]. The first evaluation was performed in November 1997 in Sydney, Australia, where twenty-four algorithms were submitted and evaluated. Following the evaluation, it was decided to create a JPEG 2000 "verification model" (VM) which was a reference implementation (in document and in software) of the working standard. The first VM (VM0) is based on the wavelet/trellis coded quantization (WTCQ) algorithm submitted by SAIC and the University of Arizona (SAIC/UA) [18]. At the November 1998 meeting, the algorithm EBCOT (embedded block coding with optimized truncation) was adopted into VM3, and the entire VM software was re-implemented in an object-oriented manner. The document describing the basic JPEG 2000 decoder (part I) reached committee draft (CD) status in December 1999. JPEG 2000 finally became an international standard (IS) in December 2000.

3.2. JPEG. In order to understand JPEG 2000, it is instructive to revisit the original JPEG. As illustrated by Figure 2, JPEG is composed of a sequence of four main modules.

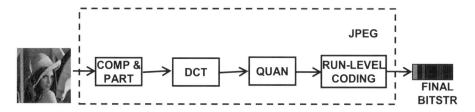

Figure 2. Operation flow of JPEG.

The first module (COMP & PART) performs *component and tile separation*, whose function is to cut the image into manageable chunks for processing. *Tile separation* is simply the separation of the image into spatially non-overlapping tiles of equal size. *Component separation* makes possible the decorrelation of color components. For example, a color image, in which each pixel is normally represented with three numbers indicating the levels of red, green and blue (RGB) may be transformed to LCrCb (luminance, chrominance red and chrominance blue) space.

After separation, each tile of each component is then processed separately according to a *discrete cosine transform* (DCT). This is closely related to the Fourier transform (see [30], for example). The coefficients are then *quantized*. Quantization takes the DCT coefficients (typically some sort of floating point number) and turns them into an integer. For example, simple rounding is a form of quantization. In the case of JPEG, we apply rounding plus a mask which applies a system of weights reflecting various psychoacoustic observations regarding human processing of images [31]. Finally, the coefficients are subjected to a form of *run-level encoding*, where the basic symbol is a run-length of zeros followed by a non-zero level, the combined symbol is then Huffman encoded.

3.3. Overview of JPEG 2000. Like JPEG, JPEG 2000 standardizes the decoder and the bitstream syntax. The operation flow of a typical JPEG 2000 encoder is shown in Figure 3.

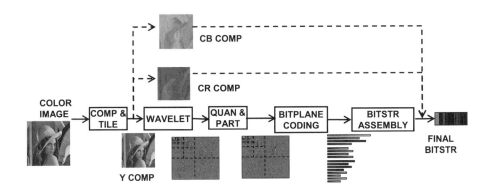

Figure 3. Flowchart for JPEG 2000.

We again start with a component and tile separation module. After this preprocessing, we now apply a *wavelet transform* which yields a sequence of *wavelet coefficients*. This is a key difference between JPEG and JPEG 2000 and we explain it in some detail in Section 4. We next quantize the wavelet coefficients which are then regrouped to facilitate localized spatial and resolution access, where by "resolution" we mean effectively the "degree" of the wavelet coefficient, as the wavelet decomposition is thought of as an expansion of the original data vector in terms of a basis which accounts for finer and finer detail, or increasing resolution. The degrees of resolution are organized into *subbands*, which are divided into non-overlapping rectangular blocks. Three spatially co-located rectangles (one from each subband at a given resolution level) form a *packet partition*. Each packet partition is further divided into *code-blocks*, each of which is compressed by a subbitplane coder into an *embedded bitstream* with a *rate-distortion curve* that records the distortion and rate at the end of each subbitplane. The embedded bitstream of the code-blocks are assembled into packets, each of which represents an increment in quality corresponding to one level of resolution at one spatial location. Collecting packets from all packet partitions of all resolution level of all tiles and all components, we form a layer that gives one increment in quality of the entire image at full resolution. The final JPEG 2000 bitstream may consist of multiple layers.

We summarize the main differences:

(1) **Transform module: wavelet versus DCT.** JPEG uses 8×8 discrete cosine transform (DCT), while JPEG 2000 uses a wavelet transform with lifting implementation (see Section 4.1). The wavelet transform provides not only better energy compaction (thus higher coding gain), but also the resolution scalability. Because the wavelet coefficients can be separated into different resolutions, it is feasible to extract a lower resolution image by using only the necessary wavelet coefficients.

(2) **Block partition: spatial domain versus wavelet domain.** JPEG partitions the image into 16×16 macroblocks in the space domain, and then applies the transform, quantization and entropy coding operation on each block separately. Since blocks are independently encoded, annoying blocking artifacts becomes noticeable whenever the coding rate is low. On the contrary, JPEG 2000 performs the partition operation in the wavelet domain. Coupled with the wavelet transform, there is no blocking artifact in JPEG 2000.

(3) **Entropy coding module: run-level coefficient coding versus bitplane coding.** JPEG encodes the DCT transform coefficients one by one. The resultant block bitstream can not be truncated. JPEG 2000 encodes the wavelet coefficients bitplane by bitplane (i.e., sending all zeroth order bits, then first order, etc. Details are in Section 4.3). The generated bitstream can be truncated at any point with graceful quality degradation. It is the bitplane entropy coder in JPEG 2000 that enables the bitstream scalability.

(4) **Rate control: quantization module versus bitstream assembly module.** In JPEG, the compression ratio and the amount of distortion is determined by the quantization module. In JPEG 2000, the quantization module simply converts the float coefficient of the wavelet transform module into an integer coefficient for further entropy coding. The compression ratio and distortion is determined by the bitstream assembly module. Thus, JPEG 2000 can manipulate the compressed bitstream, e.g., convert a compressed bitstream to a bitstream of higher compression ratio, form a new bitstream of lower resolution, form a new bitstream of a different spatial area, by operating only on the compressed bitstream and without going through the entropy coding and transform module. As a result, JPEG 2000 compressed bitstream can be reshaped (transcoded) very efficiently.

4. The Wavelet Transform

4.1. Introduction. Most existing high performance image coders in applications are *transform based coders*. In the transform coder, the image pixels are converted from the spatial domain to the transform domain through a linear orthogonal or bi-orthogonal transform. A good choice of transform accomplishes a decorrelation of the pixels, while simultaneously providing a representation in which most of the energy is usually restricted to a few (realtively large) coefficients. This is the key to achieving an efficient coding (i.e., high compression ratio). Indeed, since most of the energy rests in a few large transform coefficients, we may adopt entropy coding schemes, e.g., run-level coding or bitplane coding schemes, that easily locate those coefficients and encodes them. Because the transform coefficients are highly decorrelated, the subsequent quantizer and entropy coder can ignore the correlation among the transform coefficients, and model them as independent random variables.

The optimal transform (in terms of decorrelation) of an image block can be derived through the *Karhunen–Loeve (K-L) decomposition*. Here we model the pixels as a set of statistically dependent random variables, and the K-L basis is that which achieves a diagonalization of the (empirically determined) covariance matrix. This is equivalent to computing the SVD (singular value decomposition) of the covariance matrix (see [28] for a thorough description). However, the K-L transform lacks an efficient algorithm, and the transform basis is content dependent (in distinction, the Fourier transform, which uses the sampled exponentials, is not data dependent).

Popular transforms adopted in image coding include *block-based transforms*, such as the DCT, and wavelet transforms. The DCT (used in JPEG) has many well-known efficient implementations [26], and achieves good energy compaction as well as coefficient decorrelation. However, the DCT is calculated independently in spatially disjoint pixel blocks. Therefore, coding errors (i.e., lossy compression) can cause discontinuities between blocks, which in turn lead to annoying blocking artifacts. In contrary, the wavelet transform operates on the entire image (or a tile of a component in the case of large color image), which both gives better energy compaction than the DCT, and no post-coding blocking artifact. Moreover, the wavelet transform decomposes the image into an *L-level dyadic wavelet pyramid*. The output of an example 5-level dyadic wavelet pyramid is shown in Figure 4.

There is an obvious recursive structure generated by the following algorithm: lowpass and highpass filters (explained below, but for the moment, assume that these are convolution operators) are applied independently to both the rows and columns of the image. The output of these filters is then organized into four new 2D arrays of one half the size (in each dimension), yielding a LL (lowpass, lowpass) block, LH (lowpass, highpass), HL block and HH block. The algorithm is then applied recursively to the LL block, which is essentially a lower resolution

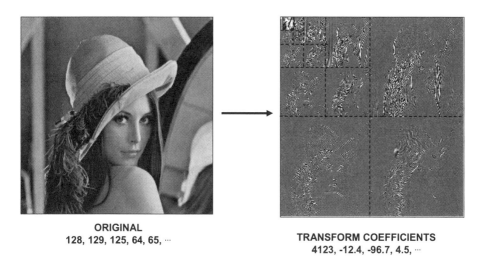

ORIGINAL
128, 129, 125, 64, 65, ⋯

TRANSFORM COEFFICIENTS
4123, -12.4, -96.7, 4.5, ⋯

Figure 4. A 5-level dyadic wavelet pyramid.

or smoothed version of the original. This output is organized as in Figure 4, with the southwest, southeast, and northeast quadrants of the various levels housing the LH, HH, and HL blocks respectively. We examine their structure as well as the algorithm in Sections 4.2 and 4.3. By not using the wavelet coefficients at the finest M levels, we can reconstruct an image that is 2^M times smaller in both the horizontal and vertical directions than the original one. The multiresolution nature (see [27], for example) of the wavelet transform is ideal for resolution scalability.

4.2. Wavelet transform by lifting. Wavelets yield a signal representation in which the low order (or lowpass) coefficients represent the most slowly changing data while the high order (highpass) coefficients represent more localized changes. It provides an elegant framework in which both short term anomaly and long term trend can be analyzed on an equal footing. For the theory of wavelet and multiresolution analysis, we refer the reader to [7; 8; 9].

We develop the framework of a one-dimensional wavelet transform using the z-transform formalism. In this setting a given (bi-infinite) discrete signal $x[n]$ is represented by the Laurent series $X(z)$ in which $x[n]$ is the coefficient of z^n. The z-transform of a FIR filter (*finite impulse response*, meaning Laurent series with a finite number of nonzero coefficients, and thus a Laurent polynomial) $H(z)$ is represented by a Laurent polynomial

$$H(z) = \sum_{k=p}^{q} h(k)z^{-k} \qquad \text{of } degree\ |H| = q - p.$$

Thus the length of a filter is the degree of its associated polynomial plus one. The sum or difference of two Laurent polynomials is again a Laurent polynomial and the product of two Laurent polynomials of degree a and b is a Laurent polynomial of degree $a + b$. Exact division is in general not possible, but division with remainder is possible. This means that for any two nonzero Laurent polynomials $a(z)$ and $b(z)$, with $|a(z)| \geq |b(z)|$, there will always exist a Laurent polynomial $q(z)$ with $|q(z)| = |a(z)| - |b(z)|$ and a Laurent polynomial $r(z)$ with $|r(z)| < |b(z)|$ such that

$$a(z) = b(z)q(z) + r(z).$$

This division is not necessarily unique. A Laurent polynomial is invertible if and only if it is of degree zero, i.e., if it is of the form cz^p.

The original signal $X(z)$ goes through a low and high-pass analysis FIR filter pair $G(z)$ and $H(z)$. These are simply the independent convolutions of the original data sequence against a pair of masks, and constitute perhaps the most basic example of a *filterbank* [27]. The resulting pair of outputs are subsampled by a factor of two. To reconstruct the original signal, the low and high-pass coefficients $\gamma(z)$ and $\lambda(z)$ are upsampled by a factor of two and pass through another pair of synthesis FIR filters $G'(z)$ and $H'(z)$. Although IIR (infinite impulse response) filters can also be used, the infinite response leads to an infinite data expansion, an undesirable outcome in our finite world. According to filterbank theory, if the filters satisfy the relations

$$G(z)G(z^{-1}) + H'(z)H(z^{-1}) = 2,$$
$$G(z)G(-z^{-1}) + H'(z)H(-z^{-1}) = 0,$$

the aliasing caused by the subsampling will be cancelled, and the reconstructed signal $Y(z)$ will be equal to the original. Figure 5 provides an illustration.

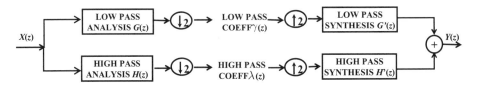

Figure 5. Convolution implementation of one dimensional wavelet transform.

A wavelet transform implemented in the fashion of Figure 5 with FIR filters is said to have a *convolutional implementation*, reflecting the fact that the signal is convolved with the pair of filters (h, g) that form the *filter bank*. Note that only half the samples are kept by the subsampling operator, and the other half of the filtered samples are thrown away. Clearly this is not efficient, and it would be better (by a factor of one-half) to do the subsampling before the filtering. This leads to an alternative implementation of the wavelet transform called *lifting* approach. It turns out that all FIR wavelet filters can be factored into lifting step. We explain the basic idea in what follows. For those interested in a deeper understanding, we refer to [10; 11; 12].

The subsampling that is performed at the forward wavelet, and the upsampling that is used in the inverse wavelet transform suggest the utility of a decomposition of the z-transform of the signal/filter into an even and odd part given by subsampling the z-transform at the even and odd indices, respectively:

$$H(z) = \sum_n h(n)z^{-n} \qquad \begin{cases} H_e(z) = \sum_n h(2n)z^{-n} & \text{(even part)}, \\ H_o(z) = \sum_n h(2n+1)z^{-n} & \text{(odd part)}. \end{cases}$$

The odd/even decomposition can be rewritten as

$$H(z) = H_e(z^2) + z^{-1}H_o(z^2) \quad \text{with} \quad \begin{cases} H_e(z) = \frac{1}{2}\big(H(z^{1/2}) + H(-z^{1/2})\big), \\ H_o(z) = \frac{1}{2}z^{1/2}\big(H(z^{1/2}) - H(-z^{1/2})\big). \end{cases}$$

With this we may rewrite the wavelet filtering and subsampling operation (i.e., the lowpass and highpass components, $\gamma(z)$ and $\lambda(z)$, respectively) using the even/odd parts of the signal and filter as

$$\gamma(z) = G_e(z)X_e(z) + z^{-1}G_o(z)X_o(z),$$
$$\lambda(z) = H_e(z)X_e(z) + z^{-1}H_o(z)X_o(z),$$

which can be written in matrix form as

$$\begin{pmatrix} \gamma(z) \\ \lambda(z) \end{pmatrix} = P(z) \begin{pmatrix} X_e(z) \\ z^{-1}X_o(z) \end{pmatrix},$$

where $P(z)$ is the polyphase matrix

$$P(z) = \begin{pmatrix} G_e(z) & G_o(z) \\ H_e(z) & H_o(z) \end{pmatrix}.$$

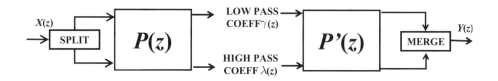

Figure 6. Single stage wavelet filter using polyphase matrices.

The forward wavelet transform now becomes the left part of Figure 6. Note that with polyphase matrix, we perform the subsampling (split) operation before the signal is filtered, which is more efficient than the description illustrated by Figure 5, in which the subsampling is performed after the signal is filtered. We move on to the inverse wavelet transform. It is not difficult to see that the odd/even subsampling of the reconstructed signal can be obtained through

$$\begin{pmatrix} Y_e(z) \\ zY_o(z) \end{pmatrix} = P(z) \begin{pmatrix} \gamma(z) \\ \lambda(z) \end{pmatrix},$$

where $P'(z)$ is a dual polyphase matrix

$$P'(z) = \begin{pmatrix} G'_e(z) & G'_o(z) \\ G'_e(z) & H'_o(z) \end{pmatrix}.$$

The wavelet transform is invertible if the two polyphase matrices are inverse to each other:

$$P'(z) = P(z)^{-1} = \frac{1}{H_o(z)G_e(z) - H_e(z)G_o(z)} \begin{pmatrix} H_o(z) & -G_o(z) \\ -H_e(z) & G_e(z) \end{pmatrix}.$$

If we constrain the determinant of the polyphase matrix to be one, i.e., $H_o(z)G_e(z) - H_e(z)G_o(z) = 1$, then not only are the polyphase matrices invertible, but the inverse filter has a simple relationship to the forward filter:

$$G'_e(z) = H_o(z), \qquad H'_e(z) = -G_o(z),$$
$$G'_o(z) = -H_e(z), \qquad H'_o(z) = G_2(z),$$

which implies that the inverse filter is related to the forward filter by the equations

$$G'_e(z) = z^{-1}H(-z^{-1}), \qquad H'(z) = -z^{-1}G(-z^{-1})$$

The corresponding pair of filters (g, h) is said to be *complementary*. Figure 6 illustrates the forward and inverse transforms using the polyphase matrices.

With the Laurent polynomial and polyphase matrix, we can factor a wavelet filter into the lifting steps. Starting with a complementary filter pair (g, h), assume that the degree of filter g is larger than that of filter h. We seek a new filter g^{new} satisfying

$$g(z) = h9z)t(z^2) + g^{\mathrm{new}}(z),$$

where $t(z)$ is a Laurent polynomial. Both $t(z)$ and $g^{\mathrm{new}}(z)$ can be calculated through long division [10]. The new filter g^{new} is complementary to filter h, as the polyphase matrix satisfies

$$P(z) = \begin{pmatrix} H_e(z)t(z) + G_e^{\mathrm{new}}(z) & H_o(z)t(z) + G_o^{\mathrm{new}}(z) \\ H_e(z) & H_o(z) \end{pmatrix}$$
$$= \begin{pmatrix} 1 & t(z) \\ 0 & 1 \end{pmatrix} \begin{pmatrix} G_e^{\mathrm{new}}(z) & G_o^{\mathrm{new}}(z) \\ H_e(z) & H_o(z) \end{pmatrix} = \begin{pmatrix} 1 & t(z) \\ 0 & 1 \end{pmatrix} P^{\mathrm{new}}(z).$$

Obviously, the determinant of the new polyphase matrix $P^{\mathrm{new}}(z)$ also equals one. By performing the operation iteratively, it is possible to factor the polyphase matrix into a sequence of lifting steps:

$$P(z) = \begin{pmatrix} K_1 & \\ & K_2 \end{pmatrix} \prod_{i=0}^{m} \left(\begin{pmatrix} 1 & t_i(z) \\ 0 & 1 \end{pmatrix} \begin{pmatrix} 1 & 0 \\ s_i(z) & 1 \end{pmatrix} \right).$$

The resultant lifting wavelet can be shown in Figure 7.

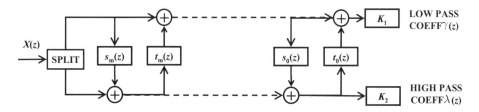

Figure 7. Multi-stage forward lifting wavelet using polyphase matrices.

Each lifting stage above can be directly inverted. Thus we can invert the entire wavelet:

$$P'(z) = P(z)^{-1} = \begin{pmatrix} 1/K_1 & \\ & 1/K_2 \end{pmatrix} \prod_{i=m}^{0} \left(\begin{pmatrix} 1 & 0 \\ -s_i(z) & 1 \end{pmatrix} \begin{pmatrix} 1 & -t_i(z) \\ 0 & 1 \end{pmatrix} \right).$$

We show the inverse lifting wavelet using polyphase matrices in Figure 8, which should be compared with Figure 7. Only the direction of the data flow has changed.

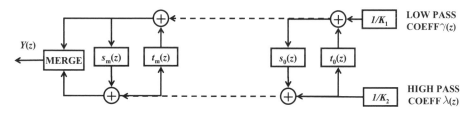

Figure 8. Multi-stage inverse lifting wavelet using polyphase matrices.

4.3. Bi-orthogonal 9-7 wavelet and boundary extension.

The default wavelet filter used in JPEG 2000 is the bi-orthogonal 9-7 wavelet [20]. It is a 4-stage lifting wavelet, with lifting filters $s_1(z) = f(a, z)$, $t_1(z) = f(b, z)$, $s_2(z) = f(c, z)$, $t_0(z) = f(d, z)$, where f, the *dual lifting step*, is of the form

$$f(p, z) = pz^{-1} + p.$$

The quantities a, b, c and d are the *lifting parameters* at each stage.

The next several figures illustrate the filterbank. The input data is indexed as $\ldots, x_0, x_1, \ldots, x_n, \ldots$, and the lifting operation is performed from right to left, stage by stage. At this moment, we assume that the data is of infinite length, and we will discuss boundary extension later. The input data are first partitioned into two groups corresponding to even and odd indices. During each lifting stage, only one of the group is updated. In the first lifting stage, the odd index data points x_1, x_3, ... are updated:

$$x'_{2n+1} = x_{2n+1} + a * (x_{2n} + x_{2n+2}),$$

where a and x'_{2n+1} are respectively the first stage lifting parameter and outcome. The entire operation corresponds to the filter $s_1(z)$ represented in Figure 8. The circle in Figure 9 illustrates one such operation performed on x_1.

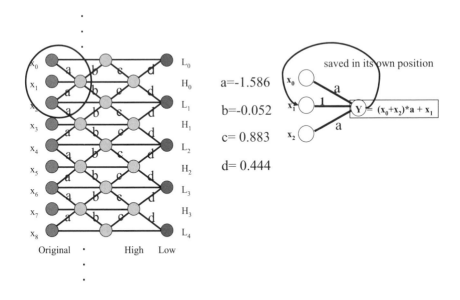

Figure 9. Bi-orthogonal 9-7 wavelet.

The second stage lifting, which corresponds to the filter $t_1(z)$ in Figure 8, updates the data at even indices:

$$x''_{2n} = x_{2n} + b * (x'_{2n-1} + x'_{2n+1}),$$

where b and x''_{2n} are the second stage lifting parameter and output. The third and fourth stage lifting can be performed similarly:

$$H_n = x'_{2n+1} + c * (x''_{2n} + x''_{2n+2}),$$
$$L_n = x''_{2n} + d * (H_{n-1} + H_n),$$

where H_n and L_n are the resultant high and low-pass coefficients. The value of the lifting parameters a, b, c, d are shown in Figure 9.

As illustrated in Figure 10, we may invert the dataflow, and derive an inverse lifting of the 9-7 bi-orthogonal wavelet.

Since the actual data in an image transform is finite in length, boundary extension is a crucial part of every wavelet decomposition scheme. For a symmetric odd-tap filter (the bi-orthogonal 9-7 wavelet falls into this category), symmetric boundary extension can be used. The data are reflected symmetrically along the boundary, with the boundary points themselves not involved in the reflection. An example boundary extension with four data points x_0, x_1, x_2 and x_3

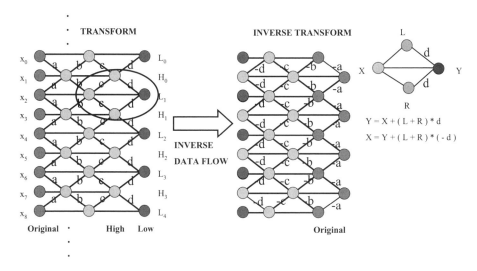

Figure 10. Forward and inverse lifting (9-7 bi-orthogonal wavelet).

is shown in Figure 11. Because both the extended data and the lifting structure are symmetric, all the intermediate and final results of the lifting are also symmetric with respect to the boundary points. Using this observation, it is sufficient to double the lifting parameters of the branches that are pointing toward the boundary, as shown in the middle of Figure 11. Thus, the boundary extension can be performed without additional computational complexity. The inverse lifting can again be derived by inverting the dataflow, as shown in the right of Figure 11. Again, the parameters for branches that are pointing toward the boundary points are doubled.

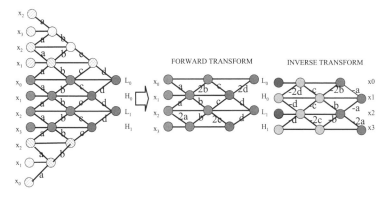

Figure 11. Symmetric boundary extension of bi-orthogonal 9-7 wavelet on 4 data points.

4.4. Two-dimensional wavelet transform. To apply a wavelet transform to an image we need to use a 2D version. In this case it is common to apply the wavelet transform separately in the horizontal and vertical directions. This approach is called the *separable 2D wavelet transform*. It is possible to design a *nonseparable* 2D wavelet (see [32], for example), but this generally increases computational complexity with little additional coding gain. A sample one-scale separable 2D wavelet transform is shown in Figure 12. The 2D data array representing the image is first filtered in the horizontal direction, which results in two subbands: a horizontal low-pass and a horizontal high-pass subband. These subbands are then passed through a vertical wavelet filter. The image is thus decomposed into four subbands: LL (low-pass horizontal and vertical filter), LH (low-pass vertical and high-pass horizontal filter), HL (high-pass vertical and low-pass horizontal filter) and HH (high-pass horizontal and vertical filter). Since the wavelet transform is linear, we may switch the order of the horizontal and vertical filters yet still reach the same effect. By further decomposing subband LL with another 2D wavelet (and iterating this procedure), we derive a *multiscale dyadic wavelet pyramid*. Recall that such a wavelet was illustrated in Figure 4.

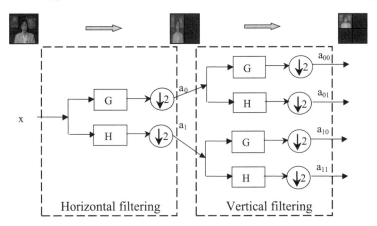

Figure 12. A single scale 2D wavelet transform.

4.5. Line-based lifting. A trick in implementing the 2D wavelet transform is *line-based lifting*, which avoids buffering the entire 2D image during the vertical wavelet lifting operation. The concept can be shown in Figure 13, which is very similar to Figure 9, except that here each circle represents an entire line (row) of the image. Instead of performing the lifting stage by stage, as in Figure 9, line-based lifting computes the vertical low- and high-pass lifting, one line at a time. The operation can be described as follows:

Step 1: Initialization, phase 1. Three lines of coefficients x_0, x_1 and x_2 are processed. Two lines of lifting operations are performed, and intermediate results x_1' and x_0'' are generated.

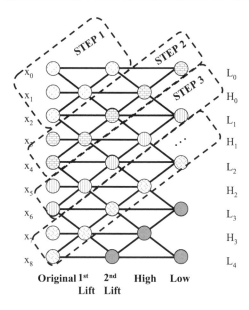

Figure 13. Line-based lifting wavelet (bi-orthogonal 9-7 wavelet).

Step 2: Initialization, phase 2. Two additional lines of coefficients x_3 and x_4 are processed. Four lines of lifting operations are performed. The outcomes are the intermediate results x_3' and x_4'', and the first line of low and high-pass coefficients L_0 and H_0.

Step 3: Repeated processing. During the normal operation, the line based lifting module reads in two lines of coefficients, performs four lines of lifting operations, and generates one line of low and high-pass coefficients.

Step 4: Flushing. When the bottom of the image is reached, symmetrical boundary extension is performed to correctly generate the final low and high-pass coefficients.

For the 9-7 bi-orthogonal wavelet, with line-based lifting, only six lines of working memory are required to perform the 2D lifting operation. By eliminating the need to buffer the entire image during the vertical wavelet lifting operation, the cost to implement 2D wavelet transform can be greatly reduced

5. Quantization and Partitioning

After the wavelet transform, all wavelet coefficients are uniformly quantized according to the rule

$$w_{m,n} = \text{sign } s_{m,n} \left\lfloor \frac{|s_{m,n}|}{\delta} \right\rfloor,$$

where $s_{m,n}$ is the transform coefficient, $w_{m,n}$ is the quantization result, δ is the quantization step size, sign(x) returns the sign of coefficient x, and $\lfloor \rfloor$ is the floor function. The effect of quantization is demonstrated in Figure 14.

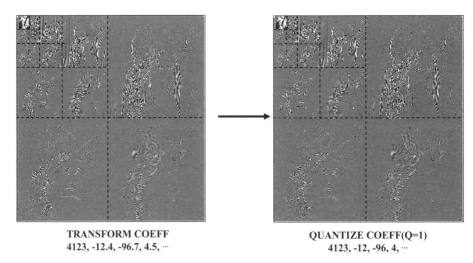

TRANSFORM COEFF   **QUANTIZE COEFF(Q=1)**
4123, -12.4, -96.7, 4.5, ⋯   4123, -12, -96, 4, ⋯

Figure 14. Effect of quantization.

The quantization process of JPEG 2000 is very similar to that of a conventional coder such as JPEG. However, the functionality is very different. In a conventional coder, since the quantization result is losslessly encoded, the quantization process determines the allowable distortion of the transform coefficients. In JPEG 2000, the quantized coefficients are lossy encoded through an embedded coder, thus additional distortion can be introduced in the entropy coding steps. Thus, the main functionality of the quantization module is to map the coefficients from floating representation into integer so that they can be more efficiently processed by the entropy coding module. The image coding quality is not determined by the quantization step size δ but by the subsequent bitstream assembler. The default quantization step size in JPEG 2000 is rather fine, e.g., $\delta = \frac{1}{128}$.

The quantized coefficients are then partitioned into packets. Each subband is divided into non-overlapping rectangles of equal size, as described above, this means three rectangles corresponding to the subbands HL, LH, HH of each resolution level. The packet partition provides spatial locality as it contains information needed for decoding image of a certain spatial region at a certain resolution.

The packets are further divided into non-overlapping rectangular code-blocks, which are the fundamental entities in the entropy coding operation. By applying the entropy coder to relatively small code-blocks, the original and working data of the entire code-blocks can reside in the cache of the CPU during the entropy coding operation. This greatly improves the encoding and decoding speed. In JPEG 2000, the default size of a code-block is 64×64. A sample partition and code-blocks are shown in Figure 15. We mark the partition with solid thick lines. The partition contains quantized coefficients at spatial location $(128, 128)$

to $(255, 255)$ of the resolution 1 subbands LH, HL and HH. It corresponds to the resolution 1 enhancement of the image with spatial location $(256, 256)$ to $(511, 511)$. The partition is further divided into twelve 64×64 code-blocks, which are shown as numbered blocks in Figure 15.

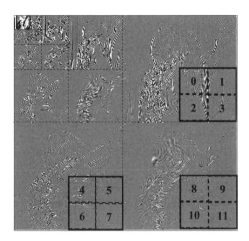

Figure 15. A sample partition and code-blocks.

6. Block Entropy Coding

Following the partitioning, each code-block is then independently encoded through a subbitplane entropy coder. As shown in Figure 16, the input of the block entropy coding module is the code-block, which can be represented as a 2D array of data. The output of the module is a embedded compressed bitstream, which can be truncated at any point and still be decodable, and a rate-distortion (R-D) curve (see Figure 16).

It is the responsibility of the block entropy coder to measure both the coding rate and distortion during the encoding process. The coding rate is derived directly through the length of the coding bitstream at certain instances, e.g., at the end of each subbitplane. The coding distortion is obtained by measuring the distortion between the original coefficient and the reconstructed coefficient at the same instance.

JPEG 2000 employs a subbitplane entropy coder. In what follows, we examine three key parts of the coder: the coding order, the context, and the arithmetic MQ-coder.

6.1. Embedded coding. Assume that each quantized coefficient $w_{m,n}$ is represented in the binary form as

$$\pm b_1 b_2 \dots b_n,$$

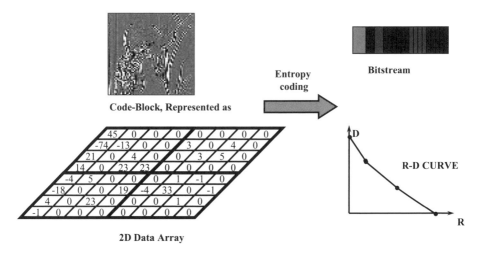

Figure 16. Block entropy coding.

where b_1 is the *most significant bit* (MSB), and b_n is the *least significant bit* (LSB), and $\pm$ represents the sign of the coefficient. It is the job of the entropy coding module to first convert this array of bits into a single sequence of binary bits, and then compress this bit sequence with a lossless coder, such as an arithmetic coder [22]. A *bitplane* is defined as the group of bits at a given level of significance. Thus, for each codeblock there is a bitplane consisting of all MSBs, one of all LSBs, and one for each of the significance levels that occur in between. By coding the more significant bits of all coefficients first, and coding the less significant bits later, the resulting compressed bitstream is said to have *the embedding property*, reflecting the fact that a bitstream of lower compression rate can be obtained by simply truncating a higher rate bitstream, so that the entire output stream has embedded in it bitstreams of lower compression that still make possible of partial decoding of all coefficients. A sample binary representation of the coefficient can be shown in Figure 17. Since representing bits in a 2D block results in a 3D bit array (the 3rd dimension is bit significance) which is very difficult to draw, we only show the binary representation of a column of coefficients as a 2D bit array in Figure 17. However, keep in mind that the true bit array in a code-block is 3D.

The bits in the bit array are very different, both in their statistical property and in their contribution to the quality of the decoded code-block. The sign is obviously different from that of the coefficient bit. The bits at different significance level contributes differently to the quality of the decoded code-blocks. And even within the same bitplane, bits may have different statistical property and contribution to the quality of decoding. Let b_M be a bit in a coefficient x. If all more significant bits in the same coefficient x are '0's, the coefficient x is said to be insignificant (because if the bitstream is terminated at this point or before, coefficient x will be reconstructed to zero), and the current bit b_M is to

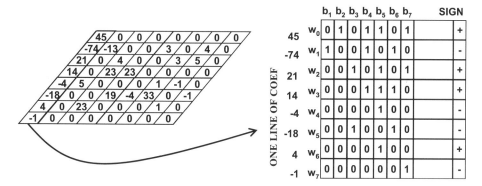

Figure 17. Coefficients and binary representation.

be encoded in the mode of significance identification. Otherwise, the coefficient is said to be significant, and the bit b_M is to be encoded in the mode of refinement. Depending on the sign of the coefficient, the coefficient can be positive significant or negative significant. We distinguish between significance identification and refinement bits because the significance identification bit has a very high probability of being 0, and the refinement bit is usually equally distributed between 0 and 1. The sign of the coefficient needs to be encoded immediately after the coefficient turns significant, i.e., a first non-zero bit in the coefficient is encoded. For the bit array in Figure 17, the significance identification and the refinement bits are shown with different shades in Figure 18.

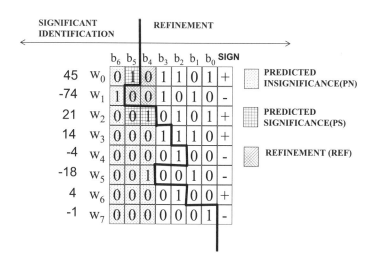

Figure 18. Embedded coding of bit array.

6.2. Context. It has been pointed out [14; 21] that the statistics of significant identification bits, refinement bits, and signs can vary tremendously. For example, if a quantized coefficient $x_{i,j}$ is of large magnitude, its neighbor coefficients may be of large magnitude as well. This is because a large coefficient locates an anomaly (e.g., a sharp edge) in the smooth signal, and such an anomaly usually causes a cluster of large wavelet coefficients in the neighborhood as well. To account for such statistical variation, we entropy encode the significant identification bits, refinement bits and signs with context, each of which is a number derived from already coded coefficients in the neighborhood of the current coefficient. The bit array that represents the data is thus turned into a sequence of *bit-context pairs*, as shown in Figure 19, which is subsequently encoded by a *context adaptive entropy coder*. In the bit-context pair, it is the bit information that is actually encoded. The context associated with the bit is determined from the already encoded information. It can be derived by the encoder and the decoder alike, provided both use the same rule to generate the context. Bits in the same context are considered to have similar statistical properties, so that the entropy coder can measure the probability distribution within each context and efficiently compress the bits.

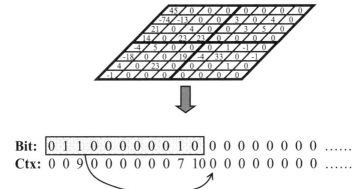

Figure 19. Coding bits and contexts. The context is derived from information from the already coded bits.

In the following, we describe the contexts that are used in the significant identification, refinement and sign coding of JPEG 2000. For the rational of the context design, we refer to [2; 19]. Determining the context of significant identification bit is a two-step process:

Step 1: Neighborhood statistics. For each bit of the coefficient, the number of significant horizontal, vertical and diagonal neighbors are counted as h, v and d, as shown in Figure 20.

Step 2: Lookup table. According to the direction of the subband that the coefficient is located (LH, HL, HH), the context of the encoding bit is indexed

LH subband (also LL) (vertically high-pass)				HL subband (horizontally high-pass)				HH subband (diagonally high-pass)		
h	v	d	context	h	v	d	context	d	$h+v$	context
2	x	x	8	x	2	x	8	≥ 3	x	8
1	≥ 1	x	7	≥ 1	1	x	7	2	≥ 1	7
1	0	≥ 1	6	0	1	≥ 1	6	2	0	6
1	0	0	5	0	1	0	5	1	≥ 2	5
0	2	x	4	2	0	x	4	1	1	4
0	1	x	3	1	0	x	3	1	0	3
0	0	≥ 2	2	0	0	≥ 2	2	0	≥ 2	2
0	0	1	1	0	0	1	1	0	1	1
0	0	0	0	0	0	0	0	0	0	0

Table 1. Context for the significance identification coding.

through one of the three tables shown in Table 1. A total of nine context categories are used for significance identification coding. The table lookup process reduces the number of contexts and enables probability of the statistics within each context to be quickly obtained.

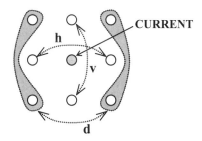

Figure 20. Number of significant neighbors: horizontal (h), vertical (v) and diagonal (d).

To determine the context for sign coding, we calculate a horizontal sign count h and a vertical sign count v. The sign count takes a value of -1 if both horizontal/vertical coefficients are negative significant; or one coefficient is negative significant, and the other is insignificant. It takes a value of $+1$ if both horizontal/vertical coefficients are positive significant; or one coefficient is positive significant, and the other is insignificant. The value of the sign count is 0 if both horizontal/vertical coefficients are insignificant; or one coefficient is positive significant, and the other is negative significant.

With the horizontal and vertical sign count h and v, an expected sign and a context for sign coding can then be calculated according to Table 2.

To calculate the context for the refinement bits, we measure if the current refinement bit is the first bit after significant identification, and if there is any significant coefficients in the immediate eight neighbors, i.e., $h + v + d > 0$. The context for the refinement bit is tabulated in Table 3.

Sign count { H	−1	−1	−1	0	0	0	1	1	1
V	−1	0	1	−1	0	1	−1	0	1
Expected sign	−	−	−	−	+	+	+	+	+
Context	13	12	11	10	9	10	11	12	13

Table 2. Context and the expected sign for sign coding.

Context 14: Current refinement bit is the first bit after significant identification and there is no significant coefficient in the eight neighbors.

Context 15: Current refinement bit is the first bit after significant identification and there is at least one significant coefficient in the eight neighbors.

Context 16: Current refinement bit is at least two bits away from significant identification.

Table 3. Context for the refinement bit.

6.3. MQ-coder: context dependent entropy coder. Through the aforementioned process, a data array is turned into a sequence of bit-context pairs, as shown in Figure 19. All bits associated with the same context are assumed to be independently and identically distributed. Let the number of contexts be N, and let there be n_i bits in context i, within which the probability of the bits taking value 1 is p_i. Using classic Shannon information theory [15; 16] the entropy of such a bit-context sequence can be calculated as

$$H = \sum_{i=0}^{N-1} n_i \left(-p \log_2 p_i - (1 - p_i) \log_2 (1 - p_i) \right). \qquad (6\text{--}1)$$

The task of the context entropy coder is thus to convert the sequence of bit-context pairs into a compact bitstream representation with length as close to the Shannon limit as possible, as shown in Figure 21. Several coders are available for such task. The coder used in JPEG 2000 is the MQ-coder. In the following, we focus the discussion on three key aspects of the MQ-coder: general arithmetic coding theory, fixed point arithmetic implementation and probability estimation. For more details, we refer to [22; 23].

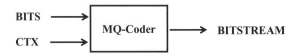

Figure 21. Input and output of the MQ-coder.

6.3.1. The Elias coder. The basic theory of the MQ-coder can be traced to the Elias Coder [24], or recursive probability interval subdivision. Let $S_0 S_1 S_2 \ldots S_n$ be a series of binary bits that is sent to the arithmetic coder. Let P_i be the probability that the bit S_i be 1. We may form a binary representation (the coding bitstream) of the original bit sequence by the following process:

Step 1: Initialization. Let the initial probability interval be $(0, 1)$. We denote the current probability interval as $(C, C+A)$, where C is the bottom of the probability interval, and A is the size of the interval. At the initialization, we have $C = 0$ and $A = 1$.

Step 2: Probability interval subdivision. The binary symbols $S_0 S_1 S_2 \ldots S_n$ are encoded sequentially. For each symbol S_i, the probability interval $(C, C+A)$ is subdivided into two sub-intervals $\big(C, \ C+A(1-P_i)\big)$ and $\big(C+A(1-P_i), \ C+A\big)$. Depending on whether the symbol S_i is 1, one of the two subintervals is selected:

$$\begin{cases} C \leftarrow C, \quad A \leftarrow A(1 - P_i), & \text{if } S_i = 0, \\ C \leftarrow A(1 - P_i), \quad A \leftarrow A P_i, & \text{if } S_i = 1. \end{cases} \tag{6-2}$$

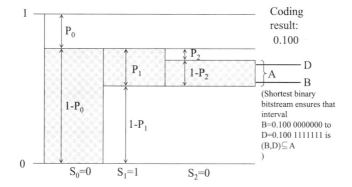

Figure 22. Probability interval subdivision.

Step 3: Bitstream output. Let the final coding bitstream be $k_1 k_2 \ldots k_m$, where m is the compressed bitstream length. The final bitstream creates an uncertainty interval where the lower and upper bound can be determined as

$$\text{Upperbound} \quad D = 0.k_1 k_2 \cdots k_m 111 \ldots,$$
$$\text{Lowerbound} \quad B = 0.k_1 k_2 \cdots k_m 000 \ldots.$$

As long as the uncertainty interval (B, D) is contained in the probability interval $(C, C+A)$, the coding bitstream uniquely identifies the final probability interval, and thus uniquely identifies each subdivision in the Elias coding process. The entire binary symbol strings $S_0 S_1 S_2 \ldots S_n$ can thus be recovered from the compressed representation. It can be shown that it is possible to find a final coding bitstream with length

$$m \leq \lceil -\log_2 A \rceil + 1$$

to represent the final probability interval $(C, C+A)$. Notice that A is the probability of the occurrence of the binary strings $S_0 S_1 S_2 \ldots S_n$, and the entropy of the original symbol stream can be calculated as

$$H = \sum_{S_0 S_1 \cdots S_n} -A \log_2 A.$$

The arithmetic coder thus encodes the binary string within 2 bits of its entropy limit, no matter how long the symbol string is. This is very efficient.

6.3.2. The arithmetic coder: finite precision arithmetic operations. Exact implementation of Elias coding requires infinite precision arithmetic, an unrealistic assumption in real applications. Using finite precision, the arithmetic coder is developed from Elias coding. Observing the fact that the coding interval A becomes very small after a few operations, we may normalize the coding interval parameter C and A as

$$C = 1.5 \cdot [0.k_1 k_2 \cdots k_L] + 2^{-L} \cdot 1.5 \cdot C_x, \qquad A = 2^{-L} \cdot 1.5 \cdot A_x,$$

where L is a normalization factor determining the magnitude of the interval A, while A_x and C_x are fixed-point integers representing values between $(0.75, 1.5)$ and $(0, 1.5)$, respectively. Bits $k_1 k_2 \ldots k_m$ are the output bits that have already been determined (in reality, certain carryover operations have to be handled to derive the true output bitstream). By representing the probability interval with the normalization L and fixed-point integers A_x and C_x, it is possible to use fixed-point arithmetic and normalization operations for the probability interval subdivision operation. Moreover, since the value of A_x is close to 1.0, we may approximate $A_x \cdot P_i$ with P_i, the interval sub-division operation (6–2) calculated as

$$\begin{aligned}
C_x &= C_x, & A_x &= A_x - P_i, & \text{if } S_i = 0, \\
C_x &= C + A_x - P_i, & A_x &= P_i, & \text{if } S_i = 1,
\end{aligned}$$

which can be done quickly without any multiplication. The compression performance suffers a little, as the coding interval now has to be approximated with a fixed-point integer, and $A_x \cdot P_i$ is approximated with P_i. However, experiments show that the degradation in compression performance is less than three percent, which is well worth the saving in implementation complexity.

6.3.3. Probability estimation. In the arithmetic coder it is necessary to estimate the probability P_i for each binary symbol S_i to take the value 1. This is where context comes into play. Within each context, it is assumed that the symbols are independently identically distributed. We may then estimate the probability of the symbol within each context through observation of the past behaviors of symbols in the same context. For example, if we observe n_i symbols in context

i, with o_i symbols to be 1, we may estimate the probability that a symbol takes on the value 1 in context i through Bayesian estimation as

$$P_i = \frac{o_i + 1}{n_i + 2}.$$

In the MQ-coder [22], probability estimation is implemented through a state-transition machine. It may estimate the probability of the context more efficiently, and may take into consideration the non-stationary characteristic of the symbol string. Nevertheless, the principle is still to estimate the probability based on past behavior of the symbols in the same context.

6.4. Coding order: subbitplane entropy coder.

In JPEG 2000, because the embedded bitstream of a code-block may be truncated, the coding order, which is the order that the data array is turned into bit-context pair sequence, is of paramount importance. A sub-optimal coding order may allow important information to be lost after the coding bitstream is truncated, and lead to severe coding distortion. It turns out that the optimal coding order first encodes those bits with the steepest rate-distortion slope, which is defined as the coding distortion decrease per bit spent [21]. Just as the statistical properties of the bits are different in the bit array, their contribution of the coding distortion decrease per bit is also different.

Consider a bit b_i in the i-th most significant bitplane, where there are a total of n bitplanes. If the bit is a refinement bit, then previous to the coding of the bit, the uncertainty interval of the coefficient is $(A, A+2^{n-i})$. After the refinement bit has been encoded, the coefficient lies either in $(A, A+2^{n-i-1})$ or in $(A+2^{n-i}, A+2^{n-i-1})$. If we further assume that the value of the coefficient is uniformly distributed in the uncertainty interval, we may calculate the expected distortion before and after the coding as

$$D_{\text{pre,REF}} = \int_A^{A+2^{n-i}} (x - A - 2^{n-i-1})^2 \, dx = \tfrac{1}{12} 4^{n-i},$$

$$D_{\text{post,REF}} = \tfrac{1}{12} 4^{n-i-1}.$$

Since the value of the coefficient is uniformly distributed in the uncertainty interval, the probability for the refinement bit to take the values 0 and 1 is equal, thus, the coding rate of the refinement bit is:

$$R_{\text{REF}} = H(b_i) = 1 \text{ bit.} \tag{6-3}$$

The rate-distortion slope of the refinement bit at the i-th most significant bitplane is thus:

$$s_{\text{REF}}(i) = \frac{D_{\text{prev,REF}} - D_{\text{post,REF}}}{R_{\text{REF}}} = \frac{\tfrac{1}{12} 4^{n-i} - \tfrac{1}{12} 4^{n-i-1}}{1} = 4^{n-i-2} \tag{6-4}$$

In the same way, we may calculate the expected distortion decrease and coding rate for a significant identification bit at the i-th most significant bitplane. Before the coding of the bit, the uncertainty interval of the coefficient ranges from -2^{n-i} to 2^{n-i}. After the bit has been encoded, if the coefficient becomes significant, it lies in $(-2^{n-i}, -2^{n-i-1})$ or $(+2^{n-i-1}, +2^{n-i})$ depending on the sign of the coefficient. If the coefficient is still insignificant, it lies in $(-2^{n-i-1}, 2^{n-i-1})$. We note that if the coefficient is still insignificant, the reconstructed coefficient before and after coding both will be 0, which leads to no distortion decrease (coding improvement). The coding distortion only decreases if the coefficient becomes significant. Assuming the probability that the coefficient becomes significant is p, and the coefficient is uniformly distributed within the significance interval $(-2^{n-i}, -2^{n-i-1})$ or $(+2^{n-i-1}, +2^{n-i})$, we may calculate the expected coding distortion decrease as

$$D_{\text{prev,SIG}} - D_{\text{post,SIG}} = p \frac{9}{4} 4^{n-i} \qquad (6\text{--}5)$$

The entropy of the significant identification bit can be calculated as

$$R_{\text{SIG}} = -(1-p)\log_2(1-p) - p\log_2 p + p \cdot 1 = p + H(p),$$

where $H(p) = -(1-p)\log_2(1-p) - p\log_2 p$ is the entropy of the binary symbol with the probability of 1 being p. In (6–5), we account for the one bit which is needed to encode the sign of the coefficient if it becomes significant.

We may then derive the expected rate-distortion slope for the significance identification bit coding as

$$s_{\text{SIG}}(i) = \frac{D_{\text{prev,SIG}} - D_{\text{post,SIG}}}{R_{\text{SIG}}} = \frac{9}{1 + H(p)/p} 4^{n-i-2}$$

From this and (6–4), we arrive at the following conclusions:

Conclusion 1. The more significant bitplane that the bit is located, the earlier it should be encoded.

A key observation is, within the same coding category (significance identification/refinement), one more significance bitplane translates into 4 times more contribution in distortion decrease per coding bit spent. Therefore, the codeblock should be encoded bitplane by bitplane.

Conclusion 2. Within the same bitplane, we should first encode the significance identification bit with a higher probability of significance.

It can be shown that the function $H(p)/p$ increases monotonically as the probability of significance decreases. As a result, the higher probability of significance, the higher contribution of distortion decrease per coding bit spent.

Conclusion 3. Within the same bitplane, the significance identification bit should be encoded earlier than the refinement bit if the probability of significance is higher than 0.01.

It is observed that the insignificant coefficients with no significant coefficients in its neighborhood usually have a probability of significance below 0.01, while insignificant coefficients with at least one significant neighbor usually have a higher probability of significance.

As a result of these three conlusions, the entropy coder in JPEG 2000 encodes the code-block bitplane by bitplane, from the most significant bitplane to the least significant bitplane; and within each bitplane, the bit array is further ordered into three subbitplanes: the predicted significance (PS), the refinement (REF) and the predicted insignificance (PN).

Using the data array in Figure 23 as an example, we illustrate the block coding order of JPEG 2000 with a series of sub-figures in Figure 23. Each sub-figure shows the coding of one subbitplane. The block coding order of JPEG 2000 is as follows:

Step 1: The most significant bitplane, the PN subbitplane of b_1. (See Figure 23(a).)

First, the most significant bitplane is examined and encoded. Since at first, all coefficients are insignificant, all bits in the MSB bitplane belong to the PN subbitplane. Whenever a 1 bit is encountered (rendering the corresponding coefficient non-zero) the sign of the coefficient is encoded immediately afterwards. With the information of those bits that have already been coded and the signs of the significant coefficients, we may figure out an uncertain range for each coefficient. The reconstruction value of the coefficient can also be set, e.g., at the middle of the uncertainty range. The outcome of our sample bit array after the coding of the most significant bitplane is shown in Figure 23(a). We show the uncertainty range and the reconstruction value of each coefficient under columns "value" and "range" in the sub-figure, respectively. As the coding proceeds, the uncertainty range shrinks, and brings better and better representation to each coefficient.

Step 2: The PS subbitplane of b_2. (See Figure 23(b).)

After all bits in the most significant bitplane have been encoded, the coding proceeds to the PS subbitplane of the second most significant bitplane (b_2). The PS subbitplane consists of bits of the coefficients that are not significant, but has at least one significant neighbor. The corresponding subbitplane coding is shown in Figure 23(b). In this example, coefficients w_0 and w_2 are the neighbors of the significant coefficient w_1, and they are encoded in this pass. Again, if a 1 bit is encountered, the coefficient becomes significant, and its sign is encoded right after. The uncertain ranges and reconstruction value of the coded coefficients are updated according to the newly coded information.

Step 3: The REF subbitplane of b_2. (See Figure 23(c).)

The coding then moves to the REF subbitplane, which consists of the bits of the coefficients that are already significant in the past bitplane. The significance status of the coefficients is not changed in this pass, and no sign of coefficients is encoded.

Step 4: The PN subbitplane of b_2. (See Figure 23(d).)

Finally, the rest of the bits in the bitplane are encoded in the PN subbit-plane pass, which consists of the bits of the coefficients that are not significant and have no significant neighbors. Sign is again encoded once a coefficient turns into significant.

Steps 2, 3, and 4 are repeated for the following bitplanes, with the subbitplane coding ordered being PS, REF and PN for each bitplane. The block entropy coding continues until certain criteria, e.g., the desired coding rate or coding quality has been reached, or all bits in the bit array have been encoded. The output bitstream has the embedding property. If the bitstream is truncated, the more significant bits of the coefficients can still be decoded. An estimate of each coefficient is thus obtained, albeit with a relatively large uncertain range.

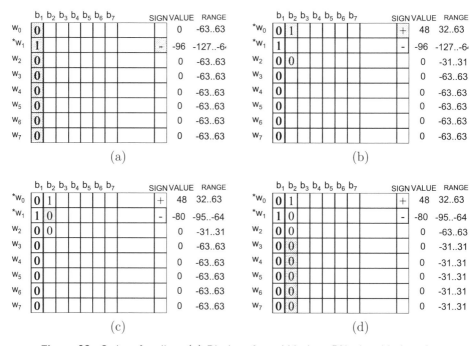

Figure 23. Order of coding: (a) Bitplane b_1, subbitplane PN, then bitplane b_2, subbitplanes (b) PS, (c) REF and (d) PN.

7. The Bitstream Assembler

The embedded bitstream of the code-blocks are assembled by the bitstream assembler module to form the compressed bitstream of the image. As described in section 6, the block entropy coder not only produces an embedded bitstream for each code-block i, but also records the coding rate R_i^k and distortion D_i^k

at the end of each subbitplane, where k is the index of the subbitplane. The bitstream assembler module determines how much bitstream of each code-block is put to the final compressed bitstream. It determines a truncation point n_i for each code-block so that the distortion of the entire image is minimized upon a rate constraint:

$$\min \sum_i D^{n_i}i, \qquad \text{with} \quad \sum_i R^{n_i}i \leq B. \qquad (7\text{-}1)$$

Since there are a discrete number of truncation points n_i, the constraint minimization problem of equation (7–1) can be solved by distributing bits first to the code-blocks with the steepest distortion per rate spent. The process of bit allocation and assembling can be performed as follows:

Step 1: Initialization. We initialize all truncation points to zero: $n_i = 0$.

Step 2: Incremental bit allocation. For each code block i, the maximum possible gain of distortion decrease per rate spent is calculated as

$$S_i = \max_{k > n_i} \frac{D_i^{n_i} - D_i^k}{R_i^k - R_i^{n_i}}.$$

We call S_i the rate-distortion slope of the code-block i. The code-block with the steepest rate-distortion slope is selected, and its truncation point is updated as

$$n_i^{\text{new}} = \arg_{k > n_i} \left(\frac{D^{n_i}i - D^k i}{R_i^k - R^{n_i}i} = S_i \right).$$

A total of $R_i^{n_i^{\text{new}}} - R_i^{n_i}$ bits are sent to the output bitstream. This leads to a distortion decrease of $D_i^{n_i} - D_i^{n_i^{\text{new}}}$. It can be easily proved that this is the maximum distortion decrease achievable for spending $R_i^{n_i^{\text{new}}} - R_i^{n_i}$ bits.

Step 3: Repeat Step 2 until the required coding rate B is reached.

The above optimization procedure does not take into account the last segment problem, i.e., when the coding bits available is smaller than $R_i^{n_i^{\text{new}}} - R_i^{n_i}$ bits. However, in practice, usually the last segment is very small (within 100 bytes), so that the residual sub-optimally is not a big concern.

Following exactly the optimization procedure above is computationally complex. The process can be speeded up by first calculating a convex hull of the R-D slope of each code-block i, as follows:

Step 1: Set $\boldsymbol{S}$ to the set of all truncation points.

Step 2: Set p to the first truncation point in $\boldsymbol{S}$.

Step 3: Do until p is the last truncation point in $\boldsymbol{S}$:

(i) Set k to the next truncation point after p in $\boldsymbol{S}$.

(ii) Set $S_i^k = \dfrac{D_i^p - D_i^k}{R_i^k - R_i^p}.$

(iii) If p is not the first truncation point in S and $S_i^k \geq S_i^p$, remove p from S and move p back one truncation point in S; otherwise, set $p = k$.

(iv) [End of current iteration. Restart at step 3(i), unless p is the last truncation point in S.]

Once the R-D convex hull is calculated, the optimal R-D optimization becomes simply the search of a global R-D slope λ, where the truncation point of each code-block is determined by:

$$n_i = \arg \max_k \left(S_i^k > \lambda \right)$$

Putting the truncated bitstream of all code-blocks together, we obtain a compressed bitstream associated with each R-D slope λ. To reach a desired coding bitrate B, we just search the minimum λ whose associated bitstream satisfies the rate inequality (7–1). The R-D optimization procedure can be illustrated in Figure 24.

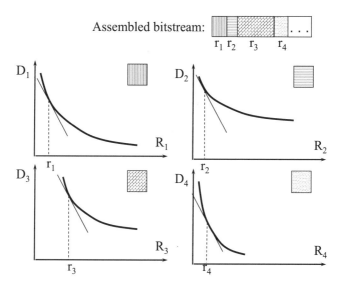

Figure 24. Bitstream assembler: for each R-D slope λ, a truncation point can be found at each code-block. The slope λ should be the minimum slope that the allocated rate for all code-blocks is smaller than the required coding rate B.

To form a compressed image bitstream with progressive quality improvement property, so that we may gradually improve the quality of the received image as more and more bitstream arrives, we may design a series of rate points, $B^{(1)}, B^{(2)}, \ldots, B^{(n)}$. A sample rate point set is 0.0625, 0.125, 0.25, 0.5, 1.0 and 2.0 bpp (bit per pixel). For an image of size 512×512, this corresponds to a compressed bitstream size of 2k, 4k, 8k, 16k, 32k and 64k bytes. First, the global R-D slope $\lambda^{(1)}$ for rate point $B^{(1)}$ is calculated. The first set of truncation point of each code-block $n_i^{(1)}$ is thus derived. These bitstream segments of the code-blocks of one resolution level at one spatial location is grouped into a packet. All packets that consist of the first segment bitstream form the first layer that represents the first quality increment of the entire image at full resolution. Then, we may calculate the second global R-D slope $\lambda^{(2)}$ corresponding to the rate point $B^{(2)}$. The second truncation point of each code-block $n_i^{(2)}$ can be derived, and the bitstream segment between the first $n_i^{(1)}$ and the second $n_i^{(2)}$ truncation points constitutes the second bitstream segment of the code-blocks. We again assemble the bitstream of the code-blocks into packets. All packets that consist of the second segment bitstreams of the code-blocks form the second layer of the compressed image. The process is repeated until all n layers of bitstream are formed. The resultant JPEG 2000 compressed bitstream is thus generated and can be illustrated with Figure 25.

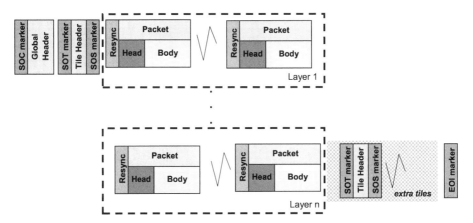

Figure 25. JPEG 2000 bitstream syntax. SOC = start of image (codestream) marker; SOT = start of tile marker; SOS = start of scan marker; EOI = end of image marker.

8. The Performance of JPEG 2000

Finally, we briefly demonstrate the compression performance of JPEG 2000. We compare JPEG 2000 with the traditional JPEG standard. The test image is the "Bike" standard image (gray, 2048×2560), shown in Figure 26. Three modes of JPEG 2000 are tested, and are compared against two modes of JPEG. The JPEG modes are progressive (P-DCT) and sequential (S-DCT) both with optimized Huffman tables [4]. The JPEG 2000 modes are single layer with the bi-orthogonal 9-7 wavelet (S-9,7), six layer progressive with the bi-orthogonal 9-7 wavelet (P6-9,7), and 7 layer progressive with the (3,5) wavelet (P7-3,5). The JPEG 2000 progressive modes have been optimized for 0.0625, 0.125, 0.25, 0.5, 1.0, 2.0 bpp and lossless for the 5×3 wavelet. The JPEG progressive mode uses

a combination of spectral refinement and successive approximation. We show
the performance comparison in Figure 27.

Figure 26. Original "Bike" test image.

JPEG 2000 results are significantly better than JPEG results for all modes
and all bit-rates on this image. Typically JPEG 2000 provides only a few dB
improvement from 0.5 to 1.0 bpp but substantial improvement below 0.25 bpp
and above 1.5 bpp. Also, JPEG 2000 achieves scalability at almost no additional

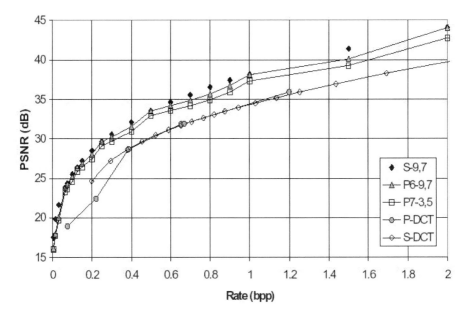

Figure 27. Performance comparison: JPEG 2000 versus JPEG. From [1], courtesy of the authors, Marcellin et al.

cost. The progressive performance is almost as good as the single layer JPEG 2000 without the progressive capability. The slight difference is due solely to the increased signaling cost for the additional layers (which changes the packet headers). It is possible to provide "generic rate scalability" by using upwards of fifty layers. In this case the "scallops" in the progressive curve disappear, but the overhead may be slightly increased.

References

[1] M. W. Marcellin, M. Gormish, A. Bilgin, M. P. Boliek, "An overview of JPEG2000", pp. 523–544 in *Proc. of the Data Compression Conference*, Snowbird (UT), March 2000.

[2] M. W. Marcellin and D. S. Taubman, *Jpeg2000: Image Compression Fundamentals, Standards, and Practice*, Kluwer International Series in Engineering and Computer Science, Secs 642.

[3] ISO/IEC JTC1/SC29/WG1/N1646R, "JPEG 2000 Part I final committee draft, version 1.0", March 2000, http://www.jpeg.org/public/fcd15444-1.pdf

[4] William B. Pennebaker, Joan L. Mitchell, *Jpeg: Still image data compression standard*, Kluwer Academic Publishers, September 1992.

[5] A. Zandi, J. D. Allen, E. L. Schwartz, and M. Boliek, "CREW: compression with reversible embedded wavelets", pp. 212–221 in *Proc. of IEEE Data Compression Conference*, Snowbird (UT), March 1995.

[6] J. Shapiro, "Embedded image coding using zerotree of wavelet coefficients", *IEEE Trans. Signal Processing* **41** (1993), 3445–3462.

[7] S. Mallat, *A wavelet tour of signal processing*, Academic Press, 1998.

[8] I. Daubechies, *Ten lectures on wavelets*, second ed., SIAM, Philadelphia, 1992.

[9] C. S. Burrus, R. A. Gopinath and H. Guo, *Introduction to wavelets and wavelet transforms, a primer*, Prentice Hall, Upper Saddle River (NJ), 1998.

[10] I. Daubechies and W. Sweldens, "Factoring wavelet transforms into lifting steps", *J. Fourier Anal. Appl.* **4**:3 (1998).

[11] W. Sweldens, "Building your own wavelets at home", in: *Wavelets in Computer Graphics*, ACM SIGGRAPH Course Notes, 1996.

[12] C. Valen, "A really friendly guide to wavelets", http://perso.wanadoo.fr/polyvalens/clemens/wavelets/wavelets.html.

[13] J. Li, P. Cheng, and J. Kuo, "On the improvements of embedded zerotree wavelet (EZW) coding", pp. 1490–1501 in *SPIE: Visual Communication and Image Processing*, vol. 2501, Taipei, Taiwan, May 1995.

[14] M. Boliek, "New work item proposal: JPEG 2000 image coding system", *ISO/IEC JTC1/SC29/WG1 N390*, June 1996.

[15] T. M. Cover and J. A. Thomas, *Elements of Information Theory*, Wiley, New York, 1991.

[16] T. M. Cover and J. A. Thomas, "Elements of information theory: online resources", http://www-isl.stanford.edu/~jat/eit2/index.shtml.

[17] ISO/IEC JTC1/SC29/WG1 N505, "Call for contributions for JPEG 2000 (ITC 1.29.14, 15444): image coding system", March 1997.

[18] J. H. Kasner, M. W. Marcellin and B. R. Hunt, "Universal trellis coded quantization", *IEEE Trans. Image Processing* **8**:12 (Dec. 1999), 1677–1687.

[19] D. Taubman, "High performance scalable image compression with EBCOT", *IEEE Trans. Image Processing* **9**:7 (July 2000), 1158–1170.

[20] M. Antonini, M. Barlaud, P. Mathieu and I. Daubechies, "Image coding using wavelet transform", *IEEE Trans. Image Processing*, **1**:2 (Apr. 1992), 205–220.

[21] J. Li and S. Lei, "An embedded still image coder with rate-distortion optimization", *IEEE Trans. Image Processing* **8**:7 (July 1999), 913–924.

[22] ISO/IEC JTC1/SC29/WG1 N1359, "Information technology — coded representation of picture and audio information — lossy/lossless coding of bi-level images", 14492 Final Committee Draft, July 1999.

[23] W. Pennebaker, J. Mitchell, G. Langdon, and R. Arps, "An overview of the basic principles of the *q*-coder adaptive binary arithmetic coder", *IBM J. Res. Develop* **32**:6 (1988), 717–726.

[24] Ian H. Witten, Radford M. Neal, and John G. Cleary, "Arithmetic coding for data compression," *Communications of the ACM* **30**:6 (1987), 520–540.

[25] J. Li and H. Sun, "A virtual media (Vmedia) interactive image browser", *IEEE Trans. Multimedia*, Sept. 2003.

[26] K. R. Rao and P. Yip, Rao, "Discrete cosine transform: algorithms, advantages, applications". Academic Press, Boston, 1990.

[27] S. Mallat, *A wavelet tour of signal processing*, Academic Press, 1998.

[28] P. P. Vaidyanathan, *Multirate systems and filter banks*, Prentice-Hall, Englewood Cliffs (NJ), 1993.

[29] R. Gonzalez and R. Woods, *Digital image processing*, Addison-Wesley, Reading (MA), 1992.

[30] K. R. Rao and D. F. Elliott, *Fast transforms: algorithms, analyses and applications*, Academic Press, New York, 1982.

[31] R. Rosenholtz and A. B. Watson, "Perceptual adaptive JPEG coding", pp. 901–904 in *Proc. IEEE International Conference on Image Processing*, Lausanne, Switzerland, 1994.

[32] G. V. Auwera, A. Munteanu, and J. Cornelis, "Evaluation of a quincunx wavelet filter design approach for quadtree-based embedded image coding", pp. 190–194 in *Proc. of the IEEE International Conference on Image Processing (ICIP)*, Vancouver, Canada, Sept. 2000.

JIN LI
MICROSOFT RESEARCH
COMMUNICATION COLLABORATION AND SIGNAL PROCESSING
ONE MICROSOFT WAY, BLD. 113/3161
REDMOND, WA 98052
jinl@microsoft.com

Modern Signal Processing
MSRI Publications
Volume **46**, 2003

Integrated Sensing and Processing
for Statistical Pattern Recognition

CAREY E. PRIEBE, DAVID J. MARCHETTE,
AND DENNIS M. HEALY, JR.

ABSTRACT. This article presents a simple version of Integrated Sensing and
Processing (ISP) for statistical pattern recognition wherein the sensor measurements to be taken are adaptively selected based on task-specific metrics.
Thus the measurement space in which the pattern recognition task is ultimately addressed integrates adaptive sensor technology with the specific
task for which the sensor is employed. This end-to-end optimization of sen-
sor/processor/exploitation subsystems is a theme of the DARPA Defense
Sciences Office Applied and Computational Mathematics Program's ISP
program. We illustrate the idea with a pedagogical example and application to the HyMap hyperspectral sensor and the Tufts University "artificial
nose" chemical sensor.

1. Introduction

An important activity, common to many fields of endeavor, is the act of refining high order *information* (detections of events, classification of objects, identification of activities, etc.) from large volumes of diverse *data* which is increasingly
available through modern means of measurement, communication, and processing. This *exploitation* function winnows the available data concerning an object
or situation in order to extract useful and actionable information, quite often
through the application of techniques from statistical pattern recognition to the
data. This may involve activities like detection, identification, and classification
which are applied to the raw measured data, or possibly to partially processed
information derived from it.

When new data are sought in order to obtain information about a specific
situation, it is now increasingly common to have many different measurement
degrees of freedom potentially available for the task. Some appreciation of the
dimensionality of available data can be obtained by considering measurements

---

This work is partially supported by DARPA Grant F49620-01-1-0395.

from one sensor, the hyperspectral camera, which is gaining broad application in fields ranging from geological remote sensing to military target identification. This sensor produces an output comprised of hundreds of megapixel images of a scene, each image corresponding to the appearance of that scene in light from a narrow band of frequencies. Taken together, these images present a finely resolved spectrum for each pixel in the scene. The data sets are often presented as cubes and can have on the order of a billion voxels per scene. Of course for real scenes, the billions of degrees of freedom exhibit correlations; nevertheless, the raw data is presented in an overwhelmingly high dimensional space.

This situation is magnified when one considers the diversity of sophisticated sensing mechanisms which might be applied to a given task. For example, remote sensing of terrain may be performed with natural light cameras, infrared cameras, hyperspectral imagers, fully polarimetric imaging radar, or combinations of all of these. This gives us many different views of the scene, but also presents a challenging requirement for effective processing and exploitation algorithms enabling reliable and affordable extraction of information from the high-dimensional spaces of sensed data.

In many situations, constraints on the available time, bandwidth, human and machine resources, and on the prior relevant experience all significantly limit the ability to deal intelligently with the many potential sensing degrees of freedom. This is particularly the case in time-critical applications. In fact, one often finds that not all of the available sensor degrees of freedom are equally useful in a given situation, suggesting the need for a reasoned approach for choosing those particular measurement types to be made and/or communicated and/or processed.

In this paper we show that it is sometimes possible to identify a particularly informative subspace of the space of all possible sensor measurements when it comes to the application of exploitation tasks on the sensed data. We will present examples in which performance is enhanced significantly by finding and working in the corresponding reduced-dimensionality subspace of sensed data. Even more, we will demonstrate in several cases that the determination of this particularly informative subspace then suggests the selection of a further subspace of measurements to improve exploitation performance yet further. This is somewhat analogous to the game of "20 questions," in which we progressively refine the scope and specificity of our questions based on partial understanding derived from previous attempts to narrow down the possibilities.

This process of focusing and targeting measurements is in fact often realizable in practice, due in part to significant engineering advances made in adaptive "smart" sensor technology. Current and projected capabilities for modifying the way certain important sensors look at the world motivate the development of mathematical methodology for guiding the adaptive selection of the types measurements made by an adaptive sensor/processor subsystem with an eye to enhancing and simplifying the exploitation of the resulting data. We present examples in which the way a sensor views a scene determines the abstract space in which the exploitation is ultimately addressed. In these cases, a judicious choice of sensor viewpoint improves exploitation performance dramatically.

Effective realization of the next generation of sensor/exploitation systems will require balanced integration and joint optimization of adaptive sensor front end functions with the pattern recognition tasks applied to sensor measurements in the system's back end. Development of methodologies for end-to-end joint optimization of sensor/processor/exploitation subsystems with respect to task-specific metrics, is a key theme of the DARPA Applied and Computational Mathematics Program's "Integrated Sensing and Processing" (ISP) effort. Various aspects of this program are currently being pursued by several groups of researchers in academia, industry, and government. Preliminary results suggest that certain applications in target detection and identification may derive significant performance enhancements by applying this concept to take full advantage of adaptive sensor technology.

In this paper, we illustrate one aspect of the ISP idea, in which the exploitation subsystem is concerned with supervised statistical pattern recognition (classification) and the observations take their value in a space with some linear ordering properties, such as multivariate time series. We illustrate the idea with a pedagogical example and application to the HyMap hyperspectral sensor (in which case the functional domain is spectral rather than temporal) and the Tufts University "artificial nose" chemical sensor. Other applications include gene expression analysis via DNA microarrays collected at multiple time instances, functional brain imaging collected at multiple time instances, etc.

2. Statistical Pattern Recognition

Pattern recognition starts with observations and returns class labels. Statistical pattern recognition addresses the problem in a probabilistic framework and applies to it statistical methods. Here we provide a brief description of the basic set up of statistical pattern recognition. For additional details, see, e.g., Fukunaga (1990), Devroye et al. (1996), Duda et al. (2000), Hastie et al. (2001), and references therein.

Let the pair (X, Y) be distributed according to probability distribution F; $(X, Y) \sim F$. Intuitively, X represents measurements made on some phenomenon of interest and Y indicates higher order information about that phenomenon, such as its membership in one of several disjoint classes.

More formally, the *feature vector* X is a Ξ-valued random variable. Usually $\Xi = \mathbb{R}^d$ or some subset thereof. More generally, Ξ may allow for more elaborate data structures such as multivariate time series, images, categorical data, dissimilarity data, etc. We will consider cases in which feature observations are multivariate time series and spectral responses. For categorical data Ξ is simply a set (unordered). In some applications, Ξ may consist of mixed data—some categorical, some continuous and some time series. For example, in a medical application one might have sex (categorical), temperature (continuous), and an EKG (time series).

The *class label* Y is a $\{1, \ldots, J\}$-valued random variable, with $J > 1$ usually finite. The label Y indicates the class to which the associated feature vector X belongs. The prior probabilities of class membership are given by $\pi_j := P[Y = j]$. We denote by F_j the *class-conditional distributions* of $X|Y = j$.

We partition statistical pattern recognition into two main categories: *supervised* and *unsupervised*. The distinguishing feature between these two categories is that for supervised pattern recognition training data exist for which the class labels Y are observed, while this is not the case in the unsupervised case. We refer to the supervised case as *classification* and the unsupervised case as *clustering*.

2.1. Classification. In the supervised case, *training data* are available. The training data set is given by $\mathcal{D}_n := \{(X_1, Y_1), \ldots, (X_n, Y_n)\}'$. That is, we have available observations for which the true categorization is known. The goal is to develop a *classifier* g which will take an unlabelled feature vector X, with true but unobserved class label Y, and estimate its class label by $\widehat{Y} = g(X)$. We hope that $\widehat{Y} = Y$ with high probability. Obviously, g should use the available training data and will have functional dependence on the particular observed training data set as well as on the measured features we are trying to classify; thus

$$g : \Xi \times (\Xi \times \{1, \ldots, J\})^n \to \{1, \ldots, J\}.$$

The use of training data to build the classifier is referred to as *training*.

In order for statistical pattern recognition methodologies to have any guarantee of success, we must assume that the training data are *representative*. Usually this means that $(X_i, Y_i) \overset{\text{iid}}{\sim} F$. Alternatively, writing $I\{E\}$ as the indicator function for event E, the *class-conditional sample sizes* given by $N_j(\mathcal{D}_n) := \sum_{i=1}^{n} I\{Y_i = j\}$ may be *design variables* rather than random variables, in which case the conditional random variables $X_i|Y_i = j$ are independent and identically distributed (iid) according to the class-conditional distributions F_j. In the former case the class-conditional sample sizes $N_j(\mathcal{D}_n)$ yield consistent estimates of the priors — $\widehat{\pi}_j(\mathcal{D}_n) := N_j(\mathcal{D}_n)/n \to \pi_j$ almost surely as $n \to \infty$. In the latter case *a priori* knowledge of the prior probabilities must be assumed.

Given a training data set $\mathcal{D}_n$, the *probability of misclassification* for classifier g is given by

$$L(g|\mathcal{D}_n) := P[g(X; \mathcal{D}_n) \neq Y|\mathcal{D}_n].$$

The *Bayes optimal probability of misclassification* is given by

$$L^\star = \min_{g:\Xi \to \{1, \ldots, J\}} P[g(X) \neq Y];$$

notice that for the purposes of defining this bound, we consider classifiers which are not constrained by a particular training set. A *Bayes rule* is any map $g^\star$ with $L(g^\star) = L^\star$. The Bayes rule can be obtained from the class-conditional distributions F_j and the prior probabilities π_j as

$$g^\star(x) = \arg\max_j \pi_j \, dF_j(x).$$

Notice that $g^\star$ depends on the distribution of (X, Y), but not on the training data set.

The goal of classification, then, is to devise a methodology for taking training data $\mathcal{D}_n$ and constructing a classifier g such that $L(g|\mathcal{D}_n)$ is as close to $L^\star$ as possible. In particular, we desire *consistency*: $L(g; \mathcal{D}_n) \to L^\star$ as $n \to \infty$ (in probability or with probability one).

2.2. The curse of dimensionality.

A common misconception in statistical pattern recognition is that "more is better". It is intuitively obvious — and wrong — that if ten features per observation are good then a hundred features are even better. This is a result of one manifestation of the so-called *curse of dimensionality* (Bellman (1961), Scott (1992)).

The curse has several manifestations. Silverman (1986) considers probability density function estimation, and provides a table for the number of observations needed to obtain a point estimate with a given accuracy as the dimension increases. The estimator considered is a nonparametric one, the kernel estimator. It is shown that the number of observations required grows from 4 for univariate data to over 800,000 for ten-dimensional data. Thus, to achieve a given accuracy for a kernel estimator at a single point, the required number of observations grows exponentially in the dimension.

Another consequence of the curse of dimensionality is discussed in Scott (1992), where he points out statistical ramifications of the fact that the volume of a cube in high dimensions resides primarily in the corners, the volume of a sphere resides mostly near the boundary. This is shown by comparing the volume of a sphere with radius r to that of an interior sphere of radius $r - \varepsilon$, and noting that for arbitrarily small $\varepsilon > 0$ the appropriate ratio of volumes goes to 0 as dimensionality goes to infinity, indicating that essentially none of the volume resides in the interior sphere. That is, "high-dimensional space is mostly empty", which in turn suggests that required sample size for fixed performance grows (rapidly) with dimension. (See also Silverman (1986), Table 4.2.)

Jain et al. (2000) discusses another aspect of the curse, first described by Trunk (1979). It is shown that in the simple case of two d-dimensional multivariate normals with equal (known) identity covariances, known priors $\pi_j = 1/2$, and means

$$\mu_j = (-1)^j \left[1, \frac{1}{\sqrt{2}}, \frac{1}{\sqrt{3}}, \dots, \frac{1}{\sqrt{d}}\right]'$$

for classes $j = 1, 2$, the probability of error for the linear classifier — the classifier which labels an observation as belonging to the class associated with the nearest of the two class-conditional sample means — goes to 0 as $d \to \infty$ if the means are known, but this probability of error converges to $\frac{1}{2}$ if the means must be estimated from any training sample of (arbitrarily large but) fixed size. In other words, adding variates that each decrease the Bayes error can actually increase the classification error when estimates must be used rather than the (unknown) truth.

2.3. Classifiers. Assume for simplicity that the class-conditional probability density functions f_j exist. Then any *density estimator* $\widehat{f}_j$ yields a plug-in classification rule:

$$\widehat{g}(x) = \arg\max_j \widehat{\pi}_j(\mathcal{D}_n)\widehat{f}_j(x; \mathcal{D}_n).$$

For iid training data the class conditional sample sizes, $\widehat{\pi}_j$, are consistent estimators for the priors; if in addition a density estimator is employed for which $\widehat{f}_j \to f_j$ in L_1 or L_2 a.s., for instance, then $L(\widehat{g}|\mathcal{D}_n) \to L^\star$ a.s.

Density estimation comes in two basic flavors, parametric and nonparametric. (We categorize "semiparametric" with nonparametric for the purposes of this discussion.) Parametric density estimation assumes that a parameterized functional form for the class-conditional densities f_j is known and focuses on estimating the (few) unknown parameters. Nonparametric methods, on the other hand, make no such parametric assumption. Parametric density estimation is an easier problem — rates of convergence are faster, for example — due to the fact that the target is finite dimensional. Of course, if the assumed parametric form is not correct, a parametric approach will not in general yield consistent classification. Nonparametric methods provide a more general guarantee of consistency, at a price of reduced efficiency if indeed a simple parametric form is appropriate. Classical examples of these two categories, which allow for a fruitful "compare and contrast" exercise, are given by finite mixture models (McLachlan and Krishnan (1997)) versus kernel estimators (Silverman (1986)).

Density estimation is, however, quite expensive in high dimensions (curse of dimensionality). Thus, for multivariate feature vectors in particular, there is much interest in developing applicable classification methodologies which somehow reduce this cost. One approach involves preprocessing to yield reduced dimensionality without seriously degrading classification performance. Thus, one might choose a projection $\mathbb{P} : \Xi \to \mathbb{R}^{d'}$, where $d' = 1$ or 2, say, and consider classification, as above, using $[(\mathbb{P}(X_1), Y_1), \ldots, (\mathbb{P}(X_n), Y_n)]'$ as the transformed training data. See, for instance, principal component analysis, independent component analysis, linear discriminant analysis, and projection pursuit. These techniques can be found in standard multivariate statistics texts such as Seber (1984), Mardia et al. (1995), Johnson and Wichern (1998), and in pattern recognition texts such as Fukunaga (1990), Duda et al. (2000), and Hastie et al. (2001).

Consideration of the maxim "classification is easier than density estimation" suggests that instead of trying to estimate the probability densities, one might choose to estimate the decision region directly. This, too, can be done parametrically or nonparametrically.

The simplest decision region is a linear one, and several methods involve either estimating the best linear separator of the data or extending to piecewise linear discriminators. See for example Sklansky and Wassel (1979).

A popular nonparametric method is the nearest neighbor classifier (and its extension, the k-nearest neighbor classifier). The idea is simple, yet powerful: choose the category associated with the nearest element of the training set. Given a training set $\mathcal{D}_n = \{(X_1, Y_1), \ldots, (X_n, Y_n)\}'$, the nearest neighbor classifier g_{nn} is defined to be

$$g_{nn}(x; \mathcal{D}_n) = Y_{\arg\min_i \{\rho(x, X_i)\}},$$

where $\rho : \Xi \times \Xi \to [0, \infty)$ is a distance function. This classifier has been studied widely — "simple rules survive!" and is a standard against which new classifiers are often tested.

It is well known that the nearest neighbor rule has asymptotic error bounded above by $2L^\star$. This means that if the classes are strictly separable, so that $L^\star = 0$, then the nearest neighbor classifier is consistent.

The k-nearest neighbor classifier is an obvious extension. Rather than considering only the nearest observation, consider the k nearest elements of the training set. A simple vote is taken amongst the classes. (More complicated voting schemes have been investigated.)

Denoting the k-nearest neighbor classifier by g_k, the following theorem of Stone (1977) establishes the universal consistency of this classifier.

THEOREM. *Given iid training data $\mathcal{D}_n$, if $k \to \infty$ and $k/n \to 0$ then*

$$EL(g_k; \mathcal{D}_n) \to L^\star$$

for all distributions.

Many other classifiers have been, and continue to be, developed. We argue, however, that for high-dimensional problems the choice of classifiers is not the most pressing problem. Rather, dimensionality reduction is the fundamental determining aspect of classification performance in high dimensions.

2.4. Misclassification rate estimation. In order to assess how good a classifier is, or to compare classifiers, we would like to know the misclassification rate (probability of misclassification) L. Unfortunately, knowing the exact value of L requires knowledge of the (unknown) class-conditional distributions. Therefore, an important issue in pattern recognition is the estimation of the misclassification rate.

One method for misclassification rate estimation is called the training/test set method: one selects a training set from which to build the classifier, and holds out an independent test set (for which the class labels are also known) upon which to evaluate the classifier. This unbiased holdout estimate of classification performance is denoted $\widehat{L}_n^m$ where n observations are used in training and m observations are used in testing. Analysis is easy: $m\widehat{L}_n^m$ is the sum of independent Bernoulli random variables, and hence follows a Binomial$(m, L(g|\mathcal{D}_n))$ distribution. A problem with this approach is that it requires the collection of additional labelled data beyond that which is used to build the classifier. Labelled data can be expensive, and one might want to use all the available labelled data for training, under the assumption that this will yield a better classifier.

The method in which one uses all the labelled data to build the classifier and then uses the same data to test the classifier is called *resubstitution*, denoted $\widehat{L}^{(R)}$. The resubstitution error rate can sometimes be useful in the analysis of classifiers, but obviously yields a biased (optimistic) estimate of the error.

An improvement on the resubstitution method, with some of the flavor of the training/test method, is *leave m-out cross-validation*, denoted $\widehat{L}_n^{(m)}$. In this, m observations are withheld from a training set of size n and are subsequently used to test the resultant classifier. This is repeated with the next m observations, until all observations have been in a test set (each observation is used in only one test set). If $m = 1$, this is simply referred to as cross-validation. For a discussion of the relative merits of various methods for estimating misclassification rate, see Devroye et al. (1996) or Ripley (1996).

2.5. Clustering.
In the unsupervised case, we have available to us feature vectors $\mathcal{X}_n := \{X_1, \ldots, X_n\}'$, with no class labels available. The goal is to *cluster* these data in such a way as to provide clusters $C_k \subset \mathcal{X}_n$, $k = 1, \ldots, K$ which correspond to some (interesting? useful?) unobserved class labels. Clustering is obviously a more difficult problem than classification. However, clustering is a likely candidate for the exploitation subsystem in some ISP applications.

Clustering can be viewed as the discovery of latent classes within the data. The clusters correspond to classes that were not identified by the collector of the data. These can represent, for example, different variants of a disease in a medical application, previously unidentified subspecies in a biological application, or different types of vehicle in an image processing application.

Unlike classification, clustering *per se* is not well posed. Before proceeding, one must define (implicitly or explicitly) a definition of cluster. Different definitions lead to different clusterings, and without *a priori* information, there is little reason to select one clustering over another. Thus, clustering depends fundamentally on the underlying cluster model.

A further distinction is that clustering requires a determination of the number of clusters. This can be done *a priori*, but usually it is done interactively, either through presentation of potential classes to the user, or through some testing procedure on the model. Thus, clustering combines all of the hard questions in statistics: model selection, model building and model assessment.

3. Integrated Sensing and Processing

The smooth functioning of industry, the government, and even our individual day-to-day activities increasingly relies on a broad spectrum of sensing systems keeping a vigilant eye (ears, nose, etc.) on myriad complex environments and tasks. We are becoming accustomed to the benefits of sophisticated sensing/exploitation systems, ranging from the CT scanners and magnetic resonance imagers that our doctors may inflict upon us, all the way to the suite of radars, thermal imagers, accelerometers, gps, and chemical sensors which some modern cars carry. (Progress.) Moreover, vast quantities of sophisticated sensor data is readily obtained for perusal in the comfort of one's home: large quantities of imagery from webcams, surveillance cameras, hyperspectral sensors, synthetic aperture radars (SAR), and X-ray astronomical data, to name only a few types, can all be quickly accessed on the internet.

The growing complexity and volume of digitized sensor measurements, the requirements for their sophisticated real time exploitation, the limitations of human attention, and increasing reliance on automated adaptive systems all drive a trend towards heavily automated computational processing of the flood of raw sensor data in order to refine out essential information and permit effective exploitation. Complex computational tasks like image formation and enhancement, feature extraction, target detection, classification, intelligent compression, indexing, and operator cueing contribute substantially to the successful operation of the ubiquitous sensing systems essential for our modern technological society.

A generic sensor system may be viewed as a machine for converting information about an object or situation through various representations. The information is initially carried in physical fields (for example, light waves entering a camera lens), transduced into a digital representation (such as the pixels of a grayscale image), which may be computationally manipulated (contrast enhanced for example), and, in many cases, converted to concentrated symbolic information (such as the identification of a particular person standing before the camera). A cartoon model of the generic sensor system is depicted in Figure 1 with the feedforward flow of information from stage to stage indicated by the horizontal arrows. Each subsystem in the figure performs its specific transformation of information in its turn, from physical fields to digital representation in the physical layer, with digital manipulations and enhancements in pre-processing, and finally exploitation to extract high level content. Digital processing generally begins on a pixel array "thrown over the fence" from the physical layer. There is generally little direct feedback from the processing layers to the physical layer that would enable a rapid adaptation of that subsystem's behavior on the basis of discoveries or requirements of processing layers. In consequence, the physical layer typically measures a rather fixed representation of the physical fields, and the digital processor endeavors to extract useful information out of this by computational processing.

Over the last 40 years the need for for effective computational processing and exploitation of digitized sensor data has been met by advances in algorithms from Digital Signal Processing (DSP) and statistical pattern recognition. These advances have combined the power of applied mathematics with the growing precision, stability, throughput, and easy availability of digital processors in an attempt to meet the growing challenges posed by modern applications. One big impact of these advances on sensor systems is the decoupling into the subsystems described previously: physical sensor layer, digital processor layer, digital/symbolic exploitation layer. This represents a significant transformation of sensor/exploitation systems from those of previous times, when exploitation tasks were not automated, and only rudimentary signal processing was performed directly on sensor measurements in the analog domain. Within the current division of labor, analog manipulation is limited to the first stages of the physical sensing, whereas recent computational mathematical developments in DSP and pattern recognition naturally concern the digital processing and exploitation layers almost exclusively.

Recent DARPA sponsored reviews of trends in sensor systems have suggested that the growth of computational complexity in sensor systems networks is quickly becoming a hard limit to scale-up through the concomitant growth of costs of hardware and software, power consumption, and specialization. As sensor data volume and dimensionality grows, computational loads appear to be outstripping the steady Moore's law growth of processor power and the sporadic algorithmic breakthroughs in throughput. One response to this is DARPA's Integrated Sensing and Processing (ISP) program, which attempts to meet this challenge by leveraging mathematical advances across *all* components of a sensing system. ISP seeks examples of sensing systems for which it is possible and advantageous to jointly optimize traditionally the decoupled subsystems of a sensor system. This contrasts sharply with standard approaches which independently optimize subsystems such as the physical layer (sensor head), and the various computational processing layers.

ISP begins with the observation that the main impact of mathematical developments for sensor systems in recent times has been in the processing and exploitation layers, where the ability to computationally adapt mathematical representations and transformations of digital data in real time enable the discovery and exploitation of structure hidden in raw sensor output. Similar but largely untapped opportunities now exist in a current generation of digitally controllable sensor heads for a broad spectrum of phenomena, suggesting new capability to adaptively sense features more informative than pixels.

To realize this capability will require effective mathematical optimizations and control strategies which intelligently integrate currently disjoint tasks of sensing and computation. This promises immediate benefit of "load balancing" between sensor head and processing, with lower signal processing burden while greatly improving the quality and information concentration of the measurements. Carrying on with this idea, ISP contemplates "back end" functions such as classifier algorithms playing an active role in dynamic control of their sensor inputs; in effect playing a mathematically optimal game of "20 questions" through tailored sensor queries suited to the task at hand and what is known or suspected up to the present time. In the new picture of a sensor system, the components have overlapping functionality and communicate data and control in an all-to-all load balanced network.

In this paper, we demonstrate several simple "proof-of-concept" examples of ISP, in which the exploitation subsystem feeds back to the sensor information on what next to sense, based on the determination of the exploitation (classifier) on the current data. Thus, based on preliminary classification of what has been observed, the sensor changes what it is collecting and how it is processing the observations. Again we refer to the cartoon presented in Figure 1. Traditionally, a sensor collects measurements which are processed in some manner and fed to a classifier. The classifier renders its decision and some action is taken based on this decision. This traditional flow is indicated by the horizontal arrows. In adaptive sensors a sensor-preprocessor feedback loop may be present. In the full ISP scenario, the classifier also modifies the set of measurements to be sensed based on exploitation-level feedback. Thus, based on analysis done in the different subsystems, sensor adjustments are fed back to the sensor to improve the overall performance of the system without adversely impacting the overall throughput.

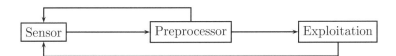

Figure 1. Integrated Sensing and Processing (ISP). The initial sensor measurements are processed in the preprocessor. This may indicate adjustments to the sensor (top arrow) — for example, to improve signal to noise ratio. Preliminary classification results at the exploitation stage suggest changes to the sensing, which information is also fed back to the sensor (bottom arrow).

One analogy for the ISP is a human doctor, viewed as an adaptive sensor/exploitation system. The doctor collects preliminary information, temperature, blood pressure, etc. Then, based on these measurements and external information (for example, information about the outbreak of a plague), the doctor selects new measurements to collect in order to improve or confirm the preliminary diagnosis. This can be viewed as adjusting the sensor to collect different or more precise information, based on a preliminary classification from the exploitation subsystem. Similarly, a hyperspectral sensor might adjust the spectral range of the sensor based on preliminary indications from the classifier of the potential class of the observed object.

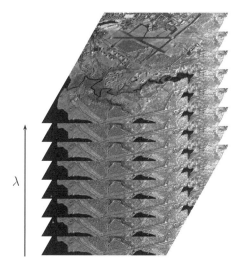

λ

Figure 2. Illustration of a hyperspectral data cube. The cube consists of spatial images (bands) taken at different wavelengths λ.

The ISP approach will be illustrated in the following sections with a pedagogical example and two experimental applications. These illustrations will demonstrate that for some simple but perhaps realistic situations the ISP idea of utilizing information obtained in the classification subsystem to drive sensor parameters can improve the overall performance.

4. Experiment: Hyperspectral Data Cube

For this experiment we have obtained from Naval Space Command a HyMap hyperspectral data set — imagery of the airport at Dahlgren, Virginia (Figure 2). The data consist of 126 images, each one representing the appearance of the scene in light which lies in a narrow spectral band. These bands are obtained throughout the visible, near infrared, and short wave infrared range. Equivalently, we can think of the data as a collection of spectra indexed by the spatial locations in the scene. Spectral imagery data of this sort can provide information about the spatial structure and chemical makeup of the objects within the scene of regard, and is being exploited for problems of detection and identification in a diversity of settings, ranging from biomedicine to defense.

Hyperspectral data gives very fine spectral resolution, but this is not always an advantage. Obviously hyperspectral data is very high-dimensional compared to multispectral imagery, which is similar in concept but comprised fewer, coarser spectral bands. One must be concerned with the curse of dimensionality in the statistical pattern recognition tasks applied to hyperspectral data. Moreover, the large data sets produced by hyperspectral imagers can also lead to significant computational and communication challenges, particularly for time-critical applications. Furthermore, the narrow spectral range of the hyperspectral bands mean that one must collect light for some time before obtaining enough photons in a given band to produce an image with reasonable signal-to-noise ratio. A multispectral sensor with fewer bands would offer coarser spectral resolution but could offer better time resolution, lower dimensional data, and less overall data burden than a hyperspectral sensor. A multispectral sensor with tunable bands could potentially offer some of the benefits of both worlds.

To explore this possibility, we used the more than 100 bands of the HyMap hyperspectral data set as the basis for simulation of a two-band ISP sensor system in which the two are chosen adaptively. For the purposes of this experiment, 6 bands with high noise were removed and 120 bands are used to give an indication of the distribution of photons over wavelength. The coarse bands of the ISP sensor are each the result of a Gaussian filter applied to the 120 band HyMap spectrum. That is, for each spatial location, a weighted sum of the the spectral intensities multiplied by the amplitude of a Gaussian with mean μ_λ and standard deviation σ_λ is returned. Thus the sensor has four adjustable parameters: the spectral means and standard deviations of the Gaussian filters.

Pixels were selected from the image and classed as corresponding to one of 7 classes, using ground truth based on a visit to the site. The 7 classes are: runway, pine, oak, grass, water, brush, swamp. A training set of 700 observations (100 from each class, selected randomly) was chosen, and the remaining (14,048) observations were designated a test set.

The experiment simulates an adaptable sensor which operates as follows. Initially the sensor collects information about the scene in two pre-specified bands (the factory setting), simulated by applying the two Gaussian windows to the HyMap data with fixed initial filter parameter settings. A classifier examines the two band data for each pixel and indicates its coarse classification in the form of the most likely (at most three) classes to which it may belong. Given the classes that this first classifier identifies as contenders, the sensor adjusts its filter parameters to collect new two band data optimized for the task of refining the initial classification by discriminating among the short list of candidates selected in round one. See Figure 3. Thus, the overall sensing and classification takes place in multiple stages with feedback to the sensor to improve the results. The classifiers must be trained and optimized; therefore for all stages, the training data has been split into two equal subsets, with one set used in classifier construction and the other used to estimate the performance of the classifier. More precisely:

Stage 1. We employ a 7-nearest neighbor classifier as the initial coarse-grained classifier. For each observation presented to it, the labels of the top three most likely classes (of the seven defined above) are returned. The filter parameters defining the two bands of the sensor are selected so as to maximize the empirical probability that this classifier places the correct class amongst the top three.

These parameters, along with the 7-nearest neighbor classifier defined by the full training set, constitutes the initial sensor/classification system. This provides the "factory setting" of the system.

Stage 2. For each of the $\binom{7}{3}$ "superclasses" (combinations of 3 candidate classes), filter parameters are selected which optimize the classification of an observation drawn from this superclass, narrowing down its classification to just one of these 3 candidates. That is, we optimize to maximize the probability that an observation is assigned to the correct class given the data available for the 3 class "superclass" identified for that observation in stage 1. The classifier applied to the sensor features tuned to a given superclass is a 1-nearest neighbor classifier based on the training data restricted to the 3 candidate classes of that superclass.

Again, performance is evaluated using the split training set, not the independent test set. The filter parameters selected for each combination of classes will be used to tune the sensor for the best possible discrimination when initial classification of a test observation indicates that particular combination of classes constitutes the candidate set.

Stage 3. The overall classifier is tested as follows. For each observation in the test set, the initial "factory setting" filter parameters are used to obtain the initial two sensor features. The 7-nearest neighbor classifier is evaluated on these initial features. Generally this will return the three leading candidate classes for the observation. In the event that all 7 nearest neighbors are labelled with the same class, unanimity is viewed as decisive and the test observation is classified accordingly without further ado. Otherwise, the filter parameters appropriate to the candidate set of classes are used to adapt the sensor and produce a new feature vector. This new feature vector is passed to the appropriate nearest neighbor classifier, which renders its decision.

The results of this experiment indicate that this optimization which includes feedback from the exploitation subsystem can yield significant performance improvement. The initial classifier places the true class of the test observation into the top three classes 94.15% of the time. This places a lower bound on the possible performance of the overall system at $\widehat{L}_{LB} = 0.0585$. Using a nearest neighbor classifier on these features produces an error of $\widehat{L}_{nn} = 0.1844$. (If instead of optimizing the parameters for the top-3 classifier we optimize for the nearest neighbor classifier we obtain an error of $\widehat{L}_{optnn} = 0.165$.) Our two-stage classifier, which adjusts the sensor based on a preliminary classification as suggested by the "feedback loop" in Figure 1, has an error of $\widehat{L}_{isp} = 0.101$. Thus this experiment demonstrates a significant improvement due to altering sensor parameters based on classification-specific feedback. Notice that we are simulating the effect of the Gaussian filter feature extraction; if implemented in a sensor system, we would expect the classification performance to be even better due to integration gains inherent in observing the spectral features directly.

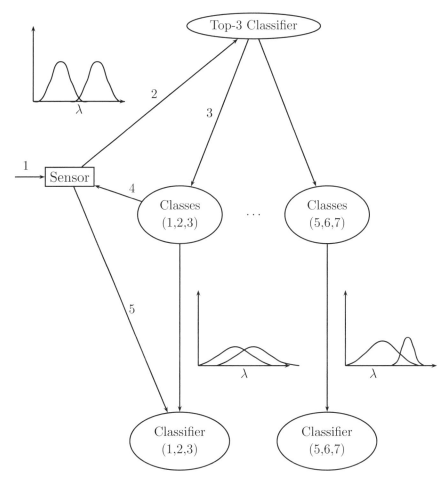

Figure 3. Illustration of the hyperspectral experiment. First, the sensor collects the default bands (1) and a classifier determines the top three classes most likely to contain the true class (2). This determines the new bands to sense (3), which is fed back to the sensor (4). The sensor collects the appropriate bands, which are passed to the ultimate classifier (5).

5. Pedagogical Example: Multivariate Time Series

As a pedagogical example of ISP, consider a case in which each observation consists of a multivariate time series (this sort of data is rather common). For each entity under investigation, the sensor is capable of observing any of $d > 1$ time series ("bands") on a time interval $[0, T]$ at a maximum resolution r_{max} — that is, at equally-spaced times $t_1 = T/r_{max}, t_2 = 2T/r_{max}, \ldots, t_{r_{max}} = r_{max}T/r_{max} = T$. However, sensor and/or channel constraints dictate a maximum throughput for each observation of $\tau < d \cdot r_{max}$. This is a reasonable simplified model of constraints which might imposed on a real systems by limitations of sensor power, available communications bandwidth, computational power, etc.

We want to perform feature selection based on exploitation-level considerations, but the exploitation subsystem cannot have access to all potential features simultaneously. We assume that the sensor/processor subsystem is capable of adapting to subsample each band at a band-specific resolution $r_b <$ r_{max} (with $b \in \{1, \ldots, d\}$) — that is, at equally-spaced times $t_1 = T/r_b, t_2 = 2T/r_b, \ldots, t_{r_b} = T$. (The direct subsampling considered here is done without any filtering of the continuous time input, and may introduce aliasing; we shall see that ISP improvement is nonetheless possible.)

Given a training sample $\mathcal{D}_n$ of entities with known class labels (class-conditional training sample sizes n_j for $j \in \{1, \ldots, J\}$ with $\sum_{j=1}^{J} n_j = n$) the goal is to optimize, based on classification performance, over the collection of band-specific resolutions. That is, we seek

$$\vec{r}^* := \arg\min_{\vec{r} \in \mathcal{R}_\tau} L_{\vec{r}}(g|\mathcal{D}_n)$$

where $L_{\vec{r}}(g|\mathcal{D}_n)$ denotes the probability of misclassification for classifier g trained on training sample $\mathcal{D}_n$ which has been subsampled in accordance with resolutions $\vec{r}$ and, for $c > 0$,

$$\mathcal{R}_c := \left\{ \vec{r} = [r_1, \ldots, r_d]' \in [0, r_{max}]^d : \sum_{b=1}^{d} r_b \leq c \right\}.$$

Thus $\mathcal{R}_\tau$ is the collection of band-specific resolutions satisfying the throughput constraint τ.

However, since the exploitation subsystem never sees all the dimensions simultaneously, this optimization must be performed iteratively. That is, we begin with an initial sensor setting (say uniform allocation of resolution, $\vec{r}^1 = [\tau/d, \ldots, \tau/d]'$) and obtain some measure of which bands are useful for the classification task at hand. This information is provided to the sensor/processor subsystem, and the resolution is increased for the more useful bands and decreased for the less useful bands. (We operate here under the guiding principle that higher resolution for bands with discriminatory information is likely to yield an improvement in classification performance. For this version of ISP to work — as opposed to yielding random search — some such guiding principle must be present to allow the sensor/processor subsystem to choose which measurements to make based on feedback from the exploitation subsystem.)

Let $L^1 := L_{\vec{r}^1}(g|\mathcal{D}_n)$ represent the mis-classification performance using features at the initial choice of resolutions, $\vec{r}^1$. The (penalized) feature selection in the first iteration,

$$\vec{r}^{1*} := \arg\min_{\vec{r} \in \mathcal{R}_\tau} L_{\vec{r}}(g|\mathcal{D}_n) + \lambda \sum_{b=1}^{d} r_b$$

yields performance $L^{1*} := L_{\vec{r}^{1*}}(g|\mathcal{D}_n)$. We expect, if d is large and the number of bands with significant discriminatory information is small, that $L^{1*} < L^1$. This expected improvement is due to the fact that this feature selection represents dimensionality reduction and, in high dimensions with finite training data, dimensionality reduction done properly can yield superior performance due to the curse of dimensionality. (Recall the Jain–Trunk example.)

A simpler version of this feature selection is to perform a band-by-band analysis to determine which bands are useful and which bands are to be discarded. This can be accomplished by considering the special unpenalized "all or nothing" choice of bands:

$$\vec{r}^{1*} := \arg\min_{\vec{r}\in\mathcal{R}'_\tau} L_{\vec{r}}(g|\mathcal{D}_n)$$

with

$$\mathcal{R}'_\tau := \{\vec{r} = [r_1,\ldots,r_d]' \in \{0,\tau/d\}^d\}.$$

At this stage, those bands b for which $r_b^{1*} = 0$ are to be discarded, with the newly-available channel capacity to be evenly allocated among those bands which have been deemed useful. Thus $\vec{r}^2 = [r_1^2,\ldots,r_d^2]'$ where

$$r_b^2 = I\{r_b^{1*} > 0\} \cdot \tau/\sum_\beta I\{r_\beta^{1*} > 0\}.$$

Finally, we define $L^2 := L_{\vec{r}^2}(g|\mathcal{D}_n)$. If our guiding principle—in this case, that higher resolution will increase the discriminatory information in the useful bands, then we expect that $L^2 < L^{1*}$.

Of course, the probability of misclassification is not generally available for use in our optimization objective. Using the available training data $\mathcal{D}_n$ we can, for any given $\vec{r}$, obtain an estimate $\widehat{L}_{\vec{r}}(g|\mathcal{D}_n)$ of the probability of misclassification. Thus we can, in principle, seek

$$\widehat{\vec{r}}^* := \arg\min_{\vec{r}\in\mathcal{R}_\tau} \widehat{L}_{\vec{r}}(g|\mathcal{D}_n).$$

Alternatively, some appropriate surrogate may be employed. For instance, a simple classifier g—a classifier for which $\widehat{L}_{\vec{r}}(g|\mathcal{D}_n)$ is readily available—can be used in the optimization. Then a more elaborate classifier g' can be used for the ultimate exploitation. This surrogate approach will be considered in the sequel. Note, however, that when exploitation means classification, as it does herein, appropriate surrogates will likely still require class label information and may need to reside at the exploitation subsystem—on the opposite side of the channel throughput constraint from the sensor/processor subsystem.

We consider for illustration the case in which each class j, band b process is autoregressive. That is, the i-th observation $X_{j,b,i}$, $i = 1,\ldots,n_j$, is given by an (independent) autoregressive $AR_{j,b}(p)$ process of order $p \geq 1$;

$$X_{j,b,i}(t_k) = \sum_{l=1}^{p} \alpha_{j,b,l} X_{j,b,i}(t_{k-l}) + \varepsilon(t_{j,b,i,k})$$

for $t_k \in \{\dots, -2T/r_{max}, -T/r_{max}, 0, T/r_{max}, 2T/r_{max}, \dots\}$, where the $\varepsilon(t_{j,b,i,k})$ are iid normal$(0, \sigma_\varepsilon^2)$. We write $\vec{\alpha}_{j,b} = [\alpha_{j,b,1}, \dots, \alpha_{j,b,p}]'$ to denote the class-specific, band-specific time series parameter vector. (Recall that a requirement for stationarity yields a constraint on $\vec{\alpha}_{j,b}$.)

In this case, no purely signal processing considerations will allow for the determination of which bands/resolutions are to be preferred. This determination must be made based on feedback from the exploitation module which is in turn based on an analysis necessarily taking into account the class labels — classification performance analysis or some appropriate surrogate.

Maximum likelihood estimates of the parameters $\vec{\alpha}_{j,b}$ can be obtained based on observations of the training entities. These estimates are consistent and asymptotically normal (Anderson (1971)). Thus the training sample provides for an asymptotically Bayes optimal classifier.

Furthermore, this provides for a reasonable surrogate. For each band b an hypothesis test of $H_0 : \vec{\alpha}_{1,b} = \vec{\alpha}_{2,b}$ against the general alternative can be performed using Hotelling's T^2 test statistic (Muirhead (1982)), for instance. Those bands for which the null hypothesis is rejected at some specified significance level are considered to be "useful" for discrimination. The consistency of the hypothesis test employed implies that, in the limit, good bands will not be discarded while most bands with no discriminatory information will be discarded. For instance, for $d = 25$ with exactly five of the bands useful for discrimination, testing at the 0.05 level of significance will be expected to reject for 19 of the 20 useless bands while rejecting for all five of the useful bands (as the estimates $\widehat{\vec{\alpha}}_{j,b}$ approach their asymptotic distributions). It follows that $L^{1\star} < L^1$ for large T.

More specifically, for the two class, two band AR(1) case ($p = 1$, $J = 2$, and $d = 2$), consider $T = 1$, $r_{max} = 100$, and initial sensor settings of $r_b = 50$ for $b = 1, 2$ ($\vec{r}^1 = [50, 50]'$). Let the class $j = 1$ model be specified by $\alpha_{1,1} = \alpha_{1,2} = 0$; similarly, let the class $j = 2$ model be specified by $\alpha_{2,1} = 0$ and $\alpha_{2,2} = 0.1$. (For $p = 1$ we drop the superfluous lag subscript l from the parameters $\alpha_{j,b,l}$.) Thus there is no discriminatory information in band $b = 1$, while band $b = 2$ at the highest resolution will allow for optimal discrimination. For these AR(1) processes, a t-test of $H_0 : \alpha_{1,b} = \alpha_{2,b}$ is an appropriate surrogate, and is here employed. To obtain $\vec{r}^{1\star}$ we optimize over $\tilde{\mathcal{R}}'_{100}$ via these t-tests, meaning that if exactly one band rejects the null hypothesis we completely eliminate the band which fails to reject and up-sample, to full resolution $r_{max} = 100$, the band which does reject the null hypothesis. Using class-conditional training sample sizes $n_j = 10$, classification performance based on these observations, as measure by a Monte Carlo estimate $\widehat{L}$ based on 50 Monte Carlo replicates of 100 test samples per class per replicate, is

$$\widehat{L}^1 = 0.2184, \qquad \widehat{L}^{1\star} = 0.2156, \qquad \widehat{L}^2 = 0.0426.$$

Thus, as designed, the exploitation-based feedback and sensor adaptation yield $\widehat{L}^2 \ll \widehat{L}^1$. As noted above, the consistency of the hypothesis test employed in this example implies that, for large enough class-conditional sample sizes, this empirically observed result can be proved; that is, $L^2 \ll L^1$. (Note that, since $d = 2$ for this case, $\widehat{L}^1 \approx \widehat{L}^{1*}$ is not surprising.)

Regarding the first feature selection, 43 times out of 50 Monte Carlo replicates this selection correctly chose band $b = 2$ ($\vec{r}^{1*} = [0, 50]'$). In five cases both bands yielded rejection in the hypothesis test, in which cases $L^2 = L^{1*} = L^1$. In one case neither band yielded rejection; again $L^2 = L^{1*} = L^1$. In one case band $b = 1$ only — the wrong selection! — yielded rejection; for this one replicate $\widehat{L}^2_{\mathrm{repl}} > \widehat{L}^{1*}_{\mathrm{repl}} > \widehat{L}^1_{\mathrm{repl}}$.

6. Experiment: "Artificial Nose" Chemical Sensor

We consider data taken from a novel chemical sensor/optical read-out system designed and constructed at Tufts University. The fundamental component of this sensor is a solvatochromic dye embedded in a polymer matrix White et al. (1996) which responds to the introduction of a chemical analyte to its environment with a change in its fluorescence intensity. These basic devices can be fabricated in a number of well characterized variants, each responding in some way to particular chemical analytes Dickinson et al. (1996). In general, the devices are cross reactive rather than specific; that is, each will respond significantly to a variety of analytes, although fortunately with differences in the details of the response signature from one analyte to another. By analyzing the responses of several of these devices one may obtain a specific identification in many cases of interest.

For application of these devices in a sensor system, the fluorescence signature must be stimulated and read-out during the exposure of a device to an analyte. For example, a device can be attached to an optical fiber through which laser illumination is provided in order to stimulate the signature fluorescence of that device. The resulting light signal is conducted back through the same fiber for read-out. Typically, an array of devices with their optical fiber readouts will be bundled together to make a sensor. See Priebe (2001) for a discussion of pattern recognition for this kind of sensor.

The Tufts data we study in this section was obtained from a bundle of 19 varying sensors attached to fibers. An observation is obtained by passing an airborne analyte (a single chemical compound or a mixture) over the fiber bundle in a four second pulse, or "sniff." The information of interest is the change over time in emission fluorescence intensity of the dye molecules for each of the 19 fiber-optic sensors (see Figure 4).

Data collection consists of recording sensor responses to various analytes at various concentrations. Each observation is a measurement of the time varying fluorescence intensity at each of two wavelengths (620 nm and 680 nm), within each sensor of the 19-fiber bundle. The sensor produces observations $X_{j,i,b}(t_k)$ where $b = 1, \ldots, d = 38$ represents the fiber-bandwidth pair $\phi \cdot \lambda$ for fibers

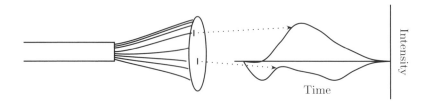

Figure 4. The Tufts artificial nose consists of optical fibers doped with a sol-vatochromic dye. Reaction of the polymer matrix with an analyte produces photons which are sampled at two wavelengths to produce a response for each fiber. These photons are captured by a CCD device, resulting in a time series of light intensity above (or below) the background intensity. The figure illustrates the response of two fibers sampled at a single wavelength.

$\phi \in \{1, \ldots, 19\}$ and wavelengths $\lambda \in \{1, 2\}$. The index $i = 1, \ldots, n$ represents the observation number. The class label j flags the presence or absence of a chemical of interest, described in more detail below. While the process is naturally described as functional with t ranging over a 20 second interval $[0, T = 20]$, the data as collected are discrete with the 20 seconds recorded at $r_{max} = 60$ equally spaced time steps $t_k = \frac{20}{60}, \frac{40}{60}, \ldots, \frac{1200}{60}$, for each response. Construction of the database involves taking replicate observations for the various mixtures of chemical analytes.

The sensor responses are inherently aligned due to the "sniff" signifying the beginning of each observation. The response for each sensor for each observation is normalized by manipulating the individual sensor baselines. This preprocessing consists of subtracting the background sensor fluorescence (the intensity prior to exposure to the analyte) from each response to obtain the desired observation: the change in fluorescence intensity for each fiber at each wavelength. Functional data analysis smoothing techniques are utilized to smooth each sensor response Ramsay and Silverman (1997).

The task at hand is the identification of an unlabelled odorant observation X. Specifically, we consider the detection of trichloroethylene (TCE) in complex backgrounds. (TCE, a carcinogenic industrial solvent, is of interest as the target due to its environmental importance as a groundwater contaminant.)

In addition to TCE in air, eight diluting odorants are considered: BTEX (a mixture of benzene, toluene, ethylbenzene, and xylene), benzene, carbon tetra-chloride, chlorobenzene, chloroform, kerosene, octane, and Coleman fuel. Dilution concentrations of 1:10, 1:7, 1:2, 1:1, and saturated vapor are considered.

We consider the training database $\mathcal{D}_n = [(X_1, Y_1), \ldots, (X_n, Y_n)]'$ to consist of 38-dimensional time series (representing odorant observations) and their associated class labels $Y_i \in \{1, 2\}$ (TCE absent and present, respectively). The database $\mathcal{D}_n$ consists of n_1 observations from class 1 and n_2 observations from class 2. Class 1, the TCE-absent class, consists of $n_1 = 352$ observations; the database $\mathcal{D}_n$ contains 32 observations of pure air and 40 observations of each of the eight diluting odorants at various concentrations in air. There are likewise $n_2 = 760$ class 2 (TCE-present) observations; 40 observations of pure TCE, 80 observations of TCE diluted to various concentrations in air, and 80 observations of TCE diluted to various concentrations in each of the eight diluting odorants in air are available. Thus there are $n = n_1 + n_2 = 1112$ observations in the training database $\mathcal{D}_n$. This database is well designed to allow for investigation of the ability of the sensor array to identify the presence of one target analyte (TCE) when its presence is obscured by a complex background; this is referred to as the "needle in the haystack" problem. This is the database considered in Priebe (2001).

As in our pedagogical autoregressive process example, we consider a through-put constraint. In this case, with $d = 38$ and $r_{max} = 60$, consider a through-put constraint of $\tau = 1140 < d \cdot r_{max} = 2280$. Then $\tau/d = 30$. Let $\vec{r}^1 = [\tau/d, \ldots, \tau/d]' = [r_{max}/2, \ldots, r_{max}/2]'$. With this initial set up we obtain $\widehat{L}^1 = 0.237$. (Probability of misclassification error rates here are obtained via 10-fold cross-validation using the one-nearest neighbor classifier.)

We obtain $\vec{r}^{1*}$ by optimizing over $\mathcal{R}'_\tau$. Actually, this still leaves 2^{38} candidate dimensionality reductions to consider, and so we "sub-optimize"; we calculate $\widehat{L}_b(g|\mathcal{D}_n)$ for each individual band $b = 1, \ldots, d$ and select the "best few". A subset of 12 of the 38 bands are selected based on this criterion, and after this optimization we obtain $\widehat{L}^{1*} = 0.121$.

The best 12 individual bands selected for $\vec{r}^{1*}$ are then upsampled, while the remaining 38 are downsampled. The components of $\vec{r}^2$ are given by

$$r_b^2 = I\{r_b^{1*} > 0\} \cdot r_{max} + I\{r_b^{1*} = 0\} \cdot r_{max}/4.$$

After optimization and feedback adjustment we obtain $\widehat{L}^2 = 0.102$.

We have, as desired, $\widehat{L}^2 < \widehat{L}^{1*} < \widehat{L}^1$. The improvement from $\vec{r}^1$ to $\vec{r}^{1*}$ is dramatic, indicating that the dimensionality reduction employed — although simplistic — was successful. Using $\vec{r}^2$ as opposed to $\vec{r}^{1*}$ yields an improvement of 1.9%. The reduction in misclassification rate is from 134 misclassified to 113 misclassified — 21 observations, or 15.7% of the previously misclassified observations. This improvement obtained by using $\vec{r}^2$ as opposed to $\vec{r}^{1*}$ is statistically significant (McNemar's test).

7. Discussion

We have presented examples illustrating "Integrated Sensing and Process-ing" (ISP) as a path towards end-to-end optimization of a sensor/processor/ exploitation system with respect to its performance in supervised statistical pat-tern recognition (classification) tasks. The approach we have studied in this paper takes the form of dimensionality reduction in sensor feature space coupled with adaptation of sensor features. These techniques are aimed explicitly at improving an exploitation objective — probability of misclassification — and are necessarily implemented iteratively due to throughput constraints.

We note that the results presented are quite preliminary and only begin exploration of the ISP concept. For instance, classifier adaptation and optimization is certainly an aim in ISP, although we have not pursued this direction in the present paper. Ultimately, ISP seeks to jointly optimize sensor function, digital preprocessing, and exploitation systems, including classifier design; however, it is our belief that this issue is secondary to that of dimensionality reduction for many high-dimensional classification applications.

Dimensionality reduction is fundamentally important for many disparate applications in pattern recognition as well as in other fields including control, modeling and simulation, operations research, and visualization. The topic is the subject of intense research in these various communities, and now becomes a fundamental enabling technology for the new discipline of ISP. In this paper we have considered only very simple dimensionality reduction methodologies, which just begin to indicate the possibilities and implications for integrating sensing and processing. Nevertheless, we feel that the results of these first experiments indicate significant promise for this line of inquiry.

A critically important aspect of the dimensionality reduction strategies considered in this paper is the identification of some guiding principle or heuristic for guiding the sensor/processor subsystem in its choices of which measurements to make based on dimensionality-reduction feedback from the exploitation subsystem. The choice of such a principle is a sensor- and application-specific task. For many multivariate time series scenarios "higher resolution in useful bands" approach taken in this paper seems to be a reasonable principle. This might be extended to include variable resolution in quantization, or in spatial sampling in other sensors. Finding appropriate guiding principle(s)for various important cases of practical interest may perhaps represent the single most important aspect of developing a workable ISP methodology.

References

T. W. Anderson. *The Statistical Analysis of Time Series*. Wiley, New York, 1971.

R. E. Bellman. *Adaptive Control Processes*. Princeton University Press, Princeton, New Jersey, 1961.

L. Devroye, L. Györfi, and G. Lugosi. *A Probabilistic Theory of Pattern Recognition*. Springer, New York, 1996.

T. Dickinson, J. White, J. Kauer, and D. Walt. A chemical-detecting system based on a cross-reactive optical sensor array. *Nature*, 382:697–700, 1996.

R. O. Duda, P. E. Hart, and D. G. Stork. *Pattern Classification*. Wiley, New York, 2000.

K. Fukunaga. *Statistical Pattern Recognition*. Academic Press, San Diego, 1990.

T. Hastie, R. Tibshirani, and J. Friedman. *The Elements of Statistical Learning: Data Mining, Inference and Prediction.* Springer, New York, 2001.

A. K. Jain, R. P. W. Duin, and J. Mao. Statistical pattern recognition: A review. *IEEE Transactions on Pattern Analysis and Machine Intelligence*, 22(1):4–37, 2000.

R. A. Johnson and D. W. Wichern. *Applied Multivariate Statistical Analysis.* Prentice Hall, New Jersey, 1998.

K. V. Mardia, J. T. Kent, and J. M. Bibby. *Multivariate Analysis.* Academic Press, New York, 1995.

G. J. McLachlan and T. Krishnan. *The EM Algorithm and Extensions.* Wiley, New York, 1997.

R. J. Muirhead. *Aspects of Multivariate Statistical Theory.* Wiley, New York, 1982.

C. E. Priebe. Olfactory classification via interpoint distance analysis. *IEEE Transactions on Pattern Analysis and Machine Intelligence*, 23:(4):404–413, 2001.

J. Ramsay and B. Silverman. *Functional Data Analysis.* Springer, New York, 1997.

B. D. Ripley. *Pattern Recognition and Neural Networks.* Cambridge University Press, Cambridge, 1996.

D. Scott. *Multivariate Density Estimation: Theory, Practice, and Visualization.* Wiley, New York, 1992.

G. A. F. Seber. *Multivariate Observations.* Wiley, New York, 1984.

B. W. Silverman. *Density Estimation for Statistics and Data Analysis.* Chapman and Hall, New York, 1986.

J. Sklansky and G. Wassel. *Pattern Classifiers and Trainable Machines.* Springer, New York, 1979.

G. V. Trunk. A problem of dimensionality: A simple example. *IEEE Transactions on Pattern Analysis and Machine Intelligence*, 1(3):306–307, 1979.

J. White, J. Kauer, T. Dickinson, and D. Walt. Rapid analyte recognition in a device based on optical sensors and the olfactory system. *Anal. Chem.*, 68:2191–2202, 1996.

CAREY E. PRIEBE
DEPARTMENT OF MATHEMATICAL SCIENCES
JOHNS HOPKINS UNIVERSITY
BALTIMORE, MD 21218-2682
UNITED STATES
   cep@jhu.edu

DAVID J. MARCHETTE
NAVAL SURFACE WARFARE CENTER, B10
DAHLGREN, VA 22448-5100
UNITED STATES
   marchettedj@nswc.navy.mil

DENNIS M. HEALY, JR.
DEPARTMENT OF MATHEMATICS
UNIVERSITY OF MARYLAND
COLLEGE PARK, MD 20742-4015
UNITED STATES
   dhealy@math.umd.edu

Modern Signal Processing
MSRI Publications
Volume **46**, 2003

Sampling of Functions and Sections for Compact Groups

DAVID KEITH MASLEN

ABSTRACT. In this paper we investigate quadrature rules for functions on compact Lie groups and sections of homogeneous vector bundles associated with these groups. First a general notion of band-limitedness is introduced which generalizes the usual notion on the torus or translation groups. We develop a sampling theorem that allows exact computation of the Fourier expansion of a band-limited function or section from sample values and quantifies the error in the expansion when the function or section is not band-limited. We then construct specific finitely supported distributions on the classical groups which have nice error properties and can also be used to develop efficient algorithms for the computation of Fourier transforms on these groups.

CONTENTS

Keywords: Sampling, nonabelian Fourier analysis, compact Lie group.

1. Introduction

The Fourier transform of a function on a compact Lie group computes the coefficients (Fourier coefficients) that enable its expression as a linear combination of the matrix elements from a complete set of irreducible representations of the group. In the case of abelian groups, especially the circle and its lower dimensional products (tori) this is precisely the expansion of a function on these domains in terms of complex exponentials. This representation is at the heart of classical signal and image processing (see [25; 26], for example).

The successes of abelian Fourier analysis are many, ranging from national defense to personal entertainment, from medicine to finance. The record of achievements is so impressive that it has perhaps sometimes led scientists astray, seducing them to look for ways to use these tools in situations where they are less than appropriate: for example, pretending that a sphere is a torus so as to avoid the use of spherical harmonics in favor of Fourier series — a favored mathematical hammer casting the multitudinous problems of science as a box of nails.

There is now however in the applied and engineering communities, a growing awareness, appreciation, and acceptance of the use of the techniques of non-abelian Fourier analysis. A favorite example is the use of spherical harmonics for problems with spherical symmetry. While this is of course classical mathematical technology (see [2; 23], for example), it is only fairly recently that serious attention has been paid to the algorithmic and computational questions that arise in looking for efficient and effective means for their computation [4; 8; 22]. Recent applications include the new analysis of the cosmic microwave background (CMB) data — in this setting, the highest order Fourier coefficients of the function that measures the CMB in all directions from a central point are expected to reveal clues to understanding events in the first moments following the Big Bang [24; 32]. Other examples include the use of spherical harmonic transforms in estimation and control problems on group manifolds [18; 19], and for the solution of nonlinear partial differential equations on the sphere, such as the PDEs of climate modeling [1]. The closely related problem of computing Fourier transforms on the Lie group SO(3) is receiving increased attention for its applicability in volumetric shape matching [13; 14; 17].

In order to bring these new transforms to bear on applications, we must bring the well-studied analytic theory of the representations of compact groups (see [33], for instance) into the realm of the computer. Generally speaking, implementation requires that two problems need to be addressed. On the one hand we need to find a reduction of the a priori continuous data to a finite set of samples of the function, and possibly of its derivatives as well, and we must solve the concomitant problem of function reconstruction, which may only be approximate, from this finite set of samples. This is the *sampling problem*. On the other hand, efficient and reliable algorithms are required in order to turn the discrete data into the Fourier coefficients. These sorts of algorithms go by the name of *Fast Fourier Transforms* or FFTs.

In the abelian case the theory and practice are by now well-known. Shannon sampling is the terminology often used to encompass the solution of the sampling problem for functions on the line, or — and more relevant to this paper — the problem of sampling for a function on the circle, while the associated FFT provides tremendous efficiencies in computation.

In this paper we focus on the sampling problem for compact Lie groups, through an investigation of quadrature rules on these groups. Following the well-known abelian case we distinguish between two situations: the *band-limited* case in which the function in question is known to have only a finite number of nonzero Fourier coefficients, and the *non-band-limited* case. In the former situation it is possible to exactly reconstruct the function from a finite collection of samples, while in the latter, the best we can hope for is an approximation to the Fourier expansion, as well as some measure of how close is this approximation.

We first describe a general setting, *a filtered algebra*, where an extension of the classical notion of band-limited, as in [28], makes sense, and adapt it to the special case of functions on a compact Lie group, G. We define a space of functions $\mathcal{A}_s$ on G, the band-limited functions with band-limit s, in such a way that $\mathcal{A}_s.\mathcal{A}_t$ is contained in $\mathcal{A}_{s+t}$. Then we develop a sampling theorem of the following form:

Assume φ is a distribution on G and f is a continuous function on G that is sufficiently differentiable for the product $f.\varphi$ to exist. There is a canonical projection, P_s, from the space of distributions onto $\mathcal{A}_s$. We describe norms, $\| \ \|$, $\| \ \|_*$, $\| \ \|_{**}$ such that

$$\|P_s(f.(\varphi - \mu))\| \leq M(s,t)\|\varphi - \mu\|_*\|(1 - P_s)f\|_{**},$$

provided that $P_{s+t}(\varphi - \mu) = 0$, where μ is Haar measure of unit mass on the group and $M(s,t)$ is a function which we explicitly bound in the case of the classical groups.

When f is band-limited this gives a condition on the distribution used to sample f that allows exact computation of the Fourier transform of f from the sampled function. When f is not band-limited it quantifies the error introduced when using the Fourier expansion of $f.\varphi$ to approximate that of f. In particular we show that for sufficiently differentiable functions the projection of the approximate expansion onto a space of band-limited functions closely approximates the projection of the original function onto this space without requiring significantly more sample values than the dimension of the band-limited space. The amount of oversampling is related to the growth function of the algebra generated by the matrix coefficients, and hence to its Gel'fand–Kirillov dimension. This is the content of Section 2.

In Section 3 we extend these results to the expansion of sections of homogeneous vector bundles in terms of basis sections coming from the decomposition of the corresponding induced representation, e.g. the expansion of a tensor field on the sphere in tensor spherical harmonics [16]. Finally in Section 4 we construct finitely supported distributions on the classical groups which are convolutions of distributions supported on one parameter subgroups and which have all the properties required by the sampling theorem, i.e. $P_{s+t}(\varphi - \mu) = 0$ and $\|\varphi - \mu\|_*$ is bounded. These distributions can be used to develop fast algorithms for the computation of Fourier transforms on these groups. A general algebraic approach for such algorithms, which uses efficient algorithms for computing with orthogonal polynomial systems [5], is presented in [21].

REMARK. This paper only considers the compact case, but the non-compact is at least as interesting. In this setting G. Chirikjian has pioneered the use of representation theoretic techniques for a broad range of interesting applications including robotics, image processing, and computational chemistry [3].

2. Sampling of Functions

Before going into the general situation it is instructive to consider the familiar case of functions on the 2-sphere S^2, identified with the subalgebra of functions on the compact Lie group $SO(3)$ that right-invariant with respect to translation by $SO(2)$, the subgroup of rotations that leave fixed the North Pole. See Section 2.2.1 for notation.

Example: The Fourier transform on S^2. Let Y_{lm}, with $|m| \leq l$, denote the spherical harmonic on S^2 of order l and degree m (see [23] for explicit definitions). Any continuous function, f, on S^2 has an expansion in spherical harmonics $\sum_{lm} a_{lm} Y_{lm}$ which converges under suitable conditions on f, e.g., when f is C^2. The coefficients a_{lm} are called the *Fourier coefficients* of the function f.

Assume s is a nonnegative integer; then f is said to be *band-limited with band-limit s* if all the coefficients a_{lm} in the expansion of f are zero for $l > s$, i.e. if $f = \sum_{|m| \leq l \leq s} a_{lm} Y_{lm}$. If we now pick $N = (s+1)^2$ points $x_1, \ldots, x_N$ on S^2 in general position, then the function values of f at these points completely determine f provided f is band-limited with band-limit s, so the linear map from function values $(f(x_i))_{1 \leq i \leq N}$ to coefficients $(a_{lm})_{|m| \leq l \leq s}$ is a vector space isomorphism. The numbers a_{lm} can be found from the function f using the formula $a_{lm} = \int_{S^2} f \cdot \overline{Y_{lm}} d\mu$, where μ is the invariant measure on the sphere of unit mass. We can also find these numbers by inverting the equations $f(x_i) = \sum_{|m| \leq l \leq s} a_{lm} Y_{lm}(x_i)$. Another method would be calculate the integrals using sums of the form

$$\sum_{i-1}^{N} f(x_i) \overline{Y_{lm}(x_i)} w_i,$$

where the w_i are numbers, called sample weights, depending only on the points x_i. This is only possible, however, if the w_i and the x_i satisfy

$$\sum_{i=1}^{N} \overline{Y_{lm}}(x_i)w_i = \delta_{(0,0),(l,m)} \qquad \text{for} \quad |m| \leq l \leq s,$$

which is not usually possible for general sets of $N = (s+1)^2$ points, but is possible for general sets of $N = (2s+1)^2$ points; the condition then determines the sample weights, w_i. This is precisely the condition that we can integrate exactly any band-limited function of band-limit $2s$ using the points and weights, and it follows from the fact that the product of two band-limited functions of band-limit s has band-limit $2s$.

What about functions that may not be band-limited? To treat this more general case we first rewrite this discussion. Let $\mathcal{A}_s$ denote the space of band-limited functions with band-limit s, let $\varphi_s = \sum w_i \delta_{x_i}$ be a finitely supported measure on S^2, and let $b_{lm} = \int_{S^2} f.\overline{Y_{lm}}d\varphi_s$ be the Fourier coefficients of the finite measure $f.\varphi_s$. If f is in $\mathcal{A}_s$ and $\langle \varphi_s - \mu, \mathcal{A}_s^2 \rangle = 0$, then $a_{lm} = b_{lm}$ for $|m| \leq l \leq s$; to obtain the condition above note that $\mathcal{A}_s^2 = \mathcal{A}_{2s}$. If f is not in $\mathcal{A}_s$, then we can not assume that we will have $a_{lm} = b_{lm}$ for $l \leq s$, but we can bound the error. It follows from the example immediately after Theorem 3.7 that, provided $\langle \varphi_s - \mu, \mathcal{A}_{2s} \rangle = 0$, we have

$$\sum_{l=0}^{s}(2l+1)\left(\sum_{m=-l}^{l}(b_{lm}-a_{lm})^2\right)^{1/2} \leq 2(s+1)^4\left(\sum_{i=1}^{N}w_i\right)\sum_{l>s}(2l+1)\left(\sum_{m=-l}^{l}a_{lm}^2\right)^{1/2}.$$

Let P_s denote the projection from the space of distributions $C^0(S^2)'$ onto $\mathcal{A}_s$ given by truncation of the expansion in spherical harmonics, then we can rewrite the above inequality to obtain

$$\|P_s(f.(\varphi_s - \mu))\|_{C_0} \leq \|P_s(f.(\varphi_s - \mu))\|_{A_0} \leq 2(s+1)^4\|\varphi_s\|_{C_0'}\|(1-P_s)f\|_{A_0}$$
$$\leq K\|\varphi_s\|_{C_0'}\|(1-P_s)f\|_{W_6},$$

where $\| \ \|_{A_0}$ is the norm of absolute summability inherited from that on $SO(3)$, $\| \ \|_{W_6}$ is the Sobolev norm on C^6, and K is a positive constant; the last inequality follows from an application of Bernstein's theorem on $SO(3)$ (see [6; 27]). Hence, of f is in C^6, and φ_s is a sequence of measures on S^2 which converges weak-$*$ to μ and for which $\langle \varphi_s, \mathcal{A}_{2s} \rangle = 0$, then $\|P_s(f.(\varphi_s - \mu))\|_{C_0}$ tends to zero as s tends tends to infinity.

This approach to the construction of quadrature rules for functions on S^2, can be generalized, and is the goal of the remainder of this section, which is divided into two parts. First we generalize the band-limited sampling of the introduction to filtered algebras and outline an approach for dealing with functions which are not band-limited. Next we treat the case of continuous functions on a compact Lie group, G. Any such function, f, has a Fourier expansion in terms of the matrix coefficients of irreducible unitary representations of G. The

Fourier transform of f is the collection of all coefficients in this expansion, and may be represented as an element of the space $\prod_\gamma \operatorname{End} V_\gamma$, where γ ranges over the irreducible unitary representations of G, and V_γ is the space on which this representation acts. Sampling a C^m function, f, corresponds to multiplying it by a distribution, φ, of order at most m. By putting norms on the space $\prod_\gamma \operatorname{End} V_\gamma$ we can, under suitable assumptions on φ, bound the difference between a finite number of the Fourier coefficients of f and $f.\varphi$.

In what follows we assume a familiarity with the basic ideas and tools of the representation theory of compact groups. There are many excellent resources for this material. Standard texts include [33; 29].

2.1. An Abstract Framework. Several of the results of this paper fit into a simple framework. Assume $\mathcal{A}$ is a complex algebra and $\{\mathcal{A}_s\}$ is a set of subspaces of $\mathcal{A}$ such that $\mathcal{A}_s.\mathcal{A}_t \subseteq \mathcal{A}_{s+t}$, where s and t range over some semigroup, which we shall take to be the non-negative integers or reals. Let $\mathcal{A}'$ denote the dual of $\mathcal{A}$, and define a $\mathcal{A}$-module structure of $\mathcal{A}'$ by

$$(a.\varphi)(g) = \varphi(g.a)$$

for any a, g in $\mathcal{A}$, and φ in $\mathcal{A}'$. Let P_s denote the projection from $\mathcal{A}'$ onto $\mathcal{A}'_s$ given by restriction of linear functionals. Then we have the following trivial result.

LEMMA 2.1. *Assume φ, μ are linear functionals in $\mathcal{A}'$ such that $P_{s+t}(\varphi - \mu) = 0$. Then*

$$P_s(f.\varphi) = P_s(f.\mu)$$

for any f in $\mathcal{A}_t$.

This lemma simply states that, if the linear functionals, φ and μ, agree on the subspace $\mathcal{A}_{s+t}$, then they also agree on the subspace $\mathcal{A}_s.\mathcal{A}_t$.

EXAMPLE. Assume $\mathcal{A}$ is a finitely generated $\mathbb{C}$-algebra with identity, and let S be a finite generating set containing the identity. Define $S_0 = \mathbb{C}.1$, and let S_k denote the span of all products of k elements of S. Then $S_k.S_l = S_{k+l}$ for any nonnegative integers k and l.

The lemma above does not necessarily hold for elements, f, which do not belong to $\mathcal{A}_t$. To deal with this case, let us introduce norms on the algebra, $\mathcal{A}$. Assume that $\| \ \|_{\mathcal{A}'_s}$ is a norm on $\mathcal{A}'_s$ and that $\| \ \|_A, \| \ \|_B$ are norms on $\mathcal{A}$. Let $\mathcal{A}^{\mathcal{A}'}$ be the continuous dual of $\mathcal{A}$ with respect to $\| \ \|_A$, let $\| \ \|'_A$ denote the dual norm, and let $\mathcal{A}^B$ be the completion of $\mathcal{A}$ with respect to $\| \ \|_B$. Now define

$$M(s,t) = \sup\{\|P_s(h.\varphi)\|_{\mathcal{A}'_s} : \|h\|_B = 1, \ \|\varphi\|'_A = 1, \ h \in \mathcal{A}, \ \varphi \in \mathcal{A}', P_{s+t}\varphi = 0\}.$$

When there is a possibility of confusion, we shall denote this $M_B^{\mathcal{A}'_s, \mathcal{A}}(s,t)$. If $M(s,t) < \infty$ then $P_s(h.\varphi)$ is well defined whenever φ is in the $\mathcal{A}$-continuous dual of $\mathcal{A}$, $P_{s+t}\varphi = 0$, and h is in the B-completion of $\mathcal{A}$. In addition, it only depends on the coset of h modulo $\mathcal{A}_t$.

LEMMA 2.2. *Assume* φ, μ *are linear functionals in* $\mathcal{A}^{A'}$ *such that* $P_{s+t}(\varphi - \mu) = 0$, *and let* $h \in \mathcal{A}^B$. *Then*

$$\|P_s(f.\varphi) - P_s(f.\mu)\|_{\mathcal{A}'_s} \leq M(s,t)\|\varphi - \mu\|'_A\|f\|_{B/\mathcal{A}_t}$$

where $\|\ \|_{B/\mathcal{A}_t}$ *denotes the quotient seminorm on* $\mathcal{A}^B/\mathcal{A}_t$.

The next section of this paper is concerned with bounding $M(s,t)$ in the case where $\mathcal{A}$ is the algebra spanned by the matrix coefficients of finite dimensional representations of a compact Lie group. We shall also bound the quantity

$$\overline{M}(s,t) = \sup\{\|e.h\|_{A/\mathcal{A}_{s+t}} : \|e\|_{\mathcal{A}_s} = 1, \ \|h\|_B = 1, \ e \in \mathcal{A}_s, \ h \in \mathcal{A}\}$$

for some particular choices of norms $\|\ \|_{\mathcal{A}_s}$ on $\mathcal{A}_s$. If $\mathcal{A}_s$ is finite dimensional and $\|\ \|_{\mathcal{A}'_s}$ is dual to $\|\ \|_{\mathcal{A}_s}$, then we have $M(s,t) \leq \overline{M}(s,t)$. Weakening $\|\ \|_A$ or $\|\ \|_{\mathcal{A}'_s}$, or strengthening $\|\ \|_B$ or $\|\ \|_{\mathcal{A}_s}$ will decrease $M(s,t)$ and $\overline{M}(s,t)$.

When the algebra $\mathcal{A}$ has a symmetric bilinear form $\langle\ ,\ \rangle$ such that $\langle a_1, a_2.a_3 \rangle = \langle a_1.a_2, a_3 \rangle$, then we have an $\mathcal{A}$-module morphism from $\mathcal{A}$ into $\mathcal{A}'$. Thus we can translate Lemma 2.1 into a statement about subspaces of $\mathcal{A}$.

LEMMA 2.3. (i) $\mathcal{A}_{s+t}^\perp.\mathcal{A}_s \subseteq \mathcal{A}_t^\perp$.
(ii) *Let* $\mathcal{A}_s^- = \cup_{t \leq s}\mathcal{A}_t$, *then* $\mathcal{A}_{s+t}^{-\perp}.\mathcal{A}_s \subseteq \mathcal{A}_t^{-\perp}$.

PROOF. Part (ii) holds because $\mathcal{A}_s.\mathcal{A}_t^- \subseteq \mathcal{A}_{s+t}^-$.   □

2.2. Sampling of Functions on a Compact Lie Group

2.2.1. Notation and conventions. In what follows, we'll assume G is a connected compact Lie group, with Lie algebra $\mathfrak{g}$. Let T be a maximal torus of G and $\mathfrak{t}$ be it's Lie algebra, then $\mathfrak{h} = \mathfrak{t}^{\mathbb{C}}$ is a Cartan subalgebra of $\mathfrak{g}^{\mathbb{C}}$. Choose a fundamental Weyl chamber and for any dominant integral weight, λ, let Δ_λ be the irreducible Lie algebra representation of highest weight λ. If $\hat{G}$ denotes the unitary dual of G, then the map sending an irreducible unitary representation, ρ, to it's highest weight allows us to identify $\hat{G}$ with a subset of the set the set of all dominant integral weights. For any λ in $\hat{G}$ denote the group representation of highest weight λ by Δ_λ as well, and set $d_\lambda = \dim \Delta_\lambda = \prod_{\alpha \in \Delta^+}(\langle \lambda + \delta, \alpha \rangle / \langle \delta, \alpha \rangle)$ where $\delta = \frac{1}{2}\sum_{\alpha \in \Delta^+} \alpha$ and $\langle\ ,\ \rangle$ is the Killing form, and Δ^+ is the set of positive roots. Let $r = \dim([G,G] \cap T)$ be the semisimple rank of G, l be the dimension of the center of G, and k be the number of positive roots of G. Then $2k + r + l = \dim G$, and d_λ is a polynomial of degree k on $\mathfrak{h}^*$. For any representation, ρ, of G, let $\rho^\vee$ be the representation dual to ρ. This gives an involution, $(\ )^\vee$ on $\hat{G}$.

Choose a norm on $\mathfrak{g}$. For any nonnegative integer, m, define a norm on $C^m(G)$, by $\|f\|_{C_m} = \sup\{\|L(X_1 \ldots X_p)f\|_\infty : 0 \leq p \leq m, \ X_1, \ldots, X_p \in \mathfrak{g}, \ \|X_1\| = \ldots = \|X_p\| = 1\}$, where L is the left regular representation. Denote the dual norm on $C^m(G)'$, by $\|\ \|_{C_{m'}}$. These norms are all invariant under the right regular representation. If we were to replace the left regular representation by the right regular representation in the above definitions, we would get an equivalent set of norms invariant under the left regular representation. For $0 \leq m \leq \infty$, denote bilinear pairing between $C^m(G)'$ and $C^m(G)$ by $\langle \, , \, \rangle$. For φ in $C^m(G)'$, and g, h in $C^m(G)$, we have $\langle \varphi, g.h \rangle = \langle \varphi.g, h \rangle$. Define an involution on $C^\infty(G)$ by $\check{f}(x) = f(x^{-1})$, and anti-involutions by $\bar{f}(x) = \overline{f(x)}$, $f^*(x) = \overline{f(x^{-1})}$. These extend to involutions and anti-involutions on $C^\infty(G)'$ by setting $\langle \check{T}, f \rangle = \langle T, \check{f} \rangle$, $\langle \bar{T}, f \rangle = \overline{\langle T, \bar{f} \rangle}$, and $T^* = \check{\bar{T}}$, for any $T \in C^\infty(G)'$ and $f \in C^\infty(G)$. If μ_G denotes Haar measure on G of unit mass, then the map $f \mapsto f.\mu_G$ gives us an inclusion $L^1(G) \subseteq C^0(G)'$, and since G is compact, we also have inclusions $L^p(G) \supseteq L^q(G)$ for $1 \leq p \leq q \leq \infty$. Denote the L^p norm on $L^p(G)$ by $\| \, \|_p$.

Let $\mathcal{A}$ denote the span of all matrix coefficients of finite dimensional unitary representations of G. Then $\mathcal{A}$ is a subalgebra of $C^\infty(G)$ under pointwise multiplication of functions. $\mathcal{A}$ is invariant under the involutions, $\bar{}, \check{}, *$, and the pairing $\langle \, , \, \rangle$ restricts to a nondegenerate bilinear form on $\mathcal{A}$. The hermitian form $\langle f, \bar{g} \rangle$ is positive definite so the bilinear form is nondegenerate on any subspace of $\mathcal{A}$ closed under $\bar{}$. In particular, if $\overline{\mathcal{A}_s} = \mathcal{A}_s$ then we can use the bilinear form to identify $\mathcal{A}_s'$ with $\mathcal{A}_s$. We shall use $\perp$ to refer to orthogonal complements taken with respect to the bilinear form. For a subspace closed under $\bar{}$ this is the same as the complement taken with respect to the hermitian form. For any $\lambda \in \hat{G}$, let $\mathcal{A}_\lambda$ be the span of the matrix coefficients of Δ_λ. The Schur relations show easily that $\mathcal{A}_\lambda^\perp = \sum_{\mu \in \hat{G} \setminus \{\lambda^\perp\}} \mathcal{A}_\mu$.

2.2.2. The Fourier transform. Let $\mathfrak{F}(\hat{G}) = \prod_{\lambda \in \hat{G}} \operatorname{End} V_\lambda$, where V_λ is the Hilbert space on which Δ_λ acts. Choose a norm on $\mathfrak{h}^*$. For $1 \leq q < \infty$ and $0 \leq m < \infty$, define on $\mathfrak{F}(\hat{G})$ the following norms, which may possibly be infinite:

$$\|A\|_{\mathfrak{F}_q} = \left(\sum_{\lambda \in \hat{G}} d_\lambda \|A_\lambda\|_{q,\lambda}^q \right)^{1/q},$$

$$\|A\|_{\mathfrak{F}_\infty} = \sup\{\|A_\lambda\|_\infty : \lambda \in \hat{G}\},$$

$$\|A\|_{A_m} = \|A_0\|_{1,0} + \sum_{\lambda \in \hat{G} \setminus \{0\}} d_\lambda \|\lambda\|^m \|A_\lambda\|_{1,\lambda},$$

$$\|A\|_{A_m'} = \sup\{\|\lambda\|^{-m} \|A_\lambda\|_{\infty,\lambda} : \lambda \in \hat{G}, \ \lambda \neq 0\} \cup \{\|A_0\|_{\infty,0}\},$$

where $\| \, \|_{\infty,\lambda}$ is the operator norm on $\operatorname{End} V_\lambda$ relative to the Hilbert space norm on V_λ, and for $1 \leq q < \infty$, $\| \, \|_{q,\lambda}$ is the norm on $\operatorname{End} V_\lambda$ given by $\|A_\lambda\|_{q,\lambda} = (\operatorname{Tr}(A_\lambda(A_\lambda)^*)^{q/2})^{1/q}$. Let $\mathfrak{F}_q(\hat{G})$, $A_m(\hat{G})$ and $A_m'(\hat{G})$ be the corresponding subspaces of $\mathfrak{F}(\hat{G})$ on which these norms are finite. For general properties of norms of these types see [11].

Recall that if H is a complex Hilbert space, and A is a linear operator on H, then A^* is a linear operator on H, and A^t is a linear operator on its dual space, H', as is $\bar{A} = A^{*t}$. Hence we can define an involution on $\mathfrak{F}(\hat{G})$, by

$(A^t)_\lambda = (A_{\lambda^\vee})^t$, for $A \in \mathfrak{F}(\hat{G})$, $\lambda \in \hat{G}$, and anti-involutions, $(A^*)_\lambda = (A_\lambda)^*$, $(\bar{A})_\lambda = \overline{A_{\lambda^\vee}}$.

We shall now assume that the norm on $\mathfrak{h}^*$ satisfies $\|\lambda^\vee\| = \|\lambda\|$ for any $\lambda \in \hat{G}$. Then the maps $(\ )^t$, $(\ )^*$, and $\overline{(\ )}$ preserve all the above norms on $\mathfrak{F}(\hat{G})$. Define a bilinear pairing between A'_m and A_m, by $\langle A', A \rangle = \sum_{\lambda \in \hat{G}} d_\lambda \operatorname{Tr}((A'^t)_\lambda A_\lambda)$. The map $T : A'_m(\hat{G}) \to A_m(\hat{G})'$ given by $T_{A'}(A) = \langle A', A \rangle$ is an isometric isomorphism, and so we shall use this map to identify $A_m(\hat{G})'$ and $A'_m(\hat{G})$ from now on.

Define the Fourier transform to be the map $\mathfrak{F} : C^\infty(G)' \to \mathfrak{F}(\hat{G})$, given by $\langle \varphi, \mathfrak{F}(s)_\lambda v \rangle = \langle s, x \mapsto \langle \varphi, \Delta_\lambda(x)v \rangle \rangle$ for any $\varphi \in V_\lambda^*$ and $v \in V_\lambda$. When f is a function in $L^1(G)$ this becomes $(\mathfrak{F}f)_\lambda = \int_G f(x)\Delta_\lambda(x)d\mu_G(x)$. To make the statement of the next lemma simpler, it is convenient to assume choose the norms on $\mathfrak{h}^*$ and $\mathfrak{g}$ so that $\|\Delta_\lambda(X)\|_{\infty,\lambda} \leq \|\lambda\|.\|X\|$; to see that this is possible, just consider the case where the norm on $\mathfrak{g}$ is Ad-invariant. This condition can always be achieved by scaling either the norm on $\mathfrak{h}^*$ or the norm on $\mathfrak{g}$. More specifically, this condition avoids additional constants in the statements of Lemma 2.4((d),(f)).

LEMMA 2.4 (PROPERTIES OF $\mathfrak{F}$). *Assume m is a nonnegative integer, $1 \leq q \leq 2$ and $1/q + 1/q' = 1$.*

(i) *$\mathfrak{F} : C^\infty(G)' \to \mathfrak{F}(\hat{G})$ is one to one.*

(ii) *$\|\mathfrak{F}f\|_{q'} \leq \|f\|_q$. These are the Hausdorff–Young inequalities.*

(iii) *$\mathfrak{F}(L^q(G)) \supseteq \mathfrak{F}_q(\hat{G})$, and for any A in $\mathfrak{F}_q(\hat{G})$ we have $\|\mathfrak{F}^{-1}(A)\|_{q'} \leq \|A\|_q$*

(iv) *$\mathfrak{F}(C^m(G)) \supseteq A_m(\hat{G})$, and for any A in $A_m(\hat{G})$ we have $\|\mathfrak{F}^{-1}A\|_{C_m} \leq \|A\|_{A_m}$.*

(v) *Assume $T \in C^m(G)'$, $A \in A_m(\hat{G})$, and $f = \mathfrak{F}^{-1}A$. Then $\langle T, f \rangle = \langle \mathfrak{F}T, \mathfrak{F}f \rangle$.*

(vi) *For any s in $C^m(G)'$ we have $\|\mathfrak{F}s\|_{A'_m} \leq \|s\|_{C_{m'}}$*

(vii) *For any s in $C^\infty(G)'$ we have $\mathfrak{F}(\bar{s}) = \overline{\mathfrak{F}s}$, $\mathfrak{F}\check{s} = (\mathfrak{F}s)^t$, and $\mathfrak{F}s^* = (\mathfrak{F}s)^*$. In particular, $\mathfrak{F}$ is real relative to the real structures on $C^\infty(G)'$ and $\mathfrak{F}(\hat{G})$ induced by the anti-involutions, $\overline{(\ )}$, on these spaces.*

(viii) *$(\mathfrak{F}(s_1 * s_2))_\lambda = (\mathfrak{F}s_1)_\lambda (\mathfrak{F}s_2)_\lambda$, for any distributions, s_1, s_2, in $C^\infty(G)'$, and any λ in $\hat{G}$, where $s_1 * s_2$ denotes the convolution of the distributions s_1 and s_2.*

(ix) *$\|\mathfrak{F}(s_1 * s_2)\|_{A'_{m_1+m_2}} \leq \|\mathfrak{F}s_1\|_{A'_{m_1}} \|\mathfrak{F}s_2\|_{A'_{m_2}}$.*

PROOF. See [20; 11]. $\qquad\square$

The image $\mathfrak{F}A$ consists of precisely those elements, A, of $\mathfrak{F}(\hat{G})$ such that $A_\lambda = 0$ except for finitely many λ. All the norms defined above are finite on $\mathfrak{F}A$, and $\mathfrak{F}A$ is dense in each of these spaces under the corresponding norm. As $\mathfrak{F}$ is one to one, we can transfer the algebra structure on A to $\mathfrak{F}A$, and hence obtain a A-module structure on the spaces A_m and A'_m. The map T, is an isomorphism of of A-modules, and we can use same formula to get a dual pairing between $\mathfrak{F}(\hat{G})$ and $\mathfrak{F}A$, and hence a A-module isomorphism between $(\mathfrak{F}A)'$ and $\mathfrak{F}(\hat{G})$.

2.2.3. Simple bounds for $\overline{M}$(s,t). Let us assume that an increasing set of finite dimensional subspaces $\{\mathcal{A}_s\}$, is given, that $\mathcal{A}_s.\mathcal{A}_t \subseteq \mathcal{A}_{s+t}$, and that $\bigcup_{s \geq 0} \mathcal{A}_s = \mathcal{A}$. Examples for such subspaces can be obtained from finite dimensional generating sets of $\mathcal{A}$, or as described in Section 2.2.4, from a norm on $\mathfrak{h}^*$. We shall bound $M(s,t)$ for several different choices of norms, $\| \ \|_A$, $\| \ \|_B$, $\| \ \|_{\mathcal{A}_s}$, on $\mathcal{A}$ and $\mathcal{A}_s$.

Using the Leibniz rule one sees that for $f, g \in C^m(G)$, we have $\|fg\|_{C_m} \leq 2^m \|f\|_{C_m} \|g\|_{C_m}$. Therefore

RESULT. Assume the A, B norms are both $\| \ \|_{C_m}$ and that $\| \ \|_{\mathcal{A}_s}$ is the restriction of $\| \ \|_{C_m}$ to $\mathcal{A}_s$. Then $\overline{M}(s,t) \leq 2^m$

When $m = 0$, this tells us that if φ is a regular bounded complex Borel measure on G satisfying $P_{s+t}(\varphi - \mu_G) = 0$, h is a continuous function on G, and $Y = (g \mapsto \langle \Delta_\lambda(g)u, v \rangle$ is a matrix coefficient in $\mathcal{A}_s$, then $\left| \int_G h.Y d\varphi - \int_G h.Y d\mu_G \right| \leq \|u\| \|v\| \|\varphi\|_{C_0'} \|h\|_{C_0/\mathcal{A}_t}$. Clearly $\|h\|_{C_0/\mathcal{A}_t}$ tends to zero as t tends to infinity.

In a similar fashion, we can bound $\overline{M}(s,t)$ for weaker choices of the norm $\| \ \|_{\mathcal{A}_s}$ on $\mathcal{A}_s$.

RESULT. Assume the A, B norms are both $\| \ \|_{C_m}$ and that $\| \ \|_{\mathcal{A}_s}$ is the restriction of $\| \ \|_{C_0'}$ to $\mathcal{A}_s$, then for some $K > 0$, independent of m,

$$\overline{M}(s,t) \leq K^m \left(1 + \sum_{\mathcal{A}_s \cap \mathcal{A}_\lambda \neq \phi} d_\lambda^2 \|\lambda\|^m \right).$$

Consider this for $s = t$. Assume that φ is a distribution of order m on G satisfying $P_{2s}(\varphi - \mu_G) = 0$, and h is a C^m function of G. Then

$$\|P_s(h.\varphi - h.\mu)\|_{C_0} \leq 2^m \left(1 + \sum_{\mathcal{A}_s \cap \mathcal{A}_\lambda \neq \phi} d_\lambda^2 \|\lambda\|^m \right) \|\varphi\|_{C_m'} \|h\|_{C_s/\mathcal{A}_s},$$

but the sum in this bound is bounded from below by a constant times $s^{2k+m+r+l}$, and we are forced to consider higher differentiability conditions on h in order to get convergence of $\|P_s(h.\varphi - h.\mu)\|_{C_0}$ to zero. Doing so leads us naturally to the consider the norms A_m, on $\mathcal{A}$, and more careful arguments with these new norms will give us more refined bounds on $M(s,t)$ in the situation above.

2.2.4. Norms on $\hat{G}$. Let $\| \ \|$ be a norm on $\mathfrak{h}^*$. For any $s \geq 0$ let $\mathcal{A}_s$ be the span of all the matrix coefficients of representations Δ_λ for $\|\lambda\| \leq s$, i.e. $\mathcal{A}_s = \sum_{\|\lambda\| \leq s} A_\lambda$. There are several properties we may require of this norm on $\mathfrak{h}^*$. We say that a norm $\| \ \|$ on $\mathfrak{h}^*$ *has property I* if whenever λ, μ, ν are in $\hat{G}$, and Δ_ν is a summand of $\Delta_\lambda \otimes \Delta_\mu$, then $\|\nu\| \leq \|\lambda\| + \|\nu\|$. We say that $\| \ \|$ *has property II* if $\|\nu'\| \leq \|\lambda\|$ whenever ν' is a weight of Δ_λ.

LEMMA 2.5. $\| \ \|$ *has property I if and only if for any $s, t > 0$, $\mathcal{A}_s.\mathcal{A}_t \subseteq \mathcal{A}_{s+t}$*

LEMMA 2.6. (i) *If $\| \ \|$ satisfies property I, and Δ_ν is a summand of $\Delta_\lambda \otimes \Delta_\mu$, then $\left| \|\lambda\| - \|\mu\| \right| \leq \|\nu\|$.*

(ii) $\| \; \|$ *has property I if and only if* $\left| \|\lambda\| - \|\nu\| \right| \leq \|\mu\|$ *whenever* Δ_ν *is a summand of* $\Delta_\lambda \otimes \Delta_\mu$.

PROOF. Part (ii) is a direct consequence of (i). To prove (i), assume I, and suppose Δ_ν is a summand of $\Delta_\lambda \otimes \Delta_\mu$. Then $\mathcal{A}_\nu \subseteq \mathcal{A}_\lambda . \mathcal{A}_\mu$. For any $s \geq 0$, let $\mathcal{A}_s^- = \sum_{\|\rho\| < s} \mathcal{A}_\rho$. Then $\mathcal{A}_\lambda \subseteq \mathcal{A}_{\|\lambda\|}^{-\perp}$, and $\mathcal{A}_\mu \leq \mathcal{A}_{\|\mu\|}$. Assume $\|\lambda\| \geq \|\mu\|$. Lemma 2.3 shows that $\mathcal{A}_{\|\lambda\|}^{-\perp} . \mathcal{A}_\mu \subseteq \mathcal{A}_{\|\lambda\| - \|\mu\|}^{-\perp}$. Hence $\mathcal{A}_\nu \subseteq \mathcal{A}_{\|\lambda\| - \|\mu\|}^{-\perp}$, and so $\|\lambda\| - \|\mu\| \leq \|\nu\|$. $\qquad \square$

To show that II implies I, we need the following lemma.

LEMMA 2.7. *Assume* λ, μ, ν *are dominant integral weights. If* Δ_ν *is a summand of* $\Delta_\lambda \otimes \Delta_\mu$, *then* $\nu = \mu + \nu'$ *where* ν' *is a weight of* Δ_λ

PROOF. Follows from Steinberg's formula for the decomposition of tensor products. See [12] $\qquad \square$

COROLLARY 2.8. *II implies I*

All the norms on $\mathfrak{h}^*$ which we will use, will satisfy property I. Let us now show that norms satisfying properties I or II really do exist.

Assume $\langle \, , \, \rangle$ is a positive definite Ad-invariant inner product on $\mathfrak{g}^{\mathbb{C}}$. Then define $\|\mu\|_{\mathrm{Ad}} = \sqrt{\langle \mu, \mu \rangle}$. This gives a norm on $\mathfrak{h}^*$ which is invariant under the Weyl group.

For calculations involving the classical groups another set of norms is more convenient. Assume G is a simple classical group and let $\lambda_1, \ldots, \lambda_r$ be the fundamental dominant weights with the standard labeling (i.e. that which appears in [12, p. 58]). Define the linear functional, H, on $\mathfrak{h}^*$ by requiring that for $\mu = \sum a_i \lambda_i$, we have

(i) $H(\mu) = \sum_{i=1}^r a_i$ when G is SU$(r+1)$ or Sp(r).
(ii) $H(\mu) = \sum_{i=1}^{r-1} a_i + \frac{1}{2} a_r$ when G is SO$(2r+1)$.
(iii) $H(\mu) = \sum_{i=1}^{r-2} a_i + \frac{1}{2}(a_{r-1} + a_r)$ when G is SO$(2r)$.

Define a norm $\| \; \|_H$ on $\mathfrak{h}^*$ by requiring that $\|\mu\|_H = H(\mu)$ for any dominant weight and $\| \; \|_H$ is invariant under the Weyl group. Note that in each of the above cases $\| \; \|_H$ is also invariant under $\vee$.

To verify that we indeed have defined norms it is easiest to use a different description. Let $\{e_i\}$ denote the usual basis of $\mathbb{C}^r$. When G is SU$(r+1)$ we have an isomorphism between $\mathfrak{h}^*$ and $\mathbb{C}^{r+1} / \langle e_1 + \ldots e_{r+1} = 0 \rangle$. such that $\lambda_i = \sum_{j=1}^i e_i$. When G is any other simple classical group we have an isomorphism between $\mathfrak{h}^*$ and $\mathbb{C}^r$ with $\lambda_i = \sum_{j=1}^{r-2} e_i$ for $1 \leq i \leq r-2$, and $\lambda_{r-1} = e_1 + \cdots + e_{r-1}$, $\lambda_r = e_1 + \cdots e_r$ for Sp(r), $\lambda_{r-1} = e_1 + \cdots + e_{r-1}$, $\lambda_r = \frac{1}{2}(e_1 + \ldots e_r)$ for SO$(2r+1)$, and $\lambda_{r-1} = \frac{1}{2}(e_1 + \cdots + e_{r-1} - e_r)$, $\lambda_r = \frac{1}{2}(e_1 + \cdots + e_r)$ for SO$(2r)$. When G is Sp(r), SO$(2r+1)$ or SO$(2r)$, the norm $\| \; \|_H$ corresponds to the sup norm on $\mathbb{C}^r$. When G is SU$(r+1)$ it corresponds to twice the quotient of the sup norm on $\mathbb{C}^{r+1}$.

LEMMA 2.9. (i) *If* $\mathfrak{g}$ *is abelian, then any norm on* $\mathfrak{h}^*$ *has property II.*

(ii) *Assume* $\| \ \|_1, \| \ \|_2$ *are norms on* $\mathfrak{g}_1$ *and* $\mathfrak{g}_2$ *which both satisfy the same property I or II. Assume* $\mathfrak{g} = \mathfrak{g}_1 \oplus \mathfrak{g}_2$, *and* $\|\lambda_1 + \lambda_2\| = \|\lambda_1\|_1 + \|\lambda_2\|_2$ *for any* $\lambda_1 \in \mathfrak{h}_1$ *and* $\lambda_2 \in \mathfrak{h}_2$. *Then* $\| \ \|$ *satisfies the corresponding property I or II on* $\mathfrak{h}^* = \mathfrak{h}_1^* \oplus \mathfrak{h}_2^*$.

(iii) $\| \ \|_{\mathrm{Ad}}$ *has property II for any* $\mathfrak{g}$.

(iv) $\| \ \|_H$ *has property II for any of the simple classical groups.*

PROOF. Parts (i) and (ii) are trivial. For (iii), note that $\mathfrak{g} = \mathfrak{z} \oplus [\mathfrak{g}, \mathfrak{g}]$ is an orthogonal direct sum, so we need only prove the result in the case where G is semisimple and $\langle \ , \ \rangle$ on it is simply the Killing form. So let's assume that this is the case, $\lambda \in \hat{G}$, and μ is a weight of λ. Since all elements of the Weyl group are isometries, we may also assume that μ is dominant. Then $\langle \lambda, \lambda \rangle - \langle \mu, \mu \rangle = \langle \lambda + \mu, \lambda - \mu \rangle$, which is greater than 0 because $\lambda + \mu$ is a dominant weight and $\lambda - \mu$ is in the positive root lattice.

Part (iv) is equivalent to the condition that $H(\alpha) \geq 0$ for any simple root α. This is easily checked by inspection of the Cartan matrices of the simple classical lie algebras.   □

There is a nice interpretation of $\mathcal{A}_s$ in the case where G is $\mathrm{SU}(r+1)$, $\mathrm{Sp}(r)$ or $\mathrm{SO}(2r+1)$, and $\| \ \| = \| \ \|_H$. In this case, $\mathcal{A}_1$ is the span of the matrix coefficients of the representations with highest weight a fundamental analytically integral dominant weight (i.e. an element of a basis for the analytically integral dominant weight over the nonnegative integers) or 0. Hence $\mathcal{A}_1$ is a finite dimensional generating set for $\mathcal{A}$, and for any positive integer s, $\mathcal{A}_s$ is the span of all products of up to s elements of $\mathcal{A}_1$. In particular, $\mathcal{A}_s.\mathcal{A}_t = \mathcal{A}_{s+t}$.

2.2.5. Further bounds for $M(s,t)$. We shall now bound $M(s,t)$, as defined in Section 2.1, where $\| \ \|_A = \| \ \|_{A_m}$, $\| \ \|_B = \| \ \|_{A_p}$. It is clear that the pairing between A'_m and A_m allows us to identify $\mathfrak{F}\mathcal{A}'_s$ with $\mathfrak{F}\mathcal{A}_s$, and that A_m and A'_m are dual norms on this finite dimensional subspace. In the definition of $M(s,t)$ we shall use $\| \ \|_{A_s} = \| \ \|_{A'_{m_1}}$, $\| \ \|_{A'_s} = \| \ \|_{A_{m_1}}$. The projection, P_s, from $\mathfrak{F}\mathcal{A}' = \mathfrak{F}(\hat{G})$ onto $\mathfrak{F}\mathcal{A}_s$ is given by $(P_s A)_\lambda = 0$ when $\|\lambda\| > s$, and $(P_s A)_\lambda = A_\lambda$ when $\|\lambda\| \leq s$. The quotient norm on $A_p(\hat{G})/\mathfrak{F}\mathcal{A}_t$ is clearly given by $\|f\|_{A_p/\mathfrak{F}\mathcal{A}_t} = \|f - P_t f\|_{A_p}$. Hence

$$M(s,t) = \sup\{\|P_s(h.\varphi)\|_{A_{m_1}} : h, \varphi \in \mathfrak{F}\mathcal{A}, \|h\|_{A_p} = 1, \|\varphi\|_{A'_m} = 1, P_{s+t}\varphi = 0\},$$

$$\overline{M}(s,t) = \sup\{\|e.h - P_{s+t}(e.h)\|_{A_m} : \|h\|_{A_p} = 1, \|e\|_{A'_{m_1}} = 1, e \in \mathfrak{F}\mathcal{A}_s, h \in \mathfrak{F}\mathcal{A}\}.$$

The bounds for $M(s,t)$ depend on the following lemma.

LEMMA 2.10. *Assume* f, g *are in* $A_0(\hat{G})$. *Then* $f.g$ *is well-defined, and*

$$\|f.g\|_{A_0} \leq \|f\|_{A_0} \|g\|_{A_0}.$$

PROOF. See [11].   □

THEOREM 2.11. *Assume the norm on $\mathfrak{h}^*$ satisfies property I. Then there is a $K > 0$ such that for any non negative integers, $p \geq m \geq 0$, and any $s, t > 1$, we have*

$$\overline{M}(s,t) \leq K_G s^{2k+2r+l+m_1}(s+t)^m t^{-p}.$$

PROOF. Assume that $e \in \mathfrak{F}A_s$, $h \in \mathfrak{F}A$ are such that $\|h\|_{A_p} = 1$, and $\|e\|_{A'_0} = 1$. For any λ in $\hat{G}$, let P_λ denote the projection from $\mathfrak{F}(\hat{G})$ onto the subspace corresponding to $\operatorname{End} V_\lambda$. Let $e_\nu = P_\nu e$, $h_\lambda = P_\lambda h$, and let $\Pi(\nu)$ denote the set of weights of Δ_ν.

Then

$$\|e.h\|_{A_m/\mathfrak{F}A_{s+t}} \leq \sum_{\|\mu\|>s+t} d_\mu \|\mu\|^m \|P_\mu(e.h)\|_{1,\mu},$$

$$\leq \sum_{\|\mu\|>s+t} d_\mu \|\mu\|^m \sum_{\substack{\|\nu\|\leq s, \lambda-\mu\in\Pi(\nu) \\ \left|\|\lambda\|-\|\mu\|\right|\leq\|\nu\|}} \|P_\mu(e_\nu.h_\lambda)\|_{1,\mu}$$

$$\leq \sum_{\|\nu\|\leq s} d_\nu^2 \max\{1,\|\nu\|^{m_1}\} \sum_{\mu,\lambda} \|\mu\|^m d_\lambda \|h_\lambda\|_{1,\lambda},$$

where we used the inequality

$$\|P_\mu(e_\nu.h_\lambda)\|_{1,\mu} \leq d_\mu^{-1} d_\lambda d_\nu \|h_\lambda\|_{1,\lambda} \|e_\mu\|_{1,\mu} \leq d_\mu^{-1} d_\lambda d_\nu^2 \|h_\lambda\|_{1,\lambda} \|e_\nu\|_{\infty,\nu},$$

which follows directly from Lemma 2.10. Now sum on μ lemma to see that for some $K > 0$, the above quantities are bounded by

$$\sum_{\|\nu\|\leq s} d_\nu^2 \max\{1,\|\nu\|^{m_1}\} \left|\Pi(\nu)\right| \sum_{\|\lambda\|>t} d_\lambda(\|\lambda\|+s)^m \|h_\lambda\|_{1,\lambda}$$

$$\leq \sum_{\|\nu\|\leq s} d_\nu^2 \max\{1,\|\nu\|^{m_1}\} \left|\Pi(\nu)\right|(\|\nu\|+t)^m t^{-p} \sum_{\|\lambda\|>t} d_\lambda \|\lambda\|^p \|h_\lambda\|_{1,\lambda}$$

$$\leq (s+t)^m s^{m_1} \left(\sum_{\|\nu\|\leq s} d_\nu^2 \left|\Pi(\nu)\right| \right) \sum_{\|\lambda\|>t} d_\lambda \|\lambda\|^p \|h_\lambda\|_{1,\lambda}$$

$$\leq K s^{2k+2r+l+m_1}(s+t)^m t^{-p} \sum_{\|\lambda\|>t} d_\lambda \|\lambda\|^p \|h_\lambda\|_{1,\lambda}.$$

The last inequality holds because there is a constant $C > 0$ such that $\left|\Pi(\nu)\right| \leq C\|\nu\|^r$. This holds for the norm $\|\ \|_{\operatorname{Ad}}$ and hence for any other norm on $\mathfrak{h}^*$. $\square$

When G is abelian we can get a more explicit bound for even more general norms on $\mathfrak{F}A$. We shall bound $M(s,t)$ for slightly more general choices of $\|\ \|_A$, $\|\ \|_B$ and $\|\ \|_{A_s}$ than we used above. We have $d_\lambda = 1$, so each $\operatorname{End} V_\lambda$ is naturally and uniquely isomorphic to $\mathbb{C}$. Define norms, on $\mathfrak{F}A$, for $1 \leq q < \infty$ and

$-\infty \le m < \infty$, by

$$\|A\|_{\mathfrak{F}_q A_m} = \left(|A_0|^q + \sum_{\lambda \in \hat{G} \setminus \{0\}} \left(\|\lambda\|^m |A_\lambda| \right)^q \right)^{1/q}$$

$$\|A\|_{\mathfrak{F}_\infty A_m} = \sup\{\|\lambda\|^m |A_\lambda| : \lambda \in \hat{G}, \ \lambda \ne 0\} \cup \{|A_0|\}.$$

If $1/q + 1/q' = 1$, then $\| \ \|_{\mathfrak{F}_{q'} A_{-m}}$ is the dual norm to $\| \ \|_{\mathfrak{F}_q A_m}$, and when both norms are restricted to $\mathcal{A}_s$, this holds for $q = \infty$ as well. When $m = 0$ we have $\| \ \|_{\mathfrak{F}_q A_0} = \| \ \|_{\mathfrak{F}_q}$, and when q is 1 or ∞, $m \ge 0$, , we have $\| \ \|_{\mathfrak{F}_1 A_m} = \| \ \|_{A_m}$ and $\| \ \|_{\mathfrak{F}_\infty A_{-m}} = \| \ \|_{A_0'}$. Now let $\| \ \|_{A_s'}$ be the restriction of $\| \ \|_{\mathfrak{F}_{q_1} A_{m_1}}$ to $\mathfrak{F}\mathcal{A}_s$, let $\| \ \|_A = \| \ \|_{\mathfrak{F}_{q_2} A_{m_2}}$ and $\| \ \|_B = \| \ \|_{\mathfrak{F}_{q_3} A_{m_3}}$.

THEOREM 2.12. *Assume G is abelian, $1 \le q_1, q_2, q_3 \le \infty$, and s and t are positive integers. Then*

$$M(s,t) \le \left(1 + \sum_{\|\nu\| \le s} (\|\nu\|^{m_1})^{q_1} \right)^{1/q_1} (s + t)^{m_2} t^{-m_3}$$

provided $q_3 \le q_2$ and $m_3 \ge m_2$.

PROOF. Similar to 2.11, except in this case, start with h, φ in $\mathfrak{F}\mathcal{A}$ and expand out the product $h.\varphi$ directly. □

2.2.6. Examples: Sampling for S^1, SO(3), and the simple classical Lie groups

The Simplest Example: Sampling on S^1. Assume m is a nonnegative integer, f is a C^m complex function on S^1, φ is a distribution of order at most m on S^1, and f, φ and $f.\varphi$ have the Fourier expansions $\sum_k c_k x^k$, $\sum_k m_k x^k$ and $\sum_k b_k x^k$ respectively. Then $\|\mathfrak{F}f\|_q = (\sum_k |c_k|^q)^{1/q}$, $\|\mathfrak{F}f\|_{A_m} = \sum_k k^m |c_k|$ and $\|\mathfrak{F}\varphi\|_{A_m'} = \sup\{k^{-m} |m_k| : k \in \mathbb{Z}\}$. Hence

$$\left(\sum_{|k| \le s} |c_k - b_k|^q \right)^{1/q} \le (2s+1)^{1/q} (1 + \frac{s}{t})^m N \sum_{|k|>t} k^m |c_k|$$

$$\le (2s+1)^{1/q} (1 + \frac{s}{t})^m N \frac{\pi}{\sqrt{3}} \left(\sum_{|k|>t} |k^{m+1} c_k|^2 \right)^{1/2},$$

provided $m_k = 0$ for $0 < |k| \le s+t$ and $m_0 = 1$, and where $N = \sup\{k^{-m} |m_k| : |k| > s+t\}$. The factor $\pi/\sqrt{3}$ could be replaced by a factor of the form $Cb^{-\varepsilon}$ for any ε strictly less than $\frac{1}{2}$. When f is C^{m+1} we can further bound this sum by a Sobolev norm, as

$$\left(\sum_{|k|>b} |k^{m+1} c_k|^2 \right)^{1/2} = \left(\frac{1}{2\pi} \int_0^{2\pi} \left| \frac{d^{m+1}}{d\theta^{m+1}} (f - P_t f)(e^{i\theta}) \right|^2 d\theta \right)^{1/2}.$$

Setting $m = 0$ and $q = \infty$ in the above gives us the results of the introduction.

Example: Sampling on SO(3). For this example we take $G = \mathrm{SO}(3)$. Then the dual $\hat{G}$ can be identified with the set of nonnegative integers. The dimension function is $d_\lambda = 2\lambda + 1$, the rank is $r = 1$, there is only one positive root, and the dimension of the center of $\mathrm{SO}(3)$ is zero. Then following the proofs above we find that when the A and B norms are $\|\ \|_{A_m}$, $\|\ \|_{A_p}$, $p \geq m$, and $\|\ \|_{A_s} = \|\ \|_{A_0'}$, we have

$$\overline{M}(s,t) \leq \left(\sum_{\nu=0}^{s} (2\nu+1)^3 \right) \left(1 + \frac{s}{t} \right)^m t^{m-p}$$

$$\leq (s+1)^2 (1 + 4s + 2s^2) \left(1 + \frac{s}{t} \right)^m t^{m-p}.$$

Example: The classical simple Lie groups. Assume G is a classical simple compact Lie group. Let the norm on $\mathfrak{h}^*$ be $\|\ \|_H$, let the A, B, and $\mathcal{A}_s$ norms be $\|\ \|_{A_m}$, $\|\ \|_{A_p}$, and $\|\ \|_{A_0'}$, where $p \geq m$. Let Λ_R be the root lattice, and let B_s denote the closed ball of radius s for $\|\ \|_H$. Then the proofs above, together with property II, show that

$$\overline{M}(s,t) \leq (s+t)^m t^{-p} \sum_{\|\nu\|_H \leq s} d_\nu^2 \big|(\nu + \Lambda_R) \cap B_{\|\nu\|_H}\big|,$$

where the sum is over analytically integral dominant weights. We can bound $\big|(\nu + \Lambda_R) \cap B_{\|\nu\|_H}\big|$ for such ν as follows.

(i) $G = \mathrm{SU}(r+1)$: $\big|(\nu + \Lambda_R) \cap B_{\|\nu\|_H}\big| \leq (s+r+1)^r$.
(ii) $G = \mathrm{Sp}(r)$: $\big|(\nu + \Lambda_R) \cap B_{\|\nu\|_H}\big| \leq 2^{r-1}(s+1)^r$.
(iii) $G = \mathrm{SO}(2r+1)$: $\big|(\nu + \Lambda_R) \cap B_{\|\nu\|_H}\big| = (2s+1)^r$.
(iv) $G = \mathrm{SO}(2r)$: $\big|(\nu + \Lambda_R) \cap B_{\|\nu\|_H}\big| \leq 2(s+1)^2(2s+1)^{r-2}$.

We can use these bounds and the Weyl dimension formula to obtain explicit bounds on $\overline{M}(s,t)$.

(i) $G = \mathrm{SU}(r+1)$:

$$\overline{M}(s,t) \leq \frac{1}{(r+3).r! \prod_{i=1}^{r} i!^2} (s+t)^m t^{-p} \left(s + \frac{r}{3} + \frac{5}{2} \right)^{r^2+3r}.$$

(ii) $G = \mathrm{Sp}(r)$:

$$\overline{M}(s,t) \leq \frac{1}{(r+1)! \prod_{i=1}^{r} (2i-1)!^2} 2^{r^2-2}(s+t)^m t^{-p} \left(s + \frac{5r}{12} + \frac{7}{4} \right)^{2r^2+2r}.$$

(iii) $G = \mathrm{SO}(2r+1)$:

$$\overline{M}(s,t) \leq \frac{1}{(r+1)! \prod_{i=1}^{r} (2i-1)!^2} 2^{r^2+2r-1}(s+t)^m t^{-p} \left(s + \frac{5r}{12} + \frac{25}{24} \right)^{2r^2+2r}.$$

(iv) $G = \mathrm{SO}(2r+1)$:

$$\overline{M}(s,t) \leq \frac{1}{r.r! \prod_{i=1}^{r-1} (2i)!^2} 2^{r^2+2r-2}(s+t)^m t^{-p} \left(s + \frac{5r}{12} + 1 \right)^{2r^2+2r}, \qquad \text{for } r \geq 3.$$

2.2.7. Differentiability and Sampling. We shall now see how the differentiability of the function being sampled plays a rôle. Define $A_m(G)$ to be the set of all continuous functions, f, on G, such that $\mathfrak{F}f$ is in $A_m(\hat{G})$. Define $\| \ \|_{A_m}$ on $A_m(G)$ by $\|f\|_{A_m} = \|\mathfrak{F}f\|_{A_m}$. Then we have the following result.

LEMMA 2.13. *Assume p is a nonnegative real number and m is a positive integer, and let $X_1,\dots,X_n$ be a basis for the complexified Lie algebra, $\mathfrak{g}^{\mathbb{C}}$ of the connected simple Lie group G. Then*

$$A_{p+m}(G) = \left\{ f \in C^{p+m}(G) : L(X_{i_1}\dots X_{i_m})f \in A_p(G) \text{ for all } 1 \le i_1,\dots,i_l \le n \right\}$$

and the following norms on A_{p+m} are equivalent

(i) $\|f\|_{A_{p+m}}$.
(ii) $\max\{\|L(X_{i_1}\dots X_{i_j})f\|_{A_p} : 0 \le j \le m, \text{ and } 1 \le i_1\dots,i_j \le n\}$
(iii) $\max\{\|L(Y_1\dots Y_j)f\|_{A_p} : 0 \le j \le m, \ Y_1,\dots,Y_j \in \mathfrak{g}^{\mathbb{C}}, \ \|Y_1\|=\dots=\|Y_j\|=1\}$.

In addition, this holds when G is an arbitrary compact connected Lie group and m is even.

PROOF. See [20]. □

LEMMA 2.14. *Assume G is a compact group of dimension n and that $m > n/2$. Then $C^m(G) \subseteq A_0(G)$, and this inclusion is continuous relative to the Sobolev norm on $C^m(G)$ given by*

$$\|f\|_{W_m} = \sup\{\|L(Y_1\dots Y_j)f\|_2 : 0 \le j \le m, \ Y_1,\dots,Y_j \in \mathfrak{g}^{\mathbb{C}}, \ \|Y_i\|=1\}$$

and the norm $\| \ \|_{A_0}$ on $A_0(G)$.

PROOF. The space $C^m(G)$ is continuously included in the Besov space $\Lambda_{1,2}^{n/2}(G)$, which in turn is continuously included in $A_0(G)$. For definitions and proof, see [27] and [6]. □

Now we can use the bounds we have been obtaining to find convergence conditions on a sequence of measures φ_s and differentiability conditions on a function f, that ensure that $\|\mathfrak{F}P_s(f - f.\varphi)\|_{C_{m_1}}$ tends to zero.

COROLLARY 2.15. *Assume that G is a n-dimensional compact connected Lie group, m, m_1, p are nonnegative integers, and φ_s is a sequence of distributions in $C^m(G)'$ converging weak-$*$ to Haar measure and satisfying $P_{2s}(\varphi - 1) = 0$. Assume f is a function on G.*

(i) *If f is in $C_{\lceil 3n/2 \rceil + r + m + m_1 + p + 1}$, then $s^p\|\mathfrak{F}P_s(f - f.\varphi_s)\|_{A_{m_1}}$ tends to zero as s tends to infinity.*
(ii) *If f is in $C_{\lceil 3n/2 \rceil + r + m + m_1 + p}$ and either G is simple or $n + m + m_1 + r + p$ is even, then $s^p\|\mathfrak{F}P_s(f - f.\varphi_s)\|_{A_{m_1}}$ tends to zero as s tends to infinity.*

PROOF. For clarity, let's just prove the case where $m_1 = p = 0$, and G is simple. Assume that f is in $C_{\lceil 3n/2 \rceil + r}$ and φ_s is a sequence of measures in $C^{m'}$ converging weak-$*$ to Haar measure and satisfying $P_{2s}(\varphi_s - 1) = 0$.

Then $\|\varphi_s\|_{A'_m}$ is bounded by a constant times $\|\varphi_s\|_{C'_m}$ is bounded, and f is in $A_{n+r+m}(G)$. Hence $\|\varphi_s\|_{A'_m}\|f\|_{A_{n+r+m}/A_s}$ converges to zero. However, our bounds for $M(s,s)$ show that

$$\|\mathfrak{F}P_s(f - f.\varphi_s)\|_{A_0} \leq K2^m s^{n+r+m} s^{-(n+r+m)} \|\varphi_s\|_{A'_m}\|f\|_{A_{n+r+m}/A_s}. \qquad \square$$

3. Sampling of Sections

It is an easy matter to generalize the above results and obtain a sampling theorem for sections of homogeneous vector bundles. As the theory here follows directly from the sampling theory for groups, I have not been as complete. Assume K is a compact subgroup of the compact Lie group G, τ is a finite dimensional unitary representation of K on E_0, and $E = G \times_\tau E_0$. Then then we can multiply a C^m section of E by a distribution on G/K to obtain a "distributional section" of E, which we will think of as a sampled version of the original section. If we project a sampling distribution on G to a distribution on G/K, then we obtain an appropriate sampling distribution on G/K. For harmonic analysis on homogeneous vector bundles over G/K, where G is compact, see [31].

3.1. Abstract Sampling for Modules. We shall now generalize the situation of Section 2.1. Let $\mathcal{A}$ be a complex algebra. For simplicity we shall assume that $\mathcal{A}$ is commutative. Assume that $\mathcal{M}$, $\mathcal{N}$ are $\mathcal{A}$-modules and that we have a $\mathcal{A}$-bilinear pairing, $\langle \, , \, \rangle$ between them. Then for any h in $\mathcal{M}$, and φ in $\mathcal{A}'$, we can define $\varphi.h$ in $\mathcal{N}' = \mathrm{Hom}_{\mathbb{C}}(\mathcal{N}'; \mathbb{C})$, by

$$(\varphi.h)(e) = \varphi(\langle e, h \rangle).$$

Let $\mathcal{A}_s$, $\{\mathcal{M}_s\}$, $\{\mathcal{N}_s\}$ be sets of subspaces of $\mathcal{A}$, $\mathcal{M}$, and $\mathcal{N}$, such that $\langle \mathcal{N}_s, \mathcal{M}_t \rangle \leq \mathcal{A}_{s+t}$. We set P_s to be the projection from $\mathcal{A}'$ onto $\mathcal{A}'_s$ or from $\mathcal{N}'$ onto $\mathcal{N}'_s$ given by restriction of linear functionals.

LEMMA 3.1. *Assume φ, μ are linear functionals in $\mathcal{A}'$ such that $P_{s+t}(\varphi - \mu) = 0$. Then*

$$P_s(\varphi.h) = P_s(\mu.h)$$

for any h in $\mathcal{M}_t$

EXAMPLE. Assume $\mathcal{M}$ is a finitely generated $\mathcal{A}$-module, X is a finite dimensional generating set for $\mathcal{M}$, and $\mathcal{A}_s.\mathcal{A}_t \subseteq \mathcal{A}_{s+t}$. Let $\mathcal{N} = \mathrm{Hom}_{\mathcal{A}}(\mathcal{M}; \mathcal{A})$, and define

$$\mathcal{M}_s = \mathcal{A}_s.X,$$
$$\mathcal{N}_s = \{f \in \mathcal{N} : f(X) \subseteq \mathcal{A}_s\}.$$

Then $\langle \mathcal{N}_s, \mathcal{M}_t \rangle \subseteq \mathcal{A}_{s+t}$.

We now return to the general situation. Let $\| \; \|_A$, $\| \; \|_B$, $\| \; \|_{\mathcal{N}_s}$, and $\| \; \|_{\mathcal{N}'_s}$ be norms on $\mathcal{N}$, $\mathcal{M}$, $\mathcal{N}_s$ and $\mathcal{N}'_s$ respectively, and denote their dual norms with a prime. Then we can define

$$N(s,t) = \sup\{\|P_s(h.\varphi)\|_{\mathcal{N}'_s} : \|h\|_B = 1, \|\varphi\|'_A = 1, h \in \mathcal{M}, \varphi \in \mathcal{A}', P_{s+t}\varphi = 0\}$$

When there is a possibility of confusion, we shall write $N_B^{\mathcal{N}'_s,A}$.

Let $\mathcal{M}^{B'}$ denote that continuous dual of $\mathcal{M}$ with respect to $\| \; \|_B$, and $\mathcal{N}^B$ be the completion of $\| \; \|_B$ with respect to $\| \; \|_B$.

LEMMA 3.2. *Assume φ, μ are linear functionals in $\mathcal{A}^{A'}$ such that $P_{s+t}(\varphi-\mu) = 0$ and $h \in \mathcal{M}^B$. Then*

$$\|P_s(f.\varphi) - P_s(f.\mu)\|_{\mathcal{N}'_s} \le N(s,t)\|\varphi - \mu\|'_A\|f\|_{B/\mathcal{M}_t},$$

where $\| \; \|_{B/\mathcal{M}_t}$ denotes the quotient seminorm on $\mathcal{M}^B/\mathcal{M}_t$.

3.2. Harmonic Analysis of Vector-Valued Functions. Assume E_0 is a finite dimensional complex vector space with norm $\| \; \|_{E_0}$. Let $C^m(G; E_0)$ be the space of C^m functions on G with values in E_0, and when m is a nonnegative integer, define $\|f\|_{C^m;E_0} = \sup\{\|L(X_1 \ldots X_p)f(x)\|_{E_0} : x \in G, 0 \le p \le m, X_1 \ldots X_p \in \mathfrak{g}, \|X_1\| = \ldots = \|X_p\| = 1\}$. All norms, $\| \; \|_{E_0}$, on E_0 will give an equivalent norms $\| \; \|_{C^m;E_0}$ on $C^m(G; E_0)$. Let $\| \; \|_{(C^m;E_0)'}$ be the dual norm to $\| \; \|_{C^m;E_0}$, and $\| \; \|_{(C^m;E_0^*)'}$ be the norm on $C^m(G; E_0^*)'$, when E_0^* is given the norm dual to that on E_0. The space $C^\infty(G; E_0^*)'$ is the space of all distributions on G with values in E_0, and $C^m(G; E_0^*)'$ is the space of all such distributions of order at most m. We can embed $C^0(G; E_0)$ continuously into $C^0(G; E_0^*)'$ by means of the map $f \mapsto \mu_G.f$, where for any h in $C^0(G; E_0^*)$, we have $\langle \mu_G.f, h \rangle = \langle \mu_G, (x \mapsto \langle h(x), f(x) \rangle) \rangle = \int_G \langle h(x), f(x) \rangle d\mu_G(x)$, and μ_G is Haar measure on G.

Let $\mathfrak{F}(\hat{G}; E_0) = \prod_{\gamma \in \hat{G}} (\mathrm{End}(V_\gamma) \otimes E_0)$, and define the Fourier transform, $\mathfrak{F}$, from $C^\infty(G; E_0^*)'$ into $\mathfrak{F}(\hat{G}; E_0)$, by

$$\langle X \otimes e^*, (\mathfrak{F}s)_\gamma \rangle = \langle s, (x \mapsto \langle X, \Delta_\gamma(x) \rangle e^*) \rangle$$

for any γ in $\hat{G}$, X in $\mathrm{End}(V_\gamma)^*$, e^* in E_0^*, and s in $C^\infty(G; E_0^*)'$. For a continuous function, f, on G with values in E_0, this becomes $(\mathfrak{F}f)_\gamma = \int_G \Delta_\gamma(x) \otimes f(x)d\mu_G(x)$.

We shall define norms on $\mathfrak{F}(\hat{G}; E_0)$ which generalize the norms $\| \; \|_{A_m}$ we had when E_0 was $\mathbb{C}$. Given two finite dimensional complex vector spaces, V and W, and norms $\| \; \|_V$ on V and $\| \; \|_W$ on W, define the tensor product of these norms, $\| \; \|_{V \otimes W}$, to be the operator norm on $V \otimes W = \mathrm{Hom}_\mathbb{C}(V^*; W)$ relative to the dual norm $\| \; \|_{V^*}$ on V^*, and the norm $\| \; \|_W$ on W. For any γ in $\hat{G}$ let $\| \; \|_{1,\gamma;E_0}$ denote the norm on $\mathrm{End}(V_\gamma) \otimes E_0$, which is the tensor product of the norms $\| \; \|_{1,\gamma}$ and $\| \; \|_{E_0}$. Define a norm $\| \; \|_{A_m;E_0}$, which is possibly infinite on $\mathfrak{F}(\hat{G}; E_0)$, by $\|A\|_{A_m;E_0} = \|A_0\|_{1,0;E_0} + \sum_{\lambda \in \hat{G}, \lambda \neq 0} d_\lambda \|\lambda\|^m \|A_\lambda\|_{1,\lambda;E_0}$. Let $A_m(\hat{G}; E_0)$ be the subspace of $\mathfrak{F}(\hat{G}; E_0)$ on which this norm is finite. This space is the space of absolutely summable Fourier transforms of distributions on G with values in E_0 whose first m derivatives also have absolutely summable transforms. The map, $\mathfrak{F}$ is one to one, and it's inverse gives a continuous from $A_m(\hat{G}; E_0)$ into $C^m(G; E_0)$.

Now, let $\mathcal{M} = \mathcal{A} \otimes E_0$, $\mathcal{N} = \mathcal{A} \otimes E_0^*$. These naturally embed in $C^\infty(G; E_0)$ and $C^\infty(G; E_0^*)$, and the spaces $\mathfrak{F}\mathcal{M}$, $\mathfrak{F}\mathcal{N}$ are the subspaces of $\mathfrak{F}(\hat{G}; E_0)$ and $\mathfrak{F}(\hat{G}; E_0^*)$ of elements with only finitely many components. Hence we can use $\mathfrak{F}$ to shift any norm on $\mathfrak{F}\mathcal{M}$ over to $\mathcal{M}$. Let $\mathcal{M}_s = \mathcal{A}_s \otimes E_0$, and $\mathcal{N}_s = \mathcal{A}_s \otimes E_0^*$. There is a natural $\mathcal{A}$-bilinear pairing between $\mathcal{M}$ and $\mathcal{N}$. Composing this form with Haar measure gives a $\mathbb{C}$-bilinear pairing between $\mathcal{M}_s$ and $\mathcal{N}_s$, which we shall use to identify $\mathcal{N}_s'$ with $\mathcal{M}_s$.

For calculation of $N(s,t)$, it is more convenient to use the norm $\| \ \|_{A_m \otimes E_0}$ defined on $A_m(\hat{G}) \otimes E_0$, by

$$\|A\|_{A_m \otimes E_0} = \sup\{\| \langle e_0^*, A \rangle_{A_m(\hat{G})} \|_{A_m} : \|e_0^*\|_{E_0^*} = 0\},$$

where $\langle \ , \ \rangle_{A_m(\hat{G})}$ is the natural $A_m(\hat{G})$-bilinear pairing between E_0^* and $\| \ \|_{A_m \otimes E_0}$. It is easy to show that $A_m(\hat{G}) \otimes E_0$ naturally embeds in $A_m(\hat{G}; E_0)$. In fact, these two spaces are equal, as the following lemma will show. First, some terminology. We say that E_0 has dual bases of unit vectors if there is a basis $\{v_i\}$ of unit vectors in E_0, with a dual basis $\{v_i^*\}$ of E_0^* consisting of unit vectors. This happens, for example, when $\| \ \|_{E_0}$ is a Hilbert space norm, or a p-norm in some basis.

LEMMA 3.3. (i) $\| \ \|_{A_m \otimes E_0} \leq \| \ \|_{A_m; E_0}$.
(ii) *If E_0 has dual bases of unit vectors, then* $\| \ \|_{A_m; E_0} \leq (\dim E_0)\| \ \|_{A_m \otimes E_0}$.
(iii) $\| \ \|_{A_m; E_0}$ *and* $\| \ \|_{A_m \otimes E_0}$ *are equivalent norms.*

Define $M(s,t)$ using the A_{m_1}, A_m, A_p norms, as we did in Section 2.2.5. We shall now relate this function to the function $N(s,t)$ for various choices of the norms on $\mathcal{N}_s' = \mathcal{M}_s$, $\mathcal{A}$, and $\mathcal{M}$.

THEOREM 3.4. (i) *If $N(s,t)$ is defined using the $A_{m_1} \otimes E_0$, A_m, $A_p \otimes E_0$ norms on $\mathcal{N}_s'$, $\mathcal{A}$ and $\mathcal{M}$, then*

$$N_{A_p \otimes E_0}^{A_{m_1} \otimes E_0, A_m}(s,t) \leq M_{A_p}^{A_{m_1}, A_m}(s,t).$$

(ii) *If $N(s,t)$ is defined using the $(A_{m_1}; E_0)$, A_m, $(A_p; E_0)$ norms on $\mathcal{N}_s'$, $\mathcal{A}$ and $\mathcal{M}$, then for some $C > 0$,*

$$N_{(A_p; E_0)}^{(A_{m_1}; E_0), A_m}(s,t) \leq C.(\dim E_0)M_{A_p}^{A_{m_1}, A_m}(s,t).$$

When E_0 has dual bases of unit vectors, we may take $C = 1$ in the above inequality.

PROOF. Assume that φ is in $\mathcal{A}$, h is in $\mathcal{M}$, and e_0^* is in E_0^*.

$$
\begin{aligned}
\| \langle e_0^*, P_s(\varphi.h) \rangle_{\mathcal{A}} \|_{A_{m_1}} &= \| P_s(\varphi. \langle e_0^*, h \rangle_{\mathcal{A}}) \|_{A_{m_1}} \\
&\leq M(s,t) \|\varphi\|_{A_m'} \| \langle e_0^*, h \rangle_{\mathcal{A}} \|_{A_p} \\
&\leq M(s,t) \|\varphi\|_{A_m'} \|e_0^*\|_{E_0^*} \|h\|_{A_p \otimes E_0}.
\end{aligned}
$$

This proves (i). The second part is an easy corollary of the first. $\qquad\square$

The proof of the first part of this theorem did not involve many special properties of the norms A_m; the basic properties used are that $\mathfrak{F}\mathcal{M}$ is dense in the $A_p(\hat{G}) \otimes E_0$ and $\mathfrak{F}\mathcal{A}$ is dense in $A_m(\hat{G})'$.

Another approach to bounding $N(s,t)$ uses an analog of Lemma 2.10 to calculate the bound directly. In some circumstances (e.g. when G is abelian), this gives better results than the combination of the previous theorem and the bounds for $M(s,t)$. In particular, we do not use the assumption that E_0 has dual bases of unit vectors.

LEMMA 3.5. *Assume f is a continuous complex function on G, g is in $C^0(G; E_0)$, and $\mathfrak{F}f \in A_0(\hat{G})$, and $\mathfrak{F}g \in A_0(\hat{G}; E_0)$. Then*

$$
\|\mathfrak{F}(f.g)\|_{A_0;E_0} \leq (\dim E_0) \|\mathfrak{F}f\|_{A_0} \|\mathfrak{F}g\|_{A_0;E_0}.
$$

PROOF. This has essentially the same proof as for the case when E_0 is simply the complex numbers, as given in [11]. $\qquad\square$

Lemma 3.5 implies that if f_λ is in the λ-isotypic subspace of $C^\infty(G)$, g_μ is in the μ-isotypic subspace of $C^\infty(G; E_0)$, under the left regular actions, and ν is in $\hat{G}$, then

$$
\|\mathfrak{F}(f_\lambda.g_\mu)\|_{1,\nu;E_0} \leq (\dim E_0) \, d_\nu^{-1} d_\lambda d_\mu \|\mathfrak{F}f_\lambda\|_{1,\lambda} \|\mathfrak{F}g_\mu\|_{1,\mu;E_0}.
$$

When $E_0 = \mathbb{C}$, this inequality our main ingredient in the bound on $M(s,t)$. The generalization gives us bounds on $N(s,t)$. The second half of the following theorem concerns the case when G is abelian. When G is abelian, define norms on $\mathfrak{F}\mathcal{M}$ for $1 \leq q < \infty$ and $-\infty \leq m < \infty$ by

$$
\|A\|_{\mathfrak{F}_q A_m} = \left(|A_0|^q + \sum_{\lambda \in \hat{G} \setminus \{0\}} \left(\|\lambda\|^m \|A_\lambda\|_{E_0} \right)^q \right)^{1/q},
$$

$$
\|A\|_{\mathfrak{F}_\infty A_m} = \sup\{ \|\lambda\|^m \|A_\lambda\|_{E_0} : \lambda \in \hat{G}, \ \lambda \neq 0 \} \cup \{|A_0|\}.
$$

THEOREM 3.6. (i) *Assume G is nonabelian, the norm on $\mathfrak{h}^*$ has property I, and $N(s,t)$ is defined using the $(A_{m_1}; E_0)$, A_m, $(A_p; E_0)$ norms on $\mathcal{N}_s'$, $\mathcal{A}$ and $\mathcal{M}$. Then for some K_G depending only on G and the norm on $\mathfrak{h}^*$,*

$$
N_{(A_p;E_0)}^{(A_{m_1};E_0),A_m}(s,t) \leq (\dim E_0) s^{r+l+m_1+1} (s+t)^{2k+r+m-1} t^{-p}.
$$

(ii) *Assume G is abelian, $1 \le q_1, q_2, q_3 \le \infty$, and s and t are positive integers. Then we have*

$$N_{\mathfrak{F}_{q_3} A_{m_3}}^{(\mathfrak{F}_{q_1} A_{m_1}),(\mathfrak{F}_{q_2} A_{m_2})}(s,t) \le \left(1 + \sum_{\|\nu\| \le s} (\|\nu\|^{m_1})^{q_1}\right)^{1/q_1} (s+t)^{m_2} t^{-m_3},$$

provided $q_3 \le q_2$ and $m_3 \ge m_2$.

PROOF. The key observation in the proof of (i) is that

$$\|P_s(h.\varphi)\|_{A_{m_1}; E_0}$$
$$\le \sum_{\|\nu\| \le s} d_\nu (1 + \|\nu\|^{m_1}) \sum_{\substack{\|\mu\| > s+t, \ \|\lambda\| > t, \\ \|\|\mu\| - \|\lambda\|\| \le \|\nu\|, \ \pi\mu = \pi\nu - \pi\lambda}} d_\nu^{-1} d_\lambda d_\mu^2 \|\mu\|^m \|(\mathfrak{F}h)_\lambda\|_{1,\lambda; E_0} \|\varphi\|_{A_m'},$$

where π is the natural projection from $\mathfrak{h}^*$ onto the dual of the center of $\mathfrak{g}$. Now sum over μ and then ν.

The proof of (ii) is essentially the same as for Theorem 2.12. □

3.3. Homogeneous Vector Bundles. Assume $E = G \times_\tau E_0$ is a homogeneous vector bundle, where τ is a unitary representation of K. E has a G-invariant unitary structure determined by the inner product on E_0. Let $\Gamma^m(E)$ denote the space of C^m sections of E with the norm $\|s\|_{\Gamma^m} = \sup\{\|L(X_1 \ldots X_p)s(x)\|_x : x \in G/K, \ 0 \le p \le m, \ X_1 \ldots X_p \in \mathfrak{g}\}$, where $\| \ \|_x$ denotes the norm on the fiber, E_x, determined by the unitary structure of E. If $\delta(G/K)$ is the density bundle and $\mu_{G/K}$ is the invariant density of unit mass on G/K, we obtain a map $\Gamma^0(E) \to \Gamma^0(E \otimes \delta(G/K)) \hookrightarrow \Gamma^0(E^*)'; f \mapsto f.\mu_{G/K}$, allowing us to identify $\Gamma(E)$ with a subspace of $\Gamma^0(E^*)'$. Thus we think of $\Gamma^\infty(E^*)'$ as the space of all distributions, or generalized sections, of E.

There is a representation ψ_τ of K by isometries on each of the spaces $C^m(G; E_0)$ and $C^m(G; E_0^*)'$, defined by $\psi_\tau(k)f(x) = \tau(k)f(x.k)$, on elements of $C(G; E_0)$, and which commutes with the left regular action of G on these spaces. The corresponding spaces of invariant functions or distributions are denoted, $C^m(G; \tau)$ and $C^{m'}(G; \tau)$. We then have an isometry[1] $j_\tau : C^{m'}(G; \tau) \to \Gamma^m(E^*)'$ which restricts to an isometry between $C^m(G; \tau)$ and $\Gamma^m(E)$. Thus questions about spaces of sections of E can be simply reduced to ones concerning ψ_τ-invariant vector valued functions on G. In particular, the multiplication map $C^m(G/K) \times \Gamma^m(E) \to \Gamma(E^*)'$ corresponds to the map $C^m(G)'^K \times C^m(G; \tau) \to C^{m'}(G; \tau)$ which is the restriction of the scalar multiplication map for distributions on G with functions in $C^m(G; E_0)$.

---

[1]The space $C^{m'}(G; \tau)$ of invariant vectors in $C^m(G; E_0^*)'$ is isometric, via the restriction map, to the space $C^{m'}(G; \tau^\vee)'$. This is because the canonical projection from $C^m(G; E_0^*)'$ onto $C^{m'}(G; \tau)$ is the transpose of the projection from $C^m(G; E_0^*)$ onto $C^m(G; \tau^\vee)$, and this last projection is also a contraction.

As in Section 3.2 we set $\mathcal{M} = \mathcal{A} \otimes E_0$ and $\mathcal{N} = \mathcal{A} \otimes E_0^*$. Let $\hat{\mathcal{M}}$, $\hat{\mathcal{N}}$ and $\hat{\mathcal{A}}$ be the subspaces of ψ_τ-, $\psi_{\tau^\vee}$-, and K-invariant vectors in $\mathcal{M}$, $\mathcal{N}$, and $\mathcal{A}$. Let $\hat{\mathcal{M}}_s$, $\hat{\mathcal{N}}_s$, $\hat{\mathcal{A}}_s$, be the intersections of the spaces above with $\mathcal{M}_s$, $\mathcal{N}_s$ and $\mathcal{A}_s$ respectively. Finally, we can use j_τ and $j_{\tau^\vee}$ to obtain corresponding subspaces, $\tilde{\mathcal{M}}$, $\tilde{\mathcal{N}}$, $\tilde{\mathcal{A}}$, $\tilde{\mathcal{M}}_s$, $\tilde{\mathcal{N}}_s$, $\tilde{\mathcal{A}}_s$ in $\Gamma^\infty(E)$, $\Gamma^\infty(E^*)$ and $C^\infty(G/K)$.

Choosing norms on $\mathcal{N}'_s = \mathcal{M}_s$, $\mathcal{A}$, and $\mathcal{M}$, allows us to define a function $N(s,t)$ as in Section 3.1. If we assume that $\mathcal{N}_s$ is invariant under the projection from $\mathcal{N}$ onto $\tilde{\mathcal{N}}$, then the dual of this projection is an injection from $\tilde{\mathcal{N}}'_s$ into $\mathcal{N}'_s$, and we may restrict the norm on $\mathcal{N}'_s$ to $\tilde{\mathcal{N}}'_s$; in fact, the $\mathbb{C}$-bilinear pairing between $\tilde{\mathcal{N}}_s$ and $\tilde{\mathcal{M}}_s$ is nondegenerate in this case. If we also restrict the norms on $\mathcal{A}$ and $\mathcal{M}$ to $\tilde{\mathcal{A}}$, and $\tilde{\mathcal{M}}$, then we can define another function $\tilde{N}(s,t)$ using these restricted norms.

THEOREM 3.7. *Assume that all the subspaces $\mathcal{A}_s$ and the norm on $\mathcal{A}$ are all invariant under the right regular action of K. Then $\tilde{N}(s,t) \leq N(s,t)$*

PROOF. First note that under these hypotheses, the subspaces $\mathcal{M}_s$, $\mathcal{N}_s$ are invariant under the representations ψ_τ, and $\psi_{\tau^\vee}$, and so the projections onto these spaces commute with the projections from $\mathcal{M}$, and $\mathcal{N}$ onto $\tilde{\mathcal{M}}$ and $\tilde{\mathcal{N}}$. Hence the definition of $\tilde{N}$ makes sense. The projection from $\mathcal{A}$ onto $\tilde{\mathcal{A}}$, P^K, is a contraction with respect to $\| \ \|_A$, and its dual, P^{K*}, is an isometric embedding of the continuous dual of $\tilde{\mathcal{A}}$ with respect to the restricted norm into the continuous dual of $\mathcal{A}$ with its norm. P^K, which is given by integration over K, commutes with the projections, from $\mathcal{A}$ onto $\mathcal{A}_s$, and hence for any φ in the continuous dual of $\tilde{\mathcal{A}}$ such that $P_s\varphi = 0$, we also have $P_s(P^{K*}\varphi) = 0$. This allows us to imbed the calculation of $\tilde{N}(s,t)$ into a calculation involving only the spaces $\mathcal{N}$, $\mathcal{M}$, $\mathcal{A}$ and the subspaces $\mathcal{N}_s$, $\mathcal{M}_s$, and $\mathcal{A}_s$, where it is obvious that $\tilde{N} \leq N$. □

We shall now define the Fourier transform map for spaces of sections of E. The representation, ψ_τ, of K on the γ-isotypic subspace of $C^\infty(G; E_0)$ corresponds, under the Fourier transform $\mathfrak{F}$, to the representation $\mathrm{Id} \otimes \Delta_\gamma^\vee \otimes \tau$, on $\mathrm{End}(V_\gamma) \otimes E_0 = V_\gamma \otimes V_\gamma^* \otimes E_0$. The subspace of invariant vectors of this space is naturally isomorphic to $V_\gamma \otimes \mathrm{Hom}_K(V_\gamma; E_0)$. So the natural space in which to define the Fourier transform of a section of E is $\mathfrak{F}(\hat{E}) = \prod_{\gamma \in \hat{G}} V_\gamma \otimes \mathrm{Hom}_K(V_\gamma; E_0)$. Define norms $\| \ \|_{A_m}$ on $\mathfrak{F}(\hat{E})$ by restricting the norms $\| \ \|_{A_m; E_0}$ on $\mathfrak{F}(\hat{G}; E_0)$, and let $A_m(\hat{E})$ denote the subspace of $\mathfrak{F}(\hat{E})$ on which the corresponding norm is finite. Let P^τ denote both the projection from $C^\infty(G; E_0^*)'$ onto the ψ_τ-invariant subspace, $C^{\infty\prime}(G; \tau)$ and also the projection from $\mathfrak{F}(\hat{G}; E_0)$ onto $\mathfrak{F}(\hat{E})$. Define the Fourier Transform map $\mathfrak{F} : \Gamma^\infty(E^*) \to \mathfrak{F}(E)$ so that $P^\tau \mathfrak{F} = \mathfrak{F}P^\tau$, then $\mathfrak{F}$ maps $\Gamma^m(E)$ into $A_m(\hat{E})$. When τ is the trivial representation, the dual space to $A_m(E)$ corresponds to the space of invariant distributions on G for which A'_m, the dual norm previously, is finite. We then have that $\|\mathfrak{F}\varphi\|_{A'_m} \leq \|\varphi\|_{(C^m)'}$ for any complex distribution, φ, on G/K. Also note that if φ is a distribution on G satisfying $P_s\varphi = 0$, then $P^K\varphi$ satisfies the same equation in $C^\infty(G/K)'$.

Example: Functions on S^2. Consider the case where $G = \mathrm{SO}(3)$, $K = \mathrm{SO}(2)$, and τ is the trivial representation of $\mathrm{SO}(2)$. Then $E = S^2 \times \mathbb{C}$ is the trivial bundle over S^2, and sections of E may be identified with complex functions on S^2. Identify the dual of $\mathrm{SO}(3)$ with the set of nonnegative integers. For any $l \geq 0$ we have $\dim \mathrm{Hom}_{\mathrm{SO}(2)}(V_l; \mathbb{C}) = 1$. Choose a $\Delta_l^\vee(\mathrm{SO}(2))$-invariant unit vector, u_l^* in V_l^* for each l. Then the map $v \mapsto v \otimes u_l^*$ gives an isomorphism between V_l and $V_l \otimes \mathrm{Hom}_{\mathrm{SO}(2)}(V_l; \mathbb{C})$. The space $V_l \otimes \mathrm{Hom}_{\mathrm{SO}(2)}(V_l; \mathbb{C})$ is naturally isomorphic to the subspace of $\mathrm{End}\, V_l = V_l \otimes V_l^*$ invariant under $\mathrm{Id} \otimes \Delta_l^\vee$. The composition of these two isomorphisms is map, $v \mapsto A_v$, from V_l into $\mathrm{End}(V_l)$ which is defined by $A_v w = u_l^*(w)v$ for any $w \in V_l$. Assume v is any vector in V_l. We shall now find $\|A_v\|_{q,l}$. Let Pr_v be the self-adjoint projection onto the linear span of v, then $A_v A_v^* = \|v\|^2 \mathrm{Pr}_v$, where $\|v\|$ is the Hilbert space norm, so

$$\|A_v\|_{q,l} = (\mathrm{Tr}\,(A_v A_v^*)^{q/2})^{1/q} = (\mathrm{Tr}(\|v\|^q \mathrm{Pr}_v))^{1/q} = \|v\|$$

Using the isomorphisms above, we can identify $\mathfrak{F}(\hat{E})$ with $\prod_{l \geq 0} V_l$, and if $y \in \mathfrak{F}(\hat{E})$, then $\|y\|_{A_m} = \sum_{l \geq 0}(2l+1)\max\{1, l^m\}\|y_l\|$. One can now use the bounds as follows. Assume f is a C^m function on S^2 with $\mathfrak{F}f = y$, and φ is a distribution of order at most m on S^2 satisfying $P_{s+t}(\varphi - 1) = 0$. Let $\mathfrak{F}(\varphi.f) = z$, then for any positive integers s, t, and any $p \geq m$,

$$\sum_{l=0}^{s}(2l+1)\|y_l - z_l\|$$
$$\leq (s+1)^2(1 + 4s + 2s^2)\left(1 + \frac{s}{t}\right)^m t^{m-p}\|\mathfrak{F}(\varphi - 1)\|_{A'_m}\sum_{l>t}(2l+1)l^p\|y_l\|$$

and $\|\mathfrak{F}(\varphi - 1)\|_{A'_m} = \sup\{l^{-m}\|(\mathfrak{F}s)_l\| : l > s + t\}$.

Example: Line bundles over S^2. For this example take $G = \mathrm{SO}(3)$, $K = \mathrm{SO}(2)$, and let $\tau = \rho_n$ be the representation of $\mathrm{SO}(2)$ with weight n, where n is a nonzero integer. Then E is a line bundle over S^2. The space $\mathrm{Hom}_{\mathrm{SO}(2)}(V_l; \rho_n)$ has dimension 1 for $l \geq |n|$ and is zero-dimensional when $0 \leq l < |n|$. When $l \geq |n|$ we may choose a unit vector, w_l^*, in the ρ_n-isotypic space of V_l and obtain an isomorphism, $v \mapsto v \otimes w_l$, between V_l and $\mathrm{Hom}_{\mathrm{SO}(2)}(V_l; \rho_n)$. As before, this allows us to identify $\mathfrak{F}(E)$ with $\prod_{l \geq |n|} V_l$, and for any $y \in \mathfrak{F}(\hat{E})$ we have $\|y\|_{A_m} = \sum_{l \geq |n|}(2l+1)l^m\|y_l\|$. To state the sampling theorem for this situation, assume f is a C^m section of E with $\mathfrak{F}f = y$, and φ is a distribution of order at most m on S^2 satisfying $P_{2b}(s-1) = 0$. Let $\mathfrak{F}(\varphi.f) = z$, and assume s, t are positive integers, and $p \geq m$, then

$$\sum_{l=|n|}^{s}(2l+1)\|y_l - z_l\|$$
$$\leq (s+1)^2(1 + 4s + 2s^2)\left(1 + \frac{s}{t}\right)^m t^{m-p}\|\mathfrak{F}(\varphi - 1)\|_{A'_m}\sum_{l \geq t+1, |n|}(2l+1)l^p\|y_l\|.$$

4. Construction of Sampling Distributions

4.1. The General Construction. Now we will outline a method for constructing distributions whose Fourier transform vanishes at a given finite set of irreducible representations. These distributions will be finitely supported, have any specified order, and will be of the form $\chi = \psi_1 * \cdots * \psi_n$, where $n = \dim G$ and each of the ψ_i are supported on a finite subset of a 1-parameter subgroup of G. In addition $\psi_1, \ldots, \psi_n$ may be chosen so that χ has bounded A_m norm as the set of irreducible representations at which its Fourier transform must vanish increases. These properties have been chosen as they are required for the development of efficient algorithms for the computation of the Fourier transform of functions sampled on the support of these distributions, as in [21]. The thesis [20] contains a description of these algorithms for functions sampled on the support of the projection of these distributions to the homogeneous spaces $\mathrm{SO}(n)/\mathrm{SO}(n-1)$ and $\mathrm{SU}(n)/\mathrm{SU}(n-1)$; they are generalizations of the algorithm for computing expansions in spherical harmonics developed by Driscoll and Healy in [4]. Here is the general construction.

Assume G is a connected compact Lie group, and K is a connected compact subgroup of G. The Fourier transforms of a distribution, $\psi \in C^\infty(K)'$, and its image $i\psi$ in $C^\infty(G)'$ are simply related; if ρ is a representation of G, then $\rho(i\psi) = (\rho|K)(\psi)$. So the relation between the two Fourier transforms is determined by the way that representations of G split on restriction to K.

For any set, Ω_0 of irreducible representations of G, define a two-sided ideal in $C^\infty(G)'$ by

$$\mathfrak{T}_{\Omega_0} = \{f \in C^\infty(G)' : \forall \psi \in \Omega_0 \ \psi(f) = 0\}.$$

We wish to show how for any finite set of representations, Ω_0, we can construct a finitely supported distribution, χ, on G, such that $\chi - 1 \in \mathfrak{T}_{\Omega_0}$. It obviously suffices to consider the case when G is simple and simply connected, the abelian case being trivial. Let us also restrict ourselves to the case when G has a rank one homogeneous space, G/K; this only leaves a few exceptional groups out of our reach.

By induction we can assume that the problem has been solved for K; this is because K is a quotient of a product of abelian groups and semisimple groups which themselves have rank 1 homogeneous spaces. Now let Ω_1 be the set of all irreducible representations of K that are contained in the restriction of some representation in Ω_0 to K. This set is finite, and $\mathfrak{T}_{\Omega_0} \subseteq i(\mathfrak{T}_{\Omega_1})$.

By induction, we can find a finitely supported distribution, $\hat{\chi}$, on K such that $\hat{\chi} - 1_K \in \mathfrak{T}_{\Omega_1}$. Let $\chi_K = i(\hat{\chi})$, then $\chi_K = c_K \pmod{\mathfrak{T}_{\Omega_0}}$, where c_K is the characteristic distribution of the submanifold, K, of G. By polar decomposition, $G = KAK$, where A is a 1 parameter subgroup of G. The idea is to choose a finitely supported distribution, ψ, with support in A, and then let $\chi = \chi_K * \psi * \chi_K$. Then, $\chi = c_K * \psi * c_K = {}^{KP^K}\psi \pmod{\mathfrak{T}_{\Omega_0}}$, where ${}^{KP^K}$ is the projection onto bi-invariant distributions. ${}^{KP^K}\psi$ has an expansion in terms of spherical functions. The polar decomposition allows us to establish an isomorphism of $[-1, 1]$ with $K\backslash G/K$ via the obvious composition of maps $[-1, 1] \to A \to G \to K\backslash G/K$. So we can lift $^K P^K \psi$ up to a finitely supported distribution on $[-1, 1]$, where its spherical function expansion corresponds to an expansion in Jacobi polynomials of some sort. By the Chebyshev property of orthogonal polynomials [20, Lemma 3.2], we can choose ψ so that the expansion of $^K P^K \psi - 1$ in spherical functions only contains spherical functions corresponding to representations that are not in Ω_0. That is, choose ψ so that $^K P^K c = 1 \pmod{\mathfrak{T}_{\Omega_0}}$. Then $\chi - 1 \in \mathfrak{T}_{\Omega_0}$.

An apparent problem with this method, is that the number of distributions in the convolution product for χ is too large. We desire exactly $\dim G$ of these factors, but the method above yields 1 factor for S^1, 3 for $SU(2)$, 4 for $S(U_2 \times U_1)$, 9 for $SU(3)$, and $2^k + 2^{k-1} - 3$ for $SU(k)$, and $\dim SU(k) = k^2 - 1$. In the examples that follow, we use relations between the ψ_i modulo $\mathfrak{T}_{\Omega_0}$ to reduce the number of factors to $\dim G$, when G is one of the classical groups.

4.1.1. Quadrature Rules. Assume that $\langle \varphi_m \rangle$ is a sequence of orthonormal polynomials relative to the positive measure $w(x) \, dx$ on $[a, c]$. Then a finitely supported distribution satisfying $\langle \psi, \varphi_m \rangle = \delta_{0m}$ for $0 \le m \le n$ is equivalent to a quadrature formula that exactly integrates polynomials of degree at most n with respect to $w(x)dx$. In the case where ψ is a measure supported at the roots of φ_n, this determines the usual Gaussian integration formula, which has the advantages that ψ is positive and $\langle \psi, \varphi_m \rangle \, \delta_{0m}$ for $0 \le m \le 2n + 1$. Similarly, by choosing the support of ψ to be the roots of the n-th l-orthogonal polynomial we may find a distribution of order $2l$, supported on these points, such that $\langle \psi, \varphi_m \rangle = \delta_{0m}$ for $0 \le m < (2l + 2)n$. For more on this, see [7].

When ψ is a positive measure, satisfying the above conditions, the total variation norm of ψ must be 1. If this measure is pushed onto a Lie group, then the resulting positive measure also has total variation norm 1, and a convolution of such measures has total variation norm 1. The construction above (and in the following examples) can therefore be required to produce measures of total variation 1 on the classical groups. When ψ is supported at the points $\cos(\pi l/n)$, $0 \le l < n$, the total variation norm of ψ tends to 1 as n tends to infinity, provided that w is a nonnegative L^1 function on $[-1, 1]$, and $0 < \int_0^\pi w(\cos \theta)d\theta < \infty$ (See [20]).

Together with Lemma 2.4 this shows that the distribution χ of the subsection above can be constructed so it is bounded in the A_m norm as the set Ω_0 varies over finite subsets of $\hat{G}$. To get an explicit formula for χ we need to know how to convolve point distributions on G; this is explained in [20].

4.2. Example: Sampling on $SO(n)$. The arguments of Section 4.1, when applied to the chain of groups

$$SO(n) \supseteq SO(n-1) \supseteq \cdots \supseteq SO(2),$$

lead to a sampling distribution on $SO(n)$ that is closely related to the parametrization of that group, by means of Euler angles. Let

$$r_m(\theta) = \begin{pmatrix} 1 & & & & & \\ & \ddots & & & & \\ & & \cos\theta & \sin\theta & & \\ & & -\sin\theta & \cos\theta & & \\ & & & & \ddots & \\ & & & & & 1 \end{pmatrix},$$

where the "rotation block" appears in columns and rows $m-1$ and m. Note
that $r_m \smile r_n$ for $|n-m| > 1$ and $SO(n) = SO(n-1).r_n([0,\pi]).SO(n-1)$. The
highest weight of a representation of $SO(2r+1)$ is determined by its coordinates
$m_{1,2r+1}, \ldots, m_{r,2r+1}$ relative to the basis $\{e_i\}$ described in Section 2.2.4. These
numbers range over all sets of integers satisfying

$$m_{1,2r+1} \geq \cdots \geq m_{r,2r+1} \geq 0.$$

The highest weight of a representation of $SO(2r)$, may also be expressed in the
coordinates of Section 2.2.4, and these coordinates are integers, $m_{1,2r}, \ldots, m_{r,2r}$,
satisfying

$$m_{1,2r} \geq \cdots \geq |m_{r,2r}|.$$

The "betweenness" relations for the restriction of representations of $SO(2r+1)$
to $SO(2r)$ and $SO(2r)$ to $SO(2r-1)$ are then

$$m_{1,2r+1} \geq m_{1,2r} \geq m_{2,2r+1} \geq \ldots \geq m_{r,2r+1} \geq |m_{r,2r}|$$

and

$$m_{1,2r} \geq m_{1,2r-1} \geq m_{2,2r} \geq \ldots \geq m_{r-1,2r-1} \geq |m_{r,2r}|,$$

where the $m_{i,j}$ are either all integral or all half integral. For convenience, we'll
assume that n is either $2k+1$ or $2k$, that the numbers $m_{1,k}, \ldots m_{k,n}$ satisfy the
appropriate restrictions, and that $n > 2$ in what follows.

Choose a positive integer, s. We shall construct a distribution, c_n on $SO(n)$,
such that $c_n - 1$ vanishes on representations Δ_λ with $\|\lambda\|_H \leq s$. In terms of the
coordinates $m_{i,j}$, this is the same as requiring that $m_{1,n} \leq s$.

The map $[0,\pi] \longleftrightarrow SO(n-1)\backslash SO(n)/SO(n-1) : \theta \mapsto SO(n-1)r_n(\theta)SO(n-1)$
is a homeomorphism, and its restriction to $(0,\pi)$ is a diffeomorphism. We may
therefore identify this double coset space with $[0,\pi]$. The class one representations for $SO(n)/SO(n-1)$ have highest weights, $(m,0,\ldots,0)$, where m is a
nonnegative integer, and the corresponding spherical functions are Gegenbauer
polynomials in $\cos(\theta)$, where $\theta \in [0,\pi]$, namely

$$\varphi_m^n = \frac{\Gamma(n-2)m!}{\Gamma(n+m-2)} . C_m^{(n-2)/2}(\cos\theta).$$

See [30] for a proof of this. For fixed n, the sequence of functions $C_m^{(n-2)/2}$ is a sequence of real orthogonal polynomials, so the sequence of functions φ_m^n is an extended Chebyshev system.

Choose real finitely supported distributions, $\tilde{\psi}_{i,k}$, on $[0,\pi]$, for $2 < i \leq k \leq n$ which each satisfy

$$\left\langle \tilde{\psi}_{i,k}, \varphi_m^i \right\rangle = \delta_{0m} \text{ for } 0 \leq m \leq s.$$

A lot of choices are involved here. In particular, the support, F, of $\tilde{\psi}_{i,k}$ may be any nonempty finite subset of $[0,\pi]$, and the order, p, of $\tilde{\psi}_{i,k}$ is likewise arbitrary provided that $(p+1)|F| \geq s+1$.

For the case $n = 2$, choose $\tilde{\psi}_{2,k}$ to be a real distribution supported on a finite subset of $[0, 2\pi)$ such that

$$\left\langle \tilde{\psi}_{2,k}, e^{im.(\ )} \right\rangle = \delta_{0m} \text{ for } |m| \leq s.$$

Define $\psi_{i,k} = (r_i)_*(\tilde{\psi}_{i,k})$ for $2 \leq i \leq k \leq n$, i.e. $\langle \psi_{i,k}, f \rangle = \langle \tilde{\psi}_{i,k}, f \circ r_k \rangle$, for any C^∞ function, f, on G. Finally we can define our sampling distributions:

$$c_2 = \psi_{2,2},$$
$$c_n = \psi_{2,n} * \cdots * \psi_{n,n} * c_{n-1}.$$

The convolution product for c_n has $\dim \mathrm{SO}(n) = \frac{n(n-1)}{2}$ factors. It is clear that we can choose the $s_{i,k}$ so that the order of c_n is 0 and c_n has support of size at most $(2s+1)^{n-1}s^{(n-1)(n-2)/2}$. If we allow c_n to have a higher order, then we can decrease the size of its support.

THEOREM 4.1. *If* $\|\lambda\|_H \leq s$, *then* $\Delta_\lambda(c_n - 1) = 0$.

PROOF. Let

$$\Omega_s^n = \{\lambda \in \widehat{\mathrm{SO}(n)} : \|\lambda\|_H \leq s\}$$
$$= \{\Delta_{(m_{1,n},\ldots,m_{k,n})} : |m_{1,n}| \leq s\}.$$

Using the embeddings $C^\infty(\mathrm{SO}(2))' \hookrightarrow \cdots \hookrightarrow C^\infty(\mathrm{SO}(n))'$ and the betweenness relations for the restriction of representations of $\mathrm{SO}(n)$ to $\mathrm{SO}(n-1)$, it is obvious that $\mathfrak{T}_{\Omega_s^2} \subseteq \cdots \subseteq \mathfrak{T}_{\Omega_s^n}$ We shall show, using induction, that $c_n = c_{\mathrm{SO}(n)}$ (mod $\mathfrak{T}_{\Omega_s^n}$), for all n. Now, from the general arguments given previously, we know that if we define $\hat{c}_k$ by

$$\hat{c}_2 = \psi_{2,2},$$
$$\hat{c}_k = \hat{c}_{k-1} * \psi_{k,k} * \hat{c}_{k-1},$$

then $\hat{c}_s = c_{\mathrm{SO}(k)}$ (mod $\mathfrak{T}_{\Omega_s^k}$), for all k. We need to show that $\hat{c}_n = c_n$. To prove this, it suffices to show that if $\psi_2, \ldots \psi_n$ are distributions with the support of ψ_k contained in $r_k(\mathbb{R})$, and satisfying $c_{\mathrm{SO}(k-1)} * \psi_k * c_{\mathrm{SO}(k-1)} = c_{\mathrm{SO}(k)}$ (mod $\mathfrak{T}_{\Omega_s^k}$), then $\hat{c}_n = \psi_2 * \cdots \psi_n * c_{n-1} \pmod{\mathfrak{I}_{\Omega_s^n}}$. By induction, we assume that this is true for numbers less than n. Then for any $\psi_2, \ldots, \psi_n$ as above, we have

$$
\begin{aligned}
\hat{c}_n &= c_{n-1} * \psi_n * c_{\mathrm{SO}(n-1)} \pmod{\mathfrak{I}_{\Omega_s^n}} \\
&= (\psi_2 * \cdots * \psi_{n-1} * c_{n-2}) * \psi_n * c_{\mathrm{SO}(n-1)} \pmod{\mathfrak{I}_{\Omega_s^n}} \\
&= \psi_2 * \cdots * \psi_{n-1} * \psi_n * c_{\mathrm{SO}(n-2)} * c_{\mathrm{SO}(n-1)} \pmod{\mathfrak{I}_{\Omega_s^n}} \\
&= \psi_2 * \cdots * \psi_n * c_{n-1} \pmod{\mathfrak{I}_{\Omega_s^n}},
\end{aligned}
$$

where we have used the facts that $c_{\mathrm{SO}(n-2)} * c_{\mathrm{SO}(n-1)} = c_{\mathrm{SO}(n-1)}$, and $c_{n-2} \smile \psi_n$. $\qquad\square$

The distribution $P^{\mathrm{SO}(n-1)}(\psi_{2,n} * \cdots * \psi_{n,n})$ on $S^{n-1} = \mathrm{SO}(n)/\mathrm{SO}(n-1)$ is zero on the associated spherical functions coming from representations of $\mathrm{SO}(n)$ satisfying $|m_{1,n}| \leq s$. In [20], it is shown that a fast transform is possible for functions sampled on the support of this distribution.

A similar argument leads to the parametrization of $\mathrm{SO}(n)$ by Euler angles.

4.3. Example: Sampling on $\mathrm{SU}(n)$. In this case, the appropriate chain of subgroups to use is,

$$
\mathrm{SU}(n) \subseteq S(U_{n-1} \times U_1) \subseteq \mathrm{SU}(n-1) \subseteq \cdots \subseteq S(U_1 \times U_1).
$$

Let $r_k(\theta)$ be the same matrix as was used in the case of $\mathrm{SO}(n)$, but also define $q_k(\theta) = \mathrm{Diag}(e^{-i\theta}, \ldots, e^{-i\theta}, e^{ik\theta}, 1, \ldots, 1)$. where there are exactly k entries of the form $e^{-i\theta}$. Note that $q_k(\theta) \smile \mathrm{SU}(k)$, that the q_k generate the usual choice of maximal torus in $\mathrm{SU}(n)$, and that

$$
\begin{aligned}
S(U_{n-1} \times U_1) &= q_{n-1}([0, 2\pi]).\,\mathrm{SU}(n-1), \\
\mathrm{SU}(n) &= S(U_{n-1} \times U_1).r_n([0, \pi/2]).S(U_{n-1} \times U_1).
\end{aligned}
$$

In fact, the map

$$
[0, \pi/2] \rightarrow S(U_{n-1} \times U_1) \backslash \mathrm{SU}(n)/S(U_{n-1} \times U_1):
$$
$$
\theta \mapsto S(U_{n-1} \times U_1)r_n(\theta)S(U_{n-1} \times U_1)
$$

is a homeomorphism, and its restriction to $(0, \pi/2)$ is a diffeomorphism.

Let $\lambda_{1,n}, \ldots \lambda_{n-1,n}$ be the coordinates of the highest weight of a representation of $\mathrm{SU}(n)$ relative to the basis, $\{e_i\}$ of the dual of the usual Cartan subalgebra, as given in Section 2.2.4. Then

$$
\lambda_{1,n} \geq \cdots \geq \lambda_{n-1,n} \geq 0.
$$

Representations of the group $S(U_{n-1} \times U_1)$, are determined by a collection of numbers $(\lambda_{1,n-1}, \ldots \lambda_{n-2,n-1}; \lambda_{n-1,n-1})$, where $(\lambda_{1,n-1}, \ldots \lambda_{n-2,n-1})$ is the highest weight of the restriction to $\mathrm{SU}(n-1)$, and $\lambda_{n-1,n-1}$ is the weight of the restriction to the subgroup $q_{n-1}(\mathbb{R})$. The relations giving the representations of $S(U_{n-1} \times U_1)$ arising are

$$\lambda_{1,n-1} = \mu_1 - \mu_{n-1},$$

$$\cdots$$

$$\lambda_{n-2,n-1} = \mu_{n-2} - \mu_{n-1},$$

$$\lambda_{n-1,n-1} = (n-1) \sum_{j=1}^{n-1} \lambda_{j,n} - n \sum_{j=1}^{n-1} \mu_j,$$

where the μ_j are integers satisfying

$$\lambda_{1,n} \geq \mu_1 \geq \lambda_{2,n} \geq \ldots \lambda_{n-1,n} \geq \mu_{n-1} \geq 0.$$

In the case $n = 2$ the appropriate relation is $\lambda_{1,2} \geq |\lambda_{1,1}|$, where $\lambda_{1,2} - \lambda_{1,1}$ must be even. To restrict to $SU(n-1)$ from $S(U_{n-1} \times U_1)$ simply throw away $\lambda_{n-1,n-1}$. If we now define for $m \geq 2$

$$\Omega_s^m = \{\Delta_\lambda : \|\lambda\|_H \leq s\} = \{\Delta_{(\lambda_{1,m},\ldots,\lambda_{m-1,m})} : \lambda_{1,m} \leq s\}$$
$$\breve{\Omega}_s^{m-1} = \{\Delta_{(\lambda;\lambda_{m-1,m-1})} : \|\lambda\|_H \leq s, |\lambda_{m-1,m-1}| \leq (m-1)s\}$$
$$= \{\Delta_{(\lambda_{1,m-1},\ldots,\lambda_{m-2,m-1};\lambda_{m-1,m-1})} : \lambda_{1,m-1} \leq s, |\lambda_{m-1,m-1}| \leq (m-1)s\}$$
$$\breve{\Omega}_s^1 = \{\Delta_{(\lambda_{1,1})} : |\lambda_{1,1}| \leq s\},$$

then using the embeddings

$$C^\infty(S(U_1 \times U_1))' \hookrightarrow C^\infty(\mathrm{SU}(2))' \hookrightarrow \ldots \hookrightarrow C^\infty(S(U_{n-1} \times U_1))' \hookrightarrow C^\infty(\mathrm{SU}(n))'$$

and the restriction relations given above, we see that

$$\mathfrak{T}_{\breve{\Omega}_s^1} \subseteq \mathfrak{T}_{\Omega_s^2} \subseteq \cdots \mathfrak{T}_{\Omega_s^{n-1}} \subseteq \mathfrak{T}_{\breve{\Omega}_s^{n-1}} \subseteq \mathfrak{T}_{\Omega_s^n}.$$

The class 1 representations of $\mathrm{SU}(n)$ relative to $S(U_{n-1} \times U_1)$ have highest weights of the form $(2m, m, \ldots)$, where $m \geq 0$, and using the map $[0, \pi/2] \longleftrightarrow S(U_{n-1} \times U_1) \backslash \mathrm{SU}(n)/S(U_{n-1} \times U_1)$ specified above, have corresponding spherical functions which are Jacobi polynomials in $\cos 2\theta$,

$$\varphi_m^n = \frac{(n-2)! m!}{(n+m-2)!} \cdot P_m^{n-2,0}(\cos 2\theta).$$

For a proof of this, see [20].

For $2 \leq i \leq k \leq n$ choose be a real finitely supported distribution, $\tilde{\psi}_{i,k}$, on $[0, \pi/2]$, that satisfies $\langle \tilde{\psi}_{i,k}, \varphi_m^i \rangle = \delta_{0,m}$ for $0 \leq m \leq \lfloor \frac{s}{2} \rfloor$. For $1 \leq j \leq k < n$, choose a real finitely supported distribution, $\tilde{\zeta}_{j,k}$, on $[0, 2\pi)$ that satisfies $\langle \tilde{\zeta}_{j,k}, e^i m(\,) \rangle = \delta_{0,m}$ for $|m| \leq jb$. Define $\tilde{\zeta}'_{n-1,n}$ in the same way, with $j = n-1$. Then set $\psi_{i,k} = (r_i)_*(\tilde{\psi}_{i,k})$, $\zeta_{j,k} = (q_j)_*(\tilde{\zeta}_{j,k})$, and define $\zeta'_{n-1,n}$ similarly. Finally define

$$c_2 = \zeta_{1,2} * \psi_{2,2} * \zeta'_{1,2},$$

$$c_n = (\zeta_{1,n} * \psi_{2,n}) * \cdots * (\zeta_{n-1,n} * \psi_{n,n}) * \zeta'_{n-1,n} * c_{n-1}.$$

THEOREM 4.2. $c_n = c_{\mathrm{SU}(n)}$ (mod $\mathfrak{T}_{\Omega_s^n}$) and $c_n * \zeta'_{-1,n} = c_{S(U_n \times U_1)}$ (mod $\mathfrak{T}_{\breve{\Omega}_s^n}$).

PROOF. We use induction on n. It suffices to show that if the ψ_k are distributions supported on $r_k(\mathbb{R})$, and ζ_k, ζ'_k satisfy $c_{S(U_{k-1} \times U_1)} * \psi_k * c_{S(U_{k-1} \times U_1)} = c_{\mathrm{SU}(k)}$, and $\zeta'_k = \zeta_k = c_{q_k(\mathbb{R})}$ modulo $\mathfrak{T}_{\Omega_s^n}$, then

$$c_{\mathrm{SU}(n)} = (\zeta_1 * \psi_2) * \cdots * (\zeta_{n-2} * \psi_{n-1}) * \zeta'_{n-2} * c_{\mathrm{SU}(n-1)} \quad (\text{mod } \mathfrak{T}_{\Omega_s^n}).$$

By induction, we can assume this holds for numbers less than n. Let Q_n be the subgroup of $\mathrm{SU}(n)$ given by $Q_n = \{\mathrm{Diag}(e^{i(n-1)\theta}, e^{-i\theta}, \ldots e^{-i\theta}) : \theta \in \mathbb{R}\}$, and note that $\zeta_{n-2} * c_{\mathrm{SU}(n-2)} * \zeta_{n-1} = \zeta_{n-1} * c_{\mathrm{SU}(n-2)} * c_{Q_n}$ (mod $\mathfrak{T}_{\Omega_s^n}$). Therefore, working modulo $\mathfrak{T}_{\Omega_s^n}$, we have

$$
\begin{aligned}
c_{\mathrm{SU}(n)} &= c_{\mathrm{SU}(n-1)} * \zeta_{n-1} * \psi_{n,n} * \zeta'_{-1} * c_{\mathrm{SU}(n-1)} \\
&= \zeta_1 * \psi_2 * \cdots * \psi_{n-1} * (\zeta'_{n-2} * c_{\mathrm{SU}(n-2)} * \zeta_{n-1}) * \psi_n * \zeta'_{n-1} * c_{\mathrm{SU}(n-1)} \\
&= \zeta_1 * \cdots * \psi_{n-1} * (\zeta_{n-1} * c_{\mathrm{SU}(n-2)} * c_{Q_n}) * \psi_n * \zeta'_{n-1} * c_{\mathrm{SU}(n-1)} \\
&= \zeta_1 * \cdots * \psi_{n-1} * \zeta_{n-1} * \psi_n * c_{\mathrm{SU}(n-2)} * c_{Q_n} * \zeta'_{n-1} * c_{\mathrm{SU}(n-1)} \\
&= \zeta_1 * \psi_2 * \cdots * \psi_{n-1} * \zeta_{n-1} * \psi_{n,n} * \zeta'_{-1,n} * c_{\mathrm{SU}(n-1)},
\end{aligned}
$$

where we used the fact that $Q_n \subseteq S(U_{n-1} \times U_1)$. $\qquad\square$

The distribution, $P^{\mathrm{SU}(n-1)}(\zeta_{1,n} * \psi_{2,n} * \cdots * \zeta_{n-1,n} * \psi_{n,n} * \zeta'_{-1,n})$, on $S^{2n-1} = \mathrm{SU}(n-1)/\mathrm{SU}(n-1)$, is zero on associated spherical functions coming from representations whose highest weight, $(\lambda_{1,n}, \ldots, \lambda_{n-1,n})$, satisfies $\lambda_{1,n} \le b$. In [20] is is shown how to perform fast transforms for functions sampled on the support of this distribution. By commutativity, $(\zeta_{1,n} * \psi_{2,n}) * \cdots * (\zeta_{n-1,n} * \psi_{n,n}) = (\zeta_{1,n} * \cdots * \zeta_{n-1,n}) * \psi_{2,n} * \cdots \psi_{n,n})$, so by replacing $\zeta_{1,n} * \cdots * \zeta_{n-1,n}$ by an appropriate distribution on the maximal torus of $\mathrm{SU}(n)$, we can obtain yet more distributions on $\mathrm{SU}(n)$, which satisfy the above theorem.

The same commutativity relations can applied to the subgroups q_i and r_j of $\mathrm{SU}(n)$. This yields a parametrization of $\mathrm{SU}(n)$, which is analogous to the Euler angles for $\mathrm{SO}(n)$.

4.4. Example: Sampling on $\mathrm{Sp}(n)$. $\mathrm{Sp}(n) = \{A \in M_n(\mathbb{H}) : A^*A = \mathrm{Id}\}$, where $\mathbb{H}$ denotes the division ring of quaternions. By elementary geometry, one can see that $\mathrm{Sp}(n)/(\mathrm{Sp}(n-1) \times \mathrm{Sp}(1))$ is isomorphic to the right quaternionic projective space, $\mathbf{P}^{n-1}\mathbb{H}$ and that the map

$$[0, \pi/2] \to (\mathrm{Sp}(n-1) \times \mathrm{Sp}(1)) \backslash \mathrm{Sp}(n)/(\mathrm{Sp}(n-1) \times \mathrm{Sp}(1))$$
$$: \theta \mapsto (\mathrm{Sp}(n-1) \times \mathrm{Sp}(1)).r_n(\theta).(\mathrm{Sp}(n-1) \times \mathrm{Sp}(1))$$

is a homeomorphism, and its restriction to $(0, \pi/2)$ is a diffeomorphism. Note that $\mathrm{Sp}(1) \hookrightarrow \mathrm{SU}(2)$.

Let

$$R_n = \left\{ \begin{pmatrix} 1 & & \\ & \ddots & \\ & & a \end{pmatrix} : a \in \mathrm{Sp}(1) \right\},$$

so that $\mathrm{Sp}(n-1) \times \mathrm{Sp}(1) = \mathrm{Sp}(n-1).R_n$.

Working in the basis $\{e_i\}$ of Section 2.2.4, the highest weights of representations of $\mathrm{Sp}(n)$ are determined by integers $m_{1,n}, \ldots, m_{n,n}$, where

$$m_{1,n} \geq \cdots \geq m_{n,n} \geq 0.$$

The highest weights, $\nu = (m_{1,n-1}, \ldots, m_{n-1,n-1})$, of those representations occurring in the restriction of the representation, $\Delta_{(m_{1,n}, \ldots, m_{n,n})}$, of $\mathrm{Sp}(n)$ to $\mathrm{Sp}(n-1)$ satisfy

$$p_1 \geq m_{1,n-1} \geq p_2 \geq \cdots \geq m_{n-1,n-1} \geq p_n,$$

where

$$m_{1,n} \geq p_1 \geq \cdots \geq m_{n,n} \geq p_n \geq 0,$$

but the corresponding multiplicities may be greater than one. The restriction of $\Delta_{(m_{1,n}, \ldots, m_{n,n})}$ to $\mathrm{Sp}(n-1) \times \mathrm{Sp}(1)$ is precisely

$$\sum_{\nu} \left(\Delta_\nu \otimes \left(\bigotimes_{i=1}^{n} \Delta_{(\min\{m_{i-1,n-1}, m_{i,n}\} - \max\{m_{i,n-1}, m_{i+1,n}\})} \right) \right),$$

where $m_{n+1,n} = m_{n,n-1} = 0$, $m_{0,n-1} = +\infty$, and ν ranges over the highest weights of irreducible representations of $\mathrm{Sp}(n)$ appearing in the restriction of $\Delta_{(m_{1,n}, \ldots, m_{n,n})}$ to $\mathrm{Sp}(n-1)$; see [33]. Hence, highest weights, m, of the representations occurring in the restriction from $\mathrm{Sp}(n)$ to R_n satisfy $m_{1n} \geq m$. It should be clear then, that if we define, for any positive integer s,

$$\Omega_s^n = \{\Delta_\lambda : \|\lambda\|_H \leq s\} = \{\Delta_{(m_{1,n}, \ldots, m_{n,n})} : m_{1,n} \leq s\},$$

then $\mathfrak{T}_{\Omega_s^1} \subseteq \cdots \subseteq \mathfrak{T}_{\Omega_s^n}$. Also, let $\Omega_s^{\mathrm{SU}(2)}$ be the set of all irreducible representations, Δ_m, of $\mathrm{SU}(2)$ such that $0 \leq m \leq b$, and denote the corresponding set of representations of R_n by $\Omega_s^{R_n}$. Using the embedding $C^\infty(R_n)' \hookrightarrow C^\infty(\mathrm{Sp}(n))'$, we see that $\mathfrak{T}_{\Omega_s^{R_n}} \subseteq \mathfrak{T}_{\Omega_s^n}$.

For any $1 \leq k \leq n$, we can construct, using previous techniques, a finitely supported measure, $v_{k,n}$, on $R_n \hookrightarrow \mathrm{SU}(2)$, such that $v_{k,n} = c_{R_k} \pmod{\mathfrak{T}_{\Omega_s^{R_k}}}$. Now assume that $n \geq 2$. The class one representations of $\mathrm{Sp}(n)$ relative to $\mathrm{Sp}(n-1) \times \mathrm{Sp}(1)$ have highest weights of the form $(m, m, 0, \ldots)$, where m is a nonnegative integer, and the corresponding spherical functions can be written using the map $[0, \pi/2] \to (\mathrm{Sp}(n-1) \times \mathrm{Sp}(1)) \backslash \mathrm{Sp}(n) / (\mathrm{Sp}(n-1) \times \mathrm{Sp}(1))$, in the form

$$\varphi_m^n = \frac{(2n-3)! m!}{(m+2n-3)!} . P_m^{2n-3,1}(\cos 2\theta).$$

For a proof of this, see [15]. Let $\tilde{\psi}_{k,n}$ be a real finitely supported distribution on $[0, \pi/2]$ that satisfies $\langle \tilde{\psi}_{k,n}, \varphi_m^k \rangle = \delta_{0,m}$ for $0 \leq m \leq s$, and set $\psi_{k,n} = (r_k)_* (\tilde{\psi}_{k,n})$. Then define c_n inductively by

$$c_1 = v_{1,1},$$

$$c_n = v_{1,n} * (\psi_{2,n} * v_{2,n}) * \cdots * (\psi_{n,n} * v_{n,n}) * c_{n-1}.$$

This finitely supported measure is the convolution product of $\dim \mathrm{Sp}(n) = 2n^2 + n$ factors each supported on a 1-parameter subgroup of $\mathrm{Sp}(n)$, and it is easy to prove the following theorem.

THEOREM 4.3. $c_n = c_{\mathrm{Sp}(n)} \pmod{\mathfrak{T}_{\Omega_s^n}}$.

PROOF. Similar to the $\mathrm{SO}(n)$ and $\mathrm{SU}(n)$ cases. $\square$

Acknowledgments

I thank Dan Rockmore for reorganizing this paper, and for rewriting the introduction to bring it up to date. I would like to thank Persi Diaconis, and Dennis Healy for many discussions and a lot of encouragement and advice along the way. I would also like to thank the Harvard University Department of Mathematics, and the Max-Planck-Institut für Mathematik, which supported me during the writing of this paper.

References

[1] J. P. Boyd, *Chebyshev and Fourier Spectral Methods*, Lecture Notes in Engineering **49**, Springer, New York, 1989.

[2] W. Byerly, *An elementary treatise on Fourier's series and spherical, cylindrical, and ellipsoidal harmonics: with applications to problems in mathematical physics*, Ginn, Boston, 1893.

[3] G. Chirikjian and A. Kyatkin, *Engineering applications of noncommutative harmonic analysis: with emphasis on rotation and motion groups*, CRC Press, Boca Raton (FL), 2000.

[4] J. R. Driscoll and D. M. Healy Jr., "Computing Fourier transforms and convolutions on the 2-sphere", *Adv. Applied Math.* **15** (1994), 202–250.

[5] J. R. Driscoll, D. M. Healy Jr., and D. Rockmore, "Fast spherical transforms on distance transitive graphs", *SIAM J. Comput.*, **26**:4, 1997, 1066–1099.

[6] G. I. Gaudrey and R. Pini, "Bernstein's theorem for compact, connected Lie groups", *Math. Proc. Cambridge Philosoph. Soc.* **99** (1986), 297–305.

[7] A. Ghizetti and A. Ossicini, *Quadrature Formulae*, Birkhäuser, Basel, 1970.

[8] D. Healy, D. Rockmore, P. Kostelec, and S. Moore, "FFTs for the 2-sphere: Improvements and variations", *J. Fourier Anal. Appl.* **9**:4 (2003), 341–384.

[9] D. Healy, P. Kostelec, and D. Rockmore, "Safe and effective higher order Legendre transforms", to appear in *App. Comp. Math.*

[10] S. Helgason, *Groups and geometric analysis*, Academic Press, New York, 1984.

[11] E. Hewitt and K. A. Ross, *Abstract harmonic analysis*, Grundlehren der mathematischen Wissenschaften **152**, Springer, Berlin, 1963.

[12] J. E. Humphreys, *Introduction to Lie algebras and representation theory*, Springer, New York, 1980.

[13] M. Kazhdan, T. Funkhouser and S. Rusinkiewicz, "Rotation invariant spherical harmonic representation of 3D shape descriptors", to appear in *Symposium on Geometry Processing* (2003).

[14] M. Kazhdan and T. Funkhouser, "Harmonic 3D Shape Matching", Technical Sketch, *SIGGRAPH* (2002).

[15] A. U. Klimyk and N.J. Vilenkin, "Relations between spherical functions of compact groups", *J. Math. Phys.* **30**:6 (June 1989), 1219–1225.

[16] P. Kostelec, D. K. Maslen, D. M. Healy, and D. Rockmore, "Computational harmonic analysis for tensor fields on the two-sphere", *J. Comput. Phys.* **162**:2 (2000), 514–535.

[17] P. Kostelec and D. Rockmore, "FFTs for SO(3)", in preparation.

[18] J. T. Lo and L. R. Eshleman, "Exponential Fourier densities on S^2 and optimal estimation and detection for directional processes", *IEEE Trans. Inform. Theory*, **23**:3 (May 1977), 321–336.

[19] J. T. Lo and L. R. Eshleman, "Exponential Fourier densities on SO(3) and optimal estimation and detection for rotational processes", *SIAM J. Appl. Math.* **36**:1 (Feb. 1979), 73–82.

[20] D. K. Maslen, *Fast transforms and sampling for compact groups*, Ph.D. Thesis, Harvard University, MA (1993).

[21] D. K. Maslen, "Efficient computation of Fourier transforms on compact groups", *J. Fourier Anal. Appl.* **4**:1 (1998), 19–52.

[22] M. P. Mohlenkamp, "A fast transform for spherical harmonics", *J. Fourier Anal. Appl.* **5**:3 (1999), 159–184..

[23] P. M. Morse and H. Feshbach, *Methods of theoretical physics*, McGraw-Hill, New York (1953).

[24] S. P. Oh, D.N. Spergel, G. Hinshaw, "An efficient technique to determine the power spectrum from the cosmic microwave background sky maps", *Astrophysical Journal* **510** (1999), 551–563.

[25] A. Oppenheim and R. Schafer, *Digital signal processing*, Prentice-Hall, Englewood Cliffs (NJ), 1975.

[26] A. Papoulis, *The Fourier integral and its applications*, McGraw-Hill, NY, 1962.

[27] R. Pini, "Bernstein's Theorem on SU(2)", *Bollettino Un. Mat. Ital.* (6) **4**-A (1985), 381–389.

[28] D. Slepian, "Some comments on Fourier analysis, uncertainty and modeling", *SIAM Review* **25**:3 (July 1983), 379–393.

[29] M. Sugiura, *Unitary representations and harmonic analysis: an introduction*, North-Holland, Amsterdam, 1990.

[30] N. J. Vilenkin, *Special functions and the theory of group representations*, Translations of Mathematical Monographs **22**, Amer. Math. Soc., Providence, 1968.

[31] N. R. Wallach, *Harmonic analysis on homogeneous spaces*, Dekker, New York, 1973.

[32] M. Zaldarriaga and U. Seljak, "An all-sky analysis of polarization in the microwave background", *Phys. Rev. D* **55** (1997), 1830–1840.

[33] D. P. Želobenko, *Compact Lie groups and their representations*, Translations of Mathematical Monographs **40**, Amer. Math. Soc., Providence, 1973.

DAVID KEITH MASLEN
SUSQUEHANNA INTERNATIONAL GROUP
401 CITY AVE., SUITE 220
BALA CYNWYD, PA 19004
U.S.A.
david@maslen.net

Modern Signal Processing
MSRI Publications
Volume **46**, 2003

The Cooley–Tukey FFT and Group Theory

DAVID K. MASLEN AND DANIEL N. ROCKMORE

ABSTRACT. In 1965 J. Cooley and J. Tukey published an article detailing an
efficient algorithm to compute the Discrete Fourier Transform, necessary
for processing the newly available reams of digital time series produced
by recently invented analog-to-digital converters. Since then, the Cooley–
Tukey Fast Fourier Transform and its variants has been a staple of digital
signal processing.

Among the many casts of the algorithm, a natural one is as an efficient
algorithm for computing the Fourier expansion of a function on a finite
abelian group. In this paper we survey some of our recent work on he
"separation of variables" approach to computing a Fourier transform on an
arbitrary finite group. This is a natural generalization of the Cooley–Tukey
algorithm. In addition we touch on extensions of this idea to compact and
noncompact groups.

Pure and Applied Mathematics: Two Sides of a Coin

The *Bulletin of the AMS* for November 1979 had a paper by L. Auslander and
R. Tolimieri [3] with the delightful title "Is computing with the Finite Fourier
Transform pure or applied mathematics?" This rhetorical question was answered
by showing that in fact, the finite Fourier transform, and the family of efficient
algorithms used to compute it, the Fast Fourier Transform (FFT), a pillar of
the world of digital signal processing, were of interest to both pure and applied
mathematicians.

Mathematics Subject Classification: 20C15; Secondary 65T10.

Keywords: generalized Fourier transform, Bratteli diagram, Gel'fand–Tsetlin basis, Cooley–
Tukey algorithm.

This paper originally appeared in *Notices of the American Mathematical Society* **48**:10 (2001),
1151–1160. Parts of the introduction are similar to the paper "The FFT: an algorithm the
whole family can use", which appeared in *Computing in Science and Engineering*, January
2000, pp. 62–67. Rockmore is supported in part by NSF PFF Award DMS-9553134, AFOSR

F49620-00-1-0280, and DOJ 2000-DT-CX-K001. He would also like to thank the Santa Fe
Institute and the Courant Institute for their hospitality during some of the writing.

Auslander had come of age as an applied mathematician at a time when pure and applied mathematicians still received much of the same training. The ends towards which these skills were then directed became a matter of taste. As Tolimieri retells it (private communication), Auslander had become distressed at the development of a separate discipline of applied mathematics which had grown apart from much of core mathematics. The effect of this development was detrimental on both sides. On the one hand applied mathematicians had fewer tools to bring to problems, and conversely, pure mathematicians were often ignoring the fertile bed of inspiration provided by real world problems. Auslander hoped their paper would help mend a growing perceived rift in the mathematical community by showing the ultimate unity of pure and applied mathematics.

We will show that investigation of finite and fast Fourier transforms continues to be a varied and interesting direction of mathematical research. Whereas Auslander and Tolimieri concentrated on relations to nilpotent harmonic analysis and theta functions, we emphasize connections between the famous *Cooley–Tukey FFT* and group representation theory. In this way we hope to provide further evidence of the rich interplay of ideas which can be found at the nexus of pure and applied mathematics.

1. Background

The finite Fourier transform or discrete Fourier transform (DFT) has several representation theoretic interpretations: either as an exact computation of the Fourier coefficients of a function on the cyclic group $\mathbb{Z}/n\mathbb{Z}$ or a function of band-limit n on the circle S^1, or as an approximation to the Fourier transform of a function on the real line. For each of these points of view there is a natural group-theoretic generalization, and also a corresponding set of efficient algorithms for computing the quantities involved. These algorithms collectively make up the *Fast Fourier Transform* or *FFT*.

Formally, the DFT is a linear transformation mapping any complex vector of length n, $f = (f(0) \ldots, f(n-1))^t \in \mathbb{C}^n$, to its *Fourier transform, $\widehat{f} \in \mathbb{C}^n$*. The kth component of $\widehat{f}$, *the DFT of f at frequency k*, is

$$\widehat{f}(k) = \sum_{j=0}^{n-1} f(j)e^{2\pi ijk/n} \tag{1-1}$$

where $i = \sqrt{-1}$, and the *inverse Fourier transform* is

$$f(j) = \frac{1}{n} \sum_{k=0}^{n-1} \widehat{f}(k)e^{-2\pi ijk/n}. \tag{1-2}$$

Thus, with respect to the standard basis, the DFT can be expressed as the matrix-vector product $\widehat{f} = \mathbb{F}_n \cdot f$ where $\mathbb{F}_n$ is the *Fourier matrix* of order n, whose j, k entry is equal to $e^{2\pi ijk/n}$. Computing a DFT directly would require n^2

scalar operations. (For precision's sake: Our count of operations is the number of complex additions of the number of complex multiplications, whichever is greater.) Instead, the FFT is a family of algorithms for computing the DFT of any $f \in \mathbb{C}^n$ in $O(n \log n)$ operations. Since inversion can be framed as the DFT of the function $\check{f}(k) = \frac{1}{n}\widehat{f}(-k)$, the FFT also gives an efficient inverse Fourier transform.

One of the main practical implications of the FFT is that it allows any cyclically invariant linear operator to be applied to a vector in only $O(n \log n)$ scalar operations. Indeed, the DFT diagonalizes any group invariant operator, making possible the following algorithm: (1) compute the Fourier transform (DFT). (2) Multiply the DFT by the eigenvalues of the operator, which are also found using the Fourier transform. (3) Compute the inverse Fourier transform of the result. This technique is the basis of digital filtering and is also used for the efficient numerical solution of partial differential equations.

Some history. Since the Fourier matrix is effectively the character table of a cyclic group, it is not surprising that some of its earliest appearances are in number theory, the subject which gave birth to character theory. Consideration of the Fourier matrix goes back at least as far as to Gauss, who was interested in its connections to quadratic reciprocity. In particular, Gauss showed that for odd primes p and q,

$$\left(\frac{p}{q}\right)\left(\frac{q}{p}\right) = \frac{\operatorname{Trace} \mathbb{F}_{pq}}{\operatorname{Trace} \mathbb{F}_p \operatorname{Trace} \mathbb{F}_q}, \qquad (1\text{–}3)$$

where $\left(\frac{p}{q}\right)$ denotes the Legendre symbol. Gauss also established a formula for the quadratic Gauss sum $\operatorname{Trace} \mathbb{F}_n$, which is discussed in detail in [3].

Another early appearance of the DFT occurs in the origins of representation theory in the work of Dedekind and Frobenius on the group determinant. For a finite group G, the group determinant Θ_G is defined as the homogeneous polynomial in the variables x_g (for each $g \in G$) given by the determinant of the matrix whose rows and columns are indexed by the elements of G with g, h-entry equal to $x_{gh^{-1}}$. Frobenius showed that when G is abelian, Θ_G admits the factorization

$$\Theta_G = \prod_{\chi \in \widehat{G}} \left(\sum_{g \in G} \chi(g) x_g \right), \qquad (1\text{–}4)$$

where $\widehat{G}$ is the set of characters of G. The linear form defined by the inner sum in (1–4) is a "generic" DFT at the frequency χ.

In the nonabelian case, Θ_G admits an analogous factorization in terms of irreducible polynomials of the form

$$\Theta_D(G) = \det\left(\sum_{g \in G} D(g) x_g \right)$$

where D is an *irreducible matrix representation* of G. The inner sum here is a generic Fourier transform over G. See [12] for a beautiful historical exposition of these ideas.

Gauss's interests ranged over all areas of mathematics and its applications, so it is perhaps not surprising that the first appearance of an FFT can also be traced back to him [10]. Gauss was interested in certain astronomical calculations, a recurrent area of application of the FFT, necessary for interpolation of asteroidal orbits from a finite set of equally-spaced observations. Surely the prospect of a huge laborious hand calculation was good motivation for the development of a fast algorithm. Making fewer hand calculations also implies less opportunity for error and hence increased numerical stability!

Gauss wanted to compute the Fourier coefficients, a_k, b_k of a function represented by a Fourier series of bandwidth n,

$$f(x) = \sum_{k=0}^{m} a_k \cos 2\pi kx + \sum_{k=1}^{m} b_k \sin 2\pi kx, \qquad (1\text{--}5)$$

where $m = (n-1)/2$ for n odd and $m = n/2$ for n even. He first observed that the Fourier coefficients can be computed by a DFT of length n using the values of f at equispaced sample points. Gauss then went on to show that if $n = n_1 n_2$, this DFT can in turn be reduced to first computing n_1 DFTs of length n_2, using equispaced subsets of the sample points, i.e., a subsampled DFT, and then combining these shorter DFTs using various trigonometric identities. This is the basic idea underlying the *Cooley–Tukey FFT*.

Unfortunately, this reduction never appeared outside of Gauss's collected works. Similar ideas, usually for the case $n_1 = 2$ were rediscovered intermittently over the succeeding years. Notable among these is the doubling trick of Danielson and Lanczos (1942), performed in the service of x-ray crystallography, another frequent employer of FFT technology. Nevertheless, it was not until the publication of Cooley and Tukey's famous paper [7] that the algorithm gained any notice. The story of Cooley and Tukey's collaboration is an interesting one. Tukey arrived at the basic reduction while in a meeting of President Kennedy's Science Advisory Committee where among the topics of discussions were techniques for off-shore detection of nuclear tests in the Soviet Union. Ratification of a proposed United States/Soviet Union nuclear test ban depended upon the development of a method for detecting the tests without actually visiting the Soviet nuclear facilities. One idea required the analysis of seismological time series obtained from off-shore seismometers, the length and number of which would require fast algorithms for computing the DFT. Other possible applications to national security included the long-range acoustic detection of nuclear submarines.

R. Garwin of IBM was another of the participants at this meeting and when Tukey showed him this idea Garwin immediately saw a wide range of potential applicability and quickly set to getting this algorithm implemented. Garwin was directed to Cooley, and, needing to hide the national security issues, told Cooley that he wanted the code for another problem of interest: the determination of the periodicities of the spin orientations in a 3-D crystal of He^3. Cooley had other projects going on, and only after quite a lot of prodding did he sit down to program the "Cooley–Tukey" FFT. In short order, Cooley and Tukey prepared their paper, which, for a mathematics/computer science paper, was published almost instantaneously—in six months!. This publication, Garwin's fervent proselytizing, as well as the new flood of data available from recently developed fast analog-to-digital converters, did much to help call attention to the existence of this apparently new fast and useful algorithm. In fact, the significance of and interest in the FFT was such that it is sometimes thought of as having given birth to the modern field of analysis of algorithms. See also [6] and the 1967 and 1969 special issues of the *IEEE Transactions in Audio Electronics* for more historical details.

The Fourier transform and finite groups. One natural group-theoretic interpretation of the Fourier transform is as a change of basis in the space of complex functions on $\mathbb{Z}/n\mathbb{Z}$. Given a complex function f on $\mathbb{Z}/n\mathbb{Z}$, we may expand f, in the basis of irreducible characters $\{\chi_k\}$, defined by $\chi_k(j) = e^{2\pi ijk/n}$. By (1–2) the coefficient of χ_k in the expansion is equal to the scaled Fourier coefficient $\frac{1}{n}\widehat{f}(-k)$, whereas the Fourier coefficient $\widehat{f}(k)$ is the inner product of the vector of function values of f with those of the character χ_k.

For an arbitrary finite group G there is an analogous definition. The characters of $\mathbb{Z}/n\mathbb{Z}$ are the simplest example of a *matrix representation*, which for any group G is a matrix-valued function $\rho(g)$ on G such that $\rho(ab) = \rho(a)\rho(b)$, and $\rho(e)$ is the identity matrix. Given a matrix representation ρ of dimension d_ρ, and a complex function f on G, the *Fourier transform of f at ρ* is defined as the matrix sum

$$\widehat{f}(\rho) = \sum_{x \in G} f(x)\rho(x). \tag{1–6}$$

Computing $\widehat{f}(\rho)$ is equivalent to the computation of the d_ρ^2 scalar Fourier transforms at each of the individual *matrix elements* ρ_{ij},

$$\widehat{f}(\rho_{ij}) = \sum_{x \in G} f(x)\rho_{ij}(x). \tag{1–7}$$

A set of matrix representations $\mathcal{R}$ of G is called *a complete set of irreducible representations* if and only if the collection of matrix elements of the representations, relative to an arbitrary choice of basis for each matrix representation in the set, forms a basis for the space of complex functions on G. The Fourier transform of f with respect to $\mathcal{R}$ is then defined as the collection of individual transforms, while *the Fourier transform on G* means any Fourier transform computed with respect to some complete set of irreducibles. In this case, the inverse transform is given explicitly as

$$f(x) = \frac{1}{|G|} \sum_{\rho \in \mathcal{R}} d_\rho \operatorname{Trace}(\widehat{f}(\rho)\rho(x^{-1})). \qquad (1\text{--}8)$$

Equation (1–8) shows us a relation between the group Fourier transform and the expansion of a function in the basis of matrix elements. The coefficient of ρ_{ij} in the expansion of f is the Fourier transform of f at the dual representation $[\rho_{ji}(g^{-1})]$ scaled by the factor $d_\rho/|G|$.

Viewing the Fourier transform on G as a simple matrix-vector multiplication leads to some simple bounds on the number of operations required to compute the transform. The computation clearly takes no more than the $|G|^2$ scalar operations required for any matrix-vector multiplication. On the other hand the column of the Fourier matrix corresponding to the trivial representation is all ones, so at least $|G| - 1$ additions are necessary. One main goal of this finite group FFT research is to discover algorithms which can significantly reduce the upper bound for various classes of groups, or even all finite groups.

The current state of affairs for finite group FFTs. Analysis of the Fourier transform shows that for G abelian, the number of operations required is bounded by $O(|G| \log |G|)$. For arbitrary groups G, upper bounds of $O(|G| \log |G|)$ remain the holy grail in group FFT research. In 1978, A. Willsky provided the first non-abelian example by showing that certain metabelian groups had an $O(|G| \log |G|)$ Fourier transform algorithm [20]. Implicit in the big-O notation is the idea that a family of groups is under consideration, with the size of the individual groups going to infinity.

Since Willsky's initial discovery much progress has been made. U. Baum has shown that the supersolvable groups admit an $O(|G| \log |G|)$ FFT, while others have shown that symmetric groups admit $O(|G| \log^2 |G|)$ FFTs (see Section 3). Other groups for which highly improved (but not $O(|G| \log^c |G|)$) algorithms have been discovered include the matrix groups over finite fields, and more generally, the Lie groups of finite type. See [15] for pointers to the literature. There is much work to be done finding new classes of groups which admit fast transforms, and improving on the above results. The ultimate goal is to settle or make progress on the following conjecture:

CONJECTURE 1. *There exist constants c_1 and c_2 such that for any finite group G, there is a complete set of irreducible matrix representations for which the Fourier transform of any complex function on the G may be computed in fewer than $c_1 |G| \log^{c_2} |G|$ scalar operations.*

2. The Cooley–Tukey Algorithm

Cooley and Tukey showed [7] how the Fourier transform on the cyclic group $\mathbb{Z}/n\mathbb{Z}$, where $n = pq$ is composite, could be written in terms of Fourier transforms on the subgroup $q\mathbb{Z}/n\mathbb{Z} \cong \mathbb{Z}/p\mathbb{Z}$. The trick is to change variables, so that the one dimensional formula (1–1) is turned into a two dimensional formula, which can be computed in two stages. Define variables j_1, j_2, k_1, k_2, through the equations

$$
\begin{aligned}
j = j(j_1, j_2) = j_1 q + j_2, \quad 0 \le j_1 < p, \quad 0 \le j_2 < q, \\
k = k(k_1, k_2) = k_2 p + k_1, \quad 0 \le k_1 < p, \quad 0 \le k_2 < q.
\end{aligned}
\tag{2-1}
$$

It follows from these equations that (1–1) can be rewritten as

$$
\widehat{f}(k_1, k_2) = \sum_{j_2=0}^{q-1} e^{2\pi i j_2 (k_2 p + k_1)/n} \sum_{j_1=0}^{p-1} e^{2\pi i j_1 k_1 / p} f(j_1, j_2).
\tag{2-2}
$$

We now compute $\widehat{f}$ in two stages:

- Stage 1: For each k_1 and j_2 compute the inner sum

$$
\tilde{f}(k_1, j_2) = \sum_{j_1=0}^{p-1} e^{2\pi i j_1 k_1 / p} f(j_1, j_2).
\tag{2-3}
$$

This requires at most $p^2 q$ scalar operations.

- Stage 2: For each k_1, k_2 compute the outer sum

$$
\widehat{f}(k_1, k_2) = \sum_{j_2=0}^{q-1} e^{2\pi i j_2 (k_2 p + k_1)/n} \tilde{f}(k_1, j_2).
\tag{2-4}
$$

This requires an additional $q^2 p$ operations.

Thus, instead of $(pq)^2$ operations, the above algorithm uses $(pq)(p+q)$ operations.

Stage 1 has the form of a DFT on the subgroup $q\mathbb{Z}/n\mathbb{Z} \cong \mathbb{Z}/p\mathbb{Z}$, embedded as the set of multiples of q, whereas stage 2 has the form of a DFT on a cyclic group of order q, so if n could be factored further, we could apply the same trick to these DFTs in turn. Thus, if N has the prime factorization $N = p_1 \cdots p_m$, then we recover Cooley and Tukey's original m-stage algorithm which requires $N \sum_i p_i$ operations [7].

A group-theoretic interpretation. Auslander and Tolmieri's paper [3] related the Cooley–Tukey algorithm to the Weil–Brezin map for the finite Heisenberg group. Here we present an alternate group-theoretic interpretation, originally due to Beth [4], that is more amenable to generalization.

The change of variables on the first line of (2–1) may be interpreted as the factorization of the group element j as the (group) product of $j_1 q \in q\mathbb{Z}/n\mathbb{Z}$, with the coset representative j_2. Thus, if we write $G = \mathbb{Z}/n\mathbb{Z}$, $H = q\mathbb{Z}/n\mathbb{Z}$, and let Y denote our set of coset representatives, the change of variables can be rewritten as

$$
g = y \cdot h, \quad y \in Y, \quad h \in H
\tag{2-5}
$$

The second change of variables in (2–1) can be interpreted using the notion of restriction of representations. It is easy to see that restricting a representation on a group G to a subgroup H yields a representation of that subgroup. In the case of $q\mathbb{Z}/n\mathbb{Z}$ this amounts to the observation that

$$e^{2\pi i j_1 q(k_2 p + k_1)/n} = e^{2\pi i j_1 k_1/p},$$

which is used to prove (2–2).

The restriction relations between representations may be represented diagramatically using a directed graded graph with three levels. At level zero there is a single vertex labeled 1, called the root vertex. The vertices at level one are labeled by the irreducible representations of $\mathbb{Z}/p\mathbb{Z}$, and the vertices at level two are labeled by the irreducible representations of $\mathbb{Z}/n\mathbb{Z}$. Edges are drawn from the root vertex to each of the vertices at level one, and from a vertex at level one to a vertex at level two if and only if the representation at the tip restricts to the representation at the tail. The directed graph obtained is the *Bratteli diagram* for the chain of subgroups $\mathbb{Z}/n\mathbb{Z} > \mathbb{Z}p/\mathbb{Z} > 1$. Figure 1 shows the situation for the chain $\mathbb{Z}/6\mathbb{Z} > 2\mathbb{Z}/6\mathbb{Z} \cong \mathbb{Z}/3\mathbb{Z} > 1$.

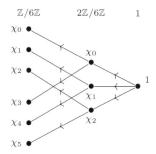

Figure 1. The Bratteli diagram for $\mathbb{Z}/6\mathbb{Z} > 2\mathbb{Z}/6\mathbb{Z} > 1$. The representation χ_k of $\mathbb{Z}/m\mathbb{Z}$ is defined by $\chi_k(l) = e^{2\pi i k l/m}$.

In this way the irreducible representations of $\mathbb{Z}/n\mathbb{Z}$ are indexed by paths (k_1, k_2) in the Bratteli diagram for $\mathbb{Z}/n\mathbb{Z} > \mathbb{Z}/p\mathbb{Z} > 1$. The DFT factorization (2–2) now becomes

$$\widehat{f}(k_1, k_2) = \sum_{y \in Y} \chi_{k_1,k_2}(y) \sum_{h \in H} f(y \cdot h) \chi_{k_1}(h). \qquad (2\text{–}6)$$

The two-stage algorithm is now restated as first computing a set of sums that depend on only the first leg of the paths, and then combining these to compute the final sums that depend on the full paths.

In summary, the group elements have been indexed according to a particular factorization scheme, while the irreducible representations (the dual group) are now indexed by paths in a Bratteli diagram, describing the restriction of representations. This allows us to compute the Fourier transform in stages, using one fewer group element factor at each stage, but using paths of increasing length in the Bratteli diagram.

3. Fast Fourier Transforms on Symmetric Groups

A fair amount of attention has been devoted to developing efficient Fourier transform algorithms for the symmetric group. One motivation for developing these algorithms is the goal of analyzing data on the symmetric group using a spectral approach. In the simpler case of time series data on the cyclic group, this approach amounts to projecting the data vector onto the basis of complex exponentials.

The spectral approach to data analysis makes sense for a function defined on any kind of group, and such a general formulation is due to Diaconis (see [8], for example). The case of the symmetric group corresponds to considering *ranked data*. For instance, a group of people might be asked to rank a list of 4 restaurants in order of preference. Thus, each respondent chooses a permutation of the original ordered list of 4 objects, and counting the number of respondents choosing each permutation yields a function on S_4. It turns out that the corresponding Fourier decomposition of this function naturally describes various coalition effects that may be useful in describing the data.

To get some feel for this notice that the Fourier transform at the matrix elements $\rho_{ij}(\pi)$ of the (reducible) defining representation count the number of people ranking restaurant i in position j. If instead ρ is the (reducible) permutation representation of S_n on unordered pairs $\{i,j\}$, then for each choice of $\{i,j\}$ and $\{k,l\}$ the individual Fourier transforms count the number of respondents ranking restaurants i and j in positions k and l. See [8] for a more thorough explanation.

The first FFT for symmetric groups (an $O(|G|\log^3|G|)$ algorithm) was due to M. Clausen. In what follows we summarize recent improvements on Clausen's result.

Example: Computing the Fourier transform on S_4. The fast Fourier transform for S_4 is obtained by mimicking the group-theoretic approach to the Cooley–Tukey algorithm. More precisely, we shall rewrite the formula for the Fourier transform using two changes of variables: one using factorizations of group elements, and the other using paths in a Bratteli diagram. The former comes from the reduced word decomposition of $g \in S_4$, by which g may be uniquely expressed as

$$g = s_2^4 \cdot s_3^4 \cdot s_4^4 \cdot s_2^3 \cdot s_3^3 \cdot s_2^2, \qquad (3\text{--}1)$$

where s_i^j is either e or the transposition $(i\ i-1)$, and $s_{i_1}^j = e$ implies that $s_{i_2}^j = e$ for $i_2 \leq i_1$. Thus any function on the group S_4 may be thought of as a function of the 6 variables $s_2^4, s_3^4, s_4^4, s_2^3, s_3^3, s_2^2$.

To index the matrix elements of S_4 paths in a Bratteli diagram are used, this time relative to the chain of subgroups $S_4 \geq S_3 \geq S_2 \geq S_1 \geq 1$. The irreducible representations of S_n are in one-to-one correspondence with partitions of the integer n, with restriction of representations corresponding to deleting a box in the Young diagram. The corresponding Bratteli diagram is called Young's lattice, and is shown in Figure 2. Paths in Young's lattice from the empty partition ϕ

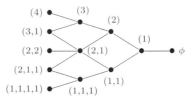

Figure 2. Young's lattice up to level 4.

to β_4, a partition of 4, index the basis vectors of the irreducible representation corresponding to β_4. Matrix elements, however, are determined by specifying a pair of basis vectors, so to index the matrix elements, we must use pairs of paths in Young's lattice, starting at ϕ and ending in the same partition of 4. Since there are no multiple edges in Young's lattice, each path may be described by the sequence of partitions $\phi, \beta_1, \beta_2, \beta_3, \beta_4$, through which it passes.

Before we can state a formula for the Fourier transform, analogous to (2–2) and (2–6), we must choose bases for the irreducible representations of S_4 in order to define our matrix elements. Efficient algorithms are known only for special choices of bases, and our algorithm uses the representations in Young's orthogonal form, which is equivalent to the following equation (3–2) for the Fourier transform in the new sets of variables.

$$
\begin{aligned}
\hat{f} &\begin{pmatrix} \beta_4\ \beta_3\ \beta_2\ \beta_1 \\ \gamma_3\ \gamma_2\ \gamma_1 \end{pmatrix} \\
&= \sum_{g=s_2^4 s_3^4 s_4^4 s_2^3 s_3^3 s_2^2\ \varphi_2, \varphi_1, \eta_1} \sum \left(P_{s_4^4}^4 \begin{pmatrix} \beta_4\ \beta_3 \\ \gamma_3\ \varphi_2 \end{pmatrix} P_{s_3^4}^3 \begin{pmatrix} \beta_3\ \beta_2 \\ \varphi_2\ \varphi_1 \end{pmatrix} P_{s_2^4}^2 \begin{pmatrix} \beta_2\ \beta_1 \\ \varphi_1 \end{pmatrix} \right. \\
&\qquad\qquad \left. \times P_{s_3^3}^3 \begin{pmatrix} \gamma_3\ \varphi_2 \\ \gamma_2\ \eta_1 \end{pmatrix} P_{s_2^3}^2 \begin{pmatrix} \varphi_2\ \varphi_1 \\ \eta_1 \end{pmatrix} P_{s_2^2}^2 \begin{pmatrix} \gamma_2\ \eta_1 \\ \gamma_1 \end{pmatrix} f(g) \right). \quad (3\text{–}2)
\end{aligned}
$$

The functions $P_{s_i^j}^i$ in equation (3–2) are defined below, and for each i, the variables $\beta_i, \gamma_i, \varphi_i, \eta_i$ are partitions of i, satisfying the restriction relations described by Figure 3. A solid line between partitions means that the right partition is obtained from the left partition by removing a box.

The relationship between (3–2) and Figure 3 is extremely close—we derived the diagram from the reduced word decomposition first, and then read the equation off the diagram. Each 2-cell in Figure 3 corresponds to a factor in the product of P functions in (3–2), and the labels on the boundary of each cell give the arguments of $P_{s_i^j}^i$. The sum in (3–2) is over those variables occurring in the interior of Figure 3. Thus, the variables describing the Fourier transformed function are exactly those appearing on the boundary of the figure.

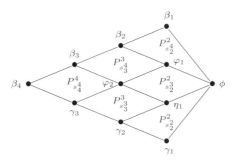

Figure 3. Restriction relations for (3–2).

Equation (3–2) can be summarized by saying that we take the product over 2-cells, and sum on interior indices, in Figure 3. This suggests a generalization of the Cooley–Tukey algorithm, that corresponds to building up the diagram one cell at a time. At each stage multiply by the factor corresponding to a 2-cell, and form the diagram consisting of those 2-cells that have been considered so far. Then sum over any indices that are in the interior of the diagram for this stage, but were not in the interior for previous stages. At the end of this algorithm we have multiplied by the factors for each 2-cell, and summed over all the interior indices, and have therefore computed the Fourier transform.

The order in which the cells are added matters, of course. The order s_2^2, s_2^3, s_3^3, s_2^4, s_3^4, s_4^4 is known to be most efficient. Here is the algorithm in detail.

- Stage 0: Start with $f(s_2^4 s_3^4 s_4^4 s_2^3 s_3^3 s_2^2)$, for all reduced words.
- Stage 1: Multiply by $P_{s_2^2}^2$. Sum on s_2^2.
- Stage 2: Multiply by $P_{s_2^3}^2$. Sum on s_2^3.
- Stage 3: Multiply by $P_{s_3^3}^3$. Sum on η_1, s_3^3.
- Stage 4: Multiply by $P_{s_2^4}^2$. Sum on s_2^4.
- Stage 5: Multiply by $P_{s_3^4}^2$. Sum on φ_1, s_3^4.
- Stage 6: Multiply by $P_{s_4^4}^3$. Sum on φ_2, s_4^4.

The indices occurring in each stage of the algorithm are shown in Figure 4.

To count the number of additions and multiplications used by the algorithm, we must count the number of configurations in Young's lattice corresponding to each of the diagrams in Figure 4. This yields a grand total of 130 additions and 130 multiplications for the Fourier transform on S_4.

The generalization to higher order symmetric groups is straightforward. The reduced word decomposition gives the group element factorization and Young's orthogonal form allows us to change variables, and the formula and algorithm for the Fourier transform can be read off a diagram generalizing Figure 3. The diagram for S_5 is shown, for example, in Figure 5.

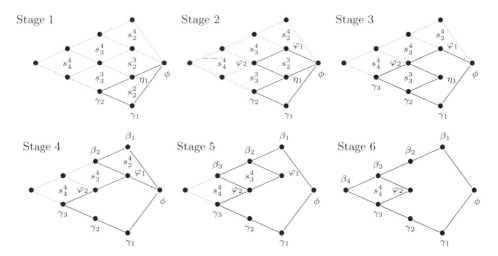

Figure 4. Variables occurring at each stage of the fast Fourier transform for S_4

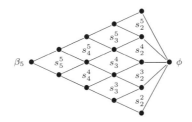

Figure 5. Restriction relations in the Fourier transform formula for S_5.

We have computed the exact operation counts for symmetric groups S_n with $n \leq 50$, and a general formula seems hard to come by. (Presumably $n \leq 50$ would cover all cases where the algorithm might ever be implemented, but the same numbers arise in FFTs on homogeneous spaces, which have far fewer elements.)

However, bounds are easier to obtain:

THEOREM 3.1 ([13]). *The number of additions (or multiplications) required by the above algorithm (as generalized to $S_n > S_{n-1} > \cdots > S_1$) is exactly*

$$n! \cdot \sum_{k=2}^{n} \frac{1}{k} \sum_{i=2}^{k} \frac{1}{(i-1)!} F_i$$

where F_i is the number of configurations in Young's lattice of the form

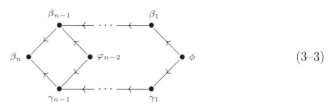

(3–3)

Furthermore, $F_i \leq 3(1 - \frac{1}{i})i!$, so the number of additions (multiplications) is bounded by $\frac{3}{4}n(n-1) \cdot n!$.

Why stop at S_n? The algorithm for the FFT on S_n generalizes to any wreath product $S_n[G]$ with the symmetric group. The subgroup chain is replaced by the chain

$$S_n[G] > S_{n-1}[G] \times G > S_{n-1}[G] > \cdots > S_2[G] > G \times G > G, \qquad (3\text{–}4)$$

and the reduced word decomposition is replaced by the factorization

$$x = s_2^n \cdots s_n^n g^n s_2^{n-1} \cdots s_{n-1}^{n-1} g^{n-1} \cdots s_s^2 g^2 g^1. \qquad (3\text{–}5)$$

Adapting the S_n argument along these lines gives the following new result.

THEOREM 3.2. *The number of operations needed to compute a Fourier transform on $S_n[G]$ is at most*

$$\left(\frac{3n(n-1)}{4}|G|d_G^2 + n\left(t_G + \frac{1}{4}|G|(h_G d_G^2 - |G|)\right) \right) |S_n[G]|$$

where h_G is the number of conjugacy classes in G, d_G is the maximal degree of an irreducible representation of G, and t_G is the number of operations required to compute a Fourier transform on G. If G is abelian, then the inner term $h_G d_G^2 - |G| = 0$.

The functions $P_{s_i^j}^i$ defining Young's orthogonal form are defined as follows: For any two boxes b_1 and b_2 in a Young diagram, we define the axial distance from b_1 to b_2 to be $d(b_1, b_2)$, where $d(b_1, b_2) = \text{row}(b_1) - \text{row}(b_2) + \text{column}(b_1) - \text{column}(b_2)$. Now suppose $\beta_i, \beta_{i-1}, \alpha_{i-1}, \alpha_{i-2}$ are partitions and that $\alpha_{i-1}, \beta_{i-1}$ are obtained from β_i by removing a box, and are obtained from α_{i-2} by adding a box. Then the skew diagrams of $\beta_i - \beta_{i-1}$ and $\beta_{i-1} - \alpha_{i-2}$ each consist of a single box, and P^i is given by

$$P_e^i \begin{pmatrix} \beta_i & \beta_{i-1} \\ \alpha_{i-1} & \alpha_{i-2} \end{pmatrix} = \begin{cases} 1 & \text{if } \alpha_{i-1} = \beta_{i-1}, \\ 0 & \text{if } \alpha_{i-1} \neq \beta_{i-1}. \end{cases}$$

$$P_{(i\ i-1)}^i \begin{pmatrix} \beta_i & \beta_{i-1} \\ \alpha_{i-1} & \alpha_{i-2} \end{pmatrix} = \begin{cases} d(\beta_i - \beta_{i-1}, \beta_{i-1} - \alpha_{i-2})^{-1} & \text{if } \alpha_{i-1} = \beta_{i-1}, \\ \sqrt{1 - d(\beta_i - \beta_{i-1}, \beta_{i-1} - \alpha_{i-2})^{-2}} & \text{if } \alpha_{i-1} \neq \beta_{i-1}. \end{cases}$$
$$(3\text{–}6)$$

For a proof of this formula, in slightly different notation, see [11], Chapter 3.

4. Generalization to Other Groups

The FFT described for symmetric groups suggests a general approach to computing Fourier transforms on finite groups. Here is the recipe.

(i) Choose a chain of subgroups

$$G = G_m \geq G_{m-1} \geq \cdots \geq G_1 \geq G_0 = 1 \qquad (4\text{–}1)$$

for the group. This determines the Bratteli diagram that we will use to index the matrix elements of G. In the general case, this Bratteli diagram may have multiple edges, so a path is no longer determined by the nodes it visits.

(ii) Choose a factorization $g = g_n \cdot g_{n-1} \cdots g_1$ of each group element g. Choose the g_i so that they lie in as small a subgroup G_k as possible, and commute with as large a subgroup G_l as possible.

(iii) Choose a system of Gel'fand–Tsetlin bases [9] for the irreducible representations of G relative to the chain (4–1). These are bases that are indexed by paths in the Bratteli diagram, that behave well under restriction of representations. Relative to such a basis, the representation matrices of g_i will be block diagonal whenever g_i lies in a subgroup from the chain, and block scalar whenever g_i commutes with all elements of a subgroup from the chain.

(iv) Now write the Fourier transform in coordinates, as a function of the pairs of paths in the Bratteli diagram with a common endpoint, and with the original function written as a function of $g_1, \ldots, g_n$. This will be a sum of products indexed by edges in the Bratteli diagram which lie in some configuration generalizing (3). This configuration of edges specifies the way in which the nonzero elements of the representation matrices appear in the formula for the Fourier transform in coordinates.

(v) The algorithm proceeds by building up the product piece by piece, and summing on as many partially indexed variables as possible.

Further considerations and generalizations. The efficiency of the above approach, both in theory, in terms of algorithmic complexity, and practice, in terms of execution time, depends on both the choice of factorization and the Gel'fand–Tsetlin bases. In particular, very interesting work of L. Auslander, R. Johnson and J. Johnson [2] shows how in the abelian case, different factorizations correspond to different well-known FFTs, each well suited for execution on a different computer architecture. This work shows how to relate the 2-cocycle of a group extension to construction of the important "twiddle factor" matrix in the factorization of the Fourier matrix. It marks the first appearances of group cohomology in signal processing and derives an interesting connection between group theory and the design of retargetable software.

The analogous questions for nonabelian groups and other important signal processing transform algorithms, that is, the problem of finding architecture-optimized factorizations, is currently being investigated by the SPIRAL project at Carnegie Mellon [19].

Another abelian idea: the "chirp-z" FFT. The use of subgroups depends upon the existence of a nontrivial subgroup. Thus, for a reduction in the case of a cyclic group of prime order, a new idea is necessary. In this case, C. Rader's "chirp-z transform" (the "chirp" here refers to radar chirp—the generation of an extremely short electromagnetic pulse, i.e., something approaching the ideal delta function) may be used [16].

The chirp-z transform proceeds by turning computation of the DFT into computation of convolution on a different, albeit related, group. Let p be a prime. Since $\mathbb{Z}/p\mathbb{Z}$ is also a finite field, there exists a generator g of $\mathbb{Z}/p\mathbb{Z}^\times$, a cyclic group (under multiplication) of order $p-1$. Thus, for any $f : \mathbb{Z}/p\mathbb{Z} \to \mathbb{C}$ and nonzero frequency index g^{-b}, we can write $\widehat{f}(g^{-b})$ as

$$\hat{f}(g^{-b}) = f(0) + \sum_{a=0}^{p-2} f(g^a)e^{2\pi i g^{a-b}/p}. \qquad (4\text{–}2)$$

The summation in (4–2) has the form of a convolution on $\mathbb{Z}/(p-1)\mathbb{Z}$, of the sequence $f'(a) = f(g^a)$, with the function $z(a) = exp^{2\pi i g^a/p}$, so that $\widehat{f}$ may be almost entirely computed using Fourier transforms of length $p-1$ for which Cooley–Tukey-like ideas may be used. It is an interesting open question to discover if the chirp-z transform has a nonabelian generalization.

Modular FFTs. A significant application of the abelian FFT is in the efficient computation of Fourier transforms for functions on cyclic groups defined over finite fields. These are necessary for the efficient encoding and decoding of various polynomial error correcting codes. Many abelian codes, e.g., the Golay codes used in deep-space communication, are defined as $\mathbf{F}_p$-valued functions on a group $\mathbb{Z}/m\mathbb{Z}$ with the property that $\widehat{f}(k) = 0$ for $k \in S$ some specified set of indices S, where now the Fourier transform is defined in terms of a primitive $(p-1)^{st}$ root of unity.

These sorts of *spectral constraints* define *cyclic codes*, and they may immediately be generalized to any finite group. Recently, this has been done in the construction of codes over $SL_2(\mathbf{F}_p)$, using connections between expander graphs and linear codes discovered by M. Sipser and D. Spielman. For further discussion of this and other applications see [17].

5. FFTs for Compact Groups

The DFT and FFT also have a natural extension to continuous compact groups. The terminology "discrete Fourier transform" derives from the algorithm having been originally designed to compute the (possibly approximate) Fourier transform of a continuous signal from a discrete collection of sample values.

Under the simplifying assumption of periodicity a continuous function may be interpreted as a function on the unit circle, and compact abelian group, S^1. Any such function f has a *Fourier expansion* defined as

$$f(e^{2\pi it}) = \sum_{l \in \mathbf{Z}} \widehat{f}(l)e^{-2\pi ilt} \qquad (5\text{–}1)$$

where

$$\widehat{f}(l) = \int_0^1 f(e^{2\pi it})e^{2\pi ilt}dt. \qquad (5\text{–}2)$$

If $\hat{f}(l) = 0$ for $|l| \geq N$, then f is *band-limited* with *band-limit* N and the DFT (1–1) is in fact a a *quadrature rule* or *sampling theorem* for f. In other words, the DFT of the function

$$\frac{1}{2N-1} f(e^{2\pi it})$$

on the group of $(2N-1)$-st roots of unity computes exactly the Fourier coefficients of the band-limited function. The FFT then efficiently computes these Fourier coefficients.

The first nonabelian FFT for a compact group was a fast spherical harmonic expansion algorithm discovered by J. Driscoll and D. Healy. Several ingredients were required: (1) A notion of "band-limit" for functions on S^2; (2) A sampling theory for such functions; and (3) A fast algorithm for the computation.

The spherical harmonics are naturally indexed according to their order (the common degree of a set of homogeneous polynomials on S^2). With respect to the usual coordinates of latitude and longitude, the spherical harmonics separate as a product of exponentials and associated Legendre functions, each of which separately has a sampling theory. Finally, by using the usual FFT for the exponential part, and a new fast algorithm (based on three-term recurrences) for the Legendre part, an FFT for S^2 is formed.

These ideas generalize nicely. Keep in mind that the representation theory of compact groups is much like that of finite groups: there is a countable complete set of irreducible representations and any square-integrable function (with respect to Haar measure) has an expansion in terms of the corresponding matrix elements. There is a natural definition of band-limited in the compact case, encompassing those functions whose Fourier expansion has only a finite number of terms. The simplest version of the theory is as follows:

DEFINITION 5.1. Let $\mathcal{R}$ denote a complete set of irreducible representations of a compact group G. A *system of band-limits on G* is a decomposition of $\mathcal{R} = \bigcup_{b \geq 0} \mathcal{R}_b$ such that

(i) $\mathcal{R}_b$ is finite for all $b \geq 0$;
(ii) $b_1 \leq b_2$ implies that $\mathcal{R}_{b_1} \subseteq \mathcal{R}_{b_2}$;
(iii) $\mathcal{R}_{b_1} \otimes \mathcal{R}_{b_2} \subseteq \text{span}_{\mathbf{Z}} \mathcal{R}_{b_1 + b_2}$.

Let $\{\mathcal{R}_b\}_{b \geq 0}$ be a system of band-limits on G and $f \in L^2(G)$. Then, f *is band-limited with band-limit b* if the Fourier coefficients are zero for all matrix elements in ρ for all $\rho \notin \mathcal{R}_b$.

The case of $G = S^1$ provides the classical example. If $\mathcal{R}_b = \{\chi_j : |j| \leq b\}$ where $\chi_j(z) = z^j$, then $\chi_j \otimes \chi_k = \chi_{j+k}$ and the corresponding notion of band-limited (as per Definition 1) coincides with the usual notion.

For a nonabelian example, consider $G = \text{SO}(3)$. In this case the irreducible representations of G are indexed by the nonnegative integers with V_λ the unique irreducible of dimension $2\lambda + 1$. Let $\mathcal{R}_b = \{V_\lambda : \lambda \leq b\}$. The Clebsch-Gordan relations

$$V_{\lambda_1} \otimes V_{\lambda_2} = \sum_{j=|\lambda_1-\lambda_2|}^{\lambda_1+\lambda_2} V_j \qquad (5\text{--}3)$$

imply that this is a system of band-limits for $SO(3)$. When restricted to the quotient $S^2 \cong SO(3)/SO(2)$, band-limits are described in terms of the highest order spherical harmonics that appear in a given expansion.

This notion of band-limit permits the construction of a sampling theory [14]. For example, in the case of the classical groups, a system of band-limits $\mathcal{R}_b^n$ is chosen with respect to a particular norm on the dual of the associated Cartan subalgebra. Such a norm $\|\cdot\|$ (assuming that it is invariant under taking duals, and $\|\alpha\| \leq \|\beta\| + \|\gamma\|$, for α occurring in $\beta \otimes \gamma$) defines a notion of band-limit given by all α with norm less than a fixed b. This generalizes the definition above. The associated sampling sets X_b^n are contained in certain one-parameter subgroups. These sampling sets permit a separation of variables analogous to that used in the Driscoll–Healy FFT. Once again, the special functions satisfy certain three-term recurrences which admit a similar efficient divide-and-conquer computational approach (see [15] and references therein.) one may derive efficient algorithms for all the classical groups, $U(n), SU(n), Sp(n)$.

THEOREM 5.2. *Assume* $n \geq 2$.

(i) *For* $U(n)$, $T_{X_b^n}(\mathcal{R}_b^n) \leq O(b^{\dim U(n)+3n-3})$.
(ii) *For* $SU(n)$, $T_{X_b^n}(\mathcal{R}_b^n) \leq O(b^{\dim SU(n)+3n-2})$.
(iii) *For* $Sp(n)$, $T_{X_b^n}(\mathcal{R}_b^n) \leq O(b^{\dim Sp(n)+6n-6})$.

Here $T_{X_b^n}(\mathcal{R}_b^n)$ *denotes the number of operations needed for the particular sample set* X_b^n *and representations* $\mathcal{R}_b^n$ *for the associated group.*

6. Further and Related Work

Noncompact groups. Much of modern signal processing relies on the understanding and implementation of Fourier analysis for $L^2(\mathbf{R})$, i.e., the noncompact abelian group $\mathbf{R}$. Nonabelian, noncompact examples have begun to attract much attention.

In this area some of the most exciting work is being done by G. Chirikjian and his collaborators. They have been exploring applications of convolution on the group of rigid motions of Euclidean space to such diverse areas as robotics, polymer modeling and pattern matching. See [5] for details and pointers to the literature.

To date, the techniques used here are approximate in nature and interesting open problems abound. Possibilities include the formulation of natural sampling, band-limiting and time-frequency theories. The exploration of other special cases such as semisimple Lie groups (see [1], for a beautifully written succinct survey

of the Harish-Chandra theory) would be one natural place to start. A sampling
and band-limiting theory would be the first step towards developing a a computational theory, i.e., FFT. "Fast Fourier transforms on semisimple Lie groups"
has a nice ring to it!

Approximate techniques. The techniques in this paper are all exact, in the
sense that if computed in exact arithmetic, they yield exactly correct answers.
Of course, in any actual implementation, errors are introduced and the utility of
an algorithm will depend highly on its numerical stability.

There are also "approximate methods", approximate in the sense that they
guarantee a certain specified approximation to the exact answer that depends
on the running time of the algorithm. For computing Fourier transforms at
nonequispaced frequencies, as well as spherical harmonic expansions, the fast
multipole method due to V. Rokhlin and L. Greengard is a recent and very important approximate technique. Multipole-based approaches efficiently compute
these quantities approximately, in such a way that the running time increases
by a factor of $\log(1/\varepsilon)$, where ε denotes the precision of the approximation. M.
Mohlenkamp has applied quasi-classical frequency estimates to the approximate
computation of various special function transforms.

Quantum computing. Another related and active area of research involves
connections with quantum computing. One of the first great triumphs of the
quantum computing model is P. Shor's fast algorithm for integer factorization on
a quantum computer [18]. At the heart of Shor's algorithm is a subroutine which
computes (on a quantum computer) the DFT of a binary vector representing an
integer. The implementation of this transform as a sequence of one- and two-
bit quantum gates, is the *quantum FFT*, is effectively the Cooley–Tukey FFT
realized as a particular factorization of the Fourier matrix into a product of
matrices composed as tensor products of certain two by two unitary matrices,
each of which is a "local unitary transform". Extensions of these ideas to the
more general group transforms mentioned above are a current important area of
research of great interest in computer science.

So, these are some of the things that go into the computation of the finite
Fourier transform. It is a tapestry of mathematics both pure and applied, woven
from algebra and analysis, complexity theory and scientific computing. It is on
the one hand a focused problem, but like any good problem, its "solution" does
not end a story, but rather initiates an exploration of unexpected connections
and new challenges.

References

[1] J. Arthur, "Harmonic analysis and group representations", *Notices Amer. Math. Soc.* **47**:1 (2000), 26–34.

[2] L. Auslander, J. R. Johnson, R. W. Johnson, "Multidimensional Cooley–Tukey algorithms revisited", *Adv. Appl. Math.* **17**:4 (1996), 477–519.

[3] L. Auslander and R. Tolimieri, "Is computing with the finite Fourier transform pure or applied mathematics?", *Bull. Amer. Math. Soc.* (N.S.) **1**:6 (1979), 847–897.

[4] T. Beth, *Verfahren der schnellen Fourier–Transformation*, Teubner, Stuttgart, 1984.

[5] G. S. Chirikjian and A. B. Kyatkin, *Engineering applications of noncommutative harmonic analysis*, CRC Press, Boca Raton (FL), 2000.

[6] J. W. Cooley, The re-discovery of the fast Fourier transform algorithm, *Mikrochimica Acta* **III** (1987), 33–45.

[7] J. W. Cooley and J. W. Tukey, "An algorithm for machine calculation of complex Fourier series", *Math. Comp.* **19** (1965), 297–301.

[8] P. Diaconis, *Group representations in probability and statistics*, IMS, Hayward (CA), 1988.

[9] I. Gel'fand and M. Tsetlin, "Finite dimensional representations of the group of unimodular matrices", *Dokl. Akad. Nauk SSSR* **71** (1950), 825–828 (in Russian).

[10] M. T. Heideman, D. H. Johnson and C. S. Burrus, "Gauss and the history of the fast Fourier transform", *Archive for History of Exact Sciences* **34**:3 (1985), 265–277.

[11] G. James and A. Kerber, *The representation theory of the symmetric group*, Encyclopedia of Mathematics and its Applications **16**, Addison-Wesley, Reading (MA), 1981.

[12] T. Y. Lam, "Representations of finite groups: a hundred years", parts I and II, *Notices Amer. Math. Soc.* **45**:3 (1998), 361–372 and **45**:4 (1998), 465–474.

[13] D. K. Maslen, "The efficient computation of Fourier transforms on the symmetric group", *Math. Comp.* **67**(223) (1998), 1121–1147.

[14] D. K. Maslen, "Efficient computation of Fourier transforms on compact groups", *J. Fourier Anal. Appl.* **4**:1 (1998), 19–52.

[15] D. K. Maslen and D. N. Rockmore, "Generalized FFTs: a survey of some recent results", pp. 183–237 in *Groups and computation*, II (New Brunswick, NJ, 1995), DIMACS Ser. Discrete Math. Theoret. Comput. Sci. **28**, Amer. Math. Soc., Providence (RI), 1997.

[16] C. Rader, "Discrete Fourier transforms when the number of data samples is prime", *IEEE Proc.* **56** (1968), 1107–1108.

[17] D. N. Rockmore, "Some applications of generalized FFTs" (an appendix with D. Healy), pp. 329–369 in *Proceedings of the DIMACS Workshop on Groups and Computation* (June 7–10, 1995), edited by L. Finkelstein and W. Kantor, 1997.

[18] P. W. Shor, "Polynomial-time algorithms for prime factorization and discrete logarithms on a quantum computer", *SIAM J. Computing* **26** (1997), 1484–1509.

[19] "SPIRAL: automatic generation of platform-adapted code for DSP algorithms", http://www.ece.cmu.edu/~spiral/.

[20] A. Willsky, "On the algebraic structure of certain partially observable finite-state Markov processes", *Inform. Contr.* **38** (1978), 179–212.

DAVID K. MASLEN
SUSQUEHANNA INTERNATIONAL GROUP LLP
401 CITY AVENUE, SUITE 220
BALA CYNWYD, PA 19004
    david@maslen.net

DANIEL N. ROCKMORE
DEPARTMENT OF MATHEMATICS
DARTMOUTH COLLEGE
HANOVER, NH 03755
    rockmore@cs.dartmouth.edu

Modern Signal Processing
MSRI Publications
Volume **46**, 2003

Signal Processing in Optical Fibers

ULF ÖSTERBERG

ABSTRACT. This paper addresses some of the fundamental problems which
have to be solved in order for optical networks to utilize the full bandwidth
of optical fibers. It discusses some of the premises for signal processing in
optical fibers. It gives a short historical comparison between the development of transmission techniques for radio and microwaves to that of optical
fibers. There is also a discussion of bandwidth with a particular emphasis on what physical interactions limit the speed in optical fibers. Finally,
there is a section on line codes and some recent developments in optical
encoding of wavelets.

1. Introduction

When Claude Shannon developed the mathematical theory of communication
[1] he knew nothing about lasers and optical fibers. What he was mostly concerned with were communication channels using radio- and microwaves. Inherently, these channels have a narrower bandwidth than do optical fibers because
of the lower carrier frequency (longer wavelength). More serious than this theoretical limitation are the practical bandwidth limitations imposed by weather
and other environmental hazards. In contrast, optical fibers are a marvellously
stable and predictable medium for transporting information and the influence
of noise from the fiber itself can to a large degree be neglected. So, until recently there was no real need for any advanced signal processing in optical fiber
communications systems. This has all changed over the last few years with the
development of the internet.

Optical fiber communication became an economic reality in the early 1970s
when absorption of less than 20 dB/km was achieved in optical fibers and life-
times of more than 1 million hours for semiconductor lasers were accomplished.
Both of these breakthroughs in material science were related to minimizing the
number of defects in the materials used. For optical fiber glass, it is absolutely
necessary to have fewer than 1 parts per billion (ppb) of any defect or transition
metal in the glass in order to obtain necessary performance.

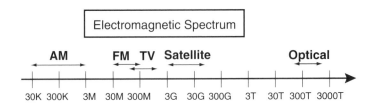

Figure 1. Electromagnetic spectrum of importance for communication. Frequencies are given in Hertz.

For the last thirty years, optical fibers have in many ways been a system engineer's dream. They have had, literally, an infinite bandwidth and as mentioned above, a stable and reproducible noise floor. So no wonder it's been sufficient to use intensity pulse-code modulation, also known as *on-off keying* (OOK), for transmitting information in optical fibers.

The bit-rate distance product for optical fibers has grown exponentially over the last 30 years. (Using bandwidth times length as a measurement makes sense, since any medium can transport a huge bandwidth if the distance is short enough.) For this growth to occur, several fundamental and technical problems had to be overcome. In this paper we will limit ourselves to three fundamental processes; absorption, dispersion and nonlinear optical interactions. Historically, absorption and dispersion were the first physical limitations that had to be addressed. As the bit-rate increase shows, great progress has been made in reducing the effects of absorption and dispersion on the effective bandwidth. As a consequence, nonlinear effects have emerged as a significant obstacle for using the full bandwidth potential of optical fibers.

These three processes are undoubtedly the most researched physical processes in optical glass fibers, which is one reason for discussing them. Another reason, of great importance to mathematicians, is that recent developments in time/frequency and wavelet analysis have introduced novel line coding schemes which seem to be able to drastically reduce the impact from many of the deleterious physical processes occurring in optical fiber communications.

2. Signal Processing in Optical Fibers

The spectrum of electromagnetic waves of interest for different kinds of communication is shown in Figure 1.

A typical communications system for using these waves to convey information is shown in Figure 2. This system assumes digitized information but is otherwise completely transparent to any type of physical medium used for the channel.

Any electromagnetic wave is *completely* characterized by its *amplitude* and *phase*:

$$\boldsymbol{E}(\boldsymbol{r},t) = \boldsymbol{A}(\boldsymbol{r},t)\exp\big(\phi(\boldsymbol{r},t)\big)$$

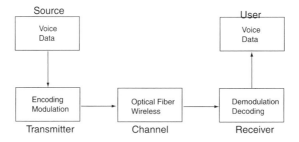

Figure 2. Typical block diagram of a digital communications system.

where $\boldsymbol{A}$ is the amplitude and $\phi(\boldsymbol{r}, t)$ is the phase. So, amplitude and phase are the two physical properties that we can vary in order to send information in the form of a wave. The variations can be in either analog or digital form. Note that even today, in our digitally swamped society, analog transmission is still used in some cases. One example is cable-TV (CATV), where the large S/N ratio (because of the short distances involved) provides a faithful transmission of the analog signal. The advantage in using analog transmission is that it takes up less bandwidth than a digital transmission with the same information content.

The first optical fiber systems in the 1970s used *time-division multiplexing*(TDM), each individual channel was multiplexed onto a trunk line using protocols called T1-T5, where T1-T5 refers to particular bit rates; see Figure 3.

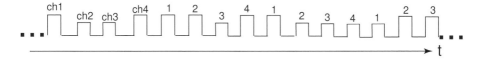

Figure 3. Time-division multiplexing.

Each individual channel was in turn encoded with the users' digital information.

TDM is still the most common scheme used for sending information down an optical fiber. Today, we are using a multiplexing protocol called *SONET* which uses the acronyms OC48, OC96, etc., where OC48 corresponds to a bit rate of 565 Mbits/sec and each doubling of the OC-number corresponds to a doubling of the bit rate. The increase in speed has been made possible by the dramatic improvement of electronic circuits and the shift from multi-mode fibers to dispersion-compensated single-mode fibers. Several large national labs are testing, in the laboratory, time-multiplexed systems up to 100 Gbits/sec, commercially most systems are still $\lesssim 2.5$ Gbits/sec.

As industry is preparing for an ever growing demand of bandwidth it is clear that electronics cannot keep up with the optical bandwidth, which is estimated to be 30 Tbits/sec for optical fibers. Because of this *wavelength-division multiplexing*(WDM) has attracted a lot of attention. In a TDM system each bit is an optical pulse, for WDM system each bit can either be a pulse or a continuous wave (CW). WDM systems rely on the fact that light of different wavelengths do not interfere with each other (in the linear regime); see Figure 4.

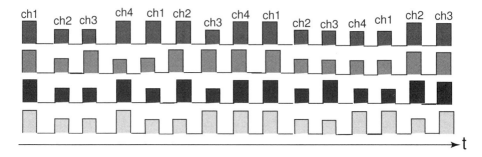

Figure 4. Wavelength-division multiplexing.

Signal processing in optical fibers has, historically, been separated into two distinct areas: pulse propagation and signal processing. To introduce these areas we will keep with tradition and describe them separately, however, please bear in mind that *the area in which mathematicians may play the most important role in future signal processing is to understand the physical limitations imposed by basic processes that are part of the pulse propagation and invent new signal processing schemes which oppose these deleterious effects.*

A pulse propagating in an optical fiber can be expressed by

$$\boldsymbol{E}(x,y,z,t) = \hat{\boldsymbol{x}}E_x(x,y,z,t) + \hat{\boldsymbol{y}}E_y(x,y,z,t) + \hat{\boldsymbol{z}}E_z(x,y,z,t),$$

where z is the direction of propagation and x, y are in the transversal plane; see Figure 5. The geometry shown in Figure 5 is for a single-mode fiber.

In such a fiber, the light has been confined to such a small region that only one type of spatial beam (mode) can propagate over a long distance. Even though this mode's spatial dependence is described by a Bessel function it is for most purposes sufficient to spatially model it as a *plane wave*. Therefore, the signal

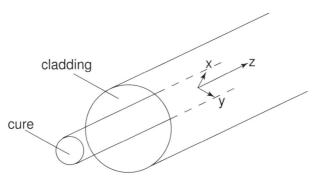

Figure 5. Optical fiber geometry.

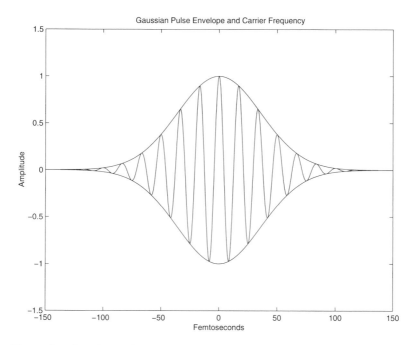

Figure 6. Gaussian pulse with the carrier frequency illustrated. The optical equivalent pulse has a 10^{15} times higher carrier frequency than shown here.

pulse representing a *bit* can mathematically be written as

$$\boldsymbol{E}(z,t) = \hat{\boldsymbol{x}} E_x(z,t),$$

where the subscript x is often ignored, tacitly assuming that we only have to deal with one (arbitrary) scalar component of the full vectorial electromagnetic field.

In a glass optical fiber the signal has to obey the following wave equation

$$\nabla^2 E(z,t) = \frac{1}{c^2} \frac{\partial^2 E(z,t)}{\partial t^2},$$

where c is the speed of light.

A solution to this equation can be written as

$$E(z,t) = p(z,t) e^{i(kz-\omega_0 t)},$$

where $p(z,t)$ is the temporal shape of the pulse (bit) representing a 1 or a 0. For a Gaussian pulse at $z = 0$,

$$p(0,t) = A e^{-t^2/(2T^2)},$$

and the electromagnetic field at $z = 0$

$$E(0,t) = A e^{-t^2/(2T^2)} e^{-i\omega_0 t}, \tag{2-1}$$

where ω_0 is the carrier frequency. This pulse is depicted in Figure 6.

To describe how this pulse changes as it propagates along the fiber we start by taking the Fourier transform (FT) of the field in equation (2–1):

$$\tilde{E}(0,\omega) = \frac{1}{\sqrt{2\pi}} \int_{-\infty}^{\infty} E(0,t)e^{i\omega t}\, \mathrm{dt}. \tag{2-2}$$

The reason for moving to the frequency domain is because in this domain the actual propagation step consists of "simply" *multiplying* the field with the phase factor e^{ikz}, where k is the *wavenumber*. To find out the temporal pulse shape after a distance z we then transform back to the time domain; that is,

$$E(z,t) = \frac{1}{\sqrt{2\pi}} \int_{-\infty}^{\infty} \tilde{E}(0,\omega)e^{-i\omega t+ikz}\, \mathrm{d}\omega.$$

So the principle is quite easy; nevertheless in reality it becomes more complicated because the phase factor, e^{ikz}, is different for different frequencies ω since $k = k(\omega)$. The wavenumber k is related to the refractive index via

$$k(\omega) = \frac{\omega n(\omega)}{c}.$$

The refractive index can be described for most materials, at optical frequencies, using the Lorentz formula

$$n(\omega) = \sqrt{n_0^2 + \sum_j \frac{b_j^2}{\omega^2 - \omega_{0j}^2 + i2\delta_j\omega}}, \tag{2-3}$$

where the different j's refer to different resonances in the media, b is the strength of the resonance and δ is the damping term ($\approx$ the width of the resonance).

For picosecond pulses (10^{-12} sec) or longer the pulse spectrum is concentrated around the carrier frequency ω_0 and we may therefore Taylor expand $k(\omega)$ around $k(\omega_0)$:

$$k(\omega) = \sum_{n=0}^{\infty} \frac{1}{n!}k_n(\omega_0)(\omega - \omega_0)^n,$$

where $k_n(\omega_0) = \frac{\partial^n k}{\partial \omega^n}|_{\omega=\omega_0}$.

Typically, it is sufficient to carry this expansion to the ω^2-term. Using this expansion we can now rewrite (2–2) as

$$E(z,t) = \frac{e^{i(k_0 z-\omega_0 t)}}{\sqrt{2\pi}} \int_{-\infty}^{\infty} \tilde{E}(0,\omega)e^{i[k(\omega_0)+k_1(\omega_0)(\omega-\omega_0)+k_2(\omega_0)(\omega-\omega_0)^2]}e^{-i\omega t}\, \mathrm{d}\omega,$$

which can be further rewritten as

$$E(z,t) = p(z,t)e^{i(k(\omega_0)z-\omega_0 t)},$$

where, for a gaussian input pulse, $p(z,t)$ is

$$p(z,t) = \frac{A}{\left(1 + k_2(\omega_0)z^2/T^4\right)^{1/4}} \exp\left(-\frac{\left(k_1(\omega_0)z - t\right)^2}{2T^2\left(1 + k_2(\omega_0)z^2/T^4\right)}\right).$$

Hence, the envelope remains Gaussian as the pulse is propagating along the optical fiber, however its width is increased and the amplitude is reduced (conservation of energy). From this type of analysis one may determine the optimum bit-rate (necessary temporal guard bands) for avoiding cross talk.

Line coding. In addition to using both time and wavelength multiplexing to increase the speed of optical fiber networks it is also necessary to use signal processing to maintain bit-error rates (BER) of $\lesssim 10^{-9}$ for voice and $\lesssim 10^{-12}$ for data. (BER is defined as the probability that the received bit differs from the transmitted bit, on average.) A ubiquitous signal processing method is *line coding* in which binary symbols are mapped onto specific waveforms; see Figure 7. In this way, pulses can be preconditioned to make them more robust to transmission impairments. Specific line codes are chosen which are adjusted differently for various physical communications media by arranging the mapping accordingly.

Line codes (three different types are shown in Figure 7) are all examples of *pulse-code modulation* or *on-off keying*. In this case it is only the amplitude which is varied; this is done by simply sending more or less light down the fiber.

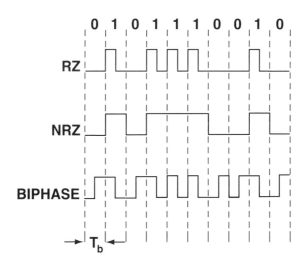

Figure 7. Three types of line codes for optical fiber communications.

The choice of line codes depends on the specific features of the communication channel that needs to be opposed [5]. Common properties among all line codes include:

(i) the coded spectrum goes to zero as the frequency approaches zero (DC energy cannot be transmitted).

(ii) the clock can be recovered from the coded data stream (necessary for detection).

(iii) they can detect errors (if not correct).

Another consideration in choosing a line code is that different coding formats will use more or less bandwidth. It is known that for a given bit-rate per bandwidth (bits/s/Hz), an ideal Nyquist channel uses the narrowest bandwidth [7]. Typically, adopting a line code will increase the needed transmission bandwidth, since redundancy is built into the system (table 1) where everything is normalized to the Nyquist bandwidth B.

Line codes	Transmission bandwidth	Bandwidth efficiency
RZ	$\pm 2B$	$\frac{1}{4}$ bit/s/Hz
NRZ	$\pm B$	$\frac{1}{2}$ bit/s/Hz
Duobinary	$\pm \frac{1}{2}B$	1 bit/s/Hz
Single Sideband	$\pm \frac{1}{2}B$	1 bit/s/Hz
M-ary ASK ($M = 2^N$)	$\pm B/N$	$\log_2 N$

Table 1. Bandwidth characteristics for different types of line codes.

Even though in the past, binary line codes were preferred to multilevel codes due to optical nonlinearities, it is now firmly established that multilevel line codes can be, spectrally, as efficient as a Nyquist channel. In particular, duobinary line coding (which uses three levels) have recently been shown to be very successful in reducing ISI due to dispersion [6].

Closely related to line coding is pulse or waveform generation. The waveform associated with a Nyquist channel is a sinc-pulse (giving rise to the "minimum" rect-shaped spectrum). The main problem with this waveform is that it requires perfect timing (no jitter) to avoid large ISI. The reason for this intolerance to timing jitter is found in the (infinitely) sharp fall-off of the spectrum. To address this problem, pulses are generated using a "raised-cosine" spectrum [1; 7] which removes the "sharp zeroes". Unfortunately, it makes the transmission bandwidth twice as large as the Nyquist channel. Lately, it has been suggested that wavelet like pulses (local trigonometric bases) are a good choice for achieving efficient time/frequency localization [8] (see section on novel line coding schemes).

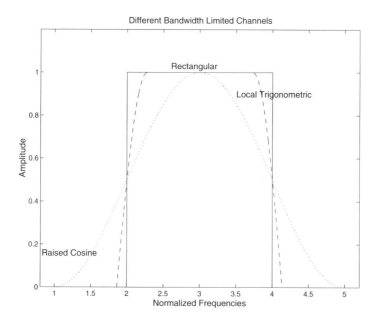

Figure 8. Examples of different bandwidth limited channels.

3. Physical Processes in Optical Fibers

Absorption. It may seem strange that the small absorption in optical fibers, which in the late 1960s was less than $20\,\mathrm{dB/km}$ (that is, over a distance of $L\ km$ we have $P_{\mathrm{in}}/P_{\mathrm{out}} \geq 10^{-20\,L/10}$), still was not sufficient to make optical communications viable (in an economical sense).

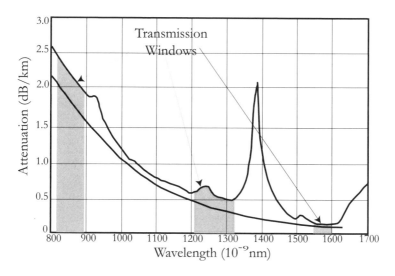

Figure 9. Absorption in optical fibers.

From 1970 to 1972 scientists managed to make fibers of even greater purity which reduced the absorption to no more than 3 dB/km at 800 nm (Figure 9). Using more or less the same type of fibers the absorption could be reduced to no more than 0.15 dB/km by going to longer wavelengths, such as 1.3 μm and 1.55 μm. This was possible through the invention of new semiconductor lasers using InGaAsP material. Despite this very low absorption, again, seen from an economical perspective, absorption was still the limiting factor. This changed with the invention of the erbium-doped fiber amplifier (EDFA). A short piece of fiber (only a few meters long) doped with Erbium and spliced to the system's fiber could now amplify the propagating pulses (bits) to "arbitrary" levels, thereby removing absorption as a system's physical limitation.

Dispersion. The next attribute which required attention was dispersion. Signal dispersion (mathematically described via the ω^2-term in equation (2–3)) a source of *intersymbol interference* (ISI) in which consecutive pulses blend into each other. Again, it turns out that optical glass fibers have inherently outstanding dispersion properties. As a matter of fact, any particular fiber has a characteristic wavelength for which the dispersion is zero. This is typically between 1.27–1.39 μm. However, as is the case for absorption, long distance transmission can cause dispersion.

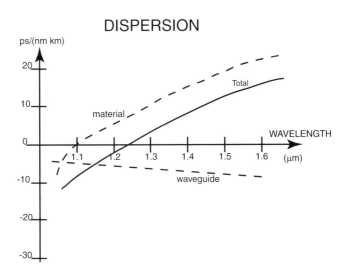

Figure 10. Dispersion in optical fibers.

There are two major contributions to dispersion: material and waveguide structure. (A waveguide is a device, such as a duct, coaxial cable, or glass fiber, designed to confine and direct the propagation of electromagnetic waves. In optical fibers the confinement is achieved by having a region with a larger refractive index.)

Material dispersion, which comes from electronic transitions in the solid, is determined as soon as the chemical constituents of the glass have been fixed. Waveguide dispersion is a function of the geometry of the core or, more precisely, how the refractive index in the core and cladding vary in space. This is important because it means that fiber manufacturers have a fair amount of flexibility in modifying the total dispersion of the fiber. Today, there is a plethora of fibers with different dispersion characteristics. However, it is not yet possible to reliably manufacture fibers with zero dispersion for all wavelengths between, say, 1400–1550 nm. Thus, even though the dispersion can be made as small as 2–4 ps/nm·km over this wavelength region, we still need to worry about dispersion for long-distance networks. Two methods used to combat dispersion are *fiber Bragg gratings* and *line coding* and combinations of the two. We now describe each of these in turn.

Optical fiber Bragg gratings are short pieces of fiber ($\lesssim 10$ cm) in which the refractive index in the core has been altered to modify the dispersion properties. Mathematically, the fiber Bragg grating is a *filter* whose properties can be described using a transfer function. Similarly, we can describe pulse propagation over a distance z in an optical fiber using a transfer function. If linear effects up to the quadratic frequency term (group-velocity dispersion) in the Taylor expansion of k in (2–3) are included, the transfer function is

$$H(\omega) = H_0 \underbrace{\exp(-\alpha\, z/2)}_{\text{amplitude}} \underbrace{\exp(-jknz)\exp(-jD\omega^2 z/(4\pi))}_{\text{phase}},$$

where k is the propagation constant, ω is the angular frequency, n is the refractive index, α is the absorption coefficient, and D is the dispersion coefficient. So for a known distance L, an EDFA can be used to amplify the amplitude and the Bragg grating (with a transfer function H^{-1}) can mostly remove the influence of the dispersion (the dispersion is primarily modeled by the $\exp(-jD\omega^2 z)$ term in the phase). The severest limitation to this scheme are *nonlinear effects* which can change both absorption and dispersion in a dramatic fashion.

Nonlinear optics. A description of electromagnetic waves interacting with matter ends up dealing with the electric and magnetic susceptibilities χ_e and χ_m, respectively. In this short exposé of nonlinear optics we will limit ourselves to non-magnetic materials, such as the glass that optical fibers are made of. The more common (in a linear description) dielectric constant, ε_r, is related to the susceptibility $\chi_e^{(1)}$ via $\varepsilon_r = 1 + \chi_e^{(1)}$. The susceptibility, in turn, has complete information about how the material interacts with electromagnetic waves. The wave equation for an arbitrary dielectric medium can be written as

$$\nabla^2 \boldsymbol{E}(\boldsymbol{r}, t) = \frac{\partial^2 \boldsymbol{P}(\boldsymbol{r}, t)}{\partial t^2},$$

where $\boldsymbol{E}(\boldsymbol{r}, t)$ is the electric field and $\boldsymbol{P}(\boldsymbol{r}, t)$ is the induced polarization field (an identical wave equation can be written for the magnetic field $\boldsymbol{H}(\boldsymbol{r}, t)$). All linear interactions can be described by assuming that the polarization field and the electric field are related via the constitutive relation,

$$\boldsymbol{P}(\boldsymbol{r}, \omega_s) = \varepsilon_0 \chi_e^{(1)}(\omega_s; -\omega_s)\boldsymbol{E}(\boldsymbol{r}, \omega_s).$$

Unfortunately, most real phenomena are not linear and this holds for electromagnetic interactions with matter. For waves whose wavelengths do not coincide with specific resonant transitions in the material, we can describe the polarization using a Taylor series expansion of the field amplitudes,

$$\boldsymbol{P}(\boldsymbol{r}, \omega_s) = \varepsilon_0 \cdot \left(\chi_e^{(1)}(\omega_s; -\omega_s)\boldsymbol{E}(\boldsymbol{r}, \omega_s) + \chi_e^{(2)}(\omega_s; \omega_1, \omega_2)\boldsymbol{E}_1(\boldsymbol{r}, \omega_1) \cdot \boldsymbol{E}_2(\boldsymbol{r}, \omega_2) \right.$$
$$\left. + \chi_e^{(3)}(\omega_s; \omega_1, \omega_2, \omega_3)\boldsymbol{E}_1(\boldsymbol{r}, \omega_1) \cdot \boldsymbol{E}_2(\boldsymbol{r}, \omega_2) \cdot \boldsymbol{E}_3(\boldsymbol{r}, \omega_3) + \ldots \right),$$

where ω_s is the frequency of the generated polarization, $\chi^{(n)}$ is the electric susceptibility of first, second and third order for $n = 1, 2, 3$, respectively, $\boldsymbol{E}(\boldsymbol{r}, \omega_n)$ are the electric field amplitudes at different carrier frequencies, ω_1, ω_2, ω_3, etc.

The susceptibilities have a general form given by

$$\chi_{i,j,k,\ldots}^{(n)}(\omega; \omega_1, \omega_2, \ldots) = \sum \frac{\langle g|r|f \rangle}{(\omega_0^2 - \omega^2 - j2\omega\gamma)} = \frac{\text{spatial dispersion}}{\text{frequency dispersion}}. \quad (3\text{--}1)$$

The subscripts i, j, k, $\ldots$, are connected with the structural symmetry of the material (spatial dispersion) and the particular polarization of the electromagnetic waves. The denominator describes the frequency dispersion with ω being the frequency of an electromagnetic wave, ω_0 being a resonant frequency in the material and γ being the width of the resonance. The summation is over all the possible states that can occur in the material while it is interacting with the electromagnetic waves. As can be seen from (3–1), the electronic susceptibilities are complex quantities. It is common to separate the susceptibilities into a real and imaginary part. For the third-order nonlinear susceptibility this could look like

$$\chi_{ijkl}^{(3)}(\omega_s; \omega_1, \omega_2, \omega_3) = \chi_{\text{Real}}^{(3)} + i \cdot \chi_{\text{Imaginary}}^{(3)}.$$

In general, the real part describes light-matter interactions that leave the material in the original energy state, while the imaginary part describes interactions that transfer energy between the electromagnetic wave and the material in such a way as to leave the material in a different energy state than the original state. Processes described by the real part are commonly referred to as parametric processes and two examples of such a process are four-photon mixing and self-phase modulation. It is interesting to note that nonlinear processes controlled by the real part require phase matching while processes due to the imaginary part do not. Examples of processes described by the imaginary part are Raman and Brillouin scattering, and two-photon absorption.

For Raman and Brillouin scattering one also needs to distinguish between spontaneous and stimulated processes. In simple terms, spontaneous Raman and Brillouin scattering are due to fluctuations in one or more optical properties caused by the internal energy of the material. Stimulated scattering is driven by the light field itself, actively increasing the internal fluctuations of the material.

Nonlinear susceptibilities of importance for tele- and data communication are all made up of electric-dipole transitions. When these transitions are between real energy levels of the material we talk about resonant processes. In general, resonant processes are strong and slow; strong because the susceptibility gets large at resonances and slow because the electrons have to be physically relocated. The nonlinear susceptibilities of importance for us are all due to non-resonant processes. These nonlinearities are distinguished by their small susceptibilities but very fast response. This is in part due to the electrons only making virtual transitions. A virtual energy level only exists for the combined system, matter and light.

In optical glass fibers, for symmetry reasons, the third-order nonlinearity, $\chi^{(3)}$, is the dominant nonlinear susceptibility. For pulse modulated systems the three most important nonlinearities are self-phase modulation, four-photon mixing and stimulated Raman scattering. The pros and cons of these nonlinearities can be summarized as follows (see [2; 3; 4]):

Self-phase modulation. Positive effects: solitons, temporal compression. Negative effects: spectral broadening, hence enhanced GVD.

Four-photon mixing. Positive effects: generation of new wavelengths. Negative effects: crosstalk between different wavelength channels.

Stimulated Raman Scattering. Positive effects: amplification (broadband and wavelength independent). Negative effects: crosstalk between different wavelength channels.

4. Novel Line Coding Schemes

With the introduction of communication channels in both time and wavelength (frequency) the challenge of fitting as much information as possible into a given time-frequency space, has become more similar to the problem that Shannon and, to some extent, Gabor were addressing in the 1940s. This is a fundamental problem — one which appears in many different fields such as; signal processing, image processing, quantum mechanics etc. Common to all of these different fields is the relation of *two* physical variables via a *Fourier transform*, which therefore, are subject to an "uncertainty relationship", which ultimately determines the information capacity; see Figure 11.

To build robust pulse forms which have good time-frequency localization properties recent research in applied mathematics has shown that shaping optical pulses as wavelets can dramatically improve the spectral efficiency and robustness of an optical fiber network [8]. In table 2 we note that present systems (2.5 Gbs) only have a 5% spectral efficiency (that is, only 5% of the available bandwidth is used for sending information). It is hoped that in five to ten years we will have 40 Gbs systems utilizing 40% of the available spectral bandwidth.

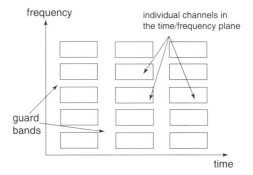

Figure 11. Time/frequency representation of the available bandwidth for any communication channel.

Bit rate (Gbs)	Channel spacing(GHz)	Spectral efficiency(%)
2.5	100/50	2.5/5.0
10	200/100/50	5/10/20
40	100	40

Table 2. Spectral efficiency for present (2.5 Gbs) and future high-speed systems.

To achieve this spectral efficiency we can use an element of an orthonormal bases $p(t)$ as our input pulse. Our total digital signal, with 1s and 0s can be described as a pulse train

$$s(t) = \sum_{j=1}^{2BT_b} a_j p(t - kT_b),$$

where B is the bandwidth of our channel, T_b is the time between pulses (Figure 7) and $p(t)$ is the temporal shape of the bits. One possible choice for $p(t)$ could be the local trigonometric bases,

$$p_{nk}(t) = w(t - n) \times \cos\big((k + \tfrac{1}{2})\pi(t - n)\big),$$

where $w(t-n)$ is a window function; see Figures 8 and 12. The window function has very smooth edges, which partly explains the good time-frequency localization of these bases (Figure 12). Compared to other waveforms—sinc pulses, for instance—the local trigonometric bases have much better systems performance, they are particularly resistant to timing jitter. So, despite the fact that sinc pulses are theoretically the best pulses they are not the best choice for an imperfect communications system.

One possible way to use these special wavelets in a network could be to partition the fiber bandwidth into many frequency channels, each defined by a particular basis function. These channels are orthogonal with out the use of guard

bands. Detection is performed by matched filters. Both the frequency partitioning and the matched filter detection can be performed all-optically, radically
increasing the network's capacity.

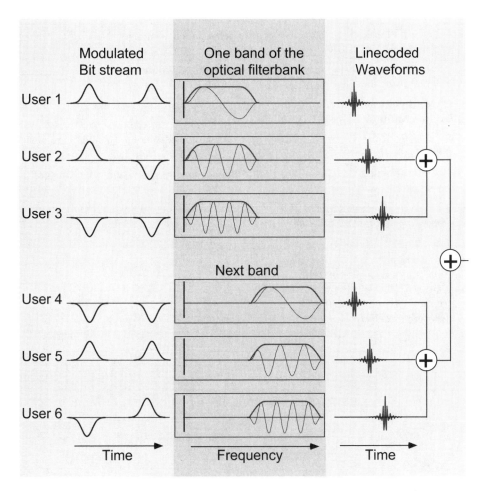

Figure 12. Encoding of orthogonal waveforms onto individual channels. Different
spectral windows, if shaped properly, can be made to overlap, making it possible
to use the full spectral bandwidth.

Conclusion. Even though dramatic improvements have been made during the
last 10 years to combat absorption, dispersion and nonlinear effects in optical
fibers it is also apparent that we need to do more if we are going to realize
the ultimate bandwidths which are possible in glass optical fibers. One very
powerful way to make a system transparent to fiber impairments is to encode
amplitude and phase information which will be immune to the negative effects
of, for example, dispersion and nonlinear interactions.

References

[1] S. Haykin, *Communication systems*, 4th Edition, Wiley, New York, 2001.

[2] D. Cotter et al., "Nonlinear optics for high-speed digital information processing", *Science* **286** (1999), 1523–1528.

[3] P. Bayvel, "Future high-capacity optical telecommunication networks", *Phil. Trans. R. Soc. Lond.* ser. A **358** (2000), 303–329.

[4] A. R. Chraplyvy, "High-capacity lightwave transmission experiments", *Bell Labs Tech. Journal*, Jan-Mar 1999, 230–245.

[5] R. M. Brooks and A. Jessop, "Line coding for optical fibre systems", *Internat. J. Electronics* **55** (1983), 81–120.

[6] E. Forestieri and G. Prati, "Novel optical line codes tolerant to fiber chromatic dispersion", *IEEE J. Lightwave Technology* **19** (2001), 1675–1684.

[7] C. C. Bissel and D. A. Chapman, *Digital signal transmission*, Cambridge University Press, 1992.

[8] T. Olson, D. Healy and U. Österberg, "Wavelets in optical communications", *Computing in Science and Engineering* **1** (1999), 51–57.

ULF ÖSTERBERG
THAYER SCHOOL OF ENGINEERING
DARTMOUTH COLLEGE
HANOVER, N.H. 03755-8000
    ulf.osterberg@dartmouth.edu

Modern Signal Processing
MSRI Publications
Volume **46**, 2003

The Generalized Spike Process, Sparsity, and Statistical Independence

NAOKI SAITO

ABSTRACT. We consider the *best sparsifying basis* (BSB) and the *kurtosis maximizing basis* (KMB) of a particularly simple stochastic process called the "generalized spike process". The BSB is a basis for which a given set of realizations of a stochastic process can be represented most sparsely, whereas the KMB is an approximation to the *least statistically-dependent basis* (LSDB) for which the data representation has minimal statistical dependence. In each realization, the generalized spike process puts a single spike with amplitude sampled from the standard normal distribution at a random location in an otherwise zero vector of length n.

We prove that both the BSB and the KMB select the standard basis, if we restrict our basis search to all possible orthonormal bases in $\mathbb{R}^n$. If we extend our basis search to all possible volume-preserving invertible linear transformations, we prove the BSB exists and is again the standard basis, whereas the KMB does not exist. Thus, the KMB is rather sensitive to the orthonormality of the transformations, while the BSB seems insensitive. Our results provide new additional support for the preference of the BSB over the LSDB/KMB for data compression. We include an explicit computation of the BSB for Meyer's discretized ramp process.

1. Introduction

This paper is a sequel to our previous paper [3], where we considered the *best sparsifying basis* (BSB), and the *least statistically-dependent basis* (LSDB) for input data assumed to be realizations of a very simple stochastic process called the "spike process." This process, which we will refer to as the "simple" spike process for convenience, puts a unit impulse (i.e., constant amplitude of 1) at a random location in a zero vector of length n. Here, the BSB is the basis of $\mathbb{R}^n$ that best sparsifies the given input data, and the LSDB is the basis of $\mathbb{R}^n$ that is the closest to the statistically independent coordinate system (regardless of whether such a coordinate system exists or not). In particular, we considered the BSB and LSDB chosen from all possible orthonormal transformations (i.e.,

$O(n)$) or all possible volume-preserving linear transformations (i.e., $SL^{\pm}(n, \mathbb{R})$, where the determinant of each element is either $+1$ or -1).

In this paper, we consider the BSB and LSDB for a slightly more complicated process, the "generalized" spike process, and compare them with those of the simple spike process. The generalized spike process puts an impulse whose amplitude is sampled from the standard normal distribution $\mathcal{N}(0, 1)$.

Our motivation to analyze the BSB and the LSDB for the generalized spike process stems from the work in computational neuroscience [22; 23; 2; 27] as well as in computational harmonic analysis [11; 7; 12]. The concept of sparsity and that of statistical independence are intrinsically different. Sparsity emphasizes the issue of compression directly, whereas statistical independence concerns the relationship among the coordinates. Yet, for certain stochastic processes, these two are intimately related, and often confusing. For example, Olshausen and Field [22; 23] emphasized the sparsity as the basis selection criterion, but they also assumed the statistical independence of the coordinates. For a set of natural scene image patches, their algorithm generated basis functions efficient to capture and represent edges of various scales, orientations, and positions, which are similar to the receptive field profiles of the neurons in our primary visual cortex. (Note the criticism raised by Donoho and Flesia [12] about the trend of referring to these functions as "Gabor"-like functions; therefore, we just call them "edge-detecting" basis functions in this paper.) Bell and Sejnowski [2] used the statistical independence criterion and obtained the basis functions similar to those of Olshausen and Field. They claimed that they did not impose the sparsity explicitly and such sparsity *emerged* by minimizing the statistical dependence among the coordinates. These motivated us to study these two criteria. However, the mathematical relationship between these two criteria in the general case has not been understood completely. Therefore we chose to study these simplified processes, which are much simpler than the natural scene images as a high-dimensional stochastic process. It is important to use simple stochastic processes first since we can gain insights and make precise statements in terms of theorems. By these theorems, we now understand what are the precise conditions for the sparsity and statistical independence criteria to select the same basis for the spike processes, and the difference between the simple and generalized spike processes. Weidmann and Vetterli also used the generalized spike process to make precise analysis of the rate-distortion behavior of sparse memoryless sources that serve as models of sparse signal representations [28].

Additionally, a very important by-product of this paper (as well as our previous paper [3]) is that these simple processes can be used for validating any independent component analysis (ICA) software that uses mutual information or kurtosis as a measure of statistical dependence, and any sparse component analysis (SCA) software that uses ℓ^p-norm ($0 < p \leq 1$) as a measure of sparsity. Actual outputs of the software can be compared with the true solutions obtained by our theorems. For example, the ICA software based on maximization of kurtosis of the inputs should not converge for the generalized spike process unless there is some constraint on the basis search (e.g., each column vector has a unit ℓ^2-norm). Considering the recent popularity of such software ([17; 5; 21]), it is a good thing to have such simple examples that can be generated and tested easily on computers.

The organization of this paper is as follows. The next section specifies notation and terminology. Section 3 defines how to quantitatively measure the sparsity and statistical dependence of a stochastic process relative to a given basis. Section 4 reviews the results on the simple spike process obtained in [3]. Section 5 contains our new results for the generalized spike process. In Section 6, we consider the BSB of Meyer's ramp process [20, p. 19], as an application of the results of Section 5. Finally, we conclude in Section 7 with a discussion.

2. Notation and Terminology

We first set our notation and the terminology. Let $\boldsymbol{X} \in \mathbb{R}^n$ be a random vector with some unknown probability density function (pdf) $f_{\boldsymbol{X}}$. Let $B \in \mathcal{D} \subset \mathbb{R}^{n \times n}$, where $\mathcal{D}$ is the so-called *basis dictionary*. For very high-dimensional data, we often take $\mathcal{D}$ to be the union of the wavelet packets and local Fourier bases (see [25] and references therein for more about such basis dictionaries). In this paper, however, we use much larger dictionaries: $\mathrm{O}(n)$ (the group of orthonormal transformations in $\mathbb{R}^n$) or $\mathrm{SL}^{\pm}(n, \mathbb{R})$ (the group of invertible volume-preserving transformations in $\mathbb{R}^n$, i.e., those with determinants equal to ± 1). We are interested in finding a basis within $\mathcal{D}$ for which the original stochastic process either becomes sparsest or least statistically dependent. Let $\mathcal{C}(B \mid \boldsymbol{X})$ be a numerical measure of *deficiency* or *cost* of the basis B given the input stochastic process $\boldsymbol{X}$. Under this setting, the *best basis* for the stochastic process $\boldsymbol{X}$ among $\mathcal{D}$ relative to the cost $\mathcal{C}$ is written as $B_\star = \arg\min_{B \in \mathcal{D}} \mathcal{C}(B \mid \boldsymbol{X})$.

We also note that log in this paper implies $\log_2$, unless stated otherwise. The $n \times n$ identity matrix is denoted by I_n, and the $n \times 1$ column vector whose entries are all ones, i.e., $(1, 1, \ldots, 1)^T$, is denoted by $\mathbf{1}_n$.

3. Sparsity vs. Statistical Independence

We now define measures of sparsity and statistical independence for the basis of a given stochastic process.

Sparsity. Sparsity is a key property for compression. The true sparsity measure for a given vector $\boldsymbol{x} \in \mathbb{R}^n$ is the so-called ℓ^0 quasi-norm which is defined as

$$\|\boldsymbol{x}\|_0 \stackrel{\text{def}}{=} \#\{i \in [1, n] : x_i \neq 0\},$$

i.e., the number of nonzero components in $\boldsymbol{x}$. This measure is, however, very unstable for even small geometric perturbations of the components in a vector.

Therefore, a better measure is the ℓ^p norm:

$$\|\boldsymbol{x}\|_p \overset{\text{def}}{=} \left(\sum_{i=1}^{n} |x_i|^p \right)^{1/p}, \quad 0 < p \leq 1.$$

In fact, this is a quasi-norm for $0 < p < 1$ since it does not satisfy the triangle inequality, but only the weaker conditions: $\|\boldsymbol{x}+\boldsymbol{y}\|_p \leq 2^{-1/p'}(\|\boldsymbol{x}\|_p+\|\boldsymbol{y}\|_p)$ where $p' = p/(p-1)$ is the conjugate exponent of p; and $\|\boldsymbol{x}+\boldsymbol{y}\|_p^p \leq \|\boldsymbol{x}\|_p^p + \|\boldsymbol{y}\|_p^p$. It is easy to show that $\lim_{p\downarrow 0} \|\boldsymbol{x}\|_p^p = \|\boldsymbol{x}\|_0$. See [11] for the details of the ℓ^p norm properties.

Thus, we use the expected ℓ^p-norm minimization as a criterion to find the best basis for a given stochastic process in terms of sparsity:

$$\mathcal{C}_p(B \mid \boldsymbol{X}) = E\|B^{-1}\boldsymbol{X}\|_p^p, \tag{3-1}$$

We propose to minimize this cost in order to select the *best sparsifying basis* (BSB):

$$B_p = \arg \min_{B \in \mathcal{D}} \mathcal{C}_p(B \mid \boldsymbol{X}).$$

REMARK 3.1. It should be noted that *minimization of the ℓ^p norm can also be achieved for each realization*. Without taking the expectation in (3–1), we can select the BSB, $B_p = B_p(\boldsymbol{x}, \mathcal{D})$ for each realization $\boldsymbol{x}$. We can guarantee that

$$\min_{B \in \mathcal{D}} \mathcal{C}_p(B \mid \boldsymbol{X} = \boldsymbol{x}) \leq \min_{B \in \mathcal{D}} \mathcal{C}_p(B \mid \boldsymbol{X}) \leq \max_{B \in \mathcal{D}} \mathcal{C}_p(B \mid \boldsymbol{X} = \boldsymbol{x}).$$

For highly variable or erratic stochastic processes, $B_p(\boldsymbol{x}, \mathcal{D})$ may change significantly for each $\boldsymbol{x}$. Thus if we adopt this strategy to compress an entire training dataset consisting of N realizations, we need to store additional information in order to describe a set of N bases.

Whether we should adapt a basis per realization or on the average is still an open issue. See [26] for more details.

Statistical independence. The statistical independence of the coordinates of $\boldsymbol{Y} \in \mathbb{R}^n$ means $f_{\boldsymbol{Y}}(\boldsymbol{y}) = f_{Y_1}(y_1)f_{Y_2}(y_2)\cdots f_{Y_n}(y_n)$, where each f_{Y_k} is a one-dimensional marginal pdf of $f_{\boldsymbol{Y}}$. Statistical independence is a key property for compressing and modeling a stochastic process because: (1) an n-dimensional stochastic process of interest can be modeled as a set of one-dimensional processes; and (2) damage of one coordinate does not propagate to the others. Of course, in general, it is difficult to find a truly statistically independent coordinate system for a given stochastic process. Such a coordinate system may not even exist for a given stochastic process. Therefore, the next best thing is to find the least statistically-dependent coordinate system within a basis dictionary. Naturally, then, we need to measure the "closeness" of a coordinate system (or random variables) $Y_1, \ldots, Y_n$ to the statistical independence. This can be measured by *mutual information* or *relative entropy* between the true pdf $f_{\boldsymbol{Y}}$ and the product of its marginal pdfs:

$$I(\boldsymbol{Y}) \overset{\text{def}}{=} \int f_{\boldsymbol{Y}}(\boldsymbol{y}) \log \frac{f_{\boldsymbol{Y}}(\boldsymbol{y})}{\prod_{i=1}^{n} f_{Y_i}(y_i)} \, d\boldsymbol{y}$$

$$= -H(\boldsymbol{Y}) + \sum_{i=1}^{n} H(Y_i),$$

where $H(\boldsymbol{Y})$ and $H(Y_i)$ are the differential entropy of $\boldsymbol{Y}$ and Y_i respectively:

$$H(\boldsymbol{Y}) = -\int f_{\boldsymbol{Y}}(\boldsymbol{y}) \log f_{\boldsymbol{Y}}(\boldsymbol{y}) \, d\boldsymbol{y},$$

$$H(Y_i) = -\int f_{Y_i}(y_i) \log f_{Y_i}(y_i) \, dy_i.$$

We note that $I(\boldsymbol{Y}) \geq 0$, and $I(\boldsymbol{Y}) = 0$ if and only if the components of $\boldsymbol{Y}$ are mutually independent. See [9] for more details of the mutual information.

Suppose $\boldsymbol{Y} = B^{-1}\boldsymbol{X}$ and $B \in \mathrm{GL}(n, \mathbb{R})$ with $\det B = \pm 1$. We denote this set of matrices by $\mathrm{SL}^{\pm}(n, \mathbb{R})$. Note that the usual $\mathrm{SL}(n, \mathbb{R})$ is a subset of $\mathrm{SL}^{\pm}(n, \mathbb{R})$. Then, we have

$$I(\boldsymbol{Y}) = -H(\boldsymbol{Y}) + \sum_{i=1}^{n} H(Y_i) = -H(\boldsymbol{X}) + \sum_{i=1}^{n} H(Y_i),$$

since the differential entropy is *invariant* under an invertible volume-preserving linear transformation:

$$H(B^{-1}\boldsymbol{X}) = H(\boldsymbol{X}) + \log |\det B^{-1}| = H(\boldsymbol{X}),$$

because $|\det B^{-1}| = 1$. Based on this fact, we proposed the minimization of the following cost function as the criterion to select the so-called *least statistically-dependent basis* (LSDB) in the basis dictionary context [25]:

$$\mathcal{C}_H(B \mid \boldsymbol{X}) = \sum_{i=1}^{n} H\left((B^{-1}\boldsymbol{X})_i\right) = \sum_{i=1}^{n} H(Y_i). \tag{3-2}$$

Now we can define the LSDB as

$$B_{LSDB} = \arg \min_{B \in \mathcal{D}} \mathcal{C}_H(B \mid \boldsymbol{X}).$$

Closely related to the LSDB is the concept of the *kurtosis-maximizing basis* (KMB). This is based on the approximation of the marginal differential entropy $H(Y_i)$ in (3–2) by higher order moments/cumulants using the Edgeworth expansion and was derived by Comon [8]:

$$H(Y_i) \approx -\frac{1}{48}\kappa(Y_i) = -\frac{1}{48}\left(\mu_4(Y_i) - 3\mu_2^2(Y_i)\right) \tag{3-3}$$

where $\mu_k(Y_i)$ is the k-th central moment of Y_i, and $\kappa(Y_i)\ /\ \mu_2^2(Y_i)$ is called the *kurtosis* of Y_i. See also Cardoso [6] for a nice exposition of the various approximations to the mutual information. Now, the KMB is defined as follows:

$$B_\kappa = \arg\min_{B\in\mathcal{D}}\mathcal{C}_\kappa(B\,|\,\boldsymbol{X}) = \arg\max_{B\in\mathcal{D}}\sum_{i=1}^{n}\kappa(Y_i), \qquad (3\text{--}4)$$

where $\mathcal{C}_\kappa(B\,|\,\boldsymbol{X}) = -\sum_{i=1}^n\kappa(Y_i)$. (This involves a slight abuse of terminology: the name is "kurtosis-maximizing basis" although what is maximized is the un-normalized κ, without the factor $1/\mu_2^2$.) Note that the LSDB and the KMB are tightly related, yet can be different. After all, (3–3) is simply an approximation to the entropy up to the fourth order cumulant. We also would like to point out that Buckheit and Donoho [4] independently proposed the same measure as a basis selection criterion, whose objective was to find a basis under which an input stochastic process looks maximally "non-Gaussian."

REMARK 3.2. Earlier work of Pham [24] also proposes minimization of the cost (3–2). We would like to point out the main difference between our work [25] and Pham's. We use the basis libraries such as wavelet packets and local Fourier bases that allow us to deal with datasets with large dimensions such as face images whereas Pham used the more general dictionary $\mathrm{GL}(n,\mathbb{R})$. In practice, however, the numerical optimization (3–2) clearly becomes more difficult in his general case particularly if we want to use this for high dimensional datasets.

4. Review of Previous Results on the Simple Spike Process

In this section, we briefly summarize the results of the simple spike process. See [3] for the details and proofs.

An n-dimensional *simple spike process* generates the standard basis vectors $\{\boldsymbol{e}_j\}_{j=1}^n \subset \mathbb{R}^n$ in a random order, where $\boldsymbol{e}_j$ has one at the j-th entry and all the other entries are zero. We can view this process as a unit impulse located at a random position between 1 and n.

The Karhunen–Loève basis. The Karhunen–Loève basis of this process is not unique and not useful because of the following proposition.

PROPOSITION 4.1. *The Karhunen–Loève basis for the simple spike process is any orthonormal basis in $\mathbb{R}^n$ containing the "DC" vector $\boldsymbol{1}_n = (1,1,\ldots,1)^T$.*

This proposition reflects the non-Gaussian nature of the simple spike process, i.e., the optimality of the KLB can be claimed only for the Gaussian processes.

The Best Sparsifying Basis. As for the BSB, we have the following result:

THEOREM 4.2. *The BSB with any $p\in[0,1]$ for the simple spike process is the standard basis if $\mathcal{D} = \mathrm{O}(n)$ or $\mathrm{SL}^\pm(n,\mathbb{R})$.*

Statistical dependence and entropy of the simple spike process. Before stating the results on the LSDB of this process, we note a few specifics about the simple spike process. First, although the standard basis is the BSB for this process, it clearly does not provide the statistically independent coordinates. The existence of a single spike at one location prohibits spike generation at other locations. This implies that these coordinates are highly statistically dependent.

Second, we can compute the true entropy $H(\boldsymbol{X})$ for this process unlike other complicated stochastic processes. Since the simple spike process selects one possible vector from the standard basis vectors of $\mathbb{R}^n$ with uniform probability $1/n$, the true entropy $H(\boldsymbol{X})$ is clearly $\log n$. This is one of the rare cases where we know the true high-dimensional entropy of the process.

The LSDB among $\mathrm{O}(n)$. For $\mathcal{D} = \mathrm{O}(n)$, we have:

THEOREM 4.3. *The LSDB among* $\mathrm{O}(n)$ *is:*

- *for $n \geq 5$, either the standard basis or the basis whose matrix representation is*

$$
\frac{1}{n}
\begin{bmatrix}
n-2 & -2 & \cdots & -2 & -2 \\
-2 & n-2 & \ddots & & -2 \\
\vdots & \ddots & \ddots & \ddots & \vdots \\
-2 & & \ddots & n-2 & -2 \\
-2 & -2 & \cdots & -2 & n-2
\end{bmatrix} ;
\tag{4-1}
$$

- *for $n = 4$, the Walsh basis, i.e.,*

$$
\frac{1}{2}
\begin{bmatrix}
1 & 1 & 1 & 1 \\
1 & 1 & -1 & -1 \\
1 & -1 & 1 & -1 \\
1 & -1 & -1 & 1
\end{bmatrix} ;
$$

- *for $n = 3$,*

$$
\begin{bmatrix}
\frac{1}{\sqrt{3}} & \frac{1}{\sqrt{6}} & \frac{1}{\sqrt{2}} \\
\frac{1}{\sqrt{3}} & \frac{1}{\sqrt{6}} & \frac{-1}{\sqrt{2}} \\
\frac{1}{\sqrt{3}} & \frac{-2}{\sqrt{6}} & 0
\end{bmatrix} ;
$$

- *for $n = 2$, $\frac{1}{\sqrt{2}} \begin{bmatrix} 1 & 1 \\ 1 & -1 \end{bmatrix}$, and this is the only case where the true independence is achieved.*

REMARK 4.4. Note that when we say the basis is a matrix as above, we really mean that the column vectors of that matrix form the basis. This also means that any permuted and/or sign-flipped (i.e., multiplied by -1) versions of those column vectors also form the basis. Therefore, when we say the basis is a matrix A, we mean not only A but also its permuted and sign-flipped versions of A. This remark also applies to all the propositions and theorems below, unless stated otherwise.

REMARK 4.5. There is an important geometric interpretation of (4–1). This matrix can also be written as:

$$B_{HR(n)} \stackrel{\text{def}}{=} I_n - 2\frac{\mathbf{1}_n}{\sqrt{n}}\frac{\mathbf{1}_n^T}{\sqrt{n}}.$$

In other words, this matrix represents the *Householder reflection* with respect to the hyperplane $\{y \in \mathbb{R}^n \mid \sum_{i=0}^n y_i = 0\}$ whose unit normal vector is $\mathbf{1}_n/\sqrt{n}$.

Below, we use the notation $B_{O(n)}$ for the LSDB among $O(n)$ to distinguish it from the LSDB among $GL(n, \mathbb{R})$, which is denoted by $B_{GL(n)}$. So, for example, for $n \geq 5$, $B_{O(n)} = I_n$ or $B_{HR(n)}$.

The LSDB among $GL(n, \mathbb{R})$. As discussed in [3], for the simple spike process, there is no important distinction in the LSDB selection from $GL(n, \mathbb{R})$ and from $SL^\pm(n, \mathbb{R})$. Therefore, we do not have to treat these two cases separately. On the other hand, the generalized spike process in Section 5 requires us to treat $SL^\pm(n, \mathbb{R})$ and $GL(n, \mathbb{R})$ differently due to the continuous amplitude of the generated spikes.

We now have a curious theorem:

THEOREM 4.6. *The LSDB among $GL(n, \mathbb{R})$ with $n > 2$ is the following basis pair (for analysis and synthesis respectively):*

$$B_{GL(n)}^{-1} = \begin{bmatrix} a & a & \cdots & \cdots & \cdots & \cdots & a \\ b_2 & c_2 & b_2 & \cdots & \cdots & \cdots & b_2 \\ b_3 & b_3 & c_3 & b_3 & \cdots & \cdots & b_3 \\ \vdots & \vdots & & \ddots & & & \vdots \\ \vdots & \vdots & & & \ddots & & \vdots \\ b_{n-1} & \cdots & \cdots & \cdots & b_{n-1} & c_{n-1} & b_{n-1} \\ b_n & \cdots & \cdots & \cdots & \cdots & b_n & c_n \end{bmatrix}, \quad (4\text{–}2)$$

$$B_{GL(n)} = \begin{bmatrix} \left(1+\sum_{k=2}^n b_k d_k\right)/a & -d_2 & -d_3 & \cdots & -d_n \\ -b_2 d_2/a & d_2 & 0 & \cdots & 0 \\ -b_3 d_3/a & 0 & d_3 & \ddots & \vdots \\ \vdots & \vdots & \ddots & \ddots & 0 \\ -b_n d_n/a & 0 & \cdots & 0 & d_n \end{bmatrix} \quad (4\text{–}3)$$

where a, b_k, c_k are arbitrary real-valued constants satisfying $a \neq 0$, $b_k \neq c_k$, and $d_k = 1/(c_k - b_k)$, $k = 2, \ldots, n$.

If we restrict ourselves to $\mathcal{D} = SL^\pm(n, \mathbb{R})$, then the parameter a must satisfy:

$$a = \pm \prod_{k=2}^n (c_k - b_k)^{-1}.$$

REMARK 4.7. The LSDB such as (4–1) and the LSDB pair (4–2), (4–3) provide us with further insight into the difference between sparsity and statistical independence. In the case of (4–1), this is the LSDB, yet it does not sparsify the simple spike process at all. In fact, these coordinates are completely dense, i.e., $\mathcal{C}_0 = n$. We can also show that the sparsity measure $\mathcal{C}_p$ gets worse as $n \to \infty$. More precisely:

PROPOSITION 4.8.

$$\lim_{n \to \infty} \mathcal{C}_p\left(B_{HR(n)} \mid \boldsymbol{X}\right) = \begin{cases} \infty & \text{if } 0 \le p < 1, \\ 3 & \text{if } p = 1. \end{cases}$$

It is interesting to note that this LSDB approaches the standard basis as $n \to \infty$. This also implies that

$$\lim_{n \to \infty} \mathcal{C}_p\left(B_{HR(n)} \mid \boldsymbol{X}\right) \neq \mathcal{C}_p\left(\lim_{n \to \infty} B_{HR(n)} \mid \boldsymbol{X}\right).$$

As for the analysis LSDB (4–2), the ability to sparsify the simple spike process depends on the values of b_k and c_k. Since the parameters a, b_k and c_k are arbitrary as long as $a \neq 0$ and $b_k \neq c_k$, we put $a = 1$, $b_k = 0$, $c_k = 1$, for $k = 2, \ldots, n$. Then we get the following specific LSDB pair:

$$B_{\mathrm{GL}(n)}^{-1} = \begin{bmatrix} 1 & 1 & \cdots & 1 \\ 0 & & & \\ \vdots & & I_{n-1} & \\ 0 & & & \end{bmatrix}, \quad B_{\mathrm{GL}(n)} = \begin{bmatrix} 1 & -1 & \cdots & -1 \\ 0 & & & \\ \vdots & & I_{n-1} & \\ 0 & & & \end{bmatrix}.$$

This analysis LSDB provides us with a sparse representation for the simple spike process (though this is clearly not better than the standard basis). For $\boldsymbol{Y} = B_{\mathrm{GL}(n)}^{-1}\boldsymbol{X}$,

$$\mathcal{C}_p = E\left[\|\boldsymbol{Y}\|_p^p\right] = \frac{1}{n} \times 1 + \frac{n-1}{n} \times 2 = 2 - \frac{1}{n}, \quad 0 \le p \le 1.$$

Now take $a = 1$, $b_k = 1$, $c_k = 2$ for $k = 2, \ldots, n$ in (4–2) and (4–3). Then

$$B_{\mathrm{GL}(n)}^{-1} = \begin{bmatrix} 1 & 1 & \cdots & 1 \\ 1 & 2 & \ddots & \vdots \\ \vdots & \ddots & \ddots & 1 \\ 1 & \cdots & 1 & 2 \end{bmatrix}, \quad B_{\mathrm{GL}(n)} = \begin{bmatrix} n & -1 & \cdots & -1 \\ -1 & & & \\ \vdots & & I_{n-1} & \\ -1 & & & \end{bmatrix}.$$

The sparsity measure of this process is

$$\mathcal{C}_p = \frac{1}{n} \times n + \frac{n-1}{n} \times \{(n-1) + 2^p\} = n + (2^p - 1)\left(1 - \frac{1}{n}\right), \quad 0 \le p \le 1.$$

Therefore, the simple spike process under this analysis basis is completely dense, i.e., $\mathcal{C}_p \ge n$ for $0 \le p \le 1$ and the equality holds if and only if $p = 0$. Yet this is still the LSDB.

Finally, from Theorems 4.3 and 4.6, we have:

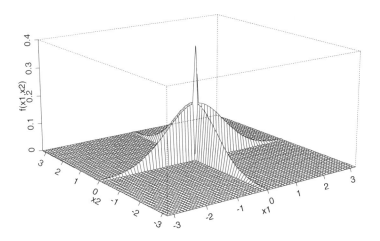

Figure 1. The pdf of the generalized spike process ($n = 2$).

COROLLARY 4.9.   *There is no invertible linear transformation providing the statistically independent coordinates for the simple spike process for $n > 2$.*

5. The Generalized Spike Process

In [13], Donoho et al. analyze the following generalization of the simple spike process in terms of the KLB and the rate distortion function, which was recently followed up in details by Weidmann and Vetterli [28]. This process first picks one coordinate out of n coordinates randomly as before, but then the amplitude of this single spike is picked according to the standard normal distribution $N(0, 1)$. The pdf of this process can be written as

$$f_{\boldsymbol{X}}(\boldsymbol{x}) = \frac{1}{n} \sum_{i=1}^{n} \left(\prod_{j \neq i} \delta(x_j) \right) g(x_i), \qquad (5\text{--}1)$$

where $\delta(\cdot)$ is the Dirac delta function, and $g(x) = (1/\sqrt{2\pi}) \cdot \exp(-x^2/2)$, i.e., the pdf of the standard normal distribution. Figure 1 shows this pdf for $n = 2$. Interestingly enough, this generalized spike process shows rather different behavior (particularly in the statistical independence) from the simple spike process in Section 4. We also note that our proofs here are rather analytical compared to those for the simple spike process presented in [3], which have a more combinatorial flavor.

The Karhunen–Loève basis. We can easily compute the covariance matrix of this process, which is proportional to the identity matrix. In fact, it is just I_n/n. Therefore, we have the following proposition, which was also stated without proof by Donoho et al. [13]:

PROPOSITION 5.1. *The Karhunen–Loève basis for the generalized spike process is any orthonormal basis in $\mathbb{R}^n$.*

PROOF. We first compute the marginal pdf of (5–1). By integrating out all x_i, $i \neq j$, we can easily get:

$$f_{X_j}(x_j) = \frac{1}{n} g(x_j) + \frac{n-1}{n} \delta(x_j).$$

Therefore, we have $E[X_j] = 0$. Since X_i and X_j cannot be simultaneously nonzero, we have

$$E[X_i X_j] = \delta_{ij} E[X_j^2] = \frac{1}{n} \delta_{ij},$$

since the variance of X_j is $1/n$, which is easily computed from the marginal pdf f_{X_j}. Therefore, the covariance matrix of this process is, as announced, I_n/n. Therefore, any orthonormal basis is the KLB. $\qquad\square$

In other words, the KLB for this process is less restrictive than that for the simple spike process (Proposition 4.1), and the KLB is again completely useless for this process.

5.1. Marginal distributions and moments under $\mathrm{SL}^\pm(n, \mathbb{R})$. Before analyzing the BSB and LSDB, we need some background. First, we compute the pdf of the process relative to a transformation $Y = B^{-1}X$, $B \in \mathrm{SL}^\pm(n, \mathbb{R})$. In general, if $Y = B^{-1}X$, then

$$f_Y(y) = \frac{1}{|\det B^{-1}|} f_X(By).$$

Therefore, from (5–1), and the fact $|\det B| = 1$, we have

$$f_Y(y) = \frac{1}{n} \sum_{i=1}^{n} \left(\prod_{j \neq i} \delta(r_j^T y) \right) g(r_i^T y), \qquad (5\text{–}2)$$

where r_j^T is the j-th row vector of B. As for its marginal pdf, we have:

LEMMA 5.2.

$$f_{Y_j}(y) = \frac{1}{n} \sum_{i=1}^{n} g(y; |\Delta_{ij}|), \qquad j = 1, \ldots, n, \qquad (5\text{–}3)$$

where Δ_{ij} is the (i, j)-th cofactor of matrix B, and $g(y; \sigma) = g(y/\sigma)/\sigma$ represents the pdf of the normal distribution $\mathcal{N}(0, \sigma^2)$.

In other words, we can interpret the j-th marginal pdf as a *mixture of Gaussians* with the standard deviations $|\Delta_{ij}|$, $i = 1, \ldots, n$. Figure 2 shows several marginal pdfs for $n = 2$. As we can see from this figure, it can vary from a very spiky distribution to a usual normal distribution depending on the rotation angle of the coordinate.

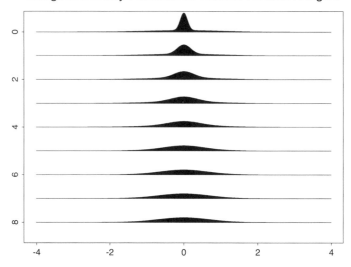

Figure 2. The marginal pdfs of the generalized spike process $(n = 2)$. All the pdfs shown here are projections of the 2D pdf in Figure 1 onto the rotated 1D axis. The axis angle in the top row is 0.088 rad., which is close to the the first axis of the standard basis. The axis angle in the bottom row is $\pi/4$ rad., i.e., 45 degree rotation, which gives rise to the exact normal distribution. The other axis angles are equispaced between these two.

PROOF. Rewrite (5–2) as

$$f_{\boldsymbol{Y}}(\boldsymbol{y}) = \frac{1}{n} \sum_{i=1}^{n} \delta(\boldsymbol{r}_1^T \boldsymbol{y}) \cdots \delta(\boldsymbol{r}_{i-1}^T \boldsymbol{y}) \delta(\boldsymbol{r}_{i+1}^T \boldsymbol{y}) \cdots \delta(\boldsymbol{r}_n^T \boldsymbol{y}) g(\boldsymbol{r}_i^T \boldsymbol{y}). \qquad (5\text{–}4)$$

The j-th marginal pdf can be written as

$$f_{Y_j}(y_j) = \int f_{\boldsymbol{Y}}(y_1, \cdots, y_n) \, dy_1 \cdots dy_{j-1} \, dy_{j+1} \cdots dy_n.$$

Consider the i-th term in the summation of (5–4) and integrate it out with respect to $y_1, \ldots, y_{j-1}, y_{j+1}, \ldots, y_n$:

$$\int \delta(\boldsymbol{r}_1^T \boldsymbol{y}) \cdots \delta(\boldsymbol{r}_{i-1}^T \boldsymbol{y}) \delta(\boldsymbol{r}_{i+1}^T \boldsymbol{y}) \cdots \delta(\boldsymbol{r}_n^T \boldsymbol{y}) g(\boldsymbol{r}_i^T \boldsymbol{y}) \, dy_1 \cdots dy_{j-1} \, dy_{j+1} \cdots dy_n.$$
$$\qquad (5\text{–}5)$$

We use the change of variable formula to integrate this. Let $\boldsymbol{r}_k^T \boldsymbol{y} = x_k$, $k = 1, \ldots, n$, and let $\boldsymbol{b}_\ell$ be the ℓ-th column vector of B. The relationship $B\boldsymbol{y} = \boldsymbol{x}$ can be rewritten as

$$B^{(i,j)} \boldsymbol{y}^{(j)} + y_j \boldsymbol{b}_j^{(i)} = \boldsymbol{x}^{(i)},$$

where $B^{(i,j)}$ is the $(n-1) \times (n-1)$ matrix by removing i-th row and j-th column, and the vectors with superscripts indicate the length $n-1$ column vectors by removing the elements whose indices are specified in the parentheses. The above equation can be rewritten as

$$\boldsymbol{y}^{(j)} = \left(B^{(i,j)}\right)^{-1}\left(\boldsymbol{x}^{(i)} - y_j \boldsymbol{b}_j^{(i)}\right).$$

Thus,

$$
\begin{aligned}
\mathrm{d}\boldsymbol{y}^{(j)} &= \mathrm{d}y_1 \cdots \mathrm{d}y_{j-1}\, \mathrm{d}y_{j+1} \cdots \mathrm{d}y_n \\
&= \frac{1}{|\det B^{(i,j)}|}\, \mathrm{d}\boldsymbol{x}^{(i)} \\
&= \frac{1}{|\Delta_{ij}|}\, \mathrm{d}x_1 \cdots \mathrm{d}x_{i-1}\, \mathrm{d}x_{i+1} \cdots \mathrm{d}x_n.
\end{aligned}
$$

We now express $\boldsymbol{r}_i^T \boldsymbol{y} = x_i$ in terms of y_j and $\boldsymbol{x}$.

$$
\begin{aligned}
\boldsymbol{r}_i^T \boldsymbol{y} &= \left(\boldsymbol{r}_i^{(j)}\right)^T \boldsymbol{y}^{(j)} + b_{ij} y_j \qquad\qquad\qquad (5\text{–}6) \\
&= \left(\boldsymbol{r}_i^{(j)}\right)^T \left(B^{(i,j)}\right)^{-1}\left(\boldsymbol{x}^{(i)} - y_j \boldsymbol{b}_j^{(i)}\right) + b_{ij} y_j \\
&= \left(\boldsymbol{r}_i^{(j)}\right)^T \left(B^{(i,j)}\right)^{-1} \boldsymbol{x}^{(i)} + y_j\left(b_{ij} - \left(\boldsymbol{r}_i^{(j)}\right)^T \left(B^{(i,j)}\right)^{-1}\boldsymbol{b}_j^{(i)}\right) \\
&\overset{(*)}{=} \left(\boldsymbol{r}_i^{(j)}\right)^T \left(B^{(i,j)}\right)^{-1} \boldsymbol{x}^{(i)} + \frac{y_j}{\Delta_{ij}}\det B \\
&= \left(\boldsymbol{r}_i^{(j)}\right)^T \left(B^{(i,j)}\right)^{-1} \boldsymbol{x}^{(i)} \pm \frac{y_j}{\Delta_{ij}},
\end{aligned}
$$

where $(*)$ follows from a lemma proved in Appendix A:

LEMMA 5.3. *For any* $B = (b_{ij}) \in \mathrm{GL}(n, \mathbb{R})$,

$$b_{ij} - \left(\boldsymbol{r}_i^{(j)}\right)^T \left(B^{(i,j)}\right)^{-1}\boldsymbol{b}_j^{(i)} = \frac{1}{\Delta_{ij}}\det B, \quad 1 \le i, j \le n.$$

Now let's go back to the integration (5–5). Thanks to the property of the delta function with Equation (5–6), we have

$$
\begin{aligned}
\int \cdots \int \delta(x_1) \cdots \delta(x_{i-1})\delta(x_{i+1}) &\cdots \delta(x_n) g(\boldsymbol{r}_i^T \boldsymbol{y}) \frac{1}{|\Delta_{ij}|}\, \mathrm{d}x_1 \cdots \mathrm{d}x_{i-1}\, \mathrm{d}x_{i+1} \cdots \mathrm{d}x_n \\
&= \frac{1}{|\Delta_{ij}|} g(\pm y_j/\Delta_{ij}) \\
&= g(y_j; |\Delta_{ij}|),
\end{aligned}
$$

where we used the fact that $g(\cdot)$ is an even function. Therefore, we can write the j-th marginal distribution as announced in (5–3). $\qquad\square$

We now compute the moments of Y_i, which will be used later. We use the fact that this is a mixture of n Gaussians each of which has mean 0 and variance $|\Delta_{ij}|^2$. The following lemma computes the higher order moments.

LEMMA 5.4.

$$E[|Y_j|^p] = \frac{\Gamma(p)}{n\, 2^{p/2-1}\Gamma(p/2)} \sum_{i=1}^{n} |\Delta_{ij}|^p, \quad \textit{for all } p > 0. \qquad (5\text{–}7)$$

PROOF. We have:

$$E[|Y_j|^p] = \frac{1}{n} \sum_{i=1}^{n} \int_{-\infty}^{\infty} |y|^p g(y; |\Delta_{ij}|) \, dy$$

$$= \frac{1}{n} \sum_{i=1}^{n} \sqrt{\frac{2}{\pi}} |\Delta_{ij}|^p \Gamma(1+p) D_{-1-p}(0)$$

by Gradshteyn and Ryzhik [14, Formula 3.462.1], where $D_{-1-p}(\cdot)$ is Whittaker's function as defined by Abramowitz and Stegun [1, pp.687]:

$$D_{-a-1/2}(0) = U(a, 0) = \frac{\sqrt{\pi}}{2^{a/2+1/4} \, \Gamma(a/2 + 3/4)}.$$

Thus, putting $a = p + 1/2$ to the above equation yields:

$$D_{-1-p}(0) = \frac{\sqrt{\pi}}{2^{1/2+p/2} \, \Gamma(1 + p/2)}.$$

Therefore,

$$E[|Y_j|^p] = \frac{1}{n} \sum_{i=1}^{n} |\Delta_{ij}|^p \frac{\Gamma(1+p)}{2^{p/2} \, \Gamma(1 + p/2)}$$

$$= \frac{1}{n} \sum_{i=1}^{n} |\Delta_{ij}|^p \frac{\Gamma(p)}{2^{p/2-1} \, \Gamma(p/2)}$$

$$= \frac{\Gamma(p)}{n \, 2^{p/2-1} \, \Gamma(p/2)} \sum_{i=1}^{n} |\Delta_{ij}|^p,$$

as we desired. □

The Best Sparsifying Basis. As for the BSB, there is no difference after all between the generalized spike process and the simple spike process.

THEOREM 5.5. *The BSB with any $p \in [0,1]$ for the generalized spike process is the standard basis if $\mathcal{D} = O(n)$ or $SL^{\pm}(n, \mathbb{R})$.*

PROOF. We first consider the case $p \in (0, 1]$. Using Lemma 5.4, the cost function (3-1) can be rewritten as

$$\mathcal{C}_p(B \mid \boldsymbol{X}) = \sum_{j=1}^{n} E[|Y_j|^p] = \frac{\Gamma(p)}{n \, 2^{p/2-1} \, \Gamma(p/2)} \sum_{i=1}^{n} \sum_{j=1}^{n} |\Delta_{ij}|^p.$$

We now define a matrix $\tilde{B} \stackrel{\text{def}}{=} (\Delta_{ij})$. Then $\tilde{B} \in SL^{\pm}(n, \mathbb{R})$ since

$$B^{-1} = \frac{1}{\det B} (\Delta_{ji}) = \pm(\Delta_{ji}),$$

and $B^{-1} \in SL^{\pm}(n, \mathbb{R})$. Therefore, this reduces to

$$\mathcal{C}_p(B \mid \boldsymbol{X}) = \frac{\Gamma(p)}{n \, 2^{p/2-1} \, \Gamma(p/2)} \sum_{i=1}^{n} \sum_{j=1}^{n} |\tilde{b}_{ij}|^p = K(p, n) \cdot \mathcal{C}_p(\tilde{B} \mid \tilde{\boldsymbol{X}}),$$

where $\tilde{\boldsymbol{X}}$ represents the simple spike process, and $K(p, n)$ is the constant before the double summations above, which is dependent only on p and n. This means that for fixed p and n, searching for the B that minimizes the sparsity cost for the generalized spike process is equivalent to searching for the $\tilde{B}$ that minimizes the sparsity cost for the simple spike process. Thus, Theorem 9.5.1 in [3] (or Theorem 4.2 in this paper) asserts that the $\tilde{B}$ must be the identity matrix I_n or its permuted or sign flipped versions. Suppose $\Delta_{ij} = \delta_{ij}$. Then, $B^{-1} = \pm(\Delta_{ji}) = \pm I_n$, which implies that $B = \pm I_n$. If (Δ_{ji}) is any permutation matrix, then B^{-1} is just that permutation matrix or its sign flipped version. Therefore, B is also a permutation matrix or its sign flipped version.

Finally, consider the case $p = 0$. Then, any linear invertible transformation except the identity matrix or its permuted or sign-flipped versions clearly increases the number of nonzero elements after the transformation. Therefore, the BSB with $p = 0$ is also a permutation matrix or its sign flipped version.

This completes the proof of Theorem 5.5.   □

The LSDB/KMB among $\mathrm{O}(n)$. As for the LSDB/KMB, we can see some differences from the simple spike process.

We first consider the case of $\mathcal{D} = \mathrm{O}(n)$. So far, we have been unable to prove the following conjecture.

CONJECTURE 5.6. *The LSDB among* $\mathrm{O}(n)$ *is the standard basis.*

The difficulty is the evaluation of the sum of the marginal entropies (3–2) for the pdfs of the form (5–3). However, a major simplification occurs if we consider the KMB instead of the LSDB, and we can prove:

THEOREM 5.7. *The KMB among* $\mathrm{O}(n)$ *is the standard basis.*

PROOF. Because $E[Y_j] = 0$, $E[Y_j^2] = \frac{1}{n} \sum_{i=1}^n \Delta_{ij}^2$, and $\mu_4(Y_j) = \frac{3}{n} \sum_{i=1}^n \Delta_{ij}^4$ by (5–7), the cost function in (3–4) becomes

$$\mathcal{C}_\kappa(B \mid \boldsymbol{X}) = \frac{3}{n} \sum_{j=1}^n \left(\sum_{i=1}^n \Delta_{ij}^4 - \frac{1}{n} \left(\sum_{i=1}^n \Delta_{ij}^2 \right)^2 \right). \tag{5–8}$$

Note that this is true for any $B \in \mathrm{SL}^\pm(n, \mathbb{R})$. If we restrict our basis search to the set $\mathrm{O}(n)$, another major simplification occurs because we have a special relationship between Δ_{ij} and the matrix element b_{ji} of $B \in \mathrm{O}(n)$:

$$B^{-1} = \frac{1}{\det B} (\Delta_{ji}) = B^T.$$

In other words,

$$\Delta_{ij} = (\det B) b_{ij} = \pm b_{ij}.$$

Therefore,

$$\sum_{i=1}^n \Delta_{ij}^2 = \sum_{i=1}^n b_{ij}^2 = 1.$$

Inserting this into (5–8), we get a simplified cost for $\mathcal{D} = O(n)$:

$$\mathcal{C}_\kappa(B \mid \boldsymbol{X}) = -\frac{3}{n}\left(1 - \sum_{i=1}^{n}\sum_{j=1}^{n}\Delta_{ij}^4\right).$$

This means that the KMB can be rewritten as

$$B_\kappa = \arg\max_{B \in O(n)} \sum_{i,j} b_{ij}^4. \tag{5–9}$$

Note that the existence of the maximum is guaranteed because the set $O(n)$ is *compact* and the cost function $\sum_{i,j} b_{ij}^4$ is continuous.

Now consider a matrix $P = (p_{ij}) = (b_{ij}^2)$. Then, from the orthonormality of columns and rows of B, this matrix P belongs to a set of *doubly stochastic matrices* $\mathcal{S}(n)$. Since doubly stochastic matrices obtained by squaring the elements of $O(n)$ consist of a proper subset of $\mathcal{S}(n)$, we have

$$\max_{B \in O(n)} \sum_{i,j} b_{ij}^4 \leq \max_{P \in \mathcal{S}(n)} \sum_{i,j} p_{ij}^2.$$

Now we prove that such P must be an identity matrix or its permuted version.

$$\max_{P \in \mathcal{S}(n)} \sum_{j=1}^{n}\sum_{i=1}^{n} p_{ij}^2 \leq \sum_{j=1}^{n}\left(\max_{\sum_{i=1}^{n} p_{ij}=1} \sum_{i=1}^{n} p_{ij}^2\right) = \sum_{j=1}^{n} 1 = n,$$

where the first equality follows from the fact that maxima of the radius of the sphere $\sum_i p_{ij}^2$ subject to $\sum_i p_{ij} = 1$, $p_{ij} \geq 0$ occur only at the vertices of that simplex, i.e., $\boldsymbol{p}_j = \boldsymbol{e}_{\sigma(j)}$, $j = 1,\ldots,n$ where $\sigma(\cdot)$ is a permutation of n items. That is, the column vectors of P must be the standard basis vectors. This implies that the matrix B corresponding to $P = I_n$ or its permuted version must be either I_n or its permuted and/or sign-flipped version. $\square$

The LSDB/KMB among $\mathrm{SL}^\pm(n,\mathbb{R})$. If we extend our search to this more general case, we have:

THEOREM 5.8. *The KMB among* $\mathrm{SL}^\pm(n,\mathbb{R})$ *does not exist.*

PROOF. The set $\mathrm{SL}^\pm(n,\mathbb{R})$ is *not* compact. Therefore, there is no guarantee that the cost function $\mathcal{C}_\kappa(B \mid \boldsymbol{X})$ has a minimum value on this set. In fact, there is a simple counterexample: let $B = \mathrm{diag}(a, a^{-1}, 1, \cdots, 1)$, where a is any nonzero real scalar. Then $\mathcal{C}_\kappa(B \mid \boldsymbol{X}) = -(a^4 + a^{-4} + n - 2)$ tends to $-\infty$ as a increases to ∞. $\square$

As for the LSDB, we do not know whether the LSDB exists among $\mathrm{SL}^\pm(n,\mathbb{R})$ at this point, although we believe that the LSDB is the standard basis. The negative result in the KMB does not necessarily imply the negative result in the LSDB.

6. An Application to the Ramp Process

Although the generalized spike process is a simple stochastic process, we have the following important interpretation. Consider a stochastic process generating a basis vector randomly selected from some fixed orthonormal basis and multiplied by a scalar varying as the standard normal distribution at a time. Then, that basis itself is simultaneously the BSB and the KMB among $O(n)$. Theorems 5.5 and 5.7 claim that once we transform the data to the generalized spike process, we cannot do any better than that, both in terms of sparsity and independence within $O(n)$.

Along this line of thought, we now consider the following stochastic process as an application of the theorems in this paper:

$$X(t) = \nu \cdot (t - H(t - \tau)), \quad t \in [0, 1), \ \nu \sim \mathcal{N}(0, 1), \ \tau \sim \mathrm{unif}[0, 1), \qquad (6\text{–}1)$$

where $H(\cdot)$ is the Heaviside step function, i.e., $H(t) = 1$ if $t \geq 0$ and 0 otherwise. This is a generalized version of the ramp process of Yves Meyer [20, p. 19]. Some realizations of the simple ramp process are shown in Figure 3.

We now consider the discrete version of (6–1). Let our sampling points be $t_k = \frac{2k+1}{2n}$, $k = 0, \ldots, n-1$. Suppose the discontinuity (at $t = \tau$) does not happen at the exact sampling points. Then all the realizations whose discontinuities are located anywhere in the open interval $\left(\frac{2k-1}{2n}, \frac{2k+1}{2n}\right)$ have the same discretized

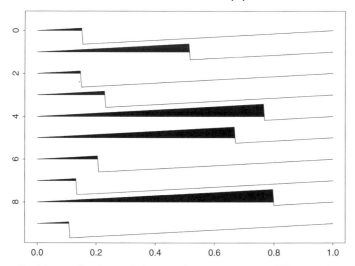

10 realizations of the ramp process

Figure 3. Ten realizations of the simple ramp process. The position of the discontinuity is picked uniformly randomly from the interval $[0, 1)$. A realization of the generalized ramp process can be obtained by multiplying a scalar picked from the standard normal distribution to a realization of the simple ramp process.

version. Therefore, any realization now has the form

$$\tilde{\boldsymbol{x}}_j = \nu \boldsymbol{x}_j = \nu(x_{0j}, \dots, x_{n-1,j})^T, \quad x_{kj} = \begin{cases} \frac{2k+1}{2n} & \text{for } k = 0, \dots, j-1, \\ \frac{2k+1}{2n} - 1 & \text{for } k = j, \dots, n-1, \end{cases}$$

where j is picked uniformly randomly from the set $\{0, 1, \cdots, n-1\}$. (Note that the index of the vector components starts with 0 for convenience). Then:

THEOREM 6.1. *The BSB pair of the discretized version of the generalized ramp process (6–1), selected from* $\mathrm{SL}^\pm(n, \mathbb{R})$, *are:*

$$B_{\mathrm{ramp}}^{-1} = (2n)^{-1/n} \begin{bmatrix} -1 & 0 & \cdots & \cdots & 0 & -1 \\ 1 & -1 & 0 & \cdots & 0 & -2 \\ 0 & \ddots & \ddots & \ddots & \vdots & \vdots \\ \vdots & \ddots & 1 & -1 & 0 & -2 \\ \vdots & & \ddots & 1 & -1 & -2 \\ 0 & \cdots & \cdots & 0 & 1 & -3 \end{bmatrix}, \tag{6-2}$$

$$B_{\mathrm{ramp}} = (2n)^{1/n} \begin{bmatrix} \boldsymbol{x}_0 \bigg| \boldsymbol{x}_1 \bigg| \cdots \bigg| \boldsymbol{x}_{n-1} \end{bmatrix}. \tag{6-3}$$

PROOF. It is straightforward to show that the matrix without the factor $(2n)^{-1/n}$ in (6–2) is the inverse of the matrix $[\boldsymbol{x}_0|\boldsymbol{x}_1|\cdots|\boldsymbol{x}_{n-1}]$. Then, the factors $(2n)^{-1/n}$ and $(2n)^{1/n}$ in (6–2) and (6–3), which are easily obtained, are necessary for these matrices to be in $\mathrm{SL}^\pm(n, \mathbb{R})$. It is now clear that the analysis basis B_{ramp}^{-1} transforms the discretized version of the generalized ramp process to the generalized spike process whose amplitudes obey $\mathcal{N}(0, (2n)^{-2/n})$ instead of $\mathcal{N}(0, 1)$. Once converted to the generalized spike process, then from Theorem 5.5, we know that we cannot do any better than the standard basis in terms of the sparsity cost (3–1). This implies that the BSB among $\mathrm{SL}^\pm(n, \mathbb{R})$ is the basis pair (6–2) and (6–3). □

In fact, this matrix is a difference operator (with DC measurement) so that it detects the location of the discontinuity in each realization, while the synthesis basis vectors (6–3) are the realizations of this process themselves modulo scalar multiplications. Clearly, this matrix also transforms the discretized version of the simple ramp process (i.e., with $\nu \equiv 1$ in (6–1)) to the simple spike process whose nonzero amplitude is $(2n)^{-1/n}$. Therefore, if the realizations of the simple or generalized ramp process is fed to any software that is supposed to find a sparsifying basis among $\mathrm{SL}^\pm(n, \mathbb{R})$, then that software should be able to find (6–2) and (6–3). As a demonstration, we conducted a simple experiment using Cardoso's JADE (Joint Approximate Diagonalization of Eigenmatrices) algorithm [6] applied to the discretized version of the simple ramp process.

The JADE algorithm was designed to find a basis minimizing the sum of the squared fourth order cross-cumulants of the input data (i.e., essentially the

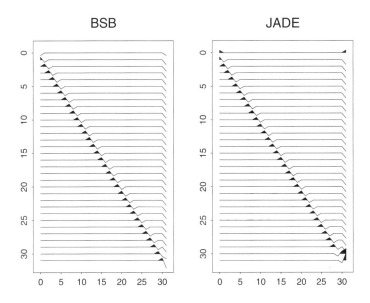

Figure 4. The analysis BSB vs. the analysis basis obtained by JADE algorithm ($n = 32$). A row permutation and a global amplitude normalization were applied to the JADE analysis basis to have a better correspondence with the BSB.

KMB) under the whitening condition, $E\boldsymbol{Y}\boldsymbol{Y}^T = I_n$. In fact, the best basis is searched for within a subset of $\mathrm{GL}(n, \mathbb{R})$, which has a very special structure: every element in this set is of the form $B = W^{-1}U$ where W is the whitening matrix of the inputs $\boldsymbol{X}$ and $U \in \mathrm{O}(n)$. Note that this subset is neither $\mathrm{O}(n)$ nor $\mathrm{SL}^{\pm}(n, \mathbb{R})$. For our numerical experiment with JADE, we modified the code available from [5] so that it does not remove the mean of the input dataset. (Otherwise, we could only extract $n - 1$ basis vectors.) In Figure 4, we compare the theoretical optimum, i.e., the analysis BSB (6–2), and the analysis basis obtained by JADE, which is almost identical to the BSB (modulo permutations and sign flips).

Now, what happens if we restrict the basis search to the set $\mathrm{O}(n)$? The basis pair (6–2) and (6–3) are not orthogonal matrices. Therefore, we will never be able to find the basis pair (6–2), (6–3) within $\mathrm{O}(n)$. Consequently, even if we found the BSB among $\mathrm{O}(n)$, the ramp process would be less sparsified by that orthonormal BSB than by (6–2). Yet, it is of interest to determine the BSB within $\mathrm{O}(n)$ due to the numerical experiments of Cardoso and Donoho [7]. They apply the JADE algorithm without imposing the whitening condition to the discretized version of the simple ramp process. This strategy is essentially equivalent to searching the KMB within $\mathrm{O}(n)$. The resulting KMB, which they call "jadelets" [7], is very similar to Daubechies's almost symmetric wavelet basis called "symmlets" [10, Sec. 6.4]. For the generalized ramp process, the KMB among $\mathrm{SL}^{\pm}(n, \mathbb{R})$ may not exist as Theorem 5.8 shows, because within

$\mathrm{SL}^{\pm}(n, \mathbb{R})$, the generalized ramp process is equivalent to the generalized spike process via (6–2) and (6–3). On the other hand, we cannot convert the generalized ramp process to the generalized spike process within $\mathrm{O}(n)$, although the KMB among $\mathrm{O}(n)$ exists for the generalized spike process. These observations indicate that the orthonormality may be a key to generate the wavelet-like multiscale basis for the generalized ramp process. At this point, however, we do not fully understand why orthonormality has to be a key for generating such a wavelet-like multiscale basis. The mystery of the orthonormality was intensified after we failed to reproduce their results using the modified JADE algorithm. This issue needs to be investigated in the near future.

7. Discussion

Unlike the simple spike process, the BSB and the KMB (an alternative to the LSDB) selects the standard basis if we restrict our basis search to the set $\mathrm{O}(n)$. If we extend our basis search to $\mathrm{SL}^{\pm}(n, \mathbb{R})$, then the BSB exists and is again the standard basis whereas the KMB does not exist. Of course, if we extend the search to nonlinear transformations, then it becomes a different story. We refer the reader to our recent articles [18; 19], for the details of a nonlinear algorithm.

The results of this paper further support the conclusion of the previous work [3]: dealing with the BSB is much simpler than the LSDB. To deal with statistical dependency, we need to consider the probability law of the underlying process (e.g., entropy or the marginal pdfs) explicitly. That is why we need to consider the KMB instead of the LSDB to prove the theorems. Also in practice, given a finite set of training data, it is a nontrivial task to reliably estimate the marginal pdfs. Moreover, the LSDB unfortunately cannot tell how close it is to the true statistical independence; it can only tell that it is the best one (i.e., the closest one to the statistical independence) among the given set of possible bases. In order to quantify the absolute statistical dependence, we need to estimate the true high-dimensional entropy of the original process, $H(\boldsymbol{X})$, which is an extremely difficult task in general. We would like to note, however, a recent attempt to estimate the high-dimensional entropy of the process by Hero and Michel [15], which uses the minimum spanning trees of the input data and does not require us to estimate the pdf of the process. We feel that this type of techniques will help assessing the absolute statistical dependence of the process under the LSDB coordinates. Another interesting observation is that the KMB is rather sensitive to the orthonormality of the basis dictionary whereas the BSB is insensitive to that. Our previous results on the simple spike process (e.g., Theorems 4.3 and 4.6) also suggest the sensitivity of the LSDB to the orthonormality of the basis dictionary.

On the other hand, the sparsity criterion neither requires estimation of the marginal pdfs nor reveals the sensitivity to the orthonormality. Simply computing the expected ℓ^p norms suffices. Moreover, we can even adapt the BSB for each realization rather than for the whole realizations, which is impossible for the LSDB, as we discussed in [3; 26]. These observations, therefore, suggest that the pursuit of sparse representations should be encouraged rather than that of statistically independent representations. This is also the viewpoint indicated by Donoho [11].

Finally, there are a few interesting generalizations of the spike processes, which need to be addressed in the near future. We need to consider a stochastic process that randomly throws in multiple spikes to a single realization. If we throw in more and more spikes to one realization, the standard basis is getting worse in terms of sparsity. Also, we can consider various rules to throw in multiple spikes. For example, for each realization, we can select the locations of the spikes statistically independently. This is the simplest multiple spike process. Alternatively, we can consider a certain dependence in choosing the locations of the spikes. The ramp process of Yves Meyer ((6–1) with $\nu \equiv 1$) represented in the wavelet basis is such an example; each realization of the ramp process generates a small number of nonzero wavelet coefficients around the location of the discontinuity of that realization and across the scales. See [4; 13; 20; 26] for more about the ramp process.

Except in very special circumstances, it would be extremely difficult to find the BSB of a complicated stochastic process (e.g., natural scene images) that truly converts its realizations to the spike process. More likely, a theoretically and computationally feasible basis that sparsifies the realizations of a complicated process well (e.g., curvelets for the natural scene images [12]) may generate expansion coefficients that may be viewed as an amplitude-varying multiple spike process. In order to tackle this scenario, we certainly need to identify interesting, useful, and simple enough specific stochastic processes, develop the BSB adapted to such specific processes, and deepen our understanding of the amplitude-varying multiple spike process.

Acknowledgment

I would like to thank Dr. Jean-François Cardoso of ENST, Paris, and Dr. Motohico Mulase and Dr. Roger Wets, both of UC Davis, for fruitful discussions. This research was partially supported by NSF DMS-99-73032, DMS-99-78321, and ONR YIP N00014-00-1-0469.

Appendix A. Proof of Lemma 5.3

PROOF. Consider the system of linear equations

$$B^{(i,j)} z^{(j)} = b_j^{(i)},$$

where $\boldsymbol{z}^{(j)} = (z_1, \cdots, z_{j-1}, z_{j+1}, \cdots, z_n)^T \in \mathbb{R}^{n-1}$, $j = 1, \ldots, n$. Using Cramer's rule (e.g., [16, pp.21]), we have, for $k = 1, \ldots, j-1, j+1, \ldots, n$,

$$z_k^{(j)} = \frac{1}{\det B^{(i,j)}} \det \left[\boldsymbol{b}_1^{(i)} \middle| \cdots \middle| \boldsymbol{b}_{k-1}^{(i)} \middle| \boldsymbol{b}_j^{(i)} \middle| \boldsymbol{b}_{k+1}^{(i)} \middle| \cdots \middle| \boldsymbol{b}_n^{(i)} \right]$$

$$\overset{(a)}{=} (-1)^{|k-j|-1} \frac{B^{(i,k)}}{B^{(i,j)}}$$

$$\overset{(b)}{=} (-1)^{|k-j|-1} \frac{\Delta_{ik}/(-1)^{i+k}}{\Delta_{ij}/(-1)^{i+j}} = -\frac{\Delta_{ik}}{\Delta_{ij}},$$

where (a) follows from the $(|k-j|-1)$ column permutations to move $\boldsymbol{b}_j^{(i)}$ located at the k-th column to the j-th column of $B^{(i,j)}$, and (b) follows from the definition of the cofactor. Hence,

$$b_{ij} - \left(\boldsymbol{r}_i^{(j)}\right)^T \left(B^{(i,j)}\right)^{-1} \boldsymbol{b}_j^{(i)} = b_{ij} - \left(\boldsymbol{r}_i^{(j)}\right)^T \boldsymbol{z}^{(j)} = b_{ij} + \frac{1}{\Delta_{ij}} \sum_{k \neq j} b_{ik} \Delta_{ik}$$

$$= \frac{1}{\Delta_{ij}} \sum_{k=1}^n b_{ik} \Delta_{ik} = \frac{1}{\Delta_{ij}} \det B.$$

This completes the proof of Lemma 5.3. $\qquad\square$

References

[1] M. Abramowitz and I. A. Stegun, *Handbook of mathematical functions*, 9th printing, Dover, New York, 1972.

[2] A. J. Bell and T. J. Sejnowski. "The 'independent components' of natural scenes are edge filters", *Vision Research*, 37:3327–3338, 1997.

[3] B. Bénichou and N. Saito, "Sparsity vs. statistical independence in adaptive signal representations: A case study of the spike process", pp. 225–257 in *Beyond wavelets*, Studies in Computational Mathematics **10**, edited by G. V. Welland, Academic Press, San Diego, 2003.

[4] J. B. Buckheit and D. L. Donoho. "Time-frequency tilings which best expose the non-Gaussian behavior of a stochastic process", pp. 1–4 in *Proc. International Symposium on Time-Frequency and Time-Scale Analysis* (Jun. 18–21, 1996, Paris), IEEE, 1996.

[5] J. F. Cardoso, "An efficient batch algorithm: JADE", available at http://sig.enst.fr/~cardoso/guidesepsou.html. See http://tsi.enst.fr/~cardoso/icacentral/index.html for collections of contributed ICA software.

[6] J.-F. Cardoso, "High-order contrasts for independent component analysis", *Neural Computation*, 11:157–192, 1999.

[7] J.-F. Cardoso and D. L. Donoho, "Some experiments on independent component analysis of non-Gaussian processes", pp. 74–77 in *Proc. IEEE Signal Processing International Workshop on Higher Order Statistics* (Cesarea, Israel), 1999.

[8] P. Comon, "Independent component analysis, a new concept?", *Signal Processing*, 36:287–314, 1994.

[9] T. M. Cover and J. A. Thomas, *Elements of information theory*, Wiley–Interscience, New York, 1991.

[10] I. Daubechies, *Ten lectures on wavelets*, CBMS-NSF Regional Conference Series in Applied Mathematics **61**, SIAM, Philadelphia, PA, 1992.

[11] D. L. Donoho, "Sparse components analysis and optimal atomic decomposition", *Constructive Approximation*, 17:353–382, 2001.

[12] D. L. Donoho and A. G. Flesia, "Can recent innovations in harmonic analysis 'explain' key findings in natural image statistics?", *Network: Comput. Neural Syst.*, 12:371–393, 2001.

[13] D. L. Donoho, M. Vetterli, R. A. DeVore, and I. Daubechies, "Data compression and harmonic analysis", *IEEE Trans. Inform. Theory*, 44(6):2435–2476, 1998.

[14] I. S. Gradshteyn and I. M. Ryzhik, *Table of integrals, series, and products*, sixth edition, Academic Press, 2000.

[15] A. O. Hero and O. J. J. Michel, "Asymptotic theory of greedy approximations to minimal k-point random graphs", *IEEE Trans. Inform. Theory*, 45(6):1921–1938, 1999.

[16] R. A. Horn and C. R. Johnson, *Matrix analysis*, Cambridge Univ. Press, 1985.

[17] A. Hyvärinen, The FastICA package for MATLAB, http://www.cis.hut.fi/projects/ica/fastica/.

[18] J.-J. Lin, N. Saito, and R. A. Levine, "An iterative nonlinear Gaussianization algorithm for resampling dependent components", pp. 245–250 in *Proc. 2nd International Workshop on Independent Component Analysis and Blind Signal Separation* (June 19–22, 2000, Helsinki), edited by P. Pajunen and J. Karhunen, IEEE, 2000.

[19] J.-J. Lin, N. Saito, and R. A. Levine, An iterative nonlinear Gaussianization algorithm for image simulation and synthesis, Technical report, Dept. Math., Univ. California, Davis, 2001. Submitted for publication.

[20] Y. Meyer, *Oscillating patterns in image processing and nonlinear evolution equations*, University Lecture Series **22**, AMS, Providence, RI, 2001.

[21] B. A. Olshausen, Sparse coding simulation software, http://redwood.ucdavis.edu/bruno/sparsenet.html.

[22] B. A. Olshausen and D. J. Field, "Emergence of simple-cell receptive field properties by learning a sparse code for natural images", *Nature*, 381:607–609, 1996.

[23] B. A. Olshausen and D. J. Field, "Sparse coding with an overcomplete basis set: A strategy employed by V1?", *Vision Research*, 37:3311–3325, 1997.

[24] D. T. Pham, "Blind separation of instantaneous mixture of sources via an independent component analysis", *IEEE Trans. Signal Process.*, 44(11):2768–2779, 1996.

[25] N. Saito, "Image approximation and modeling via least statistically dependent bases", *Pattern Recognition*, 34:1765–1784, 2001.

[26] N. Saito, B. M. Larson, and B. Bénichou, "Sparsity and statistical independence from a best-basis viewpoint. pp. 474–486 in *Wavelet Applications in Signal and*

Image Processing VIII, edited by A. Aldroubi et al., Proc. SPIE **4119**, 2000. Invited paper.

[27] J. H. van Hateren and A. van der Schaaf, "Independent component filters of natural images compared with simple cells in primary visual cortex", *Proc. Royal Soc. London*, Ser. B, 265:359–366, 1998.

[28] C. Weidmann and M. Vetterli, "Rate distortion behavior of sparse sources", submitted to IEEE Trans. Info. Theory, Oct. 2001.

NAOKI SAITO
DEPARTMENT OF MATHEMATICS
UNIVERSITY OF CALIFORNIA
DAVIS, CA 95616
UNITED STATES
saito@math.ucdavis.edu